# BEYOND
# INNOCENCE

# BEYOND INNOCENCE

## AN AUTOBIOGRAPHY
## IN LETTERS
### THE LATER YEARS

JANE GOODALL

*Edited by Dale Peterson*

HOUGHTON MIFFLIN COMPANY
BOSTON • NEW YORK
2001

For information about permission to reproduce selections
from this book, write to Permissions, Houghton Mifflin Company,
215 Park Avenue South, New York, New York 10003.

Visit our Web site: www.houghtonmifflinbooks.com.

*Library of Congress Cataloging-in-Publication Data*

Goodall, Jane, date.
Beyond innocence : an autobiography in letters : the later
years / Jane Goodall ; edited by Dale Peterson.
p.    cm.
ISBN 0-618-12520-5
1. Goodall, Jane, 1934 — Correspondence.  2. Primatologists —
Correspondence.  I. Peterson, Dale.  II. Title.
QL31.G58 A4 2001
590'.92 — dc21  [B]  00-054124

Printed in the United States of America

Book design by Robert Overholtzer

QUM 10 9 8 7 6 5 4 3 2 1

Every effort has been made to obtain permission to
reprint all photographs. If necessary, the publisher will
add the proper credit in future printings.

This book is dedicated to the
memory of my mother,
Vanne (1906–2000)

# CONTENTS

# LIST OF CORRESPONDENTS

*Family (or "All")*
Mum or Um: mother, Margaret Myfanwe (Vanne) Morris-Goodall
Jif or Jiff: sister, Judith Daphne Morris-Goodall Waters
Danny: maternal grandmother, Elizabeth Hornby Legarde Joseph
Olly or Ol: maternal aunt, Elizabeth Olwen Joseph
Aud: maternal aunt, Mary Audrey Gwyneth Joseph
Uncle Eric or Rixy or Rix: maternal uncle, William Eric Joseph
Grub or Ub or Nibs or Nibbs: son, Hugo Eric Louis van Lawick
Derek: second husband (1975–1980), Derek Noel Macleans Bryceson,
    director of Tanzania's national parks and member of Parliament

*Personal and Professional Contacts at the National Geographic Society
and Magazine*
Dr. Carmichael: Leonard Carmichael, chairman of the Committee for
    Research and Exploration and former secretary of the Smithsonian
    Institution
Ed or Mr. Snider: Edwin A. Snider, acting secretary of the Committee
    for Research and Exploration
Joanne: Joanne M. Hess, educational services, editorial services
Mary: Mary Griswold Smith, illustrations editor, later senior assistant
    editor
Neva: Neva L. Folk, editorial services
Dr. Payne: Melvin M. Payne, president
Mr. Vosburgh: Frederick G. Vosburgh, vice president and editor

*Other Professional Contacts*
Secretary Baker: James A. Baker III, U.S. secretary of state

Prince Bernhard: prince of the Netherlands

Dr. Bond: Douglas Bond, president of the Grant Foundation

Your Excellency: Basile Sindaharaye, Burundi's minister of tourism and the environment

Senator Hatch: U.S. Senator Orrin Hatch, Republican from Utah

Dr. Maletnlema: T. N. Maletnlema, director of the Tanzania Food and Nutrition Centre

Senator Melcher: U.S. Senator John Melcher, Democrat from Montana

Dr. Montagnier: Luc Montagnier, head of the oncology unit at the Pasteur Institute, Paris

Sir Peter: Sir Peter Scott, British conservationist and founder of the Waterfowl Trust, trustee of the Jane Goodall Institute (UK)

Dr. Raub: William F. Raub, deputy director of the National Institutes of Health

Mr. Rodale: Robert David Rodale, author, editor, and publisher; founder of Rodale Press

Dr. Schellekens: Huub Schellekens, director of the Netherlands TNO Primate Center


*Friends, Colleagues, Supporters, and Others*

Adrienne and Jerry: friends and supporters Adrienne and Jerry Zihlman. Adrienne was an anthropologist at the University of California at Santa Cruz; Jerry became a board member of the Jane Goodall Institute.

Alison: colleague Alison Jolly, a pioneering lemur watcher

Mr. B — : potential donor to the Bryceson scholarship fund

Barbara and Jeff: friends and supporters Barbara and Jeffrey Short

Chimpanzee sympathizer: Graziella Cotman, later manager of the Tchimpounga sanctuary

David: former Gombe student David Riss, later married to Emilie Bergmann

Mr. and Mrs. Davis: parents of Gombe student Ruth Davis

Em, Carrie, Steve: Emilie Bergmann, Carrie Hunter, and Steven Smith, students kidnapped from Gombe in 1975

Emilie: Emilie Bergmann, manager and then researcher at Gombe

FFF (Fairy Foster Father) or Louis: Louis S. B. Leakey, anthropologist, mentor, friend

Frank: Franklin M. Loew, dean of the Tufts School of Veterinary Medicine

Jim: potential supporter
Joan: Joan Travis of the L. S. B. Leakey Foundation
John: friendly critic and supporter
June: June Blackburn of the Royal Society for the Prevention of Cruelty
    to Animals
Marta and Austin: friends and supporters Marta and Austin Weeks
Mary Lynn: friend and supporter Mary Lynn Olivert
Maureen and Paul: friends and supporters Maureen Marshall and
    Paul Kase
Max: Max Pitcher, vice president for exploration at Conoco
Michael: singer Michael Jackson
Ned: Edward N. Harrison, president of the L. S. B. Leakey Foundation
Richard: colleague Richard Wrangham, a former Gombe student
Robert: Robert Hinde, professor at Cambridge University, former
    dissertation supervisor
Sallykins: Sally Cary Pugh, best friend from childhood
Mrs. Schwein: friend and supporter Virginia Schwein
Simon & Peggy: Simon and Peggy Templar, British couple living in
    Spain
Sue and Duane: Sue Savage-Rumbaugh and Duane Rumbaugh, ape
    language researchers and colleagues
Tita: Tita Caldwell of the L. S. B. Leakey Foundation
Tom: Thomas Wolflie of the National Institutes of Health
Toshi: colleague Toshisada Nishida, professor of zoology at Kyoto
    University
Vivian: Vivian Wheeler, senior manuscript editor at Harvard University
    Press

*Pet*
Cida: family dog in England

# INTRODUCTION

*Beyond Innocence* is the second volume of a two-volume autobiography based on the letters of Jane Goodall.

Jane Goodall was born on April 3, 1934. Her first letter home, scribbled probably on February 16, 1942, shows a little girl who already knew she loved animals. That little girl developed into the woman who, in 1957 at age twenty-two, took a boat to Africa, hoping somehow — naively, innocently, foolishly even — to have something to do with wild animals. In Nairobi, Kenya, she met the famed paleoanthropologist Louis Leakey and was hired to work as his personal secretary. Leakey quickly recognized in his very eager, very bright employee the ideal person to initiate a bold if eccentric scientific project he had long envisaged: to study wild apes by living among them.

So it was that Jane Goodall arrived at the Gombe Stream Chimpanzee Reserve, in what was then Tanganyika, on July 14, 1960, accompanied by her mother, Vanne, and a hired cook named Dominic — and within a few months began making the great discoveries that would revolutionize our understanding of chimpanzees and, ultimately, our appreciation of the human connection with the natural world. The National Geographic Society took over funding of her research by the end of 1960, and by August 1963 had published the first of a number of exciting *National Geographic* magazine features about Jane Goodall and the wild chimpanzees.

In 1964 Jane married Baron Hugo van Lawick, a photographer hired by the National Geographic Society to photograph her and the chimpanzees for that initial article. National Geographic continued to fund Jane's research through the decade but relatively soon terminated its support for Hugo at Gombe, feeling that the chimpanzees had been captured on film well enough. Hugo thus began photographing wildlife elsewhere in East Africa, typically in the Serengeti. As well as she could, Jane commuted between her husband's photographic sites and her own research project. She managed the ongoing work at Gombe with the help of various senior scientists, junior managers, field staff, and assistants.

This second half of her autobiography in letters begins with Jane Goodall in the summer of 1966, at age thirty-two a mature woman, her reputation firmly established, her self-confidence high, her marriage sound, driving into the Serengeti on safari and, with unexamined hope and innate high spirits, stepping grandly into the trajectory of her later years.

As time drew her beyond innocence and into experience, the later years would show many faces. Her life would turn and turn again to reveal many phases: contentment, bliss, excitement, pain, despair, hope, and contemplation. Her letter describing a nearly fatal plane crash at Ruaha National Park in early January 1974 provides, I think, a marker of sorts in the long and subtle transition of Jane Goodall's later life. Having discovered herself alive after expecting to be dead, having forded a crocodile-infested river to the park headquarters where she changed into dry clothes and shared a pot of tea with two other survivors of the crash (her son, Grub, and her companion, Derek Bryceson), Jane took a few moments to stop shaking, sip her tea, and think. The moment, one can imagine, would have been filled with both fear and exhilaration, an opportunity for reflection and renewal. She later wrote to her mother: "Africa has always been the ruling force of my life, I suppose. Now it is even more than that. Lots of things seem to have fallen into shape after nearly being dead." With an almost mystical belief in the power of fate, she resolved to do "what is best to do with the life entrusted" to her.

Clearly, one of her decisions was to marry Derek, with all the complexities and pain that would certainly bring (including divorce from her first husband, Hugo). But I believe the statement also expresses a grander sense of mission, an idealized if still rather vague sense of devotion to the future of her chimpanzees, of wildlife and wilderness, and even perhaps to the future of her adopted continent itself. Derek Bryceson, as a Tanzanian member of Parliament and director of Tanzania's national parks, was potentially a powerful force for African wildlife conservation; and in their partnership — Jane and Derek together — sustained by their love for each other and their mutual love of the African wilderness and the great and spirited African people, what could they not do?

Jane Goodall's later years, as they unfold in this second volume, follow something of that sequence again and again. Fortune's slings and arrows are a common outrage; we all walk, sometimes stumble, in a world marked by pain and trauma. But we each respond to those shocks distinctively, according to who we are and what we are made of. In the life that emerges from these letters, I see a response to the trauma of experience — or the experience of trauma — (Jane's own near death, her divorce, the kidnapping of her beloved Gombe students, the discovery of cannibalism and warfare among chimpanzees, the loss of Derek to cancer, and so on) that characteristically proceeds from full shock to deep contemplation to idealistic resolve and, finally, to determined action.

The motion might seem circular, but a more extended look suggests it is actually part of a spiral, a slow-turning rise. During the nearly thirty-five years documented in these letters we can witness, superimposed on the smaller patterns of oscillation and stasis and repetition, a larger pattern of change and growth and direction: the theme that gradually alters from private to public, the voice that slowly develops from egotist to idealist, the person excited by the drama of her own life among animals who eventually becomes the one who chooses to give everything she has to the chimpanzees and to Africa. This autobiography in letters, in short, traces a falcon's rising gyre that turns beyond innocence through experience into wisdom, and on to focused dedication.

As editor, I have been blessed with a small mountain of material: nearly two thousand letters containing between one million and two million words. From those documents I have tried to assemble an author's self-portrait that remains true both to the person I know and to the documents I see. In deference to the great verve of the writing, I have elected to keep most of Jane Goodall's infrequent spelling, punctuation, and capitalization idiosyncracies; but in an attempt to rival the coherence and drama that a more ordinary autobiography might produce, I have given the letters a larger context with chapter introductions and intermittent footnotes, and have also shortened a few of the longer passages, marking my editorial snips with the standard ellipsis dots ( . . . ). Within chapters, the letters are arranged chronologically. At the same time, since the chapters are developed and placed according to both time and subject, I have allowed a few of them to overlap in the years covered.

In combination with *Africa in My Blood,* the first volume of this autobiography, *Beyond Innocence* presents, I believe, an inspiring and surprisingly complete self-portrait of a figure unique in the history of science and human exploration.

# 1

# THE TOOL-USING VULTURE
## 1966

"He's using a tool!" Hugo and I exclaimed almost with one voice.
— "Tool-Using Bird: The Egyptian Vulture"

IN LATE JULY 1966, Jane Goodall and Hugo van Lawick, along with Hugo's brother Michael and two African assistants, Benjamen and Philip, set out from Nairobi in two vehicles on a photographic safari. It would take them south to the Serengeti Plains, an ecosystem covering some fifteen thousand square miles that included Tanzania's five-thousand-square-mile Serengeti National Park, Ngorongoro Crater, and Olduvai Gorge. Their original destination had been Ngorongoro Crater, located southeast of the official boundary of Serengeti Park, but on the advice of a "rhino man" they decided to move into the park, where they stopped and established a base camp at Seronera.

The single letter of this chapter explains in some detail what happened next. A grass fire had swept across the dry plains. When it was over, Jane and her party drove out, looking for an ostrich they had seen earlier and finding instead an abandoned ostrich nest surrounded by a swarm of birds — several different species — competing with each other for some twenty eggs, of which six remained unbroken. Ostrich eggs are large, heavy, and thick shelled; and as it turned out, only the smallest of this scrum, two "pretty little white Egyptian vultures," were able to break open three of the eggs. The yellow-beaked, white-feathered birds accomplished this feat by picking up, carrying, and throwing stones at the eggs with their beaks.

As Jane and Hugo immediately recognized, they had accidentally stumbled on a spectacular observation: another example of wild animals using objects as tools. Jane of course had been the first scientific observer to report tool using among wild chimpanzees. (Her earliest discovery was that chimpanzees use long twigs to fish for termites inside termite nests. She later witnessed several other instances of object manipulation: chimpanzees drinking with crumpled leaves as sponges, for instance, or wiping dirt and feces off themselves with noncrumpled leaves.) Aside from the chimpanzee examples, Jane and Hugo could think of only four other cases of nonhuman tool use: California sea otters breaking clams against a flat stone, Galápagos woodpecker finches probing for insects with a cactus spine, sand wasps using stones, and marine crabs holding up stinging sea anemones to threaten intruders.

It was an exciting moment, and Jane and Hugo notified their expedition sponsor, the National Geographic Society, in a telegram dispatched toward the end of the month. By then they had confirmed the stone-throwing inclinations of the Egyptian vulture with observations in other places. They also sent National Geographic several rolls of still photographs and a long strip of film on the subject, followed by letters including Jane's comment, at the end of a report of October 20 to executive vice president Melvin Payne: "We still find the whole thing hard to believe. When you consider that, apart from chimpanzees, possibly a gorilla, the sea otter, and the Galapagos Woodpecker Finch, no other vertebrates, so far, have been seen using tools in the wild — well, it does seem a fantastic piece of luck that Hugo and I have been able to observe a fifth!!" Jane's letter was quickly followed by one from Hugo, indicating that Jane was prepared "very soon if need be to write one or two small factual articles. (I especially think here of course of the vultures using tools.)"

National Geographic responded with stolid indifference. They even managed to misplace most of Hugo's photographs. And so the van Lawicks quickly produced a scientific summary and elaboration of their initial discovery and posted it to the prestigious British journal *Nature,* which published "Use of Tools by the Egyptian Vulture, *Neophron percnopterus*" the day before Christmas. That brief piece in *Nature* was itself quickly summarized in a few small newspapers in Britain, and in America in one major magazine, *Time*. The *Time* article of January 7, 1967, instantly aroused a sleepy Geographic editorial staff, who on the very same day shot out the following telegram to Hugo: "ADDITIONAL PICTURES NEEDED FOR MAGAZINE ROCK THROWING CULTURES STOP SUGGEST USING MOTOR DRIVE CAMERA STOP PLEASE ADVISE PROSPECTS STOP EDITORIAL WILL ADVISE TEXT LENGTH WHEN PHOTOGRAPHS IN HAND LETTER FOLLOWS." So began Jane Goodall's third *National Geographic* article, which ultimately appeared in the May 1968 issue.

\*     \*     \*     \*

> Seronera
> Serengeti
> 3rd August [1966] I think!

Darling family,

Well — here we are on the Serengeti. We drove down in convoy — Hugo and our new "driver" — Philip! — in the landrover (now known as Troglodyte) and me, Michael and Benjamen in the new VW (Satyre). It is super to drive, but rather like being in a very rough boat — when one meets the waves head on. Or on a bucking horse! We have decided that we must get a lot more weight in it. These buses are, of course, designed to carry about 12 fat Germans — so the springs are excellent! You realize that it is the first time I have ever driven on these roads — it was fun. We planned to go to the Crater, as I told you. We got there late one night — well, dusk. Went to see the rhino man, who works there, and he told us that it wasn't much good in the Crater. So we decided to go on to Seronera. We camped, that night, on the way down from the Crater to the Serengeti plains. And oh! the wind. We could hardly get out — it nearly blew us over. We put up one tent for Michael — Benjamen and Philip said they would sleep in the landrover. Then we saw, from our cosy little house Satyre that B. was curled up under blankets — on the roof of the landrover. Honestly, how mad can you get! However, he stuck it all night! We cooked in Satyre, really christening her for the first time. We are going to try and get stills of the inside to show you. It is just like having a tiny little house all of our own. There is a coldbox — looking like a fridge. You freeze up "jelly bags" and put them in — colder than ice. We brought with us heaps of fresh meat for us and the boys, and lots of fresh fruit and veg. Butter and fresh cheese. All kept fine in the cold box, replenished with plastic bags of ice cubes from any hotel we passed. And now we are here, in our most luxurious camp — just as luxurious as any big safari camp — we have Hugo's little fridge — you remember, Mum, the one that kept unfreezing on his films at the Reserve! It is working fine now, and even manages to freeze a jelly bag at a time for the cold box.

Before I go on to tell you other things, I have to tell you our most <u>EXCITING</u> news. So exciting we can hardly believe it (and it is dead secret at the moment till published in Nature). A NEW <u>TOOL</u>!!!!! Please don't tell Louis yet. It is a surprise for him till we tell him. Let me tell you the story from the start. Two days ago there was a huge fire raging over the plains here. Yesterday we kept well away from there because it was all so black and horrid, but today we wanted to re-visit a handsom male ostrich, with the reddest of necks, who was sitting on 5 eggs. When we visited him the first time the fire had just passed. We could not imagine how he and his eggs had escaped, but they had. He got off his eggs to try and lead us away, with a super dancing display, drooping and trailing his wings. Then he lay and looked as if he was pretending to be hatching eggs somewhere different. Well, we returned to him today. More eggs. Again he danced away. And we drove on. That is just the introduction.

Further on the fire had been worse. We saw a hyaena and some vultures over on a blackened patch, and drove over. The hyaena ran away. And we saw that he had been eating ostrich eggs. The poor bird must have abandoned the nest because of the fire — which had gone right over everything. When the hyaena went the vultures went close, several of the large type, and two of the rather pretty little white Egyptian vultures. Like the Palm Nut vulture they are not true vultures. They have feathers up the neck, and then just a small bare patch round his beak which, like the beak, is bright yellow. And bright yellow legs.

There were six unbroken eggs. The big vultures were squabbling round the broken eggs, pecking up the remains of the yolk. Suddenly one of the little Egyptian ones did something strange. Our first thought was that he had a bit of chick. And then we saw he had a big stone in his beak. Well — you can guess the rest. Between them, they broke three eggs. They took the stones in their beaks, reared up as high as they could go, and with a sudden downward movement threw the stones directly down towards the egg. Often they missed. One managed in 6 goes. The other, once, took about 12. He was a hoot. He was eating one egg, and seemed to more or less finish it — a lot ran onto the ground of course. There was a whole egg about 5 feet away. Standing by his old egg and looking at the new, he picked up the stone he had cracked the old egg with and threw it to the ground — by his old egg. Picked it up and repeated. Picked it up, took a couple of steps, threw it down. Did this three more times before he got to the new egg!!! Either sort of displacement or perhaps it was heavy for him, and it was a means of getting it there. The latter not very likely. Because, to our utter astonishment, he was able, once he had cracked the egg, to get hold of the little indentation and actually raise the whole egg — about 3 or more pounds — from the ground and bang it down. And the Egyptian vulture is one of the very smallest of the vultures. Once they had cracked open an egg, the other big vultures pushed in and drove them away. Until we drove a bit closer, and then the big cowards flew away and we could watch the little ones open another each. Then they were full and flew away. Isn't it FANTASTIC!! Hugo and I have been through all the animal tools we can think of. The sea otter, with the flat stone he puts on his chest for breaking his clams. The chimp. The Galapagos finch, with his twigs that he pokes into crevices in trees to probe out insects. The sand wasp — one, in 100 trials, used a stone to bang down sand — or something of the sort. A crab which goes around with an anemone in its claw. But we can't think of any more authentic, scientifically recorded, examples of wild animals using tools. So, that is 5 — and we have a sixth!! We are planning to write it up in a very short note to Nature, and send it off once we get one of Hugo's pictures back from the Geographic. It is so super — we feel that the whole trip has been worthwhile — which we were not sure of as the animals are not at all good round here just now.

George and Kay are installed.* It does seem funny. Their eldest, Eric, must be nearly six, mustn't he? — conceived when still with the Gorillas. Anyway, Kay brought him in to see us in her arms!!!! It reminded us of Flo when Fifi was 4!!!!! He had apparently been talking about me ever since he saw the T.V. film, so she brought him in to see if he knew me. Oh yes — Jane Goodall, he said at once! He has had a picture of me under his pillow. . . .

The "driver" I mentioned is a friend of Benjamen's. We thought it would be nice to have a driver for the other car. Also, anyway for the safari with Phyllis Jay† (one month or more) there will be four of us, so we would need an extra fellow to help. But Philip can't drive for toffee. So Hugo said he would just take him on temporarily to help B. with everything. He can make a car go — just isn't very good for it. So, in an emergency he would be useful. And, actually, on the way down we broke down — Troglodyte just stopped. Hugo and I went off to look for a mechanic (we were near a tiny village). Found that there was one, but couldn't find him. Were waiting patiently when the landrover arrived with a beaming Philip — he had mended it. We found he had worked for 2 years with a mechanic. So he has his uses. Also, he is a nice cheerful fellow. Mended a puncture for us, which saved us more time.

Before we left Nairobi Philip Leakey told us that Richard had taken a film team (which has been creating havoc out here, an ABC one, with Robert Ardrey,‡ to film wild dogs, with puppies, at Lake Olbalbal near Olduvai). We planned to go there. Then the boys at Olduvai told us that the film team had not been near Lake Olbalbal

---

* George and Kay Schaller, out to study lions.
† Primatologist and anthropologist from the University of California at Berkeley.
‡ Playwright and best-selling popularizer of anthropological theories, who was working with two of Louis Leakey's sons, Philip and Richard.

— the dogs had been seen at Seronera. Just told to Hugo to put him off the scent. Sordid.

Well, this will be the last page, as I hope somehow to find some stamps and get this posted, together with one or two other urgent ones. I have stayed in today on purpose to get all letters, etc, up to date. We havn't had any mail here at all yet — we presume that Mike hasn't yet had the message to send it here, and it will probably all be waiting for us at Ngorongoro! So don't be alarmed that I don't comment on any of your news!

The morning after I wrote the last bit of the letter, we got back at 11, and decided to try one of the ostrich eggs. Hugo chipped it open, made a hole in the shell, and gurgled it into our largest pan. It came out looking thick and dark red and thick glutinous jelly. With some froth at the end. However, determined to try something I have wanted to try for years, I tipped half into a smaller pan (equivalent of 10 or so hens' eggs, the half was) and beat and beat it. And scrambled it. It looked like a rich too wet cake mixture when I started, but gradually the consistency changed and it became like an egg. Well, believe it or not — it tasted simply super — in fact, it tasted like particularly well scrambled hens' eggs! Everyone has always said how rich it is, etc — maybe they got their eggs when they were nearly hatched, or something. Ours wasn't rich, oily or in any way different from a free ranging hen's egg.

Hugo, Michael and Benjamen left at 7.0. It is now 3.30 and they still havn't returned. Hugo said he was just going to wait with lions until they made a kill, so I guess he won't be back till dusk. We almost got one yesterday — got the whole charge, and the kill just out of sight. Same day before. And yesterday, also, we left two fat lionesses and one fat lion lying asleep at 1.0 midday. We left them for one hour to have a much needed bath. We got back — a super kill, out in the open. Hugo couldn't forgive himself for leaving, and so nothing will drag him away today. . . .

I don't think, at the moment, that there really is any more exciting news. It is quite definite that I will do a mongoose study, on and off, while writing up chimp stuff, when Hugo does the lion and hyaena stuff. I can then be a visiting scientist in the Park, which will help matters a lot, and have the chance to find out about mongooses I have wanted for years. Somehow, of course, we have to do an Egyptian Vulture study before someone else does!

> Tons and tons of love to all —
> we are thinking of Jif in America.
> Jane

P.S. If you see Louis on his way back, and <u>if</u> he is not too heavily burdened, could you give him my green anorak. I really miss it.

# 2

⁓❦ ⁓❦ ⁓❦

# POLIO EPIDEMIC

## 1966–1967

I think those few months were the darkest I have ever lived through: every time a chimp stopped visiting the feeding area, we started to wonder whether we should ever see him again or, worse, if he would reappear hideously crippled.

— *In the Shadow of Man*

THE EVOLUTIONARY CLOSENESS of chimpanzees and humans means that the two species are cousins not only emotionally, socially, and behaviorally, but biochemically as well. Their biochemical kinship means that *Pan troglodytes* and *Homo sapiens* are susceptible to many of the same diseases, including poliomyelitis.

Polio is caused by a viral infection that typically spreads orally. The virus enters its host through the mouth and settles in the digestive tract, reproducing and then generating early symptoms that may include fever and headache, or some back or neck stiffness. If a counterattack by antibodies does not end the infection at this point, the virus continues to multiply and then travels through the blood to a convenient second resting place in the host's spinal cord, ultimately destroying parts of that critical organ and thereby causing paralysis of the arm or leg muscles, or of the muscles associated with breathing and swallowing.

In the second half of 1966, a polio epidemic somehow spread from people to the chimpanzees living inside the Gombe Stream Reserve, devastating the ape community that congregated around the banana feeding site. The epidemic seems to have reached the research area in August. Jane and Hugo had spent most of that month in the Serengeti, studying and photographing animals. They returned from that safari to Nairobi, picked up a load of electronically operated banana boxes for chimpanzee provisioning, and then (accompanied by a friend and colleague, Phyllis Jay) drove back down to Kigoma, from there taking the boat to Gombe.

They had already heard the exciting news that Olly had given birth on August 7; the baby was named Grosvenor to honor Melville Bell Grosvenor of the National Geographic Society. Grosvenor was about three weeks old when the van Lawick party arrived, and Jane was at first full of enthusiasm for the beautiful little infant and his mother. "Olly's baby is so gorgeous," she wrote home in late August or very early September. And, she added, "Olly is a super Mum. Baby Grosvenor is . . . an amazingly vocal infant — he protests vigorously every time Olly moves when he is trying to have a snooze. Likes his comfort."

That was the optimistic perspective. As Jane expressed the case in "rather a gloomy letter" written one to two weeks later (the first of this sequence), "We suspected something wrong from the first — the infant was always screaming when Olly moved, as though it was hurt by her moving." Soon Baby Grosvenor became paralyzed and then quickly died. The mother tried to comfort and nurse her dead infant, and she continued to carry the lifeless carcass, flopped over her shoulder like a rag doll. Olly, a shy, long-faced female with a distinctive "fluff of hair on the back of her head,"* had two other offspring, Evered and Gilka. Evered was an adolescent by 1966 and tended to travel with the other males; Gilka, who was about six years old and still moving in her mother's orbit, was at first excited about the arrival of a baby brother. Even after he died, she tried for a while to groom and play with the baby's corpse.

Soon after Grosvenor's death, more photography work took the van Lawick safari away from Gombe, north to the national parks of Uganda. By the time they returned to the reserve at the beginning of November (bringing along from Nairobi a second set of electronic

---

* *In the Shadow of Man*, p. 33.

banana boxes and a new assistant, Alice Sorem), the epidemic was raging. Reports of human polio contagion in the villages to the south and east of the reserve had by then surfaced, while within the provisioning area several of the chimpanzees were obviously stricken with a paralytic disease. These included Gilka with a paralyzed wrist, Faben with a dangling right arm, and Madam Bee trailing a left arm.

Jane neglected to mention in her November letter home that even though none of the humans at the feeding site were infected, very few of them were actually safe. In Nairobi, Louis Leakey arranged for an emergency flight of the oral vaccine donated by Pfizer Laboratories, which (as we read in the letter written during the second week of December) was given methodically to all the Gombe people and chimpanzees — a task complicated by the social complexities of chimpanzee life. Social dominance among chimpanzees, as among humans, indicates superior access to resources; the concern was that some of the apes would take more than their share of vaccine-spiked bananas and that too much of the vaccine, derived from a live but weakened virus, might actually cause rather than prevent infection. Perhaps the worst part of the epidemic was the lingering, pathetic death of Mr. McGregor, thoroughly and movingly described in the December letter. McGregor (or Gregor) was the eccentric, egg-loving older male with a bald spot on his head who, back in the early days, had reminded Jane of the old gardener of that name in Beatrix Potter's *Tale of Peter Rabbit*.

During this same terrible period, Anyango, the well-liked cook at Gombe, died — probably of cancer. Jane's assistant, Caroline Coleman, engaged to marry a bank manager living in Kigoma, had by then decided to leave; and the secretary, Sally Avery, had become seriously ill with a kidney problem. So when Jane and Hugo left Gombe that December, the new assistant, Alice Sorem, courageously took charge of the daily observations, record keeping, and general management. A new secretary, Sue Chaytor, would soon follow.

Jane and Hugo made a couple of quick return visits around the turn of the year (mentioned in the mid-January letter). On the first trip they were accompanied by Louis Leakey's new "gorilla girl,"

Dian Fossey. On the second they went with, and by the generosity of, their friend Royal Little, logistics arranged by the Nairobi safari outfitter Ker, Downey & Selby ("Ker and Downey"). The Royal Little group came to Gombe in the middle of January 1967, by which time the polio epidemic had "finally, to all intents and purposes, been arrested." According to Jane's summary at the time (letter of January 27), some nine individuals had been affected: five who suffered from paralyzed limbs and four who died (two of them, McGregor and MacD, shot).*

\*     \*     \*     \*

The Golden Lion
Kigoma main street
Kigoma
[Around September 17, 1966]

Darling Family,

Rather a gloomy letter. Everything seems to have gone wrong just at the end of our trip. Let me first tell you the really sad sad news. Olly's baby has died. It was a most tragic affair, though not heart wringing like little Jane because none of us really knew the baby, little Grosvenor. But tragic all the same. We suspected something wrong from the first — the infant was always screaming when Olly moved, as though it was hurt by her moving. Then, 3 days ago, it really screamed loudly when she moved — when she bent to get b[anana]s out of a box — it nearly dropped to the ground. She had to support it all the time. The following morning she arrived early, and the baby was not making any attempt to hold on at all. It screamed and screamed the whole time she was moving. It was horrible. (Any ideas — it looked quite paralyzed, except for its head, and its face, and, of course, its vocal cords.) She held it most tenderly, and seemed almost to pluck up her courage to move, because she hated it screaming.

---

* Two other summaries, apparently written in response to later information, expanded those casualty figures somewhat. In *Shadow of Man* Jane concluded that fifteen were affected, of whom six died (p. 218). In *Chimpanzees of Gombe,* it was twelve affected and six dead (p. 82).

I followed. She sat down, cradling it, every few steps, and then, gradually, he quietened. She was with Gilka, who stared from time to time, and Gigi. It was specially sad because, the day before (and you should see it on the 8 mm) Gilka was allowed to reach out and touch the baby's hands, and groom his head — just as Fifi with Flint. She was so fascinated. And now — a dying little brother.

They all went up a tree, Gilka and Gigi playing, and Olly nursing this thing. It often screamed even when she didn't move. Then Gilka went up to her, and they groomed for an hour, and all the time Gilka was touching and grooming the baby — and Olly, as though she realized it was hopeless, paid no heed.

For an hour, from 10 to 11, it rained. And when Olly climbed down, after the rain, the baby was dead — or mercifully unconscious. I wanted to follow, but Olly met up with a stranger mother — well, the timid Nope. So I couldn't.

The next morning early she came. The baby was dead. I will not describe the gruesome scenes we saw — you will see these also on the 8 mm. I followed them for 6 hours, and saw Gilka playing with and grooming the corpse, carrying it, and Olly hurrying to rescue it, as Flo had rescued the live Flint from Fifi. It was unutterably horrible. And the stench was enough to make one sick. They went back to camp and then up the valley. And at 12 I lost them — they went into pig tunnels where I had to crawl, the stench of death clinging closely to the tangled vines and leaves.

But I could not keep up for long.

The next day, about lunch time, Olly came with Gilka. They had abandoned the corpse, and the little pair were back to normal. What a waste of 9 months of Olly's efforts. It was horrible.

So that is over. Merlin, I am sure, cannot survive these rains. He has pulled nearly all the hair from his legs and a lot of the rest of his body. All his hair is a pale, dull brownish colour — none of him is black. He shivers, and his face goes blue in the rain. He is still sleeping with Miff, but I am sure that soon she will kick him out — already, as he climbs up to join her, he is starting to whimper — as a youngster whimpers when it approachs to suckle and fears it will meet with no luck. Poor little scrap. . . .

Well, let me stop all these sorrows and sordidities. The sun still shines — though, to be sure, we have had three days which might have come from the middle of the rains. Rain, rain and yet more rain. Buildings flooded and chimps wet and shivering. Today is bright. Michael is drawing over at the next table. Phyllis is sitting opposite me and we are all waiting for Hugo to finish his battles so that we can start packing up the cars for the road. Murcheson Falls Park next stop. 630 miles to drive first. But, they say, the roads are good.

We are dying to hear how Jiff is getting on, but do not expect to hear first hand. So shall await the news from a letter from you. Our mail has gone and got into a muddle — goodness knows where your letters (if any of you have written) will be. We hope waiting for us at Murcheson, but some mail has been sent here — though we expressly ordered that it should not be.

There seems to be no more news for now, and I have to write three rather sordid business letters. So that, for now, I will stop this ill-typed screed — it seems to be falling off the machine anyway!

[Second week of November 1966]

Darling Family,

Just the very briefest line to you all to go in with the cards. I hope you don't mind sending them off for me Mum — I didn't dare address them to Jiff, for they would never have gone. I cannot write much for the two Geographic people are off by plane this morning. What a surprise — the book is going to be a really nice book. They have not altered the text — except that they suddenly decided it had to be in 7, instead of 13, sections! So it had to be rather rearranged, and all my carefully thought out links between chapters have been to no avail!!! No matter. If it stays as it is, the writing is all mine, and the only things they have cut are "human interest"!!!!!! And they have asked for <u>more</u> on pink ladies!!!!!!* And the drawings have been made by a man who draws animals — and, the ones we have seen, really will benefit the book. You will have to wait and see, but

---

* Adult females in estrus, advertising their sexual receptivity and potential fertility with genital swellings.

most of them are quite enchanting. There are also going to be paintings — but not by Geographic staff artists. They have hired the top illustrator in the whole of U.S.A.!!!!! So they might possibly be O.K. too. Also, the editor who came here is one of the nicest Americans I have ever met, and we had a very nice time with the two of them. The picture editor is rather a brash, pleased with himself, young man — but he's been quite fun to have around.*

Now, news in a few lines. The worst first. The chimps had a polio epidemic. It has been all around the Africans up behind the reserve (so nothing to do with the feeding area, thank goodness). And when I say all around I mean widespread, but very few cases. It was in August. Grosvenor, baby one, undoubtedly died of it. Gilka has a paralyzed wrist. Olly — is this very rare? The Dr. here said it was, but we reckon that, if, as he says, humans mostly get legs paralyzed, the chimp would get arms as it uses them most. Anyway, she is rehabilitating well. The ghastly cases are Faben and Madam Bee. Oh how horrid it is. Faben's right arm and Madam Bee's left. Completely useless. Just trailing and dangling. Faben walks all the time bipedally. It is uncanny, spooky and ghastly to watch him. You will see some film of it and agree. Madam Bee can't, with an infant, so she goes tripedal and trails the arm. It was yesterday that she appeared for the first time — we had guessed with Faben it must be polio — when we saw Madam Bee we knew. So Hugo and Dave (Geographic man) rushed into Kigoma. Vaccine (oral) is arriving today on their plane, and we shall do ourselves, and try and do some of the chimp infants. Though there is little danger now that the epidemic is still alive. Merlin, last seen two months ago, was dragging a foot. We feel he must have had it. Miff has not been seen for a month, and J.B. for quite a time. Oddly, as coincidences, Olly could not walk with one foot. And Sniff with one hand, and Melissa has had her back hurt so that her neck is too stiff to move. But none of these three are polio.† And David, yesterday, could put no weight on his leg. But they are all rather excitable at the moment. . . .

---

* Jane is referring to the final work on *My Friends the Wild Chimpanzees*. David Bridge was the picture editor who came out to Gombe.
† Possibly these three cases, and David Greybeard's, were polio infections that happened to terminate before severe spinal-cord damage.

Tons of love to all, and I will write again with the next mail now that panics are over!!!!

Tons of love,
Jane

[Second week of December 1966]

Darling Family,

This is going to be a letter of the most sordid news. I have been putting off writing it till at least I could say that the worst was over. For one thing neither Hugo, Alice nor I were safe from Polio — until yesterday. I had had one injection, but not a booster. Hugo and Alice had nothing. So we have been taking the oral vaccine — well, we took the first dose three weeks ago. Since the incubation for polio is three weeks we presumed that, if we had just caught it before taking the vaccine, we could still go down with it sometime during the three weeks. Now, however, we are safe. We have given it to all the boys and their large families, and to the scouts and wives. We are also giving it to the chimps. We have a big vaccination chart, and mark off those that have taken it. It is quite a ghastly business. More than half of those we have done have eaten their dose — injected into a banana — without a second thought. Flo, Fifi and Flint were good — though Flint gave us heart attacks because he took it out of his mouth, and kept sniffing. He knew something was wrong. But obviously didn't mind it. The smaller babies wouldn't take it. Our worst horrors came when giving it to females who come seldom and in big groups — what if a male charges a female, making her drop her vaccine, and he eats it — and has already had just one dose. We presume he would get polio. So you can imagine the tactics and worry and tension whilst these operations went on. However, apart from one flap — where Pallas accidentally dropped half her b[anana] on the ground — and we were feeding her outside the window cos a stranger was here, and were terrified someone would come and eat the half. Hugo got his arm out of the window with dettol bottle in the end, and sprayed the affected piece with dettol.* Anyway, we managed to vaccinate (not counting tiny babies or strangers that we havn't a chance with) three quarters of our chimps. The others havn't appeared yet to be done.

Well, that's the best part of the news over. The worst is that Gregor is dead. Hugo had to shoot him, and it was the most horrible time I can remember living through, and Hugo and I were in such a state about it. He managed to pull himself up to camp — and had paralysed both legs. He was moving either by sitting upright and inching backwards using his arms as crutches, or by pulling forward on his tummy — when the vegetation was strong enough — or by rolling, or, somehow by using his arms to pull his body up and turning head over heels. He had lost bladder control, and all his legs etc stank of wee. He was surrounded by clouds and clouds of flies. He <u>loathed</u> the flies. We flitted and flitted, and took him food. It was late — Hugo noticed Flo and family creeping down to the termite heap — and staring and staring. And we went to look. And there he was. To our amazement he was able to pull himself into a tree with his arms, and make a nest.

The next day he stayed in his nest until 1 o'clock. Various chimps went to stare and stare. Then he sat under the nest, and by then we had ordered a bunch of palm nuts. So we gave him nuts and bananas. He was delighted with the nuts. He then dragged himself quite a way away. We followed his trail with his tea — you know, Mum, how he loves eggs. We took him eggs. A chimp group had arrived — and I suppose the big males were scared of him. Anyway, Worzle and Huxley displayed round him, and his terror was pathetic. He couldn't move. He pulled himself even further, climbed high in a tree — terrifying to watch, and made a nest. The next day he stayed in the nest till very late, and then came down and we fed him and flitted and flitted. Oh there was a smell. And, to make matters worse, it kept deluging with rain. He just sat under his tree, and then finally climbed back, but not to his high nest. To a day nest that Humphrey had made.

This is the rather touching part of the whole horrible tragedy.

---

* A British disinfectant.

Humphrey was lost.* For three days he hardly moved from the vicinity of Gregor. Slept near him at night. Sat around in camp, or down near Gregor, during the day. But had no interaction with him.

The next day was (if you can call it that) the happiest of Gregor's days. He managed to pull himself about 200 yards right up to camp. And when the group all had boxes open, he managed to get two boxes, and he felt part of things, and not so left out. But earlier, before he came up to camp, was his worst time — so far as human observers were concerned. In fact I had to go away. Olly was pink. Humphrey was in his tree down near Gregor, and he managed to spirit Olly down with him. He has a thing with Olly. Hugh joined them in the tree. It was quite early. Gregor could see the tree from his nest. He swung down, and dragged himself to the others. Hugh was scared, and hurried to the far side of the tree, and made a nest. Gregor was giving happy grunts at arriving with the group. He sat, exhausted, under the tree. And grunted. No answering grunts. He looked up. A last effort and he pulled up, sat on a branch, and grunted. With his sad swarm of flies. And, for a moment, I thought all would be well. Humphrey went over to him. And then Humphrey rushed over to Hugh and began to groom him. And Olly joined them. And Gregor was left sitting alone. He sat there, forlorn, for about 5 minutes. Then, clumsily, he swung to the ground and sat there, occasionally grooming his arm, and then lay. Hitting his flies. And by this time his whole rump was completely raw. No skin left. From pulling over the ground. By this time I could no longer see him — he was a misty swimming figure. While the others groomed above.

Then they climbed down. Olly stepped over him as though he was a log, and he raised his head, and followed her bottom with his eyes. I'm sure it was Olly that made him pull up to camp. But what chance had he.

There was another time. He was lying under a tree. Humphrey was waiting for him. Gregor had dragged himself to eat reeds and to the stream (he wouldn't drink the water we gave him). He had been

---

* "Lost" in an emotional sense; that is, Humphrey was devastated by the appearance of his friend (and probably older brother) Gregor.

joined by Humphrey. And now Humphrey wanted his old pal to follow, as in days of yore, off up the valley and away. Gregor had come some 50 yards. Goliath came along. He went up to Gregor, lay down, his nose almost touching, his hair out, and stared. Gregor just lay, and then, fearfully, reached a hand to Goliath. Goliath walked all round him, staring and sniffing. And then went.

The worst time of all was when Gregor was in a nest and it was raining. Goliath went and displayed all round him, high in the tree, and Humphrey, bless him (so scared of Goliath), displayed at Goliath. And Gregor was clinging on, really for his life, and bowing his head as branches broke around him and his nest — made with such labour and difficulty — was destroyed. At last he really was forced to abandon his nest, and swing lower. His screams and fear face were horrible — at first it was just fear — no sound at all. Then Goliath stopped (it was his fifth display) and sat near the ground. Gregor lowered himself. And reached a tentative hand towards Goliath. And Goliath reached out and patted and patted his hand. And all was over. But it was so ghastly to watch.

Often we gave him his food up in bed. Eggs were passed up on sticks in little palm frond baskets, and palm nuts in forked sticks and bananas speared — and, of course, his wadging leaves.* And all the time we were flitting.

After five days we came to the conclusion that he would never recover anything. We knew we had to shoot him. At first we had hoped — we kept thinking we saw a foot move, or a thigh. But it was hopeless. And, having decided this, came the worst of all. We went down at 5.0 because he was not in his nest, and he usually was by then. We took him some eggs — we were planning to ask the boys to send down for the Scout and his gun. And we found that Gregor had done something awful to one arm. He had one arm left. He kept trying to pull himself places. He ate lying down. We saw him fed, and flitted the millions of flies. And then went to tell Rashidi to fetch the scout.† Soon Rashidi returned — the scout on a

---

* Leaves to mix in with the rest of his food and thereby make a satisfyingly chewy "wadge."
† Rashidi Kikwale, a senior member of the field staff who had worked at Gombe since the earliest days.

patrol and wouldn't be back till later. It was dusk. We went back to
Gregor, and couldn't find him at first. And then, there he was, under
his same tree (where he had taken over the Humphrey nest, and
where, many times, we had fed him). He was sitting under it, looking up. He couldn't balance properly, with his one bad arm. When
he tried to take an egg from my hand, he nearly fell. He ate it lying
down, with the wadge leaves we brought. He grunted happily. It got
dark. Hugo fetched a pressure lamp. And still no scout. Then we
discussed trying to inject him with morphia. Hugo went and got a
syringe, fixed most efficiently to a long stick, with another to push
it. We felt, then, that he had no feeling in his legs, as I had poked and
poked with a stick on his feet and he had not even looked. It took a
long time, getting that syringe ready. And I sat there with Gregor,
who had got quite comfortable, and who actually went to sleep. He
had his back to me, was 4 feet away, the pressure lamp burned. He
was almost snoring — deep wheezy breaths. A half eaten banana in
his hand. He had such trust in us that it was fantastic. Then Hugo
got back. But when he touched him with the needle, Gregor hit it
away. And he couldn't have seen. Hugo tried once again — again
Gregor felt. So we knew it was no good, and squirted the morphia
on the ground. We decided that, after all, he was not so frightened
because he had to sleep on the ground. It was about 9 by now. So
Hugo persuaded me to have some supper. Oh what a nightmare it
was. We sort of sat around. Then, finally, the scout came up with a
gun. Oh yes — he had a gun. But we wouldn't use it because it
wasn't cleaned. It was filthy! Too dangerous to use. So — could
they clean it — well, they said, the cleaning things were down at the
beach!! It really is hopeless. Anyway, Hugo was not keen really, to
shoot him at night. And, since he was able to sleep, we told the
scouts to come up early the next morning.

Late that night I crept down to him. Again he was asleep. He
opened a sleepy eye as I approached. I gave him a banana and he
grunted and ate it, with a few wadge leaves. Then he reached to a
little bit of twig, and bent it down under his chin. Why hadn't I
thought of it before — of course, he couldn't reach anything and he
wanted a nest. So I picked him a huge pile of green branches. And
even with all this crashing around, and torch shining, he was not

afraid. I put the pile by his good hand — he at once bent in branches under his head and neck, using good arm and teeth and chin. And then sank his head onto his curled up good hand and closed his eyes. And so I left him.

The next morning was the end. He had an egg. He was just still lying in his nest. He quite trusted Hugo behind him, just a couple of feet away. And he never even jumped or jerked — as the bullet ended his misery his head just sank slightly lower, and he lay, as if still asleep. It was much worse for us.

But this isn't the end of the horror. I was down with Gregor one day, Hugo was in Kigoma ordering vaccine, and suddenly poor Alice (what a start in chimpland for her) gave me a whistle. I went up the slope and found her in floods of tears. Who was the chimp on the doorstep she wanted to know. And I felt sick. It was Pepe. He had lost the use of one arm, and most of the use of the other. And he was moving in a squatting position, his bottom just off the ground, waddling forward on one bent leg after the other. It was so horrible. He returned the next day, and was terrified when Humphrey stared at him. Humphrey had his hair out, and was scared. And Pepe just looked up, his mouth wide open with fright, and then turned and stared behind him. What was this thing terrifying Humphrey? How could he know it was his pathetic self. And he has not been again. We fear some horrible accident has befallen him.

Merlin was last seen dragging a foot. Miff, we were terrified for. She did not come for 2 months, 2 weeks after Merlin was last seen. But 5 days ago she appeared, looking fit and well. What a relief. But we feel fairly certain we have lost dear pugnacious J.B., Willy Wally, Hornby — and now Charlie. Mandy and David have not been for nearly two weeks, and our latest horror is that Pooch and Figan have not been for some time. Our only consolation is that none of the chimps are coming regularly. But we can't help but feel sick with worry about those that don't show up. David, by the way, got over the injury to his leg. He was very lame for about 4 days, and then arrived with a big group, quite his usual self. But where is he now? It is like living in a ghastly, perpetual nightmare. Who will be the next cripple to turn up. Will we have to shoot another friend. What is, or was, the fate of those we think are gone. We can just imagine them in Gregor's state, unable to reach camp, and suffering a slow lingering death by starvation. By comparison with this, Gregor's end was merciful. Most of the time I don't suppose he was too unhappy — though the other chimps did terrify him — no more than he has many times terrified poor females. If only David and Figan would come soon it wouldn't be too bad.

Then, as if all this wasn't enough, we have another ghastly tragedy — a worse one really. Anyango was very ill, went to the best hospital — but I have told you that, and that the report said he was operated on for an abdominal mass. I wondered if it could be cancer. He got no better, so we thought we would send him home, to Kisumu, for a real rest, and a check up in Kisumu hospital. We sent Benjamen, his cousin, to look after him on the journey. And he is dead. Hugo heard when he telephoned Louis. We don't know, yet, whether he died on the journey, or just after. Isn't it ghastly.

Well, there is no more horrible news. I should have started with thank you Olly for your letter, and you, Mum for your two. We adored the Father Christmas blue* — what a super one. I thought I would get the horrors over first, and then turn to the less horrible things and end on a more normal note. I do hope that the Old Men are being kind, and helping you along with your gruesom task, Mum. I wonder if the Nature proofs have come in yet. And when, Hugo asks, is your book out — your other one.† I told him I thought it was coming out for Christmas, but that you would most undoubtedly send us a pre-copy just as soon as it was available.

Where shall we be for Christmas. On the Serengeti — just. We are leaving this sad place in four days' time. We shall fly down with the second and third doses for the chimps (of vaccine) between Christmas and New Year. Thank goodness, we are still delighted with Alice. . . . Sophie has had her baby. A little girl, named Sorem

---

* An aerogramme or single-sheet airmail letter made of blue paper, this one presumably embellished with an attractive picture of Father Christmas.

† Vanne was working on her "Old Men," a coauthored book (with Louis Leakey) entitled *Unveiling Man's Origins*. Her other book, about to appear, was a novel based on a theme of African high adventure: *In the Rainforest*, published in England by Collins.

because it arrived for the first time on Alice's birthday. I have probably told you this, but never mind. And Jomeo has brought his family. We have had fun with their names. Mum is Vodka. Youngest (1
year) is Quantro (spelling on purpose) and next up — just under
Fifi age — is Sherry. (2 birds with one stone — Sherry Washburn,
and the booze.) And, because of all this booziness, Jomeo is —
Jomeo Jin. Isn't it super. And Satan — how well you know him,
Mum! Has brought his family too. Satan, young sister Sparrow —
old Mum — Sprout!

Am being ordered to stop for a pre-supper drink. So will end off
afterwards. If there is not more time — then tons of love to you all
from all of us. Oh — where we will be by mail for Christmas. Same
address — c/o Box 2818, Nairobi.

There isn't time for more. So I will end off. It seems a long enough
letter. Hugo is, at this moment, photographing the genet. She is
<u>super.</u> Quite tame. Doesn't care 2 hoots about flashes, or talking —
or anything — she is just embarking on her second plate of curry!
Burr* sends his love.

Love from me.

As from:† Box 2818<br>Nairobi<br>15 December 1966

Dear Dr. Carmichael,

Thank you for your letter of 7 November asking me for abstracts
of the chimpanzee research project since 1963.

I'm afraid that I simply have not found the time, as yet, to prepare
such abstracts. Hugo and I have been at the Gombe Stream, and,
due to the sudden illness of the secretary, and the fact that one assistant had to have her yearly holiday, I have been working full time
here to keep the records up to date. On top of the usual hectic work,
we have been in the midst of this terrible polio epidemic — of which

---

\* A nickname for Hugo.

† Or "As if from": meaning that even though the letter was written in one place
(Gombe), any reply should be sent to a second place, the address listed (Nairobi).

I am sure you have heard by now. When we are in possession of all the details I will send a full report to the Committee — not only of the losses and disabilities that our chimp group has suffered, but also as much information as we have been able to glean as to the source of infection, and details as to how the disease spread. Let me just say for now that, to our great relief, we have been able to ascertain, more or less for certain, that the disease could not have been introduced through our research project. It began to the south of Kigoma, there were cases in Kigoma itself and, so far, we have been able to trace its occurrence in only two villages north of Kigoma — between Kigoma and the Reserve. Unfortunately, both these villages, although not in the Reserve, are, nonetheless, within the range of the chimps. In fact, several times we have seen chimps in the trees surrounding one of these villages (which is by the lake shore) during trips to or from Kigoma. The whole affair has been like living in a nightmare as one after the other of the chimps comes back, after an absence, crippled. We have had 7 affected now, three really badly. And, almost certainly, between two and four deaths.

I will work on the abstracts as soon as we leave here — which is in a couple of days from now.

Yours sincerely,
Jane

As from: Box 2818
Nairobi
15 December 1966

Dear Dr. Payne,

Thank you for your letter of 7 November. What a pity that the report-letter arrived just too late for the extended Research Committee meeting.

To answer your other queries. We have heard nothing further concerning Mr. Don Symons, and are quite in the dark as to whether he has decided to try and work at the Gombe Stream or not. We shall, of course, let you know as soon as we hear anything further from him.

With regard to the matter of providing us with negatives and prints of Hugo's colour stills of the chimps, I do agree that it is certain that we do not want copies of <u>everything.</u> I think your idea that we should try to sort this out during a visit by me to the United States is a very good one. There has been a suggestion that Hugo should visit the Geographic sometime early next year (such as April) and, if it is possible, this would obviously be the best time for me to come as well. I can quite see that a personal relationship with the Committee is of tremendous importance.

There is one other matter which I must mention — that is that I do hope that Dave Bridge passed on to you our message regarding the Grant Request for 1967. Namely that we omitted to include the salary of Mike Richmond, our Nairobi contact, in our budget. This sum amounts to £120 for the entire year.

I am afraid I have to end on a rather gloomy note. This is concerning the polio epidemic here at the Reserve. (Which is the reason why we are still here.) Apart from the two chimps with useless arms, the young male Pepe arrived with one arm useless, and the other badly affected. He is not strong enough to walk upright, and shuffles around on his bottom. Mr. McGregor arrived with both legs paralysed. For a week we searched for foods for him, and fed him — often in his nest. For he was able to pull himself up into trees in the most amazing way. His progression along the ground was nothing short of nightmarish as he dragged himself, rolled, or turned head over heels. Often he pulled himself back through his arms from a sitting position. This combination of methods of moving had worn away all the skin on his buttocks, which were raw and bleeding. And, to make the whole picture more of a horror than ever, he had lost bladder control and was constantly wet with urine so that literally millions of flies were round him all day. They nearly drove him demented, even though we went down to him many times every day to flit the flies. Finally he dislocated one good arm — we had guessed, by this time, there was no hope of recovery in either leg, and Hugo had to shoot him. It was all so horrible. And then, yesterday, poor little adolescent MacD crept into camp — both arms completely useless. A living skeleton, creeping on his buttocks like Pepe. We had to shoot him too. It is more like living in some horror story, waiting, waiting, for poor cripples to come back to us, than anything I could have imagined. We are now really worried about our favourite Figan (he has not been in for over 2 weeks) and Pooch, and the mother Mandy. J.B. is almost certainly dead — also two or three others that have not come in for 3 months.

We have managed to vaccinate all but seven of our group by now. But we still do not know if they are safe — because of the 3 weeks incubation. They might have been incubating when we gave them the vaccine. We shall know, for most of them, by Christmas. In the new year Hugo and I shall have to fly more vaccine to the Reserve for the second and third doses. (The oral type, given in bananas.) We will send a full report on the epidemic when we know all the facts.

Best regards from Hugo & me,
Yours sincerely,
Jane

[Mid-January 1967]

Darling Mum,

A very short note to wish you a very happy birthday. I think we should make a family arrangement about birthdays. All have a Special Celebration Universal Family Birthday. This to be a moveable feast, and to occur when Hugo and I are in England. Then we all give each other cards and presy's. Isn't that a good idea? And just send cables to show we have remembered the actual day — if we have! I had a super card for you — I left it at the Reserve! I am hoping I can get another from the shop where I got the first, tomorrow. Then it will still get to you by 24th.

Well, let me tell you some news. A bit brighter this time. We had just got back from the Reserve last time. I can't remember if I wrote or not? Anyway, pretending I didn't. We took the gorilla girl, Dian Fossey, down with us. We got slightly annoyed with her. Like Jif we thought she was really excellent when we first met her — and, as you know, we took her on safari for Christmas. But — and don't mention the "but" to Louis who is so pleased. She seems to have the most romantic ideas in her head. She keeps saying the meadow (you know, where the Schallers were in their cabin) is like an alpine meadow. She is determined to get a cow up there, and lots of hens. She will have a bell round the cow's neck. She wants several pets, and plans to tame all the ravens — not just two like Kay did. She plans to make bramble jam out of the wild blackberries. Well — when I began with the chimps, I had romantic notions too. But they were of how I would be able to move about with a chimp group, be accepted by them as another chimp, practise climbing through the branches — you know, a glorified Tarzan type of thing. Next we found out that she had not even read George's book carefully.* Nor has she, during the past 3 years since she planned to study gorillas, bothered to learn <u>anything</u> about primates. She said to me that she couldn't think why gorillas didn't eat wild blackberries. She was sure George was wrong. Well, as I pointed out to her, George has detailed descriptions of a big male eating wild blackberries! However, let us hope for the best. . . .

We got back with her, and, the next morning, had a note to say would we please contact the Ker and Downey office. Which we did. And this was our millionaire friend, Royal Little, saying he wanted to make a last minute change in his safari plans. Instead of driving down with his safari from a to b, which would take 4 days, he wanted to spend those days in making a visit to the chimps. He would pay our return fare, charter flight, if we would go down to show him the chimps!!! Well — anything to get there again, and a good chance to get better acquainted with Royal and party.

The same day we interviewed our prospective secretary who has been two weeks in Africa, from England. A Susanah (or Sue) Chaytor. A very nice girl, whom we engaged on the spot. No need for 2 year contracts since we didn't have to pay her fare. So we took her with us when we went up to the farm of one Guy Grant at Nanyuki. . . . We stayed there for 4 days. We liked Sue a lot — a

---

* George Schaller wrote two books about his gorilla research, one academic *(The Mountain Gorilla)* and one popular *(The Year of the Gorilla)*. Both were published by the University of Chicago Press, in 1963 and 1964 respectively.

very self effacing person, well educated, top drawer, interesting and intelligent, good sense of humor — and fun. She quite fell for Guy — but he was not interested.

When we got back we frantically shopped for lunch and supper for the millionaire day and evening at the Reserve. Took salad and ham for lunch, and 2 chickens and veg. appropriate and wine for the supper. We flew down the day before they were due to arrive, complete with Sue, in the fastest plane that Safari Air possess. A twin engine Skyknight. The stupid Ker and Downey woman made a right mess up of things. She forgot to tell Safari Air that we would not be returning the same night, and the plane was fully booked the next day. We found, also, that it was not booked to come and fetch us the right day — not booked at all. She had to hastily book it. She even forgot to tell us that we were supposed to pick up John Owen (the Tanz. National Parks Director) on the way down! But luckily he found he couldn't make it, so was not left waiting in vain at the air strip in Arusha!!! What a woman. And a vile and snooty woman too, who walked straight past Hugo and I at the Thorn Tree* when we were both looking scruffy! And is vile to her underlings!

Well, apart from a bad start — when Caroline made Hugo and I, Sue, and Alice who had come to meet us, wait for 2 hours because of two chimps that are not really scary at all, and when she could with great ease have pressed a box open behind the building and let us walk up — apart from that, I say, the two days were most successful. Not too many chimps came — it would have been better with a few more males charging about. But mums came — plus Flo of course! Babies played, Flo and Gigi had a fight, and Worzle stamped on Flo. Mike displayed and threw a rock almost into the party watching him! And they could be out all the time. Sniff and Fifi sat looking in at the windows, and Pooch played a sort of game of Peek-a-boo with Royal that delighted him. They had a colour polaroid, took a picture of Fifi, showed it to Flint — and he delighted them by kissing it! Altogether very successful. As for the night-wear of a millionaire! Sleeping accommodation was a bit tight. We had

---

* A sidewalk cafe in central Nairobi.

Royal, and the oldish woman — someone's aunt — each in one of the girls' rooms. The son with his wife in Lawick Lodge. And the four of us (we sent Caroline into Kigoma to wait with her dear Barnabus!)* slept in a row in the work room! Just as we four were about to go to bed, having laid out our various matresses, etc, the genet appeared. Royal specially wanted to see it, so we told him. And he appeared. I thought Sue was going to have an apoplectic fit when he appeared! He had on pyjamas made of sort of chill-proof stuff. The top, close fitting, was navy blue, with a tight fitting round collar — white — and tight fitting long sleeves — white cuffs. The trousers (into which the top was tucked) were white, with a navy waistband. They came just below his calves, where they were pinched in by navy cuffs. It really was the biggest hoot!

Also, only a millionaire could get away with something I found out from daughter-in-law (sweet girl) — Royal puts about 4 spoonfuls of sugar into every glass of champaigne he drinks!!!!!!!! Oh — sorry. Thought I had learnt to spell it by now. Just realized when I looked. Typed quite automatically!!!

Mum — about this girl you wrote to and tried to put off. We are hoping to get Sue to come about with us. She is ideal. And any secretary of ours had to get to know all the chimps first, so that she could whizz down there in emergencies. So we much hope that this other girl will do for the chimps. We are getting another observer to join Alice — who is still doing EXCELLENTLY. This is quite a buddy of hers — male — very highly recommended by the man who recommended her. Alice is thrilled to bits, and I really do think that, with a girl as dedicated and honest as she, it will work. I only hope that the London girl will be suitable for the Reserve so that we can have Sue — and then everything will be hunky dory. Sue is not the type of girl who will stay long in one place, but she will be very good while we have her, and will stay longer if she can travel around with us, than if she had to stay with the chimps all the time. We shall really be well away.

We were planning to go off to the Serengeti tomorrow — no, day

---

* Caroline Coleman's fiancé, a bank manager in Kigoma.

after. For two months. But phone call from the Geographic. Could we wait here until at least 24th, until the final M.S. arrives. And then, any things that are still wrong, ring up and tell over the phone! The phone call this morning must have cost nearly £100. Isn't it awful! As we have not yet seen any of the picture legends, I can envisage even longer calls in the immediate future! But they are being very good — I think the T.V. fiasco really scared them, and they are terrified of bringing Grosvenor's — or our — wrath on their heads! Jolly good show. You will be pleased to hear that although they have not completely changed the title, it is now, instead of "My Friends the Chimps" (sort of Michaela Denis type title) it is "My Friends the Wild Chimpanzees." This we think is fine — and there is now a para. in the last chapter (which I have completely rewritten) defining what I mean by friendship with a chimp. I did tell you, did I, that they had completely re-written the last chapter? We were so livid. They had put in a lot of rubbish about conservation in general, cut out the bit about conservation of chimps — or cut it to a bare minimum. Omitted to put in about the fund for the chimp reserves. And, believe it or not, added a whole long bit about the polio — which I had especially said I did not want to put in! However, they have accepted my new chapter — which is, I am certain, 50% better than the other last chapter. I think it is going to be a good book. They have even got in pictures of the musculature of man and chimp, side by side, drawings of hand positions, locomotion positions, etc. Compared with what we thought it would be like, it will be excellent. Only trouble is, they have used a number of ideas we had for our own book!!!!!!

One last bit of news. Pepe arrived in camp the day before we did — first time since when he came before and was so terrified when Humphrey and Flo were terrified. His legs have got so strong that he was walking bipedally just like Faben! Isn't that super! I felt sure there was nothing wrong with his legs except that most chimps' legs just aren't strong enough to enable them to move about upright for more than a few hundred yards. He was, of course, attacked and displayed with, and has not returned. But as Faben has now been more or less accepted back into the community, I am sure Pepe will be as well.

Let me end with more birthday wishes — many happy returns and all that. And many thanks for your last letter which I think I found at the Reserve. Thrilled to hear that the Old Men are nearing the end (if you can get Louis to do his bits which I bet you can't! Do you have to add the latest finds? The Nature Bombshell!) Did you know vulture tool using was reported fully in Time magazine & got into the Sunday papers here? Was it in any of the English papers? Time got it from Nature. Are you sending us a page from Nature?

Box 2818
Nairobi
27 January 1967

Dear Dr. Carmichael,

Very many thanks for your letter of 18 December telling us that the grant request had been approved. Unfortunately this letter never reached us — we have just received a copy! But it is wonderful news.

As we now have an external account in our Dutch bank in Nairobi, I think it would be best if the whole amount we requested be sent there, and we can arrange for small amounts to be transferred to Kigoma as and when necessary.

I have sent off the physical and literary releases to the Reserve with instructions for the two new members of our staff to return them to you when they have been signed.

You will be pleased to hear that our epidemic has finally, to all intents and purposes, been arrested. The total number of casualties, so far as we know, is now 4 deaths, two shot by us, and 5 left with paralyzed limbs. We have the body of poor Mr. McGregor in deep freeze here in Nairobi. We have now found virologists willing to examine parts of his brain and spinal cord in an effort to determine, for certain, whether or not he died of polio.

Thank you again for your letter.

Yours sincerely,
Jane

# 3

❧ ❧ ❧

## DOMESTIC INTERLUDE
### 1967

"You'll have to change your way of life now, won't you?" a number of friends said to me when they heard our family would be
enlarged.

— *Grub the Bush Baby*

FROM LATE JANUARY to the third week of February 1967, the
van Lawicks camped in the spectacular Ngorongoro Crater,
where they continued to study and photograph animals, including the stone-throwing Egyptian vultures National Geographic
had decided to feature, as well as spotted hyenas. National Geographic had contracted for the Dutch researcher Hans Kruuk to
write an article on those powerful, territorial predators. Kruuk was
to be assisted by his wife, Jane, while Hugo van Lawick had been
asked to supply the photographs.

Vultures and hyenas at Ngorongoro for three or four weeks during January and February. In July and August, down to Gombe for
chimpanzees. Then back to Ngorongoro from the second week of
September to the middle of October: more vultures and hyenas.

Since the birth of the Gombe Stream Research Center at the start
of 1964, Jane and Hugo had struggled, with the help of assistant
observers and record keepers, to maintain a continuous record from
the banana feeding station so that it operated rather like a window into the forest home of one particular chimpanzee community.
Aside from Jane's own work at Gombe during those early years, the
research taking place might be described as a maintenance-level

study: steady but somewhat generalized observations. The two research assistants who had kept that work going during much of 1966, Caroline Coleman and Sally Avery, left by the end of that year — and were replaced at first by Alice Sorem from San Diego, California.

Early in 1967, Alice was joined by a young Englishwoman, Sue Chaytor, hired by Jane and Hugo to work as a secretary. Sue left Gombe around the first of April and was replaced at that time by a young man from San Diego, Patrick McGinnis, who had come with the same recommendations as Alice Sorem and who, in fact, happened to be Sorem's "boy friend" (as mentioned in the February 26 letter to Jane's family). Whatever doubts Jane may have had about this arrangement soon disappeared. Pat McGinnis turned out to be not only "an excellent typist" but a valuable member of the research team; he later was accepted as a Ph.D. candidate at Cambridge University and, after four years of research at Gombe, finished a doctoral dissertation on "Patterns of Sexual Behaviour" among the Gombe chimpanzees.

At the same time (early April), Jane hired Nicoletta Maraschin, later known as Nita, as her personal secretary in Nairobi. She also completed the arrangements for taking on another research assistant, Patricia (Patti) Moehlman, who was expected to show up in Nairobi on June 20 but, for various reasons, failed to appear until around the middle of July. As Jane commented in a letter from Gombe (mid-August), in spite of the "bad start," Patti was "doing very well."

Another researcher arrived from Rockefeller University in New York in late June. Peter Marler, whom Jane had met two years earlier at the Wenner-Gren primate conference in Austria, came for the summer to tape-record chimpanzee vocalizations, which he would later subject to spectrographic analysis. He and Jane planned a collaborative study of chimpanzee vocalizations and facial expressions. Peter was accompanied by his wife, Judith, and their two children — and also a student, Richard (Dick) Sigmond.

Other visitors showed up that summer. The physical anthropologist and baboon expert Irven DeVore and his wife, Nancy, were guests at Gombe for three days near the middle of August. Earlier, sometime during the first week of August, the Tanzanian minister of agriculture — the only white man in the entire government — had arrived to see for himself what was going on. Derek Bryceson was his name, and although his presence barely registered at the time (and is not mentioned in any of the letters in this sequence), he would be noticed a good deal more some years later, when he became Jane's second husband. Finally, toward the end of September, one more eager young student emerged. Tim Ransom, who had studied under Phyllis Jay at the University of California at Berkeley, met up with the van Lawicks at Ngorongoro (referred to in passing at the end of the September 22 letter) on his way to Gombe to start long-term baboon research with his wife, Bonnie. Tim would eventually complete a doctoral dissertation on the ecology and social behavior of the Gombe baboons.

To summarize, during the pivotal year 1967 Jane and Hugo were regularly commuting between Ngorongoro, Gombe, and Nairobi; Jane's immediate study subjects had expanded beyond chimpanzees to include vultures and hyenas; and the pace and scope of the research at Gombe Stream had picked up markedly. At times during the summer of 1967, well over a dozen American and European researchers and their associates and family members were living in various huts and cabins at Gombe. Nairobi was the usual gateway for visitors flying into East Africa from Europe or America; and that city was often a logical meeting place for new arrivals and visitors. Jane and Hugo were fortunate in having a supportive group of friends and associates there to help with logistics, including Louis Leakey and Mike Richmond. Nevertheless, Nairobi of necessity became more and more a base of operations for Jane and Hugo during this period. Nairobi was where they met visitors, made connections, interviewed potential employees and assistants, stored and repaired equipment, kept books and papers and other research materials, and so on. In the past they had stayed in hotels. Now it made sense to buy a house.

As we can see from the letter of February 26, first in this sequence, they did so: "WE HAVE GOT A HOUSE!!!!" Located in the suburb of Limuru about 18 miles from Nairobi center, the house came complete with furniture, two dogs (Alsatians named Jessica and Rusty), and a cat (Squink), as well as a veranda that covered one entire side of the house and looked out over a panoramic view "where, on clear days, you can see for 80 miles." The closed-in veranda was, Jane wrote home, "a really lovely room — you could use it for anything — sitting in, eating, having a party, for children or pets — or anything else you can think of!" What other veranda uses Jane may have been thinking of remain unstated, but there *was* the imminent baby for whom they were just then buying "nappies" and "a little pair of sheets and a nice soft blanket." The van Lawicks finally moved into their Limuru house around the first of April, in time for Jane's thirty-third birthday (on April 3) and also in time to provide a comfortable home for their first and only child, Hugo Eric Louis van Lawick (born on March 4).

The sudden appearance of a baby may surprise many readers of these letters, since there have been no previous hints about anyone expecting one. As we can read in the second letter of February 26, addressed to Dr. Carmichael, Jane and Hugo were "planning to keep this as a sudden surprise." Jane may have had several reasons, other than a perfectly reasonable sense of privacy, for keeping quiet about the pregnancy. She was, after all, four to six months pregnant during the worst phase of the polio epidemic at Gombe. Perhaps she had hoped not to cause undue worry at home or an overreaction by her National Geographic friends and sponsors. Additionally, of course, she was a vital, energetic woman who may have been simply too busy and engaged in the immediacy of animal watching at Gombe and Ngorongoro to think about baby watching in Nairobi until an actual baby turned up.

Once the baby did arrive, though, Jane focused her extraordinary talents for observation in his direction, documenting in several letters little Hugo's development as perhaps a representative *Homo sapiens* infant. She was less deliberately documenting as well some of the typical responses of representative *Homo sapiens* parents: from "He is now a model baby!" (June) to "Little hugo . . . is undeniably teething" (July) to "He is driving us dotty" (August).

Little Hugo — Hugo Eric Louis — was named after three important men in his family: his father, his granduncle, and his "fairy foster grandfather." But in a family where virtually everyone had a nickname, it was not long before Hugo Eric Louis had one too. A year earlier, young chimpanzee Goblin had acquired his second name, Grub, as a result of some comically grubby eating habits. At some point during little Hugo's first stay at Gombe, in July of 1967, the human infant managed to win an informal competition with the chimpanzee Goblin for that long-standing nickname. The event is not directly referred to in the letters, but it must have happened in July. By August little Hugo was being called Grublin or Grublin-Gob, a mouthful that was soon shortened to Grub, which to this day remains the working name of Jane's only son.

As parents usually do, Jane and Hugo obviously doted on their new child. Just as obviously, they loved wilderness and wild animals and were deeply engaged with their lifework of watching and documenting the natural world of East Africa. Some three weeks before he was born, little Hugo was unknowingly threatened with premature delivery when three overly playful lions raided the camp at Ngorongoro one night, shredding a tent, playing cat and mouse with the Land Rover, and for an hour or so giving everyone a good scare. Three months after his birth, little Hugo was living at Gombe, protected from aggressive baboons and predatory chimpanzees (who have been known to snatch and eat human babies) by his own baby-blue cage. At age six months, little Hugo — now Grublin — was back at Ngorongoro, living with his mother and father and, as we note from the final letter of this chapter, breaking out his first tooth, singing, and watching spotted hyenas kill and be killed in a series of grisly predations and gory territorial battles between the Munge Clan and the Scratching Rocks Clan.

\*     \*     \*     \*

[Probably February 26, 1967]

Darling Family,

I must write quickly to tell you the latest news — WE HAVE GOT A HOUSE!!!! We can't move into it yet, but it is all most exciting, and we, ourselves, can hardly believe it. We saw it advertised in the paper, went to enquire about it, went out to see it that evening, and paid the deposit on it the next day.

It is at Limuru, in the very nicest, residential part. Pretty near the Moss's, about 6 miles from Cynthia* (who is, according to us, too far out to be in the nice part) and also in the same road as two very nice people we have just met, one of whom is a sculptor, mainly of animals. You turn off the main Limuru road, turn again, and there it is — all on tarmac which, of course, makes a big difference — to time of getting to Nairobi (18 miles) and to wear and tear on cars, etc.

The people have been in it 2 1/2 years. There are tears in their eyes when they talk about leaving — he is being transferred. He got the house from the estate agents — for whom he also works! So we reckoned they would not have sold an employee a dud! Now, the great thing about this house, for us, is that it is fully furnished! It has, for one thing, a huge, modern, £60 fridge, which he bought 6 months ago! 4 big beds and 4 smaller ones. Very nice dining room table. And the other things (except for matresses and cushions and curtains, etc.) all looked very nice. But it is the house itself that is such fun. From the outside it is rather weird. It is stone, with a tiled roof and a small upstairs floor. One extra wing has been added on, made (the walls) of cedar offshoots. This part we shall keep aside for someone to live — as we cannot leave it empty when we are on safari. We shall have to add one room onto it. At the moment there is one large room, a bathroom and lav — a guest wing. We shall have to add a small bedroom. Whoever lives there again . . . will share our kitchen, which is absolutely gigantic, and quite modern. Benjamen will <u>adore</u> it! It is lined with built in cupboards, has a lovely sink, and this giant fridge.

The rest of the downstairs consists of a beautiful long dining, sit-

---

* Cynthia Booth, who ran Louis Leakey's monkey breeding project at Tigoni. Louis had started this project in 1958, thinking of it as a way to provide primates for medical research without taking them from the wild. According to Leakey biographer Virginia Morrell, "Booth was then [in 1958] newly widowed, a blond, brilliant . . . young woman, and she and Louis apparently had an affair. This did not last, and by 1966, Booth, now remarried, had grown bitter and frustrated."

ting room. The sitting room half has a glorious fireplace and mantlepiece. You go up one sort of step, to a very slightly higher level, for the dining room part. This is not large, but large enough for quite big dinner parties. You step down again, towards the front of the house, into the most delightful little closed in veranda, windows all round. Looking out (as do the sitting room windows) over a view where, on clear days, you can see for 80 miles! The little guest wing leads off from this room. Then, on the other side of the sitting room, at the back of the house, is the huge kitchen and one other bedroom — or you could use it for anything. Then, the piece de resistance. Built on by the last owner, behind these two rooms, a built in veranda running the whole length of the house, windows all round, and a tiled floor. A really lovely room — you could use it for anything — sitting in, eating, having a party, for children or pets — or anything else you can think of! It made me smile to myself when the owner turned to Hugo and said "It's a good room for the wife to sit with her sewing!" . . .

As I told you, when your darling little baby clothes arrived we had bought nothing at all. We shopped a bit yesterday, and it was really rather a hoot, as we didn't know what to call anything, or what to ask for! However, we did manage to get nappies! And a little pair of sheets and a nice soft blanket. And one dear little sort of siren suit thing. We don't think we need much more in the way of clothes because small babies, we are told, grow so quickly that soon none of the tiny sized garments fit any more. . . .

How are the Old Men, Mum? Do hope they are coming on nicely. We had a letter from Louis saying the chimp book "looks excellent".* We, of course, havn't seen it! There seems to be a conspiracy on everyone's part to keep us in the dark where printed material is concerned.

Must close and write to Carmichael, Payne, Bridge, etc, etc. Thank <u>goodness</u> we have just had a cable to say Alice's boy friend is actually coming — this month. So it will not be a complete flop when Sue leaves in April. Patrick, luckily, is an excellent typist!

---

* In other words, *My Friends the Wild Chimpanzees* had just appeared, though too recently for Jane to have yet seen a copy.

Will write again soon — <u>possibly</u> it will even be after the arrival of the great-grandchild, grandchild, niece/nephew etc, etc!!

Tons & tons of love to all,

Jane

P.O. Box 2818

Nairobi

26 February 1967

Dear Dr. Carmichael,

As you may remember, I mentioned in our last grant request the possibility of Dr. Peter Marler joining the Gombe Stream research team for a short period this year. The project was a joint study with me on chimpanzee vocalizations, facial expressions, gestures, postures etc. I am now very happy to report that Dr. Marler will definitely be coming out to undertake this research. Unfortunately he is able to stay only for about 6 weeks, and we are busy working out plans so that we can work together efficiently during this short time and get a maximum of work done.

The vocalizations will be recorded on a variety of tape recorders, including a stereo recorder — one track being used for chimp calls, the other for synchronous notes.

Our most ambitious plan, however, which should yield very important results, calls for the taking of synchronous sound/film. Dr. Marler will be bringing the equipment needed for this — but we cannot do without Hugo — to take the motion picture film. We should need some film material for him of the type which he has been using.

Hugo, therefore, would need a temporary release for a short period from his assignment of photographing East African animals. He is in full support of the plan — the photography for the Animal book is proceeding excellently and the short break would not, he considers, affect the results of this photography. We hope very much, therefore, that the Society agrees to this so we can get a maximum benefit from Dr. Marler's co-operation with us.

You have undoubtedly heard, by now, that we are expecting an infant in the near future. We were planning to keep this as a sudden surprise — but, somewhat naturally, it is not easy to keep such things secret for long! We are also very excited because, at long last, we have managed to buy a house, just outside Nairobi, to serve as a home base for us, and where I can continue with my work during our necessary visits to Nairobi. We plan to divide off part of it so that someone can live there permanently and look after the place when we are away.

Also it has quite a good-sized plot (nearly 9 acres) so that, in the future, we might do such things as setting up a bush-baby colony in a huge field cage, or other research projects.

We have been doing a number of tests on Egyptian Vultures in Ngorongoro Crater with reference to their stone throwing behaviour. These have yielded much interesting information — the most important of which is that, so far as we can tell at present, the behaviour appears to be <u>learned.</u> Thus all the fully adult birds tested picked up stones as soon as they saw the ostrich egg. Some of the younger ones were also efficient in their opening technique, but other youngsters, though they tried frantically to open the egg with beak and claw for anything up to 30 minutes, never picked up a stone. Much further work remains to be done, however. We are planning a whole series of tests, and are much hoping to acquire a fledgling vulture and hand rear it. This may give us more definite clues regarding the basic patterns from which the throwing behaviour has derived.

Hugo joins me in sending warm personal regards to you and your wife.

Yours sincerely,
Jane

Mater Miseracord
(or however you [letter torn]
5th March [1967]

Darling Family,

Just a wee note to let you hear from me as well as Hugo that all is well with 'Little' Hugo Eric Louis and me. His head (& he is now about 28 hours old) is almost in its correct shape. Did Hugo tell you that he has a big head (is, in fact, a big, though not heavy, baby). Therefore it got slightly squashed during his exit to the world. He had quite pronounced jowls at birth but these are 'rising' towards his cheeks. A <u>rosebud</u> mouth. <u>Really!</u> One ear is pushed out into a funny shape, but we think that that, also, is correcting itself. I must tell you that whilst we were all having difficulties with the delivery of his head I thought of Olly's one-time sweeping statement — that babies' heads never grew!!! No babies would ever be born!! He was not red or wrinkled at birth. A nice pink colour all over. He was, by the way, a respectable 7 lbs. Even this hospital has gone back on its word — they won't let me keep him in the room. Hugo & I have given up. They all refer it to more and more inaccessible and unapproachable sisters & mothers. So, as I hope to be out in 2 more days, or 3 perhaps, we have resigned ourselves to all the possible repressions & fixations and complexes etc, etc which may develop in his personality as a consequence! Did Hugo tell you that the Night Nurse Nun who received me was so positive that nothing would happen before the following afternoon that he was peaceful enough to go back to bed! She wouldn't listen to me! Did he also tell you that he rang up a.m. & was told I was in the Labor Room, instead of the D[elivery] room. So he was discussing <u>INCOME TAX</u> whilst his son was born!!! Isn't that worthy of Hugo!! It is also a hoot about our doctor. He was <u>so</u> convinced when he went away for 10 days that nothing would happen with me!! I have a routine check up with him the day after tomorrow!!! Thanks so much for your letter, Dan — it came yesterday, Little H's birthday!

Will write more, & I hope we'll have some pictures, soon.

Love from us <u>all,</u>
Jane

The Birches
[Postmarked April 30, 1967]

My dear Sallykins,

Thank you for your letter. Isn't it a hoot — me being a Mum! All the Birches relations have lovely names — instead of Grandmother

Mum is 'Grum', Olly — Grolly. Then there is Grand, Granan and, finally, Grunkle!!

Now. He is having a hastily arranged christening in London, where Hugo & I were married. Chelsea Old Church. We are hoping you can come — but I suppose you won't get out of school in time — 5.0 p.m. on Friday 5th May. Afterwards we are having a <u>tiny</u> party in the flat — maybe you could come for that. On Saturday we all go to Cambridge for me to collect my degree — at last. And there will be a sort of tea party there too — Eric has taken his rooms — no — the Senior Fellows Guest Rooms. We are having tea there after the degree. I can't offer you a bed in Cambridge — we are staying with Lyn* — Ma, me, Jif & Grolly. And little Hugo of course. But there won't be room for anyone else!! I suspect we could offer you a sleeping bag in the flat the night before, though. Especially if you bring an eiderdown or something. But I suggest that you ring the flat on Thursday evening — 4th May. Ma & I are driving to London that day — doing the journey in stages for little Hugo's benefit.

The following weekend — can you come & stay at the Birches?

Anyway — more news when you ring — or when we see you. Must end now as the little one is stirring — almost time for his feed. I wonder if Sue's 5th has arrived yet!†

See you soon.

Love,<br>Jane

[June 2, 1967]

Darling Mum,

Well — here we are (Little Hugo & I) back in our house. It was so welcoming — full of flowers from Hugo. And, as we got out of the

---

* Lyn Lloyd Newman owned Cross Farm, near Cambridge, and lived there in a converted dove house, thus freeing the farmhouse for rental; Jane was a tenant at the farm during parts of 1964 and 1965 when she was finishing her doctoral work. Newman, incidentally, wrote the well-received *Field with Geese* (London: H. Hamilton, 1960).

† Sally's sister, Susan Cary Featherstone, was expecting a fifth child; Katy Featherstone was born ten days after this letter was written.

car, the first of Jessica's puppies was being born!! She has 7 but we are only going to keep two. And guess what — a lovely, beautiful DOUBLE BED!!!

Little Hugo was so good on the plane. He cried when we left until I fed him, was a bit scratchy after that — then slept soundly, apart from one short feed, until we reached the house! He has behaved angelically ever since. I have <u>never</u> known him [to] sleep so well as today.

The airport was not the place for fond farewells, was it? That was why I vanished rather smartly — I knew you could not have borne to kiss little Hugo goodbye. But I did want — or <u>do</u> want — to thank you for the 1000 and 1 things you did for me while I was at home, & to apologize for the 100 & 1 things I have left you to do. . . .

The temperature here is about the same as in England. Bit colder at night I think. Pleasant. Nicoletta is going to Aden to finish off her affairs there before coming to the chimps with us. We don't go until 20th June so have a nice long time in the house. I may manage to finish off what I didn't finish off when in England — like <u>AB-STRACTS!</u>

Shall not make this long as Hugo is again about to depart. He has to show the film at the Aero club where Mike Richmond shows wild life films. Poor Hugo. Eve* sends you her love — I rang her to say hello & she was so <u>thrilled</u> that Hugo had <u>dropped in</u> on them. She couldn't get over it!

<u>Later.</u> Really — I am beginning to think he must be teething! For 3 days running — Party, leaving day, and today (oh, <u>not</u> yesterday) he has cried & cried for no reason. Yet on each occasion he <u>stops</u> when you pick him up & walk round — why? Today he woke finally. Cried a bit. Stopped for music. <u>Screamed</u> when offered the breast. Ate Baby Rice. Screamed. Stopped for bath. Then laughed & kicked. Screamed. Fed for a long time — Screamed & screamed. Went peacefully to sleep. Very peculiar. <u>Since when</u> I have been

---

* Eve Mitchell had been a stalwart, motherly friend ever since Jane moved to Nairobi in 1957.

rocking, lulling, changing, repeat, repeat, ad nauseam. Hey ho. Hugo will be back soon. And I am nearly asleep and will end here.

Thank you again, more than I can say, for all that you did. I'm certain little hugo misses his Grum.

Tons of love, of course, to all,

Jane


Box 2818
Nairobi
10 June 1967

Dear Dr. Payne,

This is to express my very great delight in receiving the extra payment for the chimp book. As always, the Society is extremely generous — very many thanks indeed. It was a most pleasant surprise to greet me on my return to Africa. I am delighted to hear that the book seems to be going well.

Thank you also for sending the picture of the two baby gorilla twins. As you say it is a really wonderful picture and the protective posture of one of them is most charming.

At long long last little Hugo (we usually write the poor little chap as hugo, with a small "h"!) is becoming a model baby. He was always good, but he did go on waking up for a night feed for rather a long time. And now he has, for 6 nights running, slept right through until morning. It certainly does make a difference and I feel quite different myself. We will send some more pictures of him soon.

We are getting ready now to set off to the Gombe. There will be quite a crowd of us, but with care things can be organized all right. I think the project with Peter Marler will be fascinating. I doubt whether I shall be able to do as much work with the chimps as usual!! Little hugo's cage has already been set up in the smaller building (Lawick Lodge) and two extra windows have been put in for extra ventilation. Extra thatch on the roof too. So I do hope that he will continue to be as healthy a babe as he has been so far in his short life.

My regards to your wife, and Hugo sends his too.

Yours sincerely,
Jane

[Around June 15, 1967]

Darling Family,

Sorry not to have written sooner — but, as you know, time tends to get taken up with little hugo!! However, let me tell you that a miracle has occurred. He is now a model baby! He wakes up between 6.45 and 7.30 a.m. He feeds, plays, and goes to sleep till about 11. Again he plays, feeds, plays, and sleeps till after lunch. He then is fed and goes for a walk round the garden, looking at all the flowers (in his pram) and sleeps until about 5.30. Then he kicks by the fire, has his bath, and is fed up in our room at between 6 and 7. He at once drops off and sleeps until about 11 or 11.30. He feeds, plays in bed with us, and then sleeps throughout the night!!!!!! He has kept this up for about 5 days (with one day during which he was awake more than asleep).

But he has changed so much. He reaches out to touch things, or stares fascinated. Flowers, his bears, books, pictures — everything including faces and hands. Loves playing with fingers and trying to hold my ring. Loves hitting his father in the face — roars with laughter. Adores being bounced about on our super huge bed. Can actually get hold of the rattle if you hold it close to him. First his hands come together, like they did at first when he wanted to touch the cushion covers. Then they separate and shake about, but eventually one or both close in on the rattle. He then holds it, watching intently, and pulls it to his mouth. Either drops or waves it. I tried to film it a couple of times, but, of course, he wouldn't do it properly then. He played for the longest with his bears. I held them in front of him obliquely and he grabbed hold and pushed them up the string and then watched as they fell down. He did this for about 10 minutes at the stretch. He is a hoot when he gets fed up with something — gives a sort of despairing yell — almost a bark — and turns away. If you don't take the thing away then, he screams! He has a favourite lamp shade. We hold him up and he hits at the stuff round the bottom — this often makes the whole shade rotate (standard light) and he loves that. He is, apart from his playing and feeding, in the garden from about 9 a.m. until about 5.30 p.m. This may be why he is suddenly sleeping so well — though I don't think so because he began it when it was raining and he didn't go out at all. He is getting a good colour. . . .

I think I shall have to stop now. There is not long before he wakes, and there are heaps of letters I'm supposed to write. I got the book done first as I was fed up with all the bits of paper and things lying around — and now that it is up to date it will never be such an awful task. I can just stick in things as they come. Hugo is very keen on the Collins book and is, today, writing to Billy about it.* Did I tell you that the Geographic has given me an extra 2,000 dollars for the chimp book! So they are not so mean after all. Payne brought it over in person. Hugo said that he has never got on so well with Payne before. Seemed to really be nice. They talked about the polio — and Payne actually wiped a tear from his eye. Hugo is writing to the Geographic about the pictures in Women's Own. Oh — do you think you could get me one more copy and send the article from it — in a fairly big envelope so that the pictures are not too squashed up. I want to put it in the book — but, of course, need two copies to do that.

Oh — I didn't add, re Reserve news, that a cable came from our third research girl, Patricia Moehlman, that she is definitely arriving on 20th. So she will go down with the Hugo-Marler contingent! We have got field telephones so that no one needs to yodel or whistle when they want to come up to the observation area, so recording, observations, etc, will not be interrupted. And Payne thought it an excellent idea to give them some sort of fun <u>at</u> the Reserve — so we are getting them a little flat board type sailing boat (they are, apparently, the most fun) and water skis and goggles and snorkle and frog feet. Arn't they lucky!

In a separate envelope am putting check for Dillon's to cover peri-

---

* "Billy" was Sir William Collins, owner of the Collins publishing house in London. Collins would eventually publish the British editions of *Innocent Killers*, *In the Shadow of Man*, and *Grub the Bush Baby*.

odicals (they don't know what to charge us and so we have told them to contact you for payment). The books, however, they have made up a bill for, and we are sending that cheque direct to them. So yours you could just pay into your account and then pay them however they want to be paid. The cheque in this letter is for telephone bills etc that I never paid. Bits of petrol and things.

Miss you all — and have sung hugo songs from grum as requested.

Tons of love to you all,<br>Jane

Love from Hugo & coos from hugo.

Chimpland<br>[Postmarked July 5, 1967]

Darling Family,

I meant to write a long letter all about things here — but <u>you</u> know how it is with little hugo — on top of which there are chimps, Peter Marler and Alice badly needing a holiday and having to be sent off to laze on the beach with Peter's wife & children.

Anyhow, this is just to tell you how things are here. Little hugo is FINE. Lawick Lodge is resplendent with the CAGE. It is huge — room for his safari cot, pram and baby bouncer, plus a chair for his Moo!* They have painted it a lovely Baby Blue! When we have got everything tidy it will be nicer than it's ever been — it used to be so <u>huge.</u> Now, with the cage, it is much more cosy.

He settled down at once. He was terribly good on the trip here. Sat on my lap & watched the instrument panel, then went to sleep. Woke up in his cot (my arm having gone to sleep!) but just cooed & looked at the clouds. Was fed egg custard when he got hungry. Then I fed him when we refuelled at Tabora. He slept the last hour & a half & was awake & smiling when we got to Kigoma. He smiled at Bimje,† & then we took him over the road to choose bits of col-

---

* Meaning his mum.
† A shopkeeper in Kigoma.

oured material to play with. He at once chose a blue roll & an orange & brown one! But they produced a whole bag of sample squares & they will be tied to his cot when I get round to washing them! The only snag was trying to feed him on the boat. It wouldn't go fast — too loaded, & he got starving at about 7.00. But we made wind shields of anoraks & I fed him cosily! We got him here — Sadiki* <u>adored</u> him — & put him in his cot in the dining room where he slept through the chat & laughter of <u>9</u> people (the pilot stayed for 3 days & is posting this in Nairobi). It is gorgeous washing his nappies — I simply soak them in Napisan & rinse them in the lovely stream. Yesterday I nearly wrung out a frog! Tonight, it was nearly dark. I picked up a nappy as something brown dropped into the soap — like a twig. I picked it out & it attached itself to my finger — a large crab!!

He still wakes early. I mess around with him till about 10 & then he sleeps & I do chimps until he wakes about 1.30. Then he gets fed & played with & then sleeps till 4.30 or so. Then he has a long play, bath, feed, & sleeps until 11.30 or so. . . . He has a marvellous appetite — eats: baby rice, cereal, egg cereal, beans, banana, chicken broth, mixed vegetables, egg custard, apricot custard, fruit dessert — what a diet! He wasn't too keen on prunes & apples! Has a whole shelf of tins & we have got a food grinder to grind fresh food when we get it. We have [moved] the baby alarm from L[awick] L[odge] to Pan Palace. It works beautifully. He couldn't care less about chimp sounds — except to open his eyes rather wide at the first ones which wake him up. He is just not interested in chimps — they have all come & peered, but are only keen to get the cardboard they see. Well — that is just to set all your minds at rest. Will write more when I get more organized.

Tons of love from us all,<br>
Jane

---

* Sadiki Rukumata was a valued member of Gombe's Tanzanian field staff.

[July 1967]

Darling Family,

So much for the long letter I promised! But what with Little hugo (who is undeniably teething) and lack of help (Alice is having her holiday & Patti not yet arrived) and chimps (here all day) and tape recorders (breaking in different ways one after the other) — well, there just hasn't been time to do anything. In addition he still wakes in the night — it is AWFUL. And despite having his milk and a solids meal at 11 p.m. We are going distracted! He is eating v. well now — cereal for breakfast, vegetable or meat for lunch, fruit or egg custard for supper — banana or cereal at midnight! His cereal is mixed with the best possible baby milk. He laps up orange juice & vibena — from your blue cup, Aud-Graud. And plain water. He has his Vit D drops. He has anti-malarial dose every Monday — when he is screaming. I refuse to pop evil medicine into a mouth open & smiling for lovely food — egg custard is his favorite. He spits it out, but I get most of it in! And there are no mosi's* here now anyway at present & he sleeps under his net. He now turns over easily and repeatedly from back to tummy & progresses by sticking up his bottom, getting knees under him, straightening legs, pushing forward — on his chin! He can only sometimes roll from tummy to back — but much more frequently the last few days. I hope you will receive some films of him eventually! He has a new obsession now. When feeding. In goes a spoonful of food — and it must, immediately be followed by his thumb! Then I have to remove the thumb ready for the next spoonful. It is a hoot!

David [Greybeard] has not come yet. He apparently went off with Olly! Gilka returned today. Her hand is very good now and she has learned to make the most of the muscles she has. Saw Willy Wally today — first time since his polio. He is pathetic — keeps the bad leg drawn up (it's lucky he has the muscles for that, at least). But the whole leg is withered. He was even attacked by Fifi today. She threw a stick at him, stamped — he turned his back — she opened her mouth and flew at him, sinking her teeth into the middle of his back! They tumbled down the slope — Flo followed & gathered

---

* Mosquitoes.

up the dropped bananas! Flint has a thing about Peter Marler. He runs up & hits him at the slightest provocation! Doesn't like his beard! He has also taken to throwing stones at us — & the other chimps! He is undoubtedly copying Fifi — she gathered up 8 the other day — destined for Pooch but most of them landed almost on top of Fifi!

Now, one very <u>URGENT</u> thing — Matthews prescribed the complete course of triple DPT (diphtheria, whooping cough & whatever the other one is). It is supposed to be stored cool. Can someone find out whether it is likely to go off. It flew from our fridge in Nairobi. Did <u>not</u> get into fridge here for a day. Got <u>frozen</u> in our fridge. Will this sort of treatment affect it. Should we USE it?? URGENT.

Tons of love to all\
from Hugo, hugo & me

[Mid-August 1967]

Dear FFF,

Leakey is the heaviest chimp! But they all weigh <u>much</u> less than we thought. Leakey is 108 lbs only!!

Little Hugo, nicknamed Grublin, is thriving. He looks amazingly fit, with nice pink cheeks and a super appetite. His cage was a beautiful baby blue — painted by Alice & Pat. It is decorated with pictures & bright baubles — by me — & is super. He is out in the room a lot of the time, & outside when there are no chimps and 4 or 5 people around.

The vocalization study is going <u>EXCELLENTLY.</u> They have got 726 shots of interaction with synchronous sound! And lots of recorded sounds tied up with detailed notes. So detailed we are having to get lots typed in USA!!!

Patti Moehlman is doing very well, after the bad start! We all like her enormously.

Love\
FC*

---

* In correspondence with her mentor, Louis Leakey, Jane usually addressed him as FFF, an abbreviation for "Fairy Foster Father," which was her way of acknowledging

[Around August 18, 1967]

Darling Family,

At last I can get around to writing another brief scrawl. It is 11.10 p.m. — until now I have been writing hundreds of business letters — mostly to Payne who, as you may know by now, is the new President of the Geographic. Had you heard Grosvenor might retire? I wonder what it all means.

Grublin has just vocalized! Came over the baby alarm, and Papa has gone off to rescue him! He is coming over here whilst I finish this! He sometimes does have these midnight excursions which he loves. Perhaps it will make him sleep through the night. He is driving us dotty — waking up at 3 again, and, for three nights running, waking up twice — 3 and 5 or 3 and 6. It is ghastly but I don't know what one can do about it. Perhaps it's the moon. As for him today, I left him crawling in his cage. Which is superbly floored and lined and padded so that he can't bump himself. . . .

Did I tell you, in the last letter, that we had a brief visit from Irv DeVore? I took a bit of film of him with the others on the veranda of P[an] P[alace], including Hugo with Grublin. Thanks tons for your letter, Mum. Yes, the spectacled young man is the student of Peter's. Dick. An absolutely charming person. Nice through and through, just like Pat. The beard, as you guessed, is Peter. Other shots you will see will include Pat, who has a smaller beard. Alice with the long pigtail down her back. And Patti who has almost straight blond hair — oh, and Nicoletta (or Aunt Nita!), who has very dark hair and skin. What a crew we are to be sure! Nita and Patti are off to Kigoma tomorrow to do the shopping and try to get work permits. They are going to invade the prison garden for fresh salad, etc, as we have to give a party to repay the Marlers who have given us two parties.

Our party is for the full moon, which is day after tomorrow. Their parties are down by the lake — of course. We are finding a nice site up here for ours — near Grublin, which means that we

---

how generously and significantly he had helped advance her work. Her signature FC is short for "Fairy/Foster Child," Jane's self-applied nickname when writing to Louis.

don't have to carry him back late at night as we did after the last party. It is rather spoiling of a party, trailing a very heavy baby up a number of steep slippery slopes. I wonder what he weighs. Did I tell you we have managed to weigh the chimps — a good number of them, anyway. The heavyweight is Leakey! But he only weighs 110 lbs! We guessed wrong. Flo is about 80 lbs if I remember rightly. We will hang Grublin on there in his baby bouncer one day soon. He loves it now, but still is not very good at bouncing himself. Everyone is talking to him now, and he is smiling away and laughing. But he is not all that free with his smiles — he stares at people first, and then suddenly smiles, if he feels like it. He found out it was good to blow huge bubbles today, and then spit out lots of spitty bubbles and prod them with his finger! Also, for the first time, he showed great interest in tiny black ants going past him in a thin trail. Stared fascinated for about 5 mins. He loves watching butterflies. And, suddenly, has become absolutely thrilled with watching the chimps when they display or fight or chase. Must be movement. Little Cindy came and danced right outside his window for him this evening. I must stop — he is vocalizing again. Very happy sounds, but it is long past his bed time. Glorious full moon outside. Danny — the letter to Mrs. Marshal* is on its way. Thank you for sending on the money — wasn't it sweet of her.

Tons of love to you all
— from all of us,
Coos, gurgles and spit from Grublin,
Jane

---

* She was the mother of a young American soldier, Jack Marshal, who was temporarily stationed in Bournemouth during the war and befriended by Jane and her family. Mrs. Marshal's father, by coincidence, had been a friend of Jane's maternal grandfather when both attended Yale University. After Jack was killed in the Battle of the Bulge, a letter from Jane was found in his wallet and sent home to Mrs. Marshal. "For his mother," Vanne wrote, "it was the precious link that joined our two families in friendship, for the rest of her life."

Grublin House
Limuru
5 September 1967

Darling Family,

Have been trying to get to write a letter ever since we got back to the house about 4 days ago. But it has not been possible. When I first got here, with Pat, we had to wait for 2 days for Hugo with Grublin's foam rubber — this meant that I couldn't put him anywhere unless he was asleep, and had to cart him about. Dared not leave him on the floor, unpadded, as he can now stand up — not only can he pull himself up by a chair or other low object, but when facing a bare smooth wall. But, of course, he is liable to topple backwards, so it is not safe unless he is on his foam rubber. On his half birthday, yesterday, he crawled properly for the first time — just a few rather chameleon like paces without collapsing his tummy onto the ground. This was when we were out in the garden, he and I. He loves the dogs now — when Rusty came up and licked his hand he first looked most staring and surprised and then began to laugh. When Rusty stopped he reached out after him. He is not so partial to Jessica, who is too rough. Nor is he very keen on the cat who can out-yell him. Similarly, the cat does not like him.

Hey ho — some 3 hours later. (Can't do exclamation marks on this machine without backspacing — the full stop and the inverted comma. Most irritating. Wonder if the new typewriters will have the new punctuation mark — the boom something, isn't it?) Shall put a * for an exclamation mark in future. Can't write letters without.

This will be a rattled off letter as Hugo rang up just now to say he was returning early, so if I don't get it finished now it won't go off tomorrow again. N.B. Have just posted 3 8mm films. They should all arrive close together, therefore. So if they don't, let us know. We have the registration slips.

The interruptions were mainly Grublin. . . . He yelled. He was fed. He was suckled. He slept (so I did not dare to type but, instead, sewed up the legs of his small blue siren suit thing that we got him so long ago in Nairobi) so that it is a long sleeved romper now. The

legs were much too short for him even when he was tiny, if you remember. Then he woke, and irritated me while I tried to get some
lunch and feed the cat. Crawled about the kitchen floor while I did
his nappies, and screamed because he slipped on it and couldn't
crawl fast enough. Got put in his rucksack thing (hard to do on
one's own) while I hung them out, because the grass was wet — and
I can't put him in his little cot to leave, or his safari cot, because he
dives out of both head first*

Our garden is not so full of flowers now, but is still super. Full of
arum lilies. Just fancy* It has the nicest corn cobs you ever tasted,
and rows and rows of carrots. Some rhubarb. And, growing up, on-
ions, peas and lettuce. We have some rows of runner beans, and
some strawberries. Grublin and I raid the strawberry patch every
day and get about 4. Not 4 each, as he is not allowed to eat strawberries yet*

Just rang up Louis and heard that he got shot in the head in Israel. Honestly*** I still think he is absolutely foolish to have allowed Dian Fossey to go back to the gorillas — she's in Burundi,
not Uganda.† Chap visited us a short while ago, at the chimps, and
he had just been arrested in Burundi* Just for arriving there*
We have just given him another lot of Worzle's skin scrapes as a
double check, he knowing someone who is very interested in such
things.‡

You will have to get your brains working on how to set up a
Christmas tree that will withstand the very determined attempts of
a 9 month — no 10 month old baby to pull it down and climb up it.
Also fix the electric fire out of reach, build a guard round the fireplace — oh, you will all have your work cut out this Christmas.
I shall relax and leave the looking after him to all of you. Oh —
I didn't mention it, did I. We expect to be in England for Christ-
mas111**** (hit the wrong thing). He is now crying softly and, at
the same time, bouncing up and down on a huge blow up squeezy
rabbit sent from Holland. It wheezes squeakily when you press it. I
can't see him, only hear these sounds. Am going to see if he is stuck.

---

† This seems an error; Fossey was in Rwanda.
‡ An outbreak of an infectious skin disease had occurred among the chimpanzees.

Next day*** Ha ha. He was stuck — not dangerously for once. But I rescued him, and had a chat, and then the phone went, and that was Hugo on the way home. And, for a change, the sun suddenly came out so I whisked him into the garden where I continued to sew up his small blue suit into a romper. Then Hugo and Pat got back, Hugo with presents — super phone number thing for the phone, wastepaper basket, new yellow suit for Grublin, two ducks, etc. . . .

Hey ho* It is now 12 midnight*** Grublin woke, fell, hit his head, sobbed. Played happily after I showed him the rain, screamed and screamed, and I found he'd had a flea* Hugo got back with Pat and Super 8 films and lots of contact sheets of chimps and Grublin. Supper — one of the ducks. And now it is late. And we have tea at 6.30 a.m. tomorrow. And so I am going to ignore the rest of the news and dates and write again after Hugo goes — he goes ahead, Grublin and I follow by plane — in the plane which takes me and Alice to the crater and fetches the Marlers back again.

Tons and tons of love to all,
Jane, Hugo & Grublin

Box 2818
Nairobi
8 September 1967

Dear Mr. Snider,

Thank you for your letter of 9 August — and apologies for the delay in replying but, as you know, we have only just returned from the Gombe Stream.

Unfortunately it seems that McGregor was not preserved well enough for the experts to be able to determine the cause of the paralysis. This was mainly because, to do this properly, they need brain and spinal cord tissue that has been placed, when fresh, in the deep freeze. But, at the time, we did not know this, and just preserved him, as best we could, in formalin. This apparently has destroyed the virus.

We are very upset that this is the case. The remaining victims of the disease (which, we are convinced, really was polio since it coincided so well with the human epidemic of that disease) are managing to adapt well. Faben, in fact, is rising fast in the hierarchy despite the fact that he has only one arm. When he first was paralysed he lost his position overnight. This will be an extremely interesting situation to follow through.

Hugo (or Grublin as he is now known!) is thriving. Is already able to stand up, pulling up on a chair or something, and walk along whatever he is holding onto. Not bad at 6 months! Crawls all over the place.

With best wishes,
Yours sincerely,
Jane

Munge Cabin
Ngorongoro Crater
22 September [1967]

Darling Family, and especially Olly for your birthday (and forgive the wishes and letter arriving late, but we do all wish you a happy birthday as we said on the cable. Have not been able to send letters out (with safety) until now. Will tell you why we can now a bit later in the letter. And hope you had a very happy birthday — we shall be thinking of you on the day.)

Well. First of all. Grublin!! Today he has his first tooth. Lower left incisor. It is just visible through the skin. He is very happy but it gave him some trouble just before it came through. Grublin again. Day before yesterday he sat up for several moments when I sat him. Overbalanced when he looked round. Yesterday he sat up all by himself, three times, during playing around with his toys. For at least a minute, twice. (Filmed). Has suddenly started to love his baby bouncer. Still loves typing — you will see what happened to the last letter I started to you when you get the next batch (two) 8mm films. He is not at all bow legged or knockkneed although, from the time when I wrote to say I was worried, just before leaving the reserve, he has been standing up for about half of every day! Until three days ago he continued to sleep well at night. But now, and we hope it is teething, he refused to return to his cot after waking up at about 3 or 4 a.m. (when I say he was sleeping well, I did not mean he was sleeping all through the night). And, for the last two nights, he has been waking at 8.30 or 9 instead of 11 after his last bath and feed.

His appetite has suddenly come back. This is the fourth day of a good appetite — which he lost, really, after the first few days at the reserve. He still liked his food, but messed about with it, and did not eat much, and dribbled heaps down his chin into his neck and down his back, etc — but you have possibly seen film of that by now. He now opens his mouth and actually "gums" the food off the spoon, instead of my having to tip the spoon and scrape the food off against his upper gums. The funny thing is that he has gone back to his baby habit (which we also filmed) of sucking his thumb after every spoonful. This happened on the very day that he got his appetite back, and vanished (though I did not realize it at the time) when he lost his appetite earlier. He has been very good, till now, playing in his giant playpen. But has now started screaming. I distracted him by filling up his toys. With other toys. He has heaps of things like rubber toys, soft toys, teething rings, etc. But although he is happy to play with these things if there is nothing else around, he is happiest with other things. For instance, in his play pen now he has a red cigarette packet (empty). An empty film carton. A film can lid. 24 dud batteries!! New acquisition, and with these (they are small) I have been filling the cigarette packet and one of the coloured drinking enamel glasses from the set you gave us, Mum. A leather strap. A shawl. Several empty envelopes. Three tins of baby food. An ashtray. That's probably it. But in Limuru I used to entertain him on the kitchen floor whilst I washed nappies — with unbreakable china, egg cups and tins of custard or cocoa. These are all his favourite toys. He still loves strings of things that make a noise — so his bears, Aud, are still among his favourites, and he also has a string of coloured balls that he likes.

He is having the most extraordinary life for a baby — and thriving on it 100% as you will see from his pictures. Let me describe a typical day.

Hugo, Grublin and I wake up, in the VW, on a tiny hill right in the middle of the crater. All around us are herds of wildebeeste and zebra, moving out to the plains again from their nightly grazing grounds in the hills. Some crowned cranes fly overhead towards the lake with their plaintive haunting cry. When they land we can see them dancing their graceful display, wings up, leaping up and down as they hunt for their insect breakfast. Not far away some vultures have gathered round one of the late kills of our friends, the hyenas. This is a kill made by the Scratching Rocks Clan. The scratching rocks are just behind us, on our little hill. They are just the right height for the zebra to lean against and scratch themselves when they have been feeding all day on the open treeless plains in the hot sun. A white tailed mongoose lives in the rocks — but more of him later.

Suddenly the peace is broken. We see zebra running far off in the hills beyond the little river, and hyenas running in close pursuit. Every so often the little herd stops and the stallion wheels to attack the pursuing hyenas. They vanish into a hollow of the hills — and next thing some vultures have landed. From all around hyenas begin to run towards the scene — and we start up the motor of the landrover, fasten our safety belts, and off we go — not so fast as usual because Grublin is with us. Hurrying to the spot from closer by is another landrover — Hans and Jane Kruuk. When we arrive, finally, we are almost late on the scene — only one hyena arrives, puffing, after us.

There are 42 hyena there, divided into two growling snarling whooping groups, both with tails up aggressively. One group is feeding on the dead zebra (already half gone). The other group advances aggressively. This is a kill made by the Munge Clan in the Scratching Rock Clan territory. After a while Scratching Rocks Clan advances in a body, and chase Munge Clan from the kill. There are short individual skirmishes all over the place as one hyena after another gets a piece from the kill and rushes off, vainly trying to get away far enough to eat its spoil in peace. The high pitched nervous giggles of these animals sound from all directions.

About 5 minutes later the Munge Clan, reinforced as several of their number return from eating stolen pieces, advances in a body on Scratching Rockers. But their advance is repulsed with dreadful snarls and erect bristling manes and tails. They retreat in confusion. And again they try to reclaim their kill. This time they succeed — but only for a short time before once again the territory owners drive them off. Soon nothing remains but the head of the zebra. And Hans, who collects jaws of all hyena kills for statistical analysis of type of animal killed, rushes at the small group fighting round this last remnant until, giggling violently, the last hyena relinquishes its hold and the head ends up under Hans's car. He backs, gets out, and, with knife and axe, removes the jaw. The hyenas stand round watching — knowing, by now, that the rest will be theirs. Nonchalantly he tosses bits and pieces towards them as he works — but they wait until, wiping bloody hands, he climbs in and drives off again. Then they close once more. Still the Scratching Rockers are standing watching — some of them, that is, though the main body has drifted away back into its own territory, in twos and threes. Finally, just as the last Scratching Rocker has departed, a sleek, yellow thin form rushes towards the remaining 6 or 7 Munge Clan hyenas. A lioness. With her tail up and a snarl she charges the little group. The hyenas scatter, give their whooping alarm call, and stand watching, tails up, still aggressive. For a moment we wonder whether they will harass the hungry young lioness — but they keep a respectful distance. Then a second and a third lion arrives — but the remains of the zebra head belong now to the first arrival — she leaps at and snarls at one of her pride who tries to join her.

Through much of the action Grublin has been singing. He loves the landrover and invariably sings loudly and shoutingly as soon as the motor starts. This morning his song blended in with the yelling and calling of the hyenas. Hans and Jane drive over to us. Hans is smiling. "Young Hugo was certainly giving encouragement to the hyenas" he says, and tells us that at first he and Jane were really startled. They thought they heard a completely new hyena begging call!! Then they realized who made it!

As we drive away, back to the little grey speck that is the VW standing, where we left it, on top of the small hill, Grublin's eyes droop, his song fades away, he sleeps, heavily, in my arms. We look back towards the kill and see three great black maned lions hurrying up the hill. But nothing will avail them — when they arrive only a skull will remain.

Now it is time to test the Egyptian vultures. Off we go, Aunt Alcie,* Hugo and Grublin and I. On the way we check our "shrike thorn". When we were last in the Crater and camping in tents, I saw a shrike impale a little bird on this thorn. His nest was nearby. Next he impaled a shrew. Then we left the camp site, but when Hugo returned to check the thorn, he found fresh blood on it. That was in February this year. And now we find the bird is still using the same "larder". First we found a small bird stuck up there. Next a large grasshopper. So now we check it every time we go to the vultures. Nothing there today.

When we get to the vultures' bathing place we find we are in luck. There are, as always, about 40 birds. Mostly White Backs and Ruppells. But there are four Egyptians as well. They include two birds we know — one who is lame, and its mate — No. 2. This is a very tame pair. We drive close and set down the giant egg. It is about two feet in length, and the proportionate size in girth! As before, the vultures are most excited, and throw stones at it patiently until we remove it and set down some real hens' eggs. They get one each, and seem quite happy. The next day we plan to put out a green ostrich egg. Will they react to that? And we also plan to offer them a group of hens' eggs (which they break by throwing at the ground) and dummy eggs the same size. We shall set a big rock close by. When they find the eggs won't break open on the ground, will they try throwing them onto the rock? Poor Lame is worse today. But dominant of all the Egyptians. For the rest, today, we have Yellow and Mottled. Mottled was badly named. It arrived all splotched with wet feathers, straight from its bath. Then, by the time it was dry, it was the most beautiful snowy white — the most handsome of all!

Eventually the tests are over. The giant egg (of fibre glass) is chipped and scarred. The ground round about is littered with stones

---

* "Alcie" is "Alice" said for Grub's benefit.

and rocks of all shapes and sizes. The hens' eggs are flattened shells almost pounded into the ground. The vultures have gone. We go over to the testing grounds and gather up the rocks to be marked later. Ngorongoro Sept 67 Test No. 3. The notes are safely on tape — half by me and then, when Grublin got too active, Alcie took over and finished off the observations. As a matter of fact, it is <u>Ant</u> Alcie. The Americans pronounce it in the same manner as the Welsh! We return to the cabin for Hugo to get some sleep. Grublin has a late lunch. He sleeps for a while.

At 3.30 Grublin and I move out into the "garden". There is only one patch of shade where it is safe to lay Grublin's crawling matress. All the lovely shade under the fig tree is taboo — too many birds knocking down too many figs. They are not large figs — but Grublin's head is rather precious! Thomas* is hard at work in the kitchen, and delicious smells of roast beef drift into the afternoon air. From across the stream, where the Kruuks are camped under a huge eucalyptus tree, there are more smells of supper on the make. Grublin is playing with grass, patting it with his right hand. With a bunch of unripe figs, chewing them. With a matchbox — some of the black comes off on his face. He keeps crawling off onto the ground — his new yellow suit is rather grimy! Overhead there are some hissing squeaking chirping sounds — hard to describe the call of a young Hooded Vulture. It is greeting one of the parents who has arrived to feed it. Meal time.

And time to wake Hugo. Poor fellow — hasn't had much sleep. But he wakes soon enough when hugo is put on the matress in the little sleeping tent set up in the shade of the giant fig. Hugo crawls into and over his Pa, grabs onto the nose, pulls up by his hair, nearly overbalances onto the groundsheet. Dribbles enchantingly into Hugo's ear — and generally helps enormously in getting Hugo ready for supper.

Supper. It is 4.30. The sun is warm but not too hot as we sit on the veranda of the cabin. Hugo has to cut up my food as I have Grublin

---

* Thomas, who had been employed by Jane and Hugo at their Limuru house, came along on this safari to cook.

in one arm. Grublin wants to taste mashed potatoes — "Gggggh" — ("Not bad"). Peas — "Mmmmmmmmm" — ("Jolly good stuff, this"). A large meat bone — "Gaaaaaaa" — ("First class — excellent for teething"). And I am able to set him down on the matress beside us and finish my meal in peace. Until it gets to the chocolate pudding I have just made. Then up comes Grublin for his share. His favourite, just about.

Now a fever of activity. Hugo's cameras to be checked, tape to be checked, flash lights to be checked. And then away go Hugo and Alcie to look for the small lion cubs. Grublin and I are otherwise occupied. It is bath time for Grublins. In about 10 minutes from the time when Thomas empties a huge kettle of pale brown stream water (boiled for 5 minutes) into his yellow baby bath, together with some of our good clean water to cool it down, Moo is soaked to the skin. Grublin has water all over him, in his eyes and down his ears. But he takes it all in good part. He is laughing hysterically. He is bundled into his yellow baby towel, fluffy and soft, and rubbed and patted dry while he laughs. He laughs especially when the towel is put right over his head "Bye bye" and then whisked off "Boo". This is one of the funniest of games. Soon he is dry — between the toes, behind the ears, around the dingle dangles. Into a nightie — screams without tears. Into nappies. More screams. One tear. Into his plastic feeder. Loud yells and screams of rage. Into his baby blue chair. Quiet. Next comes Beef and Liver Broth to which his fresh peas and carrots have been added. Half of the baby tin is gone in no time. Not too grubby a baby to mop up afterwards.

Then out we go. Thomas holds the baby whilst I load the VW with forgotten things. My basket (thermos, coffee, cocoa, etc) the gas burner, a kettle, clean nappies, Olly's bag for dirty ones, spare nighty, plastic pants, and cardigan. The cot is in already. And binoculars and bedding and warm clothes, oranges, etc. I start the motor, Thomas places Grublin in my arms, and off we go, into the sunset, towards our little hill.

As we go Grublin sings. He gazes at the sunset and the black silver-fringed shapes of the wildebeeste and zebra clustered thickly on either side of our track. Up the hill, past scratching rocks and the mongoose home. And there are Hugo and Alice sitting in the Land-rover. Hugo has a group of hyaenas* under close observation.

The VW joins its sister car. Peace and evening stillness as the engine fades and dies. Grublin and I retire to the back of the bus — where the bed is made up, close beside his little cot. He is nearly asleep now — but not too sleepy for his last suckle — well, last for a little while, anyway. Oh dear — was it the right last time — or the left. Must have been right — or not? Ah, yes. The left window is open. Never got round to closing it. So it must be right. Suck ..... suck ..... suck .... Eyes close. Rhythmic breathing. Must do a burp though. The head droops heavily. No burp .... well, never mind. Into the cot. It's very hot so, for now, a blanket loosely over the top. Mosquito net on — there are one or two mosi's around. Alice's face at the window — "Are you ready? Hugo is anxious to go." Yes, ready now. Alice climbs into the VW. I join Hugo. And off we go to the hyaena group.

They are moving about, tails up, hurrying from place to place and, every so often, stopping to sniff, in a compact group. Hans has told us what they are doing — patrolling their territory. The sniffing is part of it — he calls it "social sniffing". They mark the grass in various places, or the rocks. There are five of them in the lead, and three straggling along behind. The five are females. They live in a matriarchal society, the hyaenas. It is, of course, very hard to tell the sexes apart. But the old females are fairly easy because they have large teats from feeding their pups. The stragglers are males. We follow them through the fading dusk until they are dim shapes, hard to see in the semi-darkness, and we long for moon-rise.

7.45. The sky is light behind the hills and soon the first yellow rim of the moon appears over the crater rim. Swiftly she climbs into full view — very round. It is full moon tonight. Something exciting, surely, must happen.

10.15 p.m. "How many can you see now?" I can only see two. The group we have been patiently following has split and split.

---

* Jane in this letter experiments with the spelling of "hyena," occasionally shifting to the variant "hyaena." Both spellings are correct, though the simpler version seems to be the preferred American form for popular (nonscientific) consumption.

Now there are just two lying, doing nothing. Ten minutes later only one is left of our promising group. But the night is so beautiful that it scarcely matters. Through binoculars one can see the dark forms of the grazing animals for hundreds of yards. Every so often a tiny shape moves through the dry yellow grass — which, luckily, is not too high. Luckily for Hugo's photography I mean — of course!

Two younger hyena approach our one lying female. They greet. The younger ones move off quite determinedly — we decide to follow <u>them.</u> (Hugo does not want to waste the light of the full moon — he wants <u>action.</u>) It is easy to keep the rustling forms in view. There is one chase — the hyaena are after a small mammal — we switch on our spot light for a moment and see that it is our friend the white tailed mongoose (we are not far from Scratching Rocks where he lives). But the chase does not last long and then, seemingly unperturbed, the mongoose resumes his night's hunting.

The two hyena set off in a straight line for the lake. Hugo does not want to go there. So we turn back to look for our sleeping female again. Horrors — she has gone. Hugo, cursing that he ever left her — or that he did not follow the two youngsters — begins to circle around, shining the spot light onto dark clumps of grass, or rocks, that might turn out to be hyenas. He gets desperate — we know the Scratching Rocks Clan has not killed yet. It would be terrible if we were to miss the kill because we so stupidly moved from our post. And then, quite suddenly, we find one. With a huge sigh of relief Hugo switches off the engine and we settle down for a vigil beside this welcome slumbering form.

Suddenly ears prick and our hyaena is up and off. We have only just turned off the motor — Hugo has just said "Let's have some coffee, shall we?" — and, as yet, I have not even taken one cup from the basket. We are off. About 30 yards off a second hyena is flat out after a wildebeeste. The animal, seeming to know it is the end, is giving stricken bellows. Our hyaena joins the pursuing one, and we see a third, then a fourth, rushing to the scene. The wildebeeste runs frantically to a herd and tries to escape, dodging amongst the others. But the hyaena are not to be fooled. They stick, like true hunters, to the original quarry. With eyes only on the speeding animals we have no heed for the ground ahead as the speedometer needle creeps up towards 30 m.p.h. — no mean speed for travelling over rough pot-hole (actually hyaena, jackal and fox burrow!) infested country. Luckily for us there are no holes in the way. "Don't forget to switch on the batteries" I remind Hugo — he switches them on. (Until tonight Alice or I have been holding the three great flash lights, fastened to their board and attached to batteries and photoelectric cells, and the board attached by wires and wires to Hugo's camera. But we decided it was not safe for us — as the back seat has no safety belt. So Hugo managed to fasten the board and lights into his door and was trying out driving, together with flashing, himself. But he needed to be reminded to switch on the battery which charges the lights.)

The wildebeeste makes a sudden turn. The landrover swings round and — click flash — Hugo in a superhuman manner takes a picture at the very moment that the wildebeeste is thrown. It is in mid-air with a hyena biting onto it somewhere. He is a genius.

In a few moments there are hyena running from all directions. Even so the poor wildbeeste bellows for at least three minutes as it is eaten alive. It is still calling even while hyaenas are running off with pieces of gut, giggling as they are chased.

All at once a whole new group of hyacnas arrive — followed closely by the landrover of Hans and Jane. Believe it or not but we are to witness, once again, a clash between the two clans — for we have seen a Munge kill — this time on Scratching Rock territory. As the territory owners arrive the Munge Clanners give whooping alarm calls and make off, the lucky ones each with a piece of meat. For there are many more animals in the compact group that rushes up with terrible growls. They mean business, the hyaena of the Scratching Rocks.

For a few moments all is confusion. Then things calm down. Strangely enough the hyaena are in two groups — perhaps they have torn the wildebeeste apart for certainly the Munge Clan took flight. The two groups both comprise Scratching Rock hyaenas.

"Look — it's a hyaena they've got". Hugo's voice is agitated. "I thought I noticed earlier that one of them had another by the scruff of its neck". And it is true. With unbelieving horror we watch a scene of tribal warfare carried to extremes. A pack of hyaena deliberately, and in cold blood, murdering one of their kind. A Munge hyaena that did not get away. We have never seen anything so horrible before. The moans of the tortured wildebeeste are still ringing in our ears, and we are still trembling slightly from that terrible scene. But this is infinitely more gruesome. Surely the hyaena has more brain than the wildebeeste, can feel more. And soon the tragedy that is taking place under our eyes has been dragged out for nearly 10 minutes. And still it goes on. The mauled animal is growling and screaming horribly. One hyaena has it by the scruff of its neck. Another has one ear. A third has it by the rump. There were 10 to 15 animals round it earlier, but now most have gone to eat wildebeeste, and we can clearly see the details of this murder. Two young animals are watching.

The individual holding the ear growls and shakes it as would a dog a rat. The other two follow suit. The stricken hyena screams. All is still again. Then this is repeated. And again, and again. Now a fourth adult joins in. It takes hold of a leg. The four animals pull, all in different directions. The screams are ghastly. The hyaena holding onto an ear lets go suddenly — the ear has come right off. Soon after this the stricken beast is left alone. He turns to lick his wounds — but he is so mutilated that he seems just to give up. He cannot stand. A few hyaenas go over and sniff him — he growls but cannot move away. We feel sick.

"There are the VW headlights" I see — with relief. I cannot bear to watch this mutilated animal any longer. The "action" is virtually over now. Still some animals round the remains of the kill. Hugo starts up and we drive over to the signalling VW. Grublin, screaming at the top of his voice, is in his Ant Alcie's arms. But for the noise they would look cosy in there, lit up with the little light. But oh dear — <u>what</u> a noise. Quickly I get into the car and relieve Alice of her screaming bundle. He has been offered milk already. But he wants Moo. Now he has Moo and there is peace.

Alice goes off in the Landrover with Hugo. He is taking her back to sleep in the Cabin. Thomas sleeps in the little kitchen there. Then

Hugo hurries back to the scene of the kill. Hans is roaring through the night to his camp behind the Cabin. He is getting a knock out dose for the mauled beast. He is very upset — he is fond of his hyaenas. Hugo takes pictures whilst Hans darts the poor animal. Together they examine the body. Ears torn off. Toes of three feet bitten off. Terrible mauling in the loins. Wounds all over the body. And, horrible to relate, when we go to look at the body next morning hyaenas — of his own clan — had been actually eating the carcass! (Grublin joined me at the typewriter there, and I had to stop for the time being!)

Hans goes back to bed with his Jane, to dream terrible dreams of hyaenas. Hugo watches a while longer, and sees a couple of hyaenas go up to the mauled animal and chew at its legs. Then he drives up the hill to join his Jane and his hugo. Just as he is about to switch off the headlights he sees a shadow-y shape near the VW. He turns the car towards it — and the lights pick out the form of a young lion — and another. They are moving across the hill and out towards the plains for their night's hunting — or scavenging of hyaena kills. For 10 minutes they prowl around the cars, interested that people should be in the midst of their domain in the middle of the night. One roars loudly, the exciting sound filling the air with all the savagery of the African night. The soft coughing sounds at the end gradually die away, and once again there is silence. The lions move off. When he is sure they have gone Hugo switches off the landrover lights at last and joins me in the VW. There is only a space one foot by 4 or 5 feet long for him to undress. He mutters softly to himself in this confined area as he hits his elbow on the door, his head on the roof, his toe on the gas cooker under the head of the bed. Softly — must not wake Grublin again.

But Grublin awakens. He screams and screams. I lift him, all sleepy eyed and red and screwed up with rage, from his cosy cot. Hugo talks to him. Gradually he quietens — and he stops altogether when Hugo lights a cigarette and waves the glowing end through the dim light inside the car. Grublin gazes, fascinated. He has another little suckle, and drops off to sleep. A sound sleep, I hope. I lift him gently, place him in his cot softly. He sighs, stirs, opens his eyes. He is in his cot. He is teething. He cannot bear his cot another moment. He must convince us he is in agony. He screws up his face. Opens his mouth, and yells. And yells ... and yells .....

Fifteen minutes later Jane, Hugo and hugo are all peacefully sleeping. They are in a row. Hugo ... Jane ... Grublin. Three heads in one bed. All are happy now. Outside the full moon gradually sinks lower in the sky. There is the distant roar of a lion. A moaning whoop of a hungry hyaena. A sudden yelping chorus, high pitched and ethereal, of the golden jackals. The chorus is repeated way over to the north, and then to the east. Then silence once more. Hugo and Jane and Grublin sleep until morning.

So. A typical day. Sometimes Alice goes with Hugo at night and I stay with Grublin on the hill until Hugo joins me. There is no time to write more. Grublin has interrupted me so many times — Hugo is going up to the Lodge today and can post this. It was going to go back to Nairobi with the plane which brought Tim — Mike Richmond was going to spend the night with us and return the following day. But when Hugo and co got back from meeting Tim, they did not bring Mike with them. He had been unable to stay and so I could not send the letter. However, it should reach you from the Lodge — I do hope so!

Will write again — not such an epistle! Probably a blue. Anyway — again, belated birthday wishes Olly — but I hope that the cable reached you in time.

And tons of love to you all,
Jane, Hugo & Grublin

# 4

❧ ❧ ❧

# HOPE AND LOSS
## 1968–1969

So many of the hopes we have cherished over the past few years
have been doomed.

— Untitled, unpublished manuscript submitted to
*National Geographic* in April 1969

I N JANUARY 1968, after a Christmas and New Year's celebration
in Europe, Jane, Hugo, and Grub settled back into their camp at
the Munge River in Ngorongoro Crater. They were accompanied by Hugo's mother, "Moeza," as well as Patti Moehlman (on
a break from Gombe), Benjamin Gray (a volunteer student from
FWI, the Friends World International school in Nairobi), Nicoletta
Maraschin (Jane's secretary), and Bill Talkington (an artist and
friend from Nairobi). Hugo was filming, photographing, and working on his book about East African carnivores: hyenas, jackals, and
wild dogs. *Innocent Killers,* published in 1970, was in fact a collaboration between Hugo and Jane, but during the first half of 1968
she concentrated on taking care of Grub and working on her "analysis" (letter of January 27). That analysis, an extensive revision of
the doctoral dissertation that would be published in England as a
150-page scientific monograph (in a series edited by J. M. Cullen,
appearing at last in spring of 1969), turned out to be an exhausting
project.

During this period Jane and Hugo kept in touch with Gombe via
twice-weekly radiotelephone communications and through regular
discussions with any Gombe students or researchers who were able

to visit the van Lawicks at their camp in Ngorongoro Crater or their home in Nairobi.

By mid-June 1968, the monograph was in the mail to the publisher. The van Lawicks left Nairobi on June 19 and — accompanied by Dawn Starin (an FWI volunteer), Margaret and Nick Pickford (hired to work as general administrators at Gombe), and Moro (employed as Grub's male "nanny") — drove in the Land Rover and Volkswagen bus south to Kigoma on the edge of Lake Tanganyika. After a boat ride up the lake, they arrived at the reserve (just then undergoing legal transformation into Gombe National Park) — only to be confronted by a situation that was "grim, grim, grim" (letter of July 1).

There had been an epidemic of some flulike disease among the Gombe chimpanzees earlier in the year; as a consequence, several of the apes had died, including two mothers, Circe and Sophie, and a young female named Pooch. In turn, the mothers' deaths resulted in the deaths from depression and malnutrition of their two youngest offspring. Most distressing to Jane was the loss of David Greybeard, her stalwart friend from the early years. She had been informed of David's disappearance from the first, in February, but it had seemed possible that he might eventually turn up. By July 1, it was clear that "David is no more."

The banana feeding system was still problematic. Over the years, the provisioning operation had undergone seemingly ever-increasing refinements. By the summer of 1968, the bananas that appeared from the maw of remotely operated steel boxes remained a very attractive food source for the chimpanzees. But the Gombe baboons had recently concluded that they too — if they were clever, persistent, and aggressive enough — could benefit from this strange and wonderful magic. Baboons were lingering around the feeding area, fighting with the chimpanzees, and in some instances seriously threatening researchers. In short, individuals from three primate species were crowding around the banana provisioning area. For the researchers, this unpleasant situation may have been exacerbated by their dawn-to-dark hours of observation and by the fact that some (Bonnie and Tim Ransom) were studying baboons that summer, while others (including Alice Sorem, Pat McGinnis, Geza Teleki, and Ruth Davis) were focused on the chimps. (FWI volunteers Dawn Starin and Sally Puleston were also working at Gombe that summer.)

At any rate, as we read in the July 1 letter, Jane and Hugo arrived in late June to be greeted with "delegations & despair" over the baboon and banana problem. A conference resulted in the resolution to have "far fewer feeding days" and to begin "lone following."

Lone following of individual chimps, "lone climbing about in the mountains" — the sort of approach that Jane herself had taken in her first couple of years at Gombe — seemed an exciting idea, especially because the Gombe researchers declared themselves eager to pursue it. The old matriarch Flo offered one splendid opportunity. She was pregnant that summer, and during two weeks of August Alice Sorem took it on herself to follow Flo through her wanderings into the forest, with the hope of witnessing for the first time the birth of a chimpanzee in the wild. The terrain at Gombe is very rugged, perilously so in places. There were other dangers, including buffalo, bush pigs, poisonous snakes, and, as Alice found out (letter written around August 18), bees. Despite her heroic efforts, Alice unfortunately missed the actual moment of Flame's birth.

In spite of one disturbing and never resolved event, the mysterious and apparently intentional poisoning of some baboons (noted in mid-August), the summer of 1968 was altogether a hopeful and satisfying time. There were successful visits by Gombe's distinguished scientific sponsors, David Hamburg from the Stanford University Medical School and Robert Hinde from Cambridge University, who concluded (July 19 letter) that "what is going on here is the most exciting thing in animal behaviour . . . anywhere in the world." And Tanzania's President Julius Nyerere was due to appear in September, though that visit was ultimately canceled for security and logistical reasons.

If the summer of 1968 was a time of hope, 1969 was a year of loss. Flo was ancient by the time she gave birth to Flame, old enough that Jane and several of the researchers seriously wondered whether she would "survive long enough to prevent Flame from being one of our pathetic orphans" (August 24 letter). Instead, Flo outlived Flame. The infant died early the next year, an apparent victim of another flu epidemic.

Meanwhile, Jane had been writing what was supposed to be her fourth *National Geographic* article — her third on the continuing chimpanzee study at Gombe. Since she had not previously written about the 1966 polio epidemic or the story of the orphan Merlin, this article (never given a title) covered those events among others. Various staff members at the *Geographic* had been encouraging. They were "very interested," one of them wrote, in the polio story.

The submitted draft was a disappointment. Jane realized (as we can read in the submission note of April 4) that the typescript had "rather a lot of the tragedy of the chimps." Tragedy was not the only problem. The rejection letter from Frederick Vosburgh, then vice president and editor of the magazine, summarized his in-house readers' editorial assessments. The typescript seemed to present observations "lacking in inter-relation," with not enough emphasis on "<u>why</u> from a <u>scientific</u> point of view all this work is done." Perhaps most significant was a concern that "much of the material is depressing if not downright gruesome, with vivid details of polio and influenza among the chimps and mercy killing of sick ones." Jane, in response (letter of June 28) to Vosburgh's rejection notice, agreed: "I was afraid it might be too sad, as I think I intimated in my letter. Unfortunately most of the major happenings at Gombe have been somewhat tragic — there were many more deaths than I wrote about, including a male falling out of a tree and breaking his neck!"

In a distressingly prophetic way, the rejected typescript discussed in some detail the "hazards" faced by researchers now that "the chimpanzees will tolerate being closely followed." Geza Teleki, for example, was at one point charged by enraged bush pigs; and "slim, attractive" Ruth Davis had been chased by a buffalo. These were serious incidents, and indeed the Gombe research staff had talked about the dangers of lone following. They had declared themselves opposed to the idea of a buddy system, however, believing that carrying field packs with flashlights, whistles, flares, and snakebite kits would provide adequate insurance against any likely disaster.

Jane and Hugo left Africa in late June or early July that year — to attend a wedding in the Netherlands and Jane's scientific conferences in London. It was their first trip outside Africa in well over a year. But the research center, they knew, was in capable hands: with administrator Nick Pickford and senior scientist Michael Simpson in charge, and with a seasoned team of students and researchers — including at that moment Lori Baldwin, Cathleen Clark, Tim Clutton-Brock, Pat McGinnis, Carole Gale, and Ruth Davis — ready for any eventuality.

Geza Teleki (Ruth's fiancé) had left Gombe by then and returned to Pennsylvania State University to complete his master's thesis. Ruth had stayed on, determined to prove her mettle by pursuing a physically difficult study of the relationships between far-ranging adult males. On Saturday, July 12, she disappeared, having left camp to follow chimpanzees Hugh and Charlie into a distant valley. After a search that eventually involved more than three hundred people over several days, her body was found at the bottom of a ravine, far from camp. She had fallen, it was apparent, and died instantly from a fractured skull.

Hugo flew back to Nairobi to meet Ruth's parents at the airport and accompany them on the heartbreaking flight south to Kigoma. The Davises decided that Ruth would have wanted to be buried at Gombe. So on Friday, July 24, she was (as her mother recalled in a diary) laid to rest at "a beautiful spot — a level clearing with trees and a beautiful view of the lake." In his report to Melvin Payne of the National Geographic Society, Hugo declared: "All of us have had the greatest admiration for her parents, who were at the funeral and took it all so bravely. I have a deep respect for them." But it was Jane who had to write the extraordinarily difficult letter of condolence to Ruth's parents. I have included it as the final entry in this chapter.

\*　　　\*　　　\*　　　\*

Jan 27th [1968]

Darling Family,

An unexpected chance to post a letter — but as it is 11.30 p.m. & the car goes off at 6 a.m. & Grub is awake & trying to grab the pa-

per — it can only be a short note. We are all fine and over our flue
— colds. Did you get a letter saying Moeza and I & finally Grub got
this? I was in bed 2 days & just made it in time for the trip. Grub
was just better enough to travel too. It made getting ready rather
chaotic & hectic.

We have Patti (from the Reserve) with us. And Ben — a chap
from the same strange school as Carole & Sanno (who are the 2 volunteer girls at the Reserve). He is helping Hugo with his cameras.
Nicoletta is leaving! She is all mixed up! More of her anon! She is
off back to Nairobi with Bill Talkington — who has to rush back to
do something or other with his exhibition & is then returning to go
on working. Nita will go to Aden, where her father is.

Grub is well & is having the time of his life. He loves it. Is standing very well on his own — works at it all day long for the past 4
days. Fed himself for the first time 2 days ago with your spoon, Aud.
He simply <u>loves</u> birds. I have rigged up a nice bird table and already
a lot of birds including the Superb Starlings have found it. He especially loves the Egyptian geese that fly past morning & evening to
roost in our tree.

Our major set back was that we couldn't bring the 2 VW's down
— my travelling office & Bill's. The only road suitable for normal
cars — <u>without</u> 4 wheel drive — is closed because of rains.

I have started [my] analysis in a big way. Have the tent you slept
in at the Reserve, Mum, as my work tent. By the stream in the thick-
est shade it is cool — almost <u>cold</u> — all day long. The old Reserve
work tent is our dining/sitting room. The Cabin is Grub's nursery
and our bedroom. He is sleeping a <u>bit</u> better — <u>once</u> he slept from
11 p.m. till morning!! Bill has Hugo's old tent from the Reserve & a
huge tarpaulin under which he paints. He is going to move further
away to do his sculpting — as it makes so much noise! Moeza has a
small tent just behind the cabin. Also, by her tent, another small one
shared by Patti & Nita (soon to be Patti's) and one for Ben. And the
gay VW tent is — or was — Nita's office. Is now Hugo's writing
tent. He is getting on v. well with his book, by the way.

Grub has just finished his course of medicine for his E. coli. It
gave him diarrhea which is now better. Apart from being stung by a
hairy caterpillar he is fine.

Oh — what a panic-y departure from London. Many apologies for it all, all over again. How are the Old Men, Mum? They must be just about finished — surely? I do hope so. Will write a decent letter for posting in a few days — when Mike flies back after bringing Billy.* Oh — Flo had a bad cold & had to spend 2 nights on the ground. We are in a state about her. Poor Flo. And Flint is properly weaned. Grub has begun to cry. So must stop & not start new page.

Tons & tons of love,<br>Jane

Chimpland<br>1 July 1968

Darling Family,

I was hoping to get a long letter written for the first mail from here, but things have been too hectic. The journey was fine. Hugo, Grub, me and Dawn in the landrover — heavily overloaded as usual — & Margaret, Nick and Moro in the VW. We went in convoy & had only a few spots of trouble. Once a trailer spring broke. Once we thought the LR gear box had gone, but after driving about 100 miles at slow speed we discovered it had made itself all right, somehow.

We arrived in Kigoma on Sunday — dead as a doornail. Paused long enough to hire a water taxi, load our things & park the cars — then we were off. Grub was splendid on the trip, apart from the first day when he cried a bit. Probably as he was cutting 2 molars. He now watches outside the car with great interest for long stretches of time, waving to approaching people or vehicles, & getting frantically excited when he sees cows or other animals close by.

The one nasty thing was a most ghastly accident. Nick was ahead of us & nearly collided with a tractor. It was weaving over the road & driving twice as fast as tractors should (they have no springs). Luckily Nick was keeping a wary eye on it, & had said to Margaret he bet it would soon be involved in an accident — the driver

---

* Mike Richmond handled Jane and Hugo's travel arrangements from Nairobi and sometimes piloted; Billy Collins was their British publisher.

suddenly pulled up to chat to a friend. Anyhow, Nick avoided the crash & drove on. We drove up about 5 [minutes] later. An African woman, very pregnant, was riding on it (illegal) & a little boy was on the driver's lap. The woman noticed us coming up behind & said something to the driver. We were still quite a way behind. He began pulling over to the side of the road and, <u>without slowing down</u> bounced onto the verge. Well, that tractor behaved like a wild thing, leaping in the air. The driver fell off first. The huge back wheel went right over his chest. And then the woman. The same wheel went over her <u>head.</u> The driver got up, ran after the tractor, & stopped it. The woman lay twitching. Then she <u>got up,</u> though Hugo, with a blanket on the road, was trying to make her lie down. The driver was weaving all over the road, spitting blood. The woman spat blood. The child had lost a tooth & was scratched a bit but otherwise O.K. Another car stopped — German missionary. Was eventually persuaded to take the man. We took the woman & child until we got up to Nick, who was waiting, & then put them in the VW — smoother ride. We got them to what they called a 'hospital' — only a tiny dispensary. But we were in the middle of nowhere — about 50 miles from a hospital. The ride would have killed them. Nick thought the woman would die anyway. Oh, it was so horrible.

Anyway, Grub enjoyed the taxi ride, & threw his favourite toy into the lake — gone forever! And, since I <u>know</u> I'll forget, if you hear of anyone coming to Nairobi I need some Paddi Pants — 1 large and 1 extra large or 2 of each. Can't get them out here any more.

Well. The reserve. At first all the news was grim, grim, grim. I'll have to say, now, that David is no more. Nor Pooch. And Faben gone for 3 months. Baboons attacking humans. Baboon had a tooth broken by Geza throwing a stone. Ruth attacked. Carole wanting to leave. Gloom. Hurried conversations, stopping when Hugo & I appeared. Delegations & despair. What a way to be greeted.

And then we had a conference. I decreed that, or suggested that, we have far fewer feeding days — one in 5 or 6 days. That people could follow. That no more stones should be thrown at babs. That boxes should <u>always</u> be kept closed, but, if empty, opened as soon as the chimps inspected them — at present they are always open if empty. This so that, eventually, chimps may be less frustrated by closed boxes because, after all, they might be empty. By feeding less we feel the babs may stop hanging around waiting for the signal of screaming chimps to descend on the camp.

Well. You know how I have always wanted people to try & follow the chimps? And none ever have? Well — Geza, Ruth, Carole (& our two temporary FWI students, Dawn & Sally) all want to follow, lone following. Lone climbing about in the mountains. It is so exciting now — 2 people follow each day, & one stays in camp. The chimps are back to their old 1963 habits — sometimes they wander into camp & sometimes they don't. Today FABEN came BACK! So exciting. Yesterday Goliath caught a baboon infant, & shared it with Worzle & Flo. And it would have been a super day except that it was Goblina's baby — her first. Tim's favorite infant, called Huxley — (Aldous) (the Hippie hero).*

Finally the beach house. I was dreading living here. Hot. Awful. Imagine. Well, the cage is gigantic.† Wait till you see pictures. Cool as cool. Almost need a sweater all day, & this is the hot part of the year. The house is cool. And does Grub love it all. The baboons pass each day & he is so excited. A stray kitten — from a cat imported by Iddi‡ (who sends Um, Mum, his salaams) was adopted by Tim & Bonnie — & Grub & it get on fine & play like anything — nearly all non-contact play. Grub roars with laughter when it pounces on & plays with his toys. He is wild on the lake. Simply loves it. Loves to go out sailing in his "boat" — his yellow paddling pool. Margaret is v. good with him, & loves him, & is my age & sensible, so can be trusted to look after him when I go up to the chimps. Which, in 8 days, I haven't done till today!! Except for yesterday the meat eating which took place almost over the kitchen!

Nick is a genius at making things. And so nice. He has fixed us up

---

* Aldous Huxley had recently authored an account of his mescaline experiences, *The Doors of Perception.*

† This particular cabin, by the beach, had been built the year before; a wire mesh extension (the cage) with concrete floor was added, primarily to protect Grub from aggressive baboons or chimps.

‡ Iddi Matata was, by virtue of his significant age and dignity, already "honorary headman" of a small village near the mouth of Kasekela Stream when Jane and her mother first arrived at Gombe in 1960.

with shelves & cupboards. Is building a <u>dark</u> <u>room.</u> (He is <u>very</u> good at developing & printing.) Also is making a little <u>harbour</u> for the boats, & a <u>huge</u> aquarium, waist deep, where we plan to get as many lake fish as poss to look at through a glass bottomed thing. He has made all the boxes work. Best of all he is <u>very</u> good with the boys and they are all working all day long and <u>cheerfully!</u>

Tons & tons of love to all<br>
(it is 12.30 & must go to bed),<br>
Jane & Grub & love from Hugo too

<u>19 July 1968</u>

Darling Family,

Have now found a typewriter, so there's some hope you'll be able to read some of what I write! Well, there's lots to say — it's a pity Grub leaves me so little time to do anything except attend to him. Although that's not strictly true because I have someone look after him every morning while I do chimp observations "upstairs,"* but then I feel I should devote the afternoon to him. Sometimes he has a nap — at others he stays awake all day — even then he doesn't usually sleep all night, though he is getting better — his 10 to 11 o'clock wakefulnesses are getting shorter and shorter, and sometimes he doesn't wake after that. I think it depends on his teeth.

Well, thank you for your letters, Danny, Olly and Mum. All much appreciated. I think I didn't get several of your letters Mum. Robert† says he thinks you may have written about a young man — a possible research assistant? And, while I think of it, if there's any possible chance of Rosemary David-Smith coming <u>any</u> earlier it will be a good thing. Robert wants me to work her in personally. So even a week's difference would be good. Grub has just rushed in, dirty faced, chewing something, grabbed a pen, a box of matches, and run off. He really is very super now. He can pick up so many things

---

* The banana feeding and main observation area was called "upstairs" because it was situated up a trail some distance from the buildings on the beach.
† Professor Robert Hinde. Rosemary David-Smith never appeared.

out of books — pictures I mean. Just to put it on the record, cos I never seem to get time to make a record for myself, he knows (and not only in his own books, but to choose out of any old magazine, first asking) things including these: little girl (all ages), little boy, horse, dog (all sorts of breeds), bird (any kind), ostrich, lion, cat, tree, flower, man, apple, ball (decent type), hat, eye (of anything), nose and mouth of people, cow, mouse, beetle, book, plate, cut, bellows (and this was a pair of bellows lying by a fire which I showed him in a book) three weeks after leaving Limuru (where he used to play with them). He had never been told what they were in a picture. Toys. Teddy bear. Monkey, pig, duck, chicken, boat, foot, hand — he even picked out the foot of a tortoise!, tortoise, lizard, bee, fly, hair. Can't think of more at present. . . .

Well, the beach house, contrary to all my fears, is cool and beautiful and I'm thoroughly enjoying it, even though I'm not with the chimps so much. Grub has never been so happy anywhere. He has little red water wings, and he sails about in his yell[ow] paddling pool (that you saw from the Crater pictures) and he loves the water. He keeps fetching his wings and putting his arm through, and asking us (with gestures only!) to blow them up. He really is funny with his talking. He shakes his head firmly if you ask him to repeat a word — will readily repeat nonsense or baboon or chimp sounds, or imitate coughs. But he does not fancy talking till he has mastered it properly I think. Being Grub, and so uncannily clever about everything else, it is not at all worrying, but rather funny.

Robert's visit is a huge enormous success. He has gone down well with everyone. Margaret thinks he's a sweet poppet, Geza is thrilled with his intellect, as is Pat, Alice likes anything in trousers, and Robert (who says he forgot to bring trunks) bathes in his black bikini pants (I'm sure on purpose!) He keeps away from others for the bathing, so you see the elegant figure with the tiny black strip around his loins, in the distance. Most dashing. Alice saw him once thus, and I'm sure was bowled over! Nick likes him. He adores Grub, and he has quite fallen for Geza's Ruth* — who is willowy,

---

* Geza Teleki had been accepted to do research at Gombe earlier; Ruth Davis, his friend, had arrived more recently.

quiet, and intelligent. Poor Ruth hurt her foot, so was quite a hero-ine for a couple of days. Grub is back with his grin and his apple. He is just getting his canines.

Robert is thrilled with the work here, the set up, the chimps, and the monograph. He says he thinks Cullen would be a fool not to publish it as it is because it is "beautifully written". He couldn't have been more complimentary about it. Thinks it's exciting. Rob-ert and Dave think that what is going on here is the most exciting thing in animal behaviour that is going on anywhere in the world. Robert is madly going to help us get funds and people. And Dave. Dave is pretty sure he can get the funds for us to do this editing of research film — which will be 18 months to 2 years in our own house! Just had a letter from the pregnant Terry Stobbs who has found us a tenant for the house, and says that Jessie and pups are well — did you know that Jessie had 9 daughters and 2 sons just af-ter we left?

Now. Do you know that FLO IS PREGNANT!!! Can you believe it? Nova lost a baby in November. Pallas lost a baby two weeks ago — she disappeared just before it was due, and came back a week later with no baby. But Flo won't! Bet Fifi gets that way soon. Mike is still dominant, with Humphrey coming up fast. Figan will fight for the position too. Faben is still magnificent even with his bad arm. Willy Wally, after holding one leg up close to his body for 2 years, has just begun to use the withered limb for walking, and is rapidly getting more and more use. Pepe is still pathetic, but has started displaying again, and even beats his chest with his good arm.

We have started a new system of records. It was funny. Robert wanted lots and lots of information left out of the records because of the pile of notes building up. I agreed with lots, but we fought over lots too. He wanted lots of charts made, which I said I didn't want to analyze because I'd never be sure that people had made them up right. Anyway, I said we'd give his way a try. And now, two days later, when he has seen his scheme in operation, he has agreed that I was right! Well, not quite so clear cut, but gradually things have been changed, and now it is quite super. Did I tell you that eve-ryone now, at last, loves to follow chimps. We have a completely new feeding system — feeding only every four or five days. And the groups of chimps have gone back to how they used to be, coming in much less often. I am happy about it for the first time since it started! Robert thinks we should get funds for the mother/offspring relations to be studied in detail all the time — so one person on those records every year. Pat we have persuaded, thank Goodness, to return to the fold. He has given up his colobus (thankfully, I know) and is going to do six months of sexual behaviour, go to Cambridge for 6 months, return here for two years of sexual behaviour, write up for a year in Cambridge, and leave with a PhD — at least, there seems little doubt of that. His subject is vast — how do females differ in their behaviour in different stages of their cycles. How do males differ when there is or is not a pink female present. How do male and female infants differ. What about the various touching gestures which people like Peter Marler think are sexually orientated and which I think are not. Etc. What a subject — that is all as well as the more obvious aspects. He will make a super job of it. One thing which I suddenly thought of — you know that sometimes one male will take off [with] a young female — they are not seen again until she is no longer pink. Well, if he can follow them for those 10 days or so (what a job!) and be sure that no other males have access to the female, and if it so happens that she does not menstruate again after that, then we shall know at last who is the FATHER of the infant.

We have a new sort of record now — each of the general researchers takes a chimp in turn — about every 3 days for each of them — and takes detailed timed notes on its behaviour. They follow it from camp on that day for as long as they can. It really will be super. And then Pat will have the same sort of information on his females, and the mother-infant person on the infants. Geza is returning after a year to study locomotion. Everything is working so well. Oh yes — we are also to get a Senior Scientist, on a yearly basis, to generally supervise everyone, and this will mean that a lot of universities will make grants for students to come here that would not do so otherwise — because most supervisors like their students to have constant supervision in the field. It will be very super indeed, and will take a huge load of responsibility from Hugo's and my shoulders — with Grub, and film editing, and book writing, etc, it is really too much to be solely responsible for a place that has grown so large and so fast as this. To see the chimps completely ignoring something like 12 people (this is with the visitors all up there) is a sight that must be seen to be believed. Robert just can't get over it.

Finally, to you Mum. I didn't suggest you come this summer, cos I thought that this house would be so hot, and I thought you'd loath it. But now I know how super it is, it will be different. They have just started to get cases of sleeping sickness at Seronera, so we cannot go there with Grub. Hugo has to go there to do leopards in January, so I can come here. Can you come out after Christmas? And have a month here, and then, I think, a month in the Crater. Though I'm not sure quite where Hugo's going after Seronera. He isn't either.

Do hope, Danny, you got your cable and letter in time for your birthday. . . .

Tons and tons of love,
Jane

[late July 1968]

Darling Family,

Again this will be a fairly hurried note. We had some most unwelcome visitors foisted on us — they arrived on the sordid new boat which has been bought for the tourist plans for here — horrible thought that we really do have to do something about getting a feeding area ready for them.* Anyway, these three arrived — a rather dear old American Ma in Law, with a son in law who is some high up bod in the National Parks — Administrator I think, and a daughter who is the son in law's wife — really! Anyway, Ma in law has behaved fine. The other two — honestly, they marched in as though the whole place was theirs now it's a Park. They wandered

---

* Part of the plan for Gombe Stream National Park was to habituate a new group of chimpanzees, south of the research area, for tourists to view. A fancy new trimaran, the *Triton*, had just been purchased to handle the anticipated influx of tourists.

about up with the chimps in a way no one has before. Unfortunately
we didn't tell them not to — we never thought of it because no one
else ever has. And, after the first day, it was almost impossible to do
so, as you can imagine. Well, they had two days here, and are now
about to go, in this large Triton which, as I say, has been bought for
potential tourists — even though we have told Parks there can be
no hope of having any chimps ready for tourists before the end of 2
years — at a minimum. How we shall ever get it going I simply can't
imagine. What a task.

Well. What news. Grub is fine, though he has his periodic diarrhea again which is a nuisance. He still, point blank, refuses to talk.
Will imitate even a donkey now, let alone the non-human primates.
He is still loving it here — his walks along the beach in the cool of
morning and evening, his swims, his rides in his yellow rubber boat.
He adores watching the baboons when they come along and sit
around the cage at lunch time. He has a kikapu on ropes* in the
cage, and he often snoozes off whilst Thomas' wife, Theresa, swings
him gently to and fro. Thomas and Theresa, and sometimes Moro,
look after him in the morning while I go up to the chimps, or do
some paper work. He is so good with them — and they with him.
He seldom cries even once when I am gone which is, of course, a big
relief. . . .

I am getting so sorry for poor old Flo. Flint is going through a real
baby stage now that, at long last (3 months before the new baby is
due) he is weaned. He rides about on her the whole time. Carole
spent 6 hours with the two of them the other day. When Flo sat
down to rest or eat, Flint, whimpering, invariably went up behind
her and pushed until she moved on — at which he jumped dorsal.
When she dared climb down a tree without him ventral, he flew
down after her in the most terrible temper tantrum. And if she
grooms anyone but him, he whimpers and pushes inbetween! But
the really ridiculous thing is when Fifi is with them — which is
nearly always except when she is pink and wanting to be with the
men! Then Fifi wants to be groomed. She pulls Flo's hands away

---

* A woven shopping basket made, in this case, to function as an infant's swing.

from Flint, she whimpers like a small spoilt child! Two days ago, when Hugo was filming, Flo managed to get away from Flint for a short lie down — Flint went off to play with Athena's gorgeous nine month old, Atlas. But Fifi noticed. She went over to Flo, and groomed her for a moment. Then she pushed Flo, and when Flo merely rolled over onto the other side, Fifi began to whimper. She picked up Flo's arm and pulled the hand towards her, she whimpered, she pushed — until poor old Flo, in self defence, had to laboriously sit up and do as her terrible daughter demanded!

Shall be most interested to hear what Robert says in his letter. He became more than humanized.* He says he will always now think of zoo chimps as being in prison — oh and many other things. He left with tears in his eyes — off to . . . Dian and the gorillas. Shall be really fascinated to hear his report on her. She does seem to be getting super things — George is getting more and more mad about it! Did you know George is taking three months off from his lions to go and look for the abominable snowman!! Really. Dave Hamburg also left with tears.

Hugo is champing for the typewriter, and I have to re-write the Geographic vulture article for Grzimek which is an awful bore.† And I must make all the alterations for the monograph and send them off — though I havn't heard a single word from Cullen yet. For all I know he may have rejected the MS or put it into print. Anyway, don't let anything go through until you have received a whole batch of alterations from me. . . .

Oh dear. Grub is absolutely screaming, and I shall just have to stop because I can't think, and he is attaching himself to my arm and trying to climb all over me — just like Flint.

Am not sending off films yet — Dave left overweight,‡ and the

---

* That is, Professor Hinde, having spent time with wild chimpanzees in their natural state, now understood how disturbing it is to see captive chimps in cages.
† H. C. Bernhard Grzimek was director of the Frankfurt Zoo and a conservationist and author. One of the creators of the Serengeti National Park, in the 1960s and 1970s he was still an important presence in Tanzania. Jane was probably rewriting her article about tool-using Egyptian vultures in accordance with Grzimek's requirements for a publication he edited.
‡ With too much weight for the plane flying him out.

films were lost when he went. So Hugo will post them when he leaves in 2 weeks. From Nairobi. Dare not post them from here.

Tons and tons of love to all,
Do hope you'll forgive this disjointed epistle,
Jane, Grub & Hugo


[Late July or early August 1968]

Darling Family,

It is 11.15 and everyone has gone to bed save for Hugo and I — and Sadiki who is guarding the cage and Grub. Hugo and I are in the little dining room building down on the lake shore — only a short way from sleeping Grub, but I could never hear him crying for the pounding of the little waves.

Have spent most of to-day doing the oddments and changes that Cullen suggested for the Monograph. Shall send you a copy, Mummy, by the next mail, when I have done all there is to do. It sounds as though there is no violent rush and that he is planning to send the proofs out here — which will be nice for you if you don't have that sordid job. I did tell you, didn't I, that Cullen finally did write, sounding awfully nice, and saying that he planned to publish the whole thing?

We have been having a dread time with the baboons. They all started dying — well, Hugo and I found one on the beach, and thought nothing of it. Then, same day, Alice found one when she was following Flo and Flint. Then we managed to find, during the next 2 days, 3 more, and two traces. Tim has gone away for 2 weeks (he left with Phyllis to look at babs elsewhere — silly clot) so we began to suspect poison. But were also scared the chimps might catch something if it wasn't poison. So Hugo got onto the radio telephone, all sorts of precautions were taken, and we arranged for Monks, the veterinary chemist, and his wife, a qualified vet, to come down by charter plane the next day. They duly arrived. We had one corpse fresh enough for examination — though pretty smelly. Certainly poison, but Monks was staggered by the nature of it. The baboons were literally perfectly O.K. until just about the moment they died. Monks said that the first indication, in any animal, that it wasn't feeling well, was going off its food. This baboon still had food in the esophagus! Also, in most irritant poisons, the gut is irritated right down from the stomach to the small intestines. This baboon showed irritation in its stomach wall and 2 inches of the large intestine — and that was all. Anyhow, he and his slides have gone off back to Nairobi. He isn't at all sure they'll be able to trace the poison since he thinks it may be quite unknown to Europeans. They have now had a scare — the fishermen — and no more baboons have died. Tim has missed some absolutely fascinating things. The changes in hierarchy led to some fantastic fights — when attacked the females and youngsters rush right into the lake!* Did you ever see that, Mum?

One bit of news will delight you, Mum. Guess who turned up on the beach 2 nights ago, in the darkness? Dominic!! Wanting work. So, since we have to get another cook, we have re-employed the old rogue. He is off buying food and blanket and fishing line today, and will start work tomorrow. And [he will] import Chiko and Ado (who is "mkubwa sana sasa" he says) at the beginning of next month.†

Grub. Well. Not much new on him. He still refuses to utter a single word — he doesn't talk jargon either, except very very rarely, usually when he's in bed at night, or frightfully preoccupied with his own things. But he knows more and more. And, touch wood, he is beginning to sleep better at night, especially since the first of his lower canines has come through. He is quite fearless in the sea — loves the waves. And has just begun to love to hurl himself on top of Hugo or I if we are lying on the bed. He is quite utterly mad at these times — stands absolutely upright and then lets himself go. He also climbs about on me as though I'm a Flo or something — even to the tune of climbing up my back and diving head first over my shoulder onto my lap! He loves charging round his cage pulling his toy canoe

* The death of certain presumably high-status male baboons led to competition for status in the hierarchy among other males.
† Dominic Charles Bandola had come with Jane and her mother on their very first expedition to Gombe Stream in 1960, to work as their cook. Chiko was his wife. Their daughter, Ado, was (Dominic says here), "all grown up now."

behind him, filled with toys. Or a string with the cat chasing after the end. I did tell you about his make believe drinking of tea, pouring into a cup from an empty tea pot and then pretending to drink nothing? About a week after we got here he did that. He is now terribly good at fitting together his "pipes" — plastic tubes which fit together into long shapes, turn corners, etc. He is really good at it now. And then pushes the finished things along the ground as if they were cars. He understands almost too much now. I think he will really burst forth into excellent English when he does condescend to utter. Can you tell us about spina bifidas, Olly? Is there any hope for ones that are "tapped" at birth? Park warden here has a new daughter who had this done. See I must stop.

> Tons and tons of love to all of you,
> Jane, Hugo & Grub

> Box 185
> Kigoma
> [Mid-August 1968]

Darling Family,

It's almost impossible to find time to write letters these days — it's all work, work, work. Have just had to do final alterations to Monograph based on Cullen's, Robert's, and my suggestions. I enclose them, Mum, in case you might have to proof read — though, as I said, Cullen seems to think he is sending all proofs to me. I enclose my letter to him, as this has one or two other oddments other than the pages. If you do have to proof read — which, for your sake, I certainly hope you won't! — the best thing would be to cut out the longer bits and add them to the — no, stick them over the — wrong or changed pieces. The shorter bits change in ink. Let's hope it all comes here, where I have willing helpers. . . .

Report back from Nairobi that the baboons were 99% certainly poisoned. So we are trying to move fishermen along the beach and away from Tim's baboon troop's beaches. We also plan to move our staff headquarters over the stream to the Scout's place — the Scout will be moved re. the Parks scheme to where the second feeding area will, one day, have to be. Then two sweet little stone houses will go where all the mess of the Africans' quarters are now — and there are 6 uniports there now, plus kitchen, plus store, plus boathouse, plus bits and pieces. It will be super to have that gone. The stone houses are for Margaret and Nick, and one for the Senior Scientist — when we get one. Now that the place has changed anyway, we might as well make it nice changing rather than mess changing. There will be a roof, for a dining room, where the Africans are now, too. And a tiny rough stone darkroom, kitchen and store tucked away in the bushes by the stream.

We have been having conference after conference to try and sort out people being able to live together. The line between Tim, Bonnie, the FWI students, and everyone else, is a thick and seemingly impenetrable line. But, by getting everyone together, and bringing out personal grudges and grievances — as we did last night over dinner, — we seem to have got people to at least think that they can talk to each other politely. And no more FWIs!!

Flo's infant is really any minute now. Alice lost her this morning. So I thought I'd find her and see the birth! I found her, purely by luck, along the path. But she still hasn't given birth! Poor thing — Flint is still riding dorsal. She lies in nests half the day.

Oh — re the 8mm. You won't be getting more for a bit I'm afraid, since the camera has broken. As soon as anyone goes to Nairobi it will be mended — and there will be quite a few black and whites to send, too.

D[ominic] sends his love, Mum. It's amazing — it took him 3 days to reestablish himself at the top of the dominance hierarchy, together with Moro. They sort of avoid each other, as each senses the other's prestige! Tons and tons of love — it's pitch dark, so can't start new sheet. Pregnancy tests for chimps have arrived — & work!!

Jane

P.S. Will send the pages of alterations next mail — no big envelopes.

[Around August 18, 1968]

Darling Family,

Really a very brief note to let you know all is well. Hugo, first, & then me, have just finished recovering from malaria. Hugo's usual bi-visitly attack — my first since 1963! So it knocked me out somewhat. How (the thing I was resting on gave way!) — ever, I am fighting fit again now. Grub, of course, is fine. No signs of any illness for him, thank goodness. Still no word. In Gesell it says that infants who miss out the 'jargon' stage are apt to show "super-intelligence" later.* Grub has never used jargon. On the other hand, even dim children usually say one word at 1 year, & an average of 10–15 at 18 months. However, since a) G is only 17 mos, & b) he is behaving, in <u>ALL</u> other respects, like Gesell's 2, 2 1/2 (even, in some things 3) year olds, we are not concerned! He can even walk up to a ball and kick it on command. I am going to make an inventory of his accomplishments for when he is 18 months. Will send a copy.

Flo has <u>still</u> not produced. Alice is really redeeming herself — has followed her daily for 6 days now — or more. And got stung into the bargain, as Flo raided a bees' nest, climbed down, & headed straight for A & Pat who were following. So <u>Flo</u> lost the bees!! A lost Flo, but Pat ran in Flo's direction, so one of them remained with her. Flint is <u>still</u> riding on Flo's back. This is probably why Flo keeps traveling through tunnels in thick undergrowth — seeming to go out of her way to do so. Because then Flint <u>can't</u> ride dorsal! When she makes an early nest, Flint pesters her so for grooming that she has to leave.

Oh — meant to comment first on your super long letter Mum. Of course we want you that much. Grub is longing to see Grum again. The letter to Hugo will probably be in the mail tomorrow. So glad you, O, are enjoying your cessation of the 'deadly grind' of the daily trails to S. Road. Great news about Jiff & I do hope USA goes well — hoot about Wilkie. Should be lots of pictures of Grub — and

---

* Probably refers to Frances Ilg, Louise Ames, and Sidney Baker, *Child Behavior,* from the Gesell Institute of Human Development.

some of me! when H goes to Nairobi in 3 weeks. Do hope you're feeling OK Dan.

Tons [&] tons of love to all,
Jane, H & G

24 August 1968

Darling Family,

The baby has been born. Poor Alice, who had followed Flo for 10 days, only losing her for short times here and there, lost her the crucial morning. She got to the nest at 6.30 in the morning and Flo had already gone. Tim came across Flo at about 9.30 or earlier as he watched his baboons by the Game Scouts, and Flo had the baby. Hugo, Alice and I all converged.

It is the sweetest little girl, Flame. Typical Flo family — born full pink! She did not detach the placenta — it is still attached, and the baby is at least 48 hours. But Alice is still with her, so we shall know this evening whether it is off yet — it stinks. Flo very carefully cradles it, along with the baby, but once it dropped as Flo moved through the branches. Flo caught it again, but when she made a huge leap away from Leakey a few minutes later, we all had our hearts in our mouths lest it drop and get caught again. It didn't though. Also, until 3.00 the day it was born the cord was twice round its waist. Had it been around the neck I'm sure the little thing would have been strangled. She is almost completely hairless! Has hair on her head, and a few long white beard and moustache hairs. For the rest she looks quite naked, but close inspection reveals a few short downy sort of hairs. She is very lively and wiry, and already capable of moving a few inches about on Flo. Flint to everyone's amazement is behaving beautifully. I wish we knew if anything drastic happened when the infant was first born. Even the day before the birth (which was yesterday) Flint was riding dorsal. We never saw him even try to climb dorsal yesterday, nor today. He did sleep in Flo's nest though. And probably will again. Flo met Fifi this morning. She peered, and several times just touched a hand or foot, but was not as overjoyed as we had hoped. And Faben simply ignored Flame's existence. Figan is on a safari with Melissa and doesn't know yet.

Which brings me to the hooting thing about Leakey. He has gone slightly berserk, dear old fellow. He must, but must, always have a woman with him. Pink or not pink, it doesn't matter.* First he took Olly, then Fifi, then Olly again. Then Olly got away (this all took place over 2 months or so, each female going with him for about 2 weeks). Then, when I was up there the other morning, he tried to take them both together! I've never seen anything so funny. He branched, hair out, and Olly rushed up, panting. He continued to branch Fifi, thus sending Olly into hysteria. This continued all across camp. Then Fifi was a bit slower than usual — so when she finally arrived Leakey attacked her. And during the attack Olly made a quick get away, with furtive backward looks. Leakey, after calming down, was livid that Olly had gone, and made Fifi follow him in circles all round camp while he peered to try and see Olly. We were all in hysterics! . . .

Well, there really is no time for more. The last of the mob is drinking coffee all around — Pat & Alice, Nick & Margaret, Dawn and us. Everyone is discussing whether or not Flo can survive long enough to prevent Flame from being one of our pathetic orphans. There's always hope that Fifi will take her on, but she might have her own by then. In fact we were saying this morning we hoped Flo could make it till Fifi gets her first — <u>what</u> a family!

Grub. Well, nothing new since I last wrote. <u>Still</u> no words. Getting wilder & wilder — hurls himself about — at us, out of his "boat" into the water, running along the beach, hurling rocks. Can eat fine on his own provided it's a type of food that won't make a mess if he spills it. He hates spilling. Points at the roll of bumf† until we wipe it up. Nor will he get into his chair unless it is clean!

Must end.

Tons & tons of love, Jane, Hugo & Grub

---

* Leakey is one of the adult male chimpanzees; "pink," of course, describes a female's very visible genital swelling during estrus. When Leakey took Olly and Fifi on consortship, he used the usual male technique (branch-shaking and hair-raising threat displays) to coerce or persuade the females to follow him.
† Slang for toilet paper, a shortening of the original Royal Air Force expression "bum fodder."

[Postmarked September 19, 1968]

Darling Family,

I meant to write more than a sordid blue, but life has just been too hectic. We were supposed to have a visit by Nyerere this week, so Hugo, poor Hugo, delayed his safari to the Crater to cover the visit for the Geographic. Then, at the last minute, the authorities decided, as we had known all along, that the whole thing was utterly impractical. For one thing, we told them that all the chimps would run away if more than 6 people came up. So how could he be adequately bodyguarded? For another, it takes 20 mins to walk upstairs, and he had to open a dispensary in Mwamgongo. And he couldn't be sure of seeing chimps unless he stayed at least an hour. The whole thing was hopeless.

However, we offered our boat (only one now since we lost 2 engines driving John Owen of Tanzania National Parks back to Kigoma when the boat sank — did you hear about that?) So, finally they told us he couldn't make it. But still Nick was told he would be needed to drive the Triton — this ghastly trimaran the Parks has bought for the ultimate tourist area in the Gombe. And could the Boston Whaler (our speedboat) drive the Area Commissioner and party to Mwamgongo so that they could meet the president on arrival. So Hugo planned to be off early tomorrow. He, Nick and Pat drove in at 7.00 this morning. Pat was to drive the Area C to Mwam. and then bring back the boat. Tim was to take a second load of luggage to Kigoma to be loaded on the landrover and VW for the trip. Pat didn't appear and didn't appear. At 12.30 we were planning emigration to the hills and I was wondering whether clothes or food was most important for Grub — cos we thought perhaps Nyerere had been assassinated and all our people arrested or shot! However, just after that the welcome sound of our boat. Pat rushed the Area Commissioner plus party to Mwamgongo, returned here, and collected another load for packing in Kigoma.

He set off at 1.00. The President with his convoy of boats — the Triton plus the Police boat plus two fisheries boats — didn't pass until 2.30! Next we got worried cos Pat and the Whaler didn't get back. But finally the President and party came past again — we had flags and waved. Wanted to get a picture of Grub waving to President. He did it once (got picture) and then he firmly walked to water's edge, turned back to boats, and removed his pants!

Well, next the Whaler came back. Poor Pat and his passengers had got soaked to the skin, plus the load. Then Dawn's train had come in — she went to Nairobi for us, had to go to hospital, finally started back on a plane, didn't arrive on the train she was booked on last week — panic utter. She turned out to be in Tabora Hotel waiting for Hugo's precious equipment which had got sent on to Dar because a plane from Uganda Police had backed three times into Dawn's plane on the runway, so causing utter chaos! Anyway, she got back, with everything, yesterday. Had made airways pay all her hotel bills, etc. Jolly good.

Pat then had to go and fetch the Area Commissioner back from Mwamgongo — he was hoping to get to Kigoma ahead of the President to welcome him and make final arrangements for the party. So. Pat got back with him & two other officials — one of whom had lain flat out on the floor, terrified of the speed boat, and begged and begged to be dumped ashore! Tim and Bonnie (Tim going to see Bonnie off to the dentist on a plane arriving today) set off at 6.00 with load and Area Commissioner. We relaxed. Soon Hugo and Nick would be back, the others sleeping on the Triton, and Hugo, Nick and Margaret ready to go in early this morning with the last load. Supper time came and went. Super apple pie from Dominic. No Hugo and Nick. Finally Margaret and I went to bed about 1 o'clock wondering what on earth had happened. (I started this letter yesterday so the sequence may jump rather — i.e. there may be two todays!) Then, about 2.00, we heard the Whaler. Tim had broken down. For an hour he tried to start the engine. For an hour he made the Area Com. row! Then the Area Com. left ship, took a canoe, and set off to paddle to Kigoma! Tim finally got the engine going. Finally got to Kigoma but couldn't find the Area Comm. on the way. Hugo, by then, had alerted the Police. A deathly pale Regional Com. left the party and feared the worst. They were holding council of war when Tim arrived from the boat. The Regional Com. relaxed — he presumes all was under control? No, says Tim, the Area Com.

is lost in a canoe! So they all went down to get a search light on the boat — and then the canoe paddled into the harbour.

Dramas and more dramas, all day! So now they are about to go. Hugo has given last minute lectures in cine film to Pat and Geza to cover Flame developments. The Jacobis, from Amsterdam Zoo, are coming by plane to spend 5 days here. I leave with them for the Crater, when they go, to join Hugo. I spend a month in the Crater. Then return here, after a short trip to Kigoma — Nairobi I mean. Had better stop because I can't think any more.

Tons and tons of love,

Jane

Chimpland

23 September [1968]

Darling Olly,

Why do I always feel so sure your birthday is in October until it's too late to do anything about it. It's odd, because I don't normally have difficulty in remembering months. Anyway, as you see, I have thought of you on THE day, and I wish you many many happy returns of today. Grub sends Grolly a juicy kiss. My, he really does have juicy kisses these days — some of them are quite indecent, when he bites lips!

Thanks for the letter about spina bifs. I can't tell you any more because I don't like to ask the man concerned to give me intimate details. Alice saw the baby. Says the little tap thing is in the child's hair, she can't sit up because she has weak neck muscles. She can't move her feet — but Alice didn't say about her legs. She says she is a lively little thing otherwise, and seems to have normal intelligence.

As I look out of my window the waves are huge. Almost like the sea. We've been having some mighty wave storms lately. Odd thing is that it never seems to be windy at all when these great waves start pounding the shore. Must be frightfully windy somewhere else on the lake. You'd adore living down here on the beach. You could live in the water. Never too hot, sometimes (for here!) chilly. Sometimes so flat you can see 40 yards or more to the bottom — super for goggling. Sometimes all wild and wavy like now. Only occasionally really murky after a storm.

Grub is just drawing in black biro* all over his body, my legs, and my shirt. Now my arm. It is all meant to be on a piece of paper. Oh, I see. He had used up all the [paper]. He has now stolen a fresh piece, pulling the bottom bit from a pile of notes which are all over the floor. Just a mo [typing runs off page]

So. Order restored. Grub singing and humming and pointing delightedly (for his own benefit) to his various works of art. He has twice copied a cross — was so pleased the first time he managed to do this that he leapt up and gave me a large kiss! How does his behaviour (other than his lack of speech!) compare with the little girl of Phylly's secretary?

Grub and I are getting ready to join Hugo tomorrow. We go into Kigoma early and catch the plane to the Crater at 12 sharp. Should be with Hugo about 3. Don't much look forward to Grub in a plane! He has been very helpful this afternoon. I spent a long time trying to fit everything into the smallest space possible. When I had to go and answer the telephone (you did know we had field telephones?) Grub decided to find out the quickest way of emptying a small tightly and carefully packed suitcase. He made a pretty good job of it in 1 minute! He also escaped with all his newly washed, just dried clothes and dunked them all in the lake, then rubbed them in the sand for good measure. Brought them in, saw a pool of his wee, and with great glee wiped it up with his wet and sandy burden! However, we are packed now. The heat of the day has gone. The red sun is hovering over the horizon that is the invisible Congo. That is always the funny thing. In the dry season, when you simply cannot make out the land on the far side of the lake, the sun set is quite bizarre. The sun suddenly vanishes into thin air!

I meant to write a long long letter. Alas. Life decrees otherwise. I never got any more written last night after that spectacular plunge into nothingness of the red ball of fire. Grub loves to wave to the sinking sun. He only waves to it when it sinks, never when it is

---

* Ballpoint pen (named for its Hungarian inventor).

high in the sky. He certainly knows the difference between sun and moon, even though he hasn't seen all that many moons. Now it's 6.30 a.m., and there is still packing to be done. . . .

Tons and tons of love to you,
Olly, Danny,
Mum, Audrey and Rixey,
Jane & Grub

Serengeti
15 February 1969

Dear Ed,

Thank you very much for sending part of the grant money which I hear has arrived safely. As we are on safari I haven't yet had the bank statements, but presume that Shs. 30,000 arrived.

In the meantime we have had an opportunity to go through the grant request and determine what is needed each quarter. I enclose a copy of the grant request with the quarter in which we should like the money sent added after each item. Could you please subtract what has been sent already from what we are requesting for the first quarter, and send the remainder, as soon as possible, to the Chimpanzee Research account in Nairobi.

I have just left the chimps where everything is going very well indeed. Except that when I left there Flo was ill and had not been seen for several days. Now we hear that she has reappeared, but is without the new infant, Flame. This will be a tragic loss — both from the personal angle, and the scientific one too.

Hugo sends his regards.

Yours sincerely,
Jane

P.O. Box 2818
Nairobi
4 April 1969

Dear Mr. Vosburgh,

I am very sorry I have been so long in getting an article written, but life has been more than unusually hectic of late, and we have had innumerable problems to sort out at the Gombe Stream.

The enclosed article seems to have rather a lot of the tragedy of the chimps. Yet perhaps this is a good thing, for it is one of the aspects which becomes so pronounced in a long term study. The high death rate of infants and the illness. I actually had to take out several of the deaths about which I had written and try to substitute them with happier things!

I am writing separately to Mary Griswold* about the picture coverage, as it seems that many of the pictures which should illustrate this article may still be with Special Publications — the early polio ones and those of little Merlin. Incidentally, I hope you will agree that the Merlin story should come in this article. It was in the book, but I have gone on the assumption firstly that many readers of the magazine will not have seen the book, and secondly that those who did never knew the fate of the orphan — in the book he was still alive at the end.†

Hugo and I shall probably be leaving Nairobi on 13th April, but the above address will reach us quite speedily I think.

I hope everyone is well at the Geographic — we are all fine, including Little Hugo, who is now running, talking — and going to school every morning! At only 2 he knows 9 letters of the alphabet, can make them with matches, and can count up to 3 — not bad!?

Hugo, and my mother who is with us at present, join me in sending warm personal regards to you and your wife.

Yours sincerely,
Jane

---

* Illustrations editor at the *National Geographic* magazine.
† The book, *My Friends the Wild Chimpanzees,* was published by the National Geographic Society in 1967.

P.O. Box 2818
Nairobi
5 April 1969

Dear Mary,

This is in answer to Hugo's letter — I mean your letter to Hugo! He asks me to apologize profusely for the fact that he has not answered it before — but he really has been completely hectic, on top of which he had to fly down to the Gombe to try and sort out problems down there.

The legends for the chimp pictures you have are all on tape. The tape recorder has broken down, but is being repaired, and I will type them out and send them to you forthwith. I have now done an article — I have just posted it to Mr. Vosburgh, so if he approves of it, or the gist of it, perhaps you will see it soon.

The story covers the following: 1) the polio epidemic (pictures should be with Special Publications of old Mr. McGregor being peered at by Fifi, etc, and possibly others) and Hugo should have some good pictures of Faben walking bipedally holding paralyzed arm by the wrist with his good hand. There may be some of him scratching with a foot — something a normal chimp never does. But the Gregor locomotion, I think, was only on film. 2) Merlin being orphaned. Unfortunately I don't think there are any of him with Miff. But there are some excellent ones of him shivering and miserable, again with Special Publications. Did Edna Koning, at that time (1965), send any colour transparencies to the Geographic? If so, there might be one of him with Miff. 3) Meat eating. 4) Birth of Flame — and Hugo I think sent you some good ones. In addition, one of our researchers has an excellent one of Flint dorsal and Flame ventral which she is sending you. We are sending one of Flo, Flame and Flint all in one nest. And Hugo, last summer, I think got some shots of Flint in temper tantrums? (Again, it may have been all on film.) I am checking with our researchers if they have any colour slides of Flint or Fifi with Flame, and have asked them to try and get one of Flint, today, still riding on poor old Flo! 5) Brothers. If Hugo did not have pictures of Figan and Faben together, we can get one quite easily. I have written to ask them to try and cover these two brothers, just in case. 6) Grub and baboons. In case Hugo didn't get it, we have written to Tim Ransom asking him to try and get a group of baboons peering into the big cage, with people inside. Incidentally, Hugo had some very good pictures of Little Hugo in his first small cage. So far as we could see, <u>all</u> of these were returned to us — by Special Publications I think. If this is so, then we should obviously return some to you — also some of everyone at dinner with the little genet right in the circle eating.

Special Publications should also have a number of Hugo's super genet pictures — close up. And I have asked someone at Gombe to get a picture of Ruth Davis following a big male in thick undergrowth (You'll see why when you read the story).

Please could you let us know quickly whether you think you have, or will have, a good enough picture coverage for the article. We shan't be in Nairobi after about 13th April, but the above address will soon reach us.

Please also forgive strange spacing — my space lever has broken. It's driving me mad!

Hugo joins me in sending very best wishes.

Yours,
Jane

As from: 1 York Mansions
Earl's Court
London, S.W.
28 June 1969

Dear Mr. Vosburgh,

Thank you for your letter of 3rd June. We are very sorry that the article was not suitable for the National Geographic Magazine, although I must admit this was not a great surprise. I was afraid it might be too sad, as I think I intimated in my letter. Unfortunately most of the major happenings at Gombe have been somewhat tragic — there were many more deaths than I wrote about, including a male falling out of a tree and breaking his neck!

Although I could probably change the article to some extent we should have difficulty in obtaining sufficient new photos. We did ask the researchers, some months back, to shoot additional colour stills for the article, but due to the pressure of other work I'm afraid the results have been meagre to say the least.

We therefore feel it would be best to delay the article. It is very possible that Fifi will soon have a baby which would give us an excellent story, especially if Flo is still alive. Old Flo might even surprise us by producing again herself, though, for her sake, I hope not. What do you feel about this?

Things are going very well down at Gombe now. We have the best team there that we have ever had. Pat McGinnis, as you may have heard, was threatened by the draft, but has been rejected and is now on his way back to Gombe after his first 2 terms at Madingley.* Geza Teleki, who also returned to the States for his medical, has been rejected too, and will be returning to Gombe in January — when he will be married to Ruth Davis (the one charged by a buffalo in the article). Hugo's work is going very well too, although it is taking a year longer than planned, with the result that we shall be penniless by the end of it!

Please give our regards to your wife.

Yours sincerely,
Jane

6th August 1969

Dear Mr. and Mrs. Davis,

I have no written words to express to you my most heartfelt sympathy in your terrible loss. I am so sorry that I was not able to be with you in Africa to talk to you and take you down to the Gombe Stream with Hugo. I fully realize how simply awful it must have been for you both to see, in such tragic circumstances, the place where Ruth has been so happy.

You know from Geza, and I am sure you heard from Ruth, how really and truly she loved working at the Gombe. All of us who

---

* Madingley Zoological Field Station at Cambridge University.

knew her there realize that the peace and solitude of the mountains gave her contentment of mind and that her work utterly absorbed and satisfied her. I should like you to know, too, that her work was first class, and I shall see to it that her results do not go unacknowledged.

Those of us who knew her in Africa will always remember Ruth with affection and with admiration: her enthusiasm, clear thinking, and considerable moral & physical courage. It seems doubly tragic that she should have lost her life just as she was about to realize another kind of happiness with Geza. I'm glad he was able to be with you during those terrible days of waiting. His presence must have been a comfort to you.

I find it impossible to find words that can adequately convey my distress. This accident shouldn't have happened. I cannot help but feel in some way responsible; but for my work there, Ruth would have never gone to the Gombe. Yet she herself told me that she could never hope to have found a way of life, and work, that would have given her such happiness.

Yours in sympathy,
Jane van Lawick-Goodall

# 5

# INNOCENT KILLERS

## 1968–1970

The magnificence of the wild country that stretched out below
was completely hidden from us by the mist; had we been merely
passing tourists we should have missed forever that fantastic
view. Just as, had our lives run on different courses, we should
never have learned of the vivid personalities of Mrs Brown the
old hyena mother, or Jason the golden jackal, or Genghis the
leader of the wild dog pack.

— *Innocent Killers*

THIS CHAPTER brings us to another subject and (briefly skip-
ping back a year) a different time. Hans Kruuk, the Dutch
researcher who studied hyenas at Ngorongoro, saw the publication of his *National Geographic* article in July of 1968, with
photographs by Hugo van Lawick. Thus, after their long 1968 summer at Gombe, by the time the van Lawicks returned to Ngorongoro in October, Hugo was entirely free to focus on his own work
— which at that point had become the book on East African carnivores entitled *Innocent Killers*.

By October 1968, moreover, Grub was big enough to stand, to
stagger, and even, as Jane eagerly anticipated, to speak. Jane had by
then finished the analysis and writing of the burdensome scientific
monograph. She too felt ready to chase hyenas.

Hans Kruuk's study was a pioneering work. Kruuk, who kept
track of some fifty hyenas in Ngorongoro and about two hundred in
the Serengeti by knocking them out with an anesthetic and clipping
distinctive notches in their ears, arrived at some fundamental data:

around 420 adult hyenas inhabited the 100-square-mile area of the crater, separated into eight communities or clans, each of which fiercely defended its own territory against incursions from the others. Jane and Hugo chose to work less analytically, more in the style that had served them so well with chimpanzees. They observed specific groups very closely, learned to recognize individuals by their distinctive features and personalities, and focused probably more than Kruuk did on the relationships between individuals.

Both the van Lawicks and Kruuk recognized two more startling facts about the spotted hyenas. First, their clans are maintained as matriarchies; and second, contrary to what was then the common wisdom, the hyenas hunted more than scavenged. In the crater, as a matter of fact, lions were the major scavengers, seldom killing for themselves, characteristically waiting for an opportunity to grab the leavings of a hyena predation.*

Jane's early work with the chimpanzees of Gombe was a stunning breakthrough, a milestone in natural history studies. No equivalent breakthrough was possible with the savanna carnivores. But of course original research was only half the purpose. Jane and Hugo went to Ngorongoro as both researchers and communicators — or popularizers, intent on revealing secret worlds to a large and largely nonscientific public. As they had done with chimpanzees, Jane and Hugo pried open those secret worlds, the emotional and social and perceptual lives of intelligent animals, by using names that evoked personalities, with dramatic examples and tales and vignettes, and through the unalloyed power of their own profound empathy with their subjects.

Since hyenas tend to be active at night, the research schedule at Ngorongoro turned nocturnal, especially when there was enough of a moon to enhance visibility. Jane's participation in the study tended to consist of long vigils under the moon, sitting in the front of the VW bus with Grub asleep in the back, parked outside a hyena den and waiting for something to happen (as we read in the first let-

---

* See Hans Kruuk, "Hyenas: The Hunters Nobody Knows," *National Geographic* (July 1968): 44–57.

ter). Hugo, along with Nick and Margaret Pickford (on holiday from their administrative duties at Gombe), and for a time Cathleen Clark (a research assistant on her way to Gombe), would strap on crash helmets and race their car across a blue and shadowy landscape, trying to avoid holes and dens and rocks while "prowling for kills." Jane loved those quiet nights and her moon-slathered visions of the hyenas: "Oh to see these gross old ladies, their stomachs only inches from the ground, gambolling after each other and frolicking with the pups in the moonlight!" She also loved her close times with Grub.

A young British journalist named Timothy Green flew out to the crater (mentioned in both October 1968 letters), intent on interviewing Jane for a "profile," part of his book about four "contemporary travelers." *The Adventurers* includes the following candid snapshots of the van Lawick family as they appeared just after the journalist's Piper Apache came to a jolting stop on what passed for a landing strip at Ngorongoro. Hugo van Lawick stepped forward: "a short young man, with rather unbrushed dark brown hair, a face burnt red-brown by the African sun, and tired eyes that seemed constantly slightly screwed up in defence against the strong light." Soon after, "a moving cloud of dust" appeared in the distance, out of which gradually emerged a white Volkswagen bus. "A tall, very slim girl with long blonde hair, tied simply behind her head with a band, jumped out. She wore a light blue shirt and blue jeans; her feet were bare. She lifted down after her a blond haired little boy, with a rather dirty face, dressed in a red and white tee shirt and brown shorts."*

With help from friends and volunteers, Jane and Hugo watched, followed, studied, and photographed spotted hyenas and jackals in the crater until late December of 1968. They celebrated Christmas in Nairobi, and then packed up once again and moved into the Serengeti National Park — eventually erecting a half-dozen tents in the shade of acacia trees at the edge of Lake Legaja, hoping from there to locate the third of their "innocent killers," the Serengeti

---

* Timothy Green, *The Adventurers: Four Profiles of Contemporary Travelers* (London: Michael Joseph, 1970), p. 160.

wild dogs. Jane's mother, Vanne, came in early January 1969 for a visit. She stayed with them at the Legaja camp in January and February, and at their Nairobi home in March and early April, helping to care for Grub. As we read in the letter to Sally Cary Pugh of April 11, carried back to England by "Postman Mum," Jane and Hugo had returned to Nairobi principally so that Grub would have a chance to "go to school and get used to other children"; but now, with Vanne bound for London, they were heading back to the Serengeti.

Although in most of her published writings on the subject Jane tends to downplay the physical dangers of living on the Serengeti, for young Grub those dangers — from lions and hyenas to an outbreak of bubonic plague in nearby Arusha — were serious enough that he had to be watched carefully and constantly. For that task, Jane interviewed a sister of one of Grub's teachers in Nairobi. The eighteen-year-old unfortunately was bitten by one of the van Lawick household dogs on her first "trial morning" at the house. In the end, three strapping African men assisted with the "ayahing" of Grub that spring (letter of April 28): Moro, Alexander, and Thomas. Alexander was replaced in September 1969 by Isaac, and Thomas in March 1970 by Mucharia. From all accounts, Grub enjoyed his toddlerhood in the Serengeti. It is not clear how seriously he missed playing with children his own age. In any case, he did have a playmate back in Nairobi — Cherise, daughter of Jane's neighbor Judy Strong. Judy and Cherise flew out to help celebrate Grub's third birthday in March of 1970.

Hugo was well assisted by two volunteers, "Roger and Jack" (Roger Polk and Jean-Jacques Mermod), who had proudly managed (letter of April 28, 1969) to stay with the wild dogs "almost every day in three weeks" when the van Lawicks were in Nairobi that spring. In later months James Malcolm, Simon Petit, and Andrew Duits helped Hugo with the wild dog studies, while David Bygott, one of the Gombe researchers at the time, agreed to contribute some of his superb line drawings to *Innocent Killers*.

Their camp was in the center of the Serengeti — a rough, 30-mile drive from the tiny cluster of houses and shops near park headquarters at Seronera. It was surrounded by an awesome and sometimes rather bleak natural spectacle, pleasantly shaded in an acacia grove and overlooking the beautiful Lake Legaja. The lake was indeed beautiful: blue and serene. Or sometimes, during the wildebeest migration, for example, not so serene — as "those stupid idiotic wildebeeste" (March 14, 1970) tended to stampede crazily into the lake and drown. And sometimes, in the morning light, for instance, more pink than blue. The pink came from the feathers of several thousand flamingos that regularly congregated at the edges of the lake.

Lake Legaja was what people called a soda lake; the water was alkaline and quite undrinkable. So getting water suitable for drinking and washing was one problem with the Serengeti camp. On the other side of the lake, however, an eccentric Englishman named George Dove, with red hair and long, expressively pointed red mustaches, maintained a tented safari camp for tourists known as Ndutu Lodge. It was a vast landscape they were surrounded by, the van Lawicks on one side of the lake and George Dove on the other, and it was probably inevitable that "Dov" and the van Lawicks saw a lot of one another that year. They became good friends.

Another problem was the mice: "all very sweet, but . . . just as bad as rats" (April 28, 1969).

A third problem with Lake Legaja was how to spell it. Was it "Legadja," as Jane first attempted in the note of April 26 — or was it, as the letter of April 28 would indicate, "Legarga"? A year and a half later (letter of September 16, 1970), the lake had become "Legaja," a spelling that was the official version for *Innocent Killers*. Almost simultaneously, however, Timothy Green had produced his book *The Adventurers,* where the same lake was "Lagaja" — and a couple of years subsequently, Hugo van Lawick, in his second book on the Serengeti wild dogs, *Solo,* decided that the lake was "Lagarja" — rather close to the spellings with which Jane had first experimented. Bluff and hearty old George Dove, living on the other side of the lake, had always called his own camp Ndutu, and eventually some sensible person solved the spelling problem with an inspired appropriation. By the time Hugo published his grand photographic book *Among Predators and Prey* (1986), Lake Legaja had been discreetly replaced by Lake Ndutu.

Hugo's brother Godert was married in the summer of 1969, and "Uncle Godi" and his wife, Bobby, came to visit that September. Godi, unhappily, broke a leg during his time on the Serengeti and flew to Nairobi in early October to have the cast removed. In December the van Lawicks went to Gombe, where they celebrated Christmas. Godi and Bobby remained there and took over as general administrators, a responsibility they fulfilled for some three months. They were replaced in about March 1970 by Gerald Rilling.

As for *Innocent Killers,* what had started out as Hugo's book became increasingly a joint venture, as Hugo came to rely more and more on Jane's writing talents. In the letter of April 11, 1969, Jane notes that their friend, editor, and publisher, Sir William (Billy) Collins, had concluded that "it will be fine to have one chapter by me." In fact, the final book was officially half written by Jane (two of the four chapters). Unofficially, probably more than half. Jane appears to have been one of those rare authors who takes publishers' schedules seriously, and the looming deadline of January 13, 1970, for her finished manuscript prompted much angst and actual activity, as we can conclude from her "are we hectic!" letter of January 8. The situation deteriorated when in February Billy Collins came out to the Serengeti for a visit and Jane was seriously ill, probably with malaria. Nevertheless, a late book is better than a lame one, and thus a month later (March 14) she was still "shut in the VW, day and evening, redoing the hyena chapter." By September 16 Jane was able to ask her family with justifiable pride, "Have you seen Innocent Killers?"

So *Innocent Killers* was in the book stores by then. It would soon be followed by Jane's *Grub the Bush Baby* (1970); Hugo's *Solo: The Story of an African Wild Dog* (1973); and, of course, Jane's classic popularized summary of her first ten years of research at Gombe, *In the Shadow of Man* (1971), the first draft of which she apparently had finished ("chimp book off my mind") by the last letter in this sequence.

*     *     *     *

12 October 1968
P.O. Box 751
ARUSHA
Tanzania

Darling Family,

This is the first evening I've had to write in for over a week. We've all been flat out on hyena! Hugo, Margaret and Nic, all in seat belted, crash-helmeted safety, are prowling for kills. Grub and I have spent our nights at the "Golden Grass Den". In the evening the setting sun gives every dried blade a gleam of gold, brilliant as metal. Our companions are, from the littlest black pup upwards: Walpole, Toffee, Fudge, Coal, H. H., Coke, Sheltie, M, and Woolsey for the pups. Then there are the 'old bags'. The great fat old Mums (who suckle their young, comparatively, as long as the chimps): Coffee, Mrs. Brown, Mrs. Wart, Mrs Straggle, Scoop. And the males we don't really know yet — since both sexes are so alike you have to be lucky enough to see them lying almost on their backs before you can be sure!

Oh to see these gross old ladies, their stomachs only inches from the ground, gambolling after each other and frolicking with the pups in the moonlight! It is a sight that must be seen to be believed! One old bag played with 6 young ones. Often she was completely obliterated save for an occasional glimpse of a paw. And then Mrs Brown, always digging for her youngster HH (Half & Half because 1/2 black, 1/2 adult colour). I don't yet know why she digs for it all the time. She digs down the burrow but when he finally emerges — usually from another hole, she only licks him or something.

We set off at about 5.45, with Nic & Margaret in the VW. On Scratching Rocks hill, or at Golden Grass Den, we meet Hugo in the landrover. Then Margaret & Nic don crash helmets & join Hugo, & Grub & I go to, or stay at, the Den. At first the pups were scared of Grub's exuberant squeals of pleasure, caused by their comic spotted selves. But today he can yell, wave his arms at them, even (and I blush to say it) spit at them!, and they sometimes do not even glance up. They are too intent on chewing on everything they can reach on the car. Luckily the only damage they have been able to wreak has consisted of chewing through the horn & spotlight wires! Even if I get out of the car they only look — one pup, making a terrible noise when Grub was asleep, even ignored my squirting him with flit — he did raise a somewhat injured nose to savour the polluted air!

As it gets dark Grub has his supper (he also has lunch at 12, sleeps, and then, when we have our 'supper' at 3 p.m. he joins us with gusto!). Then he & I lie cosily in the back with his books until he flies off to sleep in his 'aeroplane bird' somewhere on his way to the moon or a star. This is a story which holds him enthralled, every night, and causes grins and chuckles of pleasure when he hears that only very clever little boys can fly aeroplane birds to the moon and find & kiss a 'pretty lady of the moon'!

Then I creep to the front, enwrap myself in blankets, & settle down to my moon lit vigil. Gas stove on the floor beside me, coffee when I want it — oh, but how cold!

Between us, we are getting so much information. I honestly think that we know more about the subtle aspects of social behaviour than Hans already. True he's 'only' an ecologist — but he's been doing hyena for years now.

Let me relate the most exciting episode Hugo saw. 2 nights ago. My old bags raced off to Scratching Rocks. I heard sounds of eating hyenas, saw Hugo's flash, & knew a kill had been made. Then alarm calls. A lion, I guessed, had arrived & pinched their kill. That was true, but I didn't guess the rest. Hugo was taking pictures of the clan fighting for food, close against the little ridge of rocks on top of the hill. Suddenly, out of the blackness of the night, a lion came charging over the rocks & leapt amongst the feasters. They had not seen him coming. And one did not escape. With a ferocious hatred which Hugo said was terrifying to behold, the lion pounced on one hyena that was cowering, trapped, against the rocks. The lion seized it by the back, in its jaws, and shook it savagely. Then it rushed after another hyena. The first managed to sit up but not to move. It sat there, a terrible grin of fear on its face, as a second lion charged over the rocks and also leapt at the stricken beast. It lay, almost motionless. Even so, a bit later, one of the lions again pounced on it & worried it — mercifully ending its misery. But even stranger.

When the second lion was actually mauling that hyena, a hyena from the rival clan, Munge Clan (which had been watching the feasting hyenas all along) rushed to feed on the dead wildebeeste. So the first lion grabbed it by the neck & shook it about. It escaped over the rocks, the lion in hot pursuit, but obviously got away.

Hugo, Nic & Margaret were still shaking when they came to tell me the news, an hour later. The sheer blind hatred behind the attack.

That night Grub woke and refused to go back to sleep. Usually I switch on the engine when he stirs & he sleeps deeply. Anyway, I had to go & ask Hugo for a mike, as I broke mine. So Grub saw the lions. Oh, was he excited! He waved goodbye to them all the way down the hill & back to the Den!

The next evening the Clan ate the dead hyena. Even tonight one old bag was working on the last remains — the head!

One thing would amuse you. When Grub 1/2 wakes up I switch on engine & sing. Then when I switch off I have to go on singing a bit. So if hyena do anything, I have to sing it.* Oh how funny it sounds — a quiet droning voice singing "An old bag — comes in and tail wags — and leaps away from Mrs Brown — with wild giggles" etc. . . .

A dear little striped mouse — do you remember Timkin, Mum? — has just come into the cabin. Grub is so excited by animals. On the way back last night we saw, <u>close</u> to the road, his first buffalo & his first elephant — on this trip. He was <u>so</u> excited & waved goodbye to the elephant for the next 20 mins & hoped for another.

<u>Must</u> end. Didn't post in Arusha yesterday as Nic is off to Nairobi by plane today, & it's quicker from there. The plane bringing Timothy Green!

Tons & tons of love to all,
Jane, Hugo & Grub

Hope you got my late birthday letter, O.

<u>Mum</u> Urgent for Hugo. A book, just published: — 42/ — "Wild Fox" by Roger Burrows, Pub by David & Charles.

---

* In other words, she is singing as she takes notes with a tape recorder.

c/o Ngorongoro Crater Lodge
P.O. Box 751
Arusha
21 October 1968

Darling Family,

For the past 3 days I have been sitting down to getting all the sordid things off my agenda that have been weighing me down for the past few weeks. . . . We are going up to the top tomorrow for supplies, and I'm hoping to get everything typed and ready to be actually posted. Super thought. Then I ought to be able to start flat out on my facial expressions only I shan't be able to because the moon is coming up and there will be hyena work non-stop for 10 days! After which it takes me a week to catch up on lost sleep!

Mummy. We shall be sending you money for Mike Simpson's airfare soon. I have just written to him and told him to contact you about it. I know Mike quite well, though apparently he doesn't think so since he addressed me as Baroness van Lawick-Goodall! You can tell all the scientific bods, by the way, that I prefer to be Dr. vL instead of Baroness. Not that I really care much. I also told him you knew about the whys and wherefores of the immigration, but I'm not sure that you do. Anyone coming to work at the Gombe Stream should get a Visitor's Pass — doesn't matter how long valid for — and say they are coming on a holiday. This is a visitor's pass for <u>Kenya.</u> Once they are in Kenya we then arrange the things for Tanzania. Did I tell you we have fixed up a thing with John Owen and that I have just been done — complete exemption from all Tanzanian immigration requirements for 2 years! Super. When you come, Mum, you should get Visitor's Passes for Kenya and Tanzania, if possible, valid, I'd say to be safe, for 3 months.

My plans for next year are to be in England for July and August while Hugo is on the Serengeti again. For part of this time Peter Marler will be over with the chimp film we did together,* and we shall have to go through it all — in B'mth. Do you happen to know if — gosh, I've forgotten his name — from the zoo film unit is still

---

* Marler had studied chimpanzee vocalizations at Gombe in the summer of 1967.

operating at that little film studio which's name I've also forgot. Hope you approve of the English.

Our latest new girl, Cathy Clark, has just arrived — another San Diegan! She came through quite different channels [from] Alice and Pat though. She is one of the nicest girls we've had. We both like her most frightfully and, unlike most of these Americans, she's prepared to rough it, and does not expect caviar twice a week — nor does she take vitamin pills!

She and I are working on the hyenas here. We have the most gorgeous collection of names now. Mrs. Brown, Mrs. Wart, Mrs. Straggle, Coffee, Lady Dracula, Ten Ton Tessie, Harolda (blind in left eye) and Double O are the "old bags". Toffee, Fudge, H.E., Cole, Coke, "M", Splodge, Woolsey and Walpole, Sheltie are the pups. And the young females or males (so far unsexed) are Nelson (blind in right eye), Waterloo, Black Watch, Quizz. Oh and there's Lady Astor! Hugo's two jackals are Jason (it's the Golden Jackal) and Jewel (also my names). Yesterday Cathy and Moro were going to look at hyena in the morning and they found a Serval and kitten. Unfortunately the kitten is already half grown. Anyway, Hugo went yesterday evening and this morning to try and get pictures, and this morning actually saw them again — the grass was too long! However, it is very near the cabin so there is hope.

No more new things re Grub. But he is as clever, and uncommunicative, as ever! He has started drawing things, i.e. he made one of his million circles imposed on each other yesterday, looked at it carefully, and then pointed excitedly from the drawing to a tree and back, and so on. He had drawn a tree! Oh, Timothy Green. He will be coming to see you eventually, Mum. He is nice, and I said I'd let him do this profile. You can tell him anything about me, only don't show him letters, and don't tell him more than has been written about re. early chimp days. He wants to see Pongo* I think! Is she alive?

Tons of love,
Jane, Grub, Hugo

---

* A housekeeper at the Birches.

Box 2818
Nairobi
11 April 1969

Dear Sallykins,

Don't be surprised at the postmark — I'm not in England. But I thought I'd make use of Postman Mum to ensure that this letter reached you. Most of our letters have not done so recently.

So very many thanks for the super present for Grub. He was thrilled with it, and it couldn't be more useful for safari. Incidentally, I havn't been as tardy in acknowledging it as the date might seem — it didn't reach us on the Serengeti until about 3 weeks ago, having waited in Nairobi for a plane to be visiting us. This is what has been happening to all our mail. It just sits around in people's offices and drawers and one day, perhaps, we get it!

Grub is now walking, running, climbing, jumping, wheelbarrowing and — yes, actually talking! He has just broken up after a 3 1/2 week term (we weren't here for more).* For the first week there were tears when we left (Mum stayed with him the first morning) but after that he couldn't wait to get there. Awfully nice having a whole free morning. And we are about to employ one of the assistant teacher's sisters as an ayah for him. Oh dear — I'm on the verge of getting his cold. He has a real snorter. The poor little thing (Grub's prospective ayah) arrived this morning for a trial morning — to see if she and Grub got on before going off on safari — and she got bitten badly by one of our dogs on her way in. She is only 18, and it was really sad. We rushed her off to the local hospital — where she had to wait for one and a half hours before having 2 stitches. However, we gave her compensation, and we think that, if she braves the house again, she may be quite a good sort!

There is, of course, too much news to start trying to tell it!! The best thing would be for you to pay a visit to Mum sometime and she can bring you up to date! I'm supposed to be coming to England either in July or September to see the family. And to do a lecture tour in America to try and get some money. Now Hugo is no longer free

---

* Jane is describing Grub's day care as if it were school. The day care was stopped ("broken up") after three and a half weeks (the "term").

lancing in a tied-to-the-Geographic manner (if you see what I mean) money is difficult. But his book — or rather two books — are going to be really first rate and super duper.

One very sad bit of news is that dear old Flo chimp had a baby and lost it when it was 6 months old. She, Flo, got the most ghastly flu cold and nearly died herself. A search party went out to look for her and found her, when she had been lost for a week. But no sign of Flame, as her daughter was called. However, you remember Flint, her last son for whose birth Hugo and I cut short our honeymoon? He has now become, once more, Mummy's baby. He rides on her back, rides ventral, sleeps in her nest, shares her food. Even has started to suckle again, though as yet Flo does not appear to have produced any milk!!!! As he is now 5 years it is really staggering!

It's very funny right now. Grub is sitting on the grass outside the house, with his cold, and with all three dogs around him, tails wagging, ears pricked. He is picking stones [out] of the rockery there and throwing them down the slope with a loud triumphant yell accompanying each one. The dogs are catching them with their teeth! (Alsatians.)

I shall sorely miss Mummy. She is simply super with Grub, and he adores her. Calls her Um, short for Grum, short for Grandmother! Grandmum, that is! She is also marvellous for reading bits of manuscripts, chapters, articles, and so forth. My last disappointment was that my monograph on the chimps, the result of 8 years work, has been produced in the most miserable little paper-backed edition, with a few pages of lousily produced photographs, and the script so cramped up it just isn't true. Why I let myself be bullied into publication in this journal, instead of a book, I just can't imagine. Never mind. Dr. Leakey thinks he can manage to get it to come out in a hard cover with more photos in about a year's time. So Mum is off to see another publisher, armed with letter and photos etc, to give battle. Good old Mum!

We have been in Nairobi about a month now — the main reason for returning from the Serengeti being to give Grub a chance to go to school and get used to other children. Which, of course, went off fine. Mum leaves for London tomorrow, and Hugo and I and Grub and our cook and, perhaps, our little ayah, leave for the Serengeti the day after. Hugo has two assistants there continuing work for him whilst we are away. Nice boys both of them, very keen, and both completely volunteer. We couldn't afford them otherwise. Soon we're going to visit the Crater again and do some more work on hyenas. I find that I have to write the hyena chapter in the book. Billy Collins thinks it will be fine to have one chapter by me. Just wait till you read all about our gorgeous hyenas. They are more like the chimps than any other animal I've met in Africa — or any-where, for that matter. They have super characters. So that will mean some more lovely moonlight nights at their burrows with Grub sleeping in the back of the car.

Oh — yells of anguish from the Garden. I'd better stop and go and see what's up. Oh — Wellington (Grub's own dog) has run off with Grub's cardigan. Mummy is hot in pursuit. However, I'll end anyway.

Thank you again very very much for the present.

Love,<br>Jane

P.S. Love to Daphne, Sue & Robert.

[Around April 26, 1969]

Darling Family,

Very quick note from Arusha Hotel. We are on our way to Le-gadja. My flue hasn't properly gone, but as Roger and Jack are leav-ing camp today, we got to go! Anyway, the worst is over. Did you get eye and head aches Mum? Ghastly brand of flue, wasn't it?

These are just some of the pictures. Fotofinishers printed them the wrong size and only one print of each. So we are having them re-done, but I don't quite know when you'll get them — Roger is col-lecting them. Half of this lot went to Michael. At present Grub, af-ter demanding my attention for ages, is playing with your lot of photos so they may be a bit dog-eared! The ones you havn't got are rather nice, too. Oh — isn't the one of Hugo and baby Grub sweet. . . .

Grub was marvellous last night — he is quite better by the way.

When we got here it was about 5.30. So we had some tea in the garden, for him. Which he loved, and kept running away, and having to be retrieved. I didn't feel like the dining room, so we went out to a little snack bar. Had a snack, with him, walked home, and thought we'd read in bed. Found I had brought up his nappies, but no plastic pants. So laid all the towels I could find in his bed. He went to sleep about 8.30. And, at 7.00 this morning, — was DRY!! Just imagine. Wasn't that marvellous. Must end, as Hugo has to type a sordid letter to immigration. Poor Hugo. Still problems. Will write to you all again from Legadja. I wonder how you do spell it? Do hope you and Danny are quite better, Mummy — bet you're not, Mum, as you only got it a day before me, and I'm not! But still,

Tons & tons of love,
Jane, Hugo & Grub

Lake Legarga
28 April 1969

Darling Family,

How are you all I wonder. How are you Danny? Is your flue better Mummy? Mine is gone except for a sort of peculiar sinusy thing all round my left eye which is most peculiar. It comes every morning, and goes by about lunch time and then returns the next morning! Did you have anything like that? By the way, the name of those capsules which are so good for inhaling is KARVOL — by Crookes. Inhalant capsules. They are made in England so you should be able to get them quite easily.

Returned here to find we are inundated with dormice! All very sweet, but, as Dov says, they are just as bad as rats. I was really distraught when, after being in bed here for a day and a half I got up, went to the suitcase we had brought with us from Nairobi, and found, to my horror, that not only had they chewed up half of my super yellow sweater, but also part of my egg-blue one! Wasn't it absolutely sordid. And wasn't it lucky you brought the green one for me, Mum.

The ayahing of Grub is going very well indeed. The three take it in turns, and he is very well looked after. As I type now Alec is sitting in a chair on the veranda of the tent and Grub is sitting in his chair, kicking his heel on the ground, and eating cornflakes at 10.30! He suddenly decided he wanted some and is tucking in like anything! He has suddenly taken to calling me Jane, interspersed with Mummy, Dammy and Mum. It does sound so funny — the Jane. It's usually more like Dane, actually! Thomas is 'Omas. And whilst on Thomas — his Theresa has just had a baby! He is so thrilled, and must be dying to go see it. I say "it" because he has just heard about the event from Alexander who hadn't heard the sex!

We returned here to find the boys in fine form. They had managed to keep with four wild dogs for almost every day in three weeks, and were very pleased with themselves. They had also got pictures of a cheetah killing, which is super — if they come out. They set off the next morning for Nairobi to see to Immigration matters, etc. Hugo was pretty pleased with them. Since their departure the best news is that Hugo has found a Striped Hyena den. He's not sure yet whether there is a cub down it, but doesn't think so. Anyway, he found a dead tommy and pulled it there — and the hyena got quite tame. The following night the same hyena came — to eat a bit of our meat, and about 3 others came, with their crests on end. To-night he may find out whether there is a cub. Very exciting anyway. He also saw a cheetah kill and could have got pictures — but his camera stuck!

I think Grub really is dry now — not at night. But in the day time. Takes his own pants off. Most days he refuses to sleep in the day time, but this makes him sleep extra well at night, of course. So I don't mind, especially when the boys look after him so well. There was a dormouse in his toy box when he tipped it over this morning with his usual sweeping nonchalance. It leapt out and clung to his leg. For a moment he was slightly shocked, but quickly recovered and decided it was great fun — as the dormouse leapt down and ran off! It had eaten all the stuffing — or pulled it out rather — from one leg of Bear. Luckily not much material had been eaten, so I was able to sew up the leg good as new.

Dov's workmen appear to have been abandoned! They walked over the other day to say they had run out of food. Jolly as we nearly

have too. Hugo drove to Seronera to get food, but found the Pennel-
Bayers closed down, virtually. They couldn't be bothered to open
the shop even though there were a few tourists who wanted it. She
told Hugo she had nothing in the shop anyway, but then agreed to
open it up to get sugar for him. Unfortunately she forgot herself sufficiently to let him follow her in — and he saw the coffee with
his own eyes that she had told him was not there! However, she
wouldn't relent on those things not visible to the naked eye — she
wouldn't sell him any salt or matches (said they had no matches,
can you believe it!) or cigarettes. And apparently she told Roger and
Jack, when they went over with Dov's starving boys, that it was
most inconvenient, us keeping on wanting things, and she would
only sell to us in future if we were starving! And when you think of
the early offers of help — nothing would be too much trouble. Part
of it, of course, stems from the fact that many of the offers were
made by him, independently of her! Anyhow, she's a sordid woman.
If our two, Jack and Roger, don't get back, as planned, on Tuesday,
we shall have to drive up to Ngorongoro not only for food for Dov's
boys, but for ourselves.

I have got the "Book" completely up to date now.* Wish you
could see it, Mum — and everyone. All letters in — even those between me and Hugo. All photos stuck in and captioned, etc. I did it
whilst recovering from Flue. Very useful, Flue!

There is no more exciting news for the moment. Everyone here
expects a drought — horrible. The migration is way over on the
other side of the Serengeti towards Mwanza. Tommies scattered
about. Not many animals left here, but enough. Hugo and Grub
and I, with Grub's ayah in chief, plan to go to the Crater mid-May
for a month. After that, Seronera for lion and leopard and cheetah
— though the cheetah here would be better, the lion would be good
— but only Seronera is good for the leopard.† Pity. Back to the tset-

---

* Jane is referring to a scrapbook, the source for most of *Grub the Bush Baby*. Originally "never intended for publication," it was "put together as a collection of photographs" as a Christmas present for Grub's two grandmothers. However, Billy Collins
saw the collection and said to Jane, "I *must* publish this. It's marvelous!"
† A projected second volume of *Innocent Killers* would cover lions, leopards, and
cheetahs.

ses and so forth. I'll stop for now, and continue later if there is more news, unless someone passes (ha ha) who could post a letter. It is absolutely super re tourists — not a single tourist. Though it does mean there is no one to help us find Havoc or Black Angel.* By the way, Dov rang from Arusha (or were you still there, Mum?) to say that he never managed to get to Nairobi. That's why he didn't come to see us. I'll end, in case I don't continue!

Tons and tons of love from us three,
Jane, Hugo, Grub

P.S. Flue quite better now. Will be going to Crater in 2 days so will write again.

Lake Lagarja
26 May 1969

Dear Mary,

Thank you for your last letter — I hope you have got the legends by now — just to be sure I have sent you the original and a carbon copy on different dates! So many of our letters get lost these days. We now have an additional risk to our mail — Arusha, through which everything gets forwarded, is closed due to Bubonic Plague. Just fancy! Luckily someone is coming to visit us this week so can post and bring mail, and also food. Everywhere round here — Seronera, Ngorongoro, Manyara — all get food from Arusha, and we are very low.

I enclose a copy of a letter I wrote in reply to Mr. van Erp — mad, but still. I suppose I am correct in that you still have the originals. I see no harm in him using the two in his Rotarian Magazine — do you?!

Hugo sends his regards — Little Hugo is chatting and rushing around and great fun generally.

Yours sincerely,
Jane

---

* Tourists from Ndutu Camp, driven around the area to look at wildlife, often provided information about where the wild dogs were.

Lake Legarja
23 September 1969

Darling Family,

I didn't write before because there wasn't any way of posting until tomorrow. Dov is still away, and it is so dry here that there are not really any tourists.

How are you all? Grub still thinks of you, adding you all into his morning and nightly list of names of people who are nice. He always ends his list with either "Lots of people nice" or "Everybody nice". He starts the list, sometimes, before he is properly awake in bed in the morning. I am now teaching him to read in this new way. It is quite fascinating, and requires virtually no time at all. He was a scream though. The kick off is mummy in very large letters in red. For 2 days you hold this up, every so often during half hour sessions at odd moments in the day, and say "This says mummy". You do not ask what it says until the third day. Well, he got rather bored with this. The first time I held it up on the second day he said "Now write daddy". This is the second step in the exercise! How we all laughed. When I started the rigmarole with Daddy, he took a look and said "Shut that book". And now we are on to parts of the body. He learnt hand and foot easily. The second time I asked him what it said on the "foot" paper he stared, grinned, and said "tummy". He is a hoot. He is drawing nicely now. Heads with big eyes and ears and mouths and noses and hair all in the right places. Arms often come out of the head, as in enclosed drawing. He talks more and more, coming out with all sorts of surprising words, like his hands "awfully dirty". Still no more first consonants than before!

The dogs are marvellous. Hugo is getting really good stuff on the pack, with all sorts of fascinating interactions between the four bitches, and interesting relationships between different males and females. The pups are quite big now, but still most attractive. Yesterday, on the spur of the moment, we went to Seronera. To do immigration. On the way there we checked on the wild dogs, checked on a pair of courting hyenas near the den, and then, just as we were coming into Seronera, what did we find? 17 wild dogs! This is the pack that had 16 pups 1 1/2 years ago. 10 of the pups had survived — 2 with horrible awful twitches, as distemper swept through the pack. We called in on Hugh Lamprey and the Kruuks.* Jane Kruuk is having a baby at last! It is making her really really sick — they fear it won't make it, I think. She looks ghastly. Honestly, all these poor creatures with their complications. Anyway, we drove back cross country to the hills and kopjes† between Legarga and Seronera. What did we find? The 7 pack of dogs — you remember, Mum. The Havoc pack? Where Cassidy had the lame leg, and Ramona was jealous when Long John mated Havoc. Hugo and I stayed with them all night if you recollect. Well, there were 10 pups. The odd thing was that it almost looked as though both Havoc and Ramona had had pups — their nipples looked exactly the same. It was super seeing them. 2 extra dogs had joined the pack. The pups were about 6 months old. The pack no longer at a den. Now it only remains to find the pack of 4 and we shall have really super information.

There is not really much more news. We are off tomorrow — having delayed one day because of Thomas needing another injection. Alex is, at last, on his way out. Hugo found him with his cigarettes in his suitcase. We have taken on a nice Kikuyu called Isaac. Oh — poor Moro went on leave. He should have been back on the 5th, and yesterday morning still wasn't back. Hugo was livid and said he'd jolly well better have a good excuse. Well, he got back yesterday evening — his house had fallen on top of him! We might not have believed it, but he has a broken arm, and his little girl of Grub's age a broken leg, poor little thing.

Poor Dov had a gala supper ready to welcome Grub back all ready for us. But, of course, we couldn't make it. He is off on safari with an oil millionaire. He may be going to Gombe at the end of the month, in which case we will be able to go. The crowd now are going back together by train — quite a crowd. Lori and Ann Shouldice, Washington and Leanne Taylor‡. . . .

---

* Hugh Lamprey and Hans Kruuk, directors of the Serengeti Research Institute, were living in SRI housing at Seronera.
† The flat or gently hilly grassland of the Serengeti is occasionally interrupted by dramatic rock outcroppings or rock hills, known as kopjes.
‡ Gombe research assistants Lori Baldwin, Ann Shouldice, Neville Washington, and Leanne Taylor (studying baboons).

Tons and tons of love, and thanks for everything — oh, Hugo loved the dress, and his sweaters. The pants fitted him exactly.

Hugo sends lots of love,

Jane

c/o George Dove Safaris

Kimba

P.O. Box 284

ARUSHA

Tanzania

[Late September 1969]

Dear Louis,

I had a horrible feeling that you would not have received the photo and list of references etc. It was in the same batch as a letter to Gombe which we have just heard never arrived. I'm sending this with Godi who is going to Nairobi for the day to have his plaster off, and I'm sorry I can only enclose the negative. I hope Godi will be able to locate it and enclose it, that is.

I'd like to do the lectures before Christmas next year and as near to Christmas as possible. I get so muddled with when the lecture series begin and end, and realize that this may mean November. Anyway, I hope that is O.K.

I'm not quite sure whether you wanted references of everything, or just scientific, or what, so I've put them all — enclosed is the copy of the list I sent you two or three weeks ago.

Hugo got simply super stuff on the wild dogs — it was so nice that he got a den in the end, after all that hunting and searching in Feb, March and April. Anyhow, he is about to disprove most current theories about wild dog social structure — hunting dog, that is. The pack has just left, with the small pups, and so we are going to the Crater for a month to get the final data on the hyenas. Then we shall sit down, finish the first book, and then I shall try and get started on the chimp book, whilst Hugo starts on the cats.

I do hope your leg is better now. I hear you were so mauled about by the specialist that you couldn't sit down. Terrible. Did you manage to get to the Coast? Knowing you, you probably didn't, but I do hope you did.

I must close now, or I'll be too late to send this with the plane. Grub is thriving, talking more and more and better and better, but still minus most first consonants. He can read his first 8 words, using the new system, and is enjoying it hugely.

Hope you'll be in Nairobi week starting 5 November?

Jane

25 Oct 1969

Full moon

Crater

Half a letter. Rest follows.

Darling Family,

What a bad letter writer I have become. But when one is up all night observing hyenas, plus mornings and evening, and trying to get pictures of Ub and vultures all mid-days and trying to keep up with tape typing for the rest of the time — well — it is a bit difficult, to say the least!

Thank you for your last letter Mum — no, I never got a previous communication about David Bygott's money, but we have sorted it all out with him. My first impression of him was quite wrong — I think he must have been very nervous and on edge. In fact, he is one of the nicest people we have yet had. He is quite marvellous with Grub — spends all day making him drawings, aeroplanes, cats and rabbits out of paper, and catching frogs with him in the stream. He is really clever at drawing, and we have tentatively asked him to do drawings for Hugo's book. These will be small line drawings, portraying either things like the different tail positions, or things we couldn't photograph — like two hyenas creeping up to lick the bottom of a sleeping dog! Anyway, he has done 5 which we are going to send to Billy as a sample to see what Billy thinks of the idea. Personally I think it will be excellent. He is super at cartoons, too. He just rattles them off — lots of Egyptian vultures, and a lovely one of Hugo, his flash aimed hopefully out of the window at non-existent hyenas, whilst all the hyenas are hiding under the car or piled up against the sides! This was after the first experience he had watching all the hyenas chewing the car and playing round it!

The hyenas are not being at all co-operative. Not at all. Mainly because there is no rain and so they are in their dens or those horrible reeds all day. However, we are getting nice things, and it all adds up. Only I am not going to get the answer to their "that certain behaviour"* which means that a lot of things in the book will have to be described but not explained — except as a guess. Hey ho. Anyway, it is nice to see all the familiar faces again, and to recognize grown up children, and to find a lot of so called young males now with cubs! Also Hugo has got some photos of most spectacular hunts — if the lighting, exposure, shutter speed etc, etc, was right!

George himself is driving Godi, Bobby, and David to Gombe in about 10 days. He is definitely selling Kimba in about 2 weeks to be free to do Gombe buildings! Fine, except that we have no funds yet! However, we'll see. Still no word from R[obert], and we think the best thing to do is to send him a cable saying shall we ask for one more year, anyway, from Geographic, to give him more time, and because we are worried that otherwise we may be landed with no money next year, and Geographic grant must be in by mid-November. As you can imagine, we are getting in quite a flap about it!

Now, Mum. Finances. Could you enquire from Billy in a nice sort of way whether he would be prepared to make us a LOAN! — I didn't mean the exclamation mark! (Which I don't disapprove of, Mum, but Philip Ziegler† does!) As you know, we can pay Billy back. I hope you know what I mean. Anyway, the thing to mention is that Louis is arranging these lectures for me, he has put the price at $1,000 per lecture. I will add, when Hugo gets back, what loan he wants. Over and above this lecture money we can guarantee Billy to repay his loan, if you comprehend. Hoping you do, which is to say we are writing to you and not Billy, who wouldn't. And —

---

* Meaning sex. The phrase originated with Danny, Jane's grandmother, who had a Victorian sensibility about such matters.
† An editor at Collins.

mum! Savez-vous? Mum on paper. Dear Mum, a nice long chat with Billy boy.

Godi's leg is making rapid improvement and he is now walking pretty well, and driving a lot. Crutches a thing of the past — except when they serve as occasional steed for Grub. It was Godi's birthday a few days ago and we all went up to Kimba to celebrate. George was on his way back from Arusha for the event, and we waited and waited and waited. No George. He turned up at 10.00 — had broken down, with Mike, on the way and had an awful time. It was a mercy they broke down on a straight bit of road — the brakes and gear box all broke at the same time. Can you imagine anything more horrible. George says he's never known it [to] happen before on a car — only on big lorries it's quite common, and is the reason for many of the lorry crashes.

Oh — a lovely story. A VW was driving down into the Crater, down that steep road. I forget what happened to it, but these bods never bother to use their gears for the steep descent, but just brakes. I think the brakes went. Anyway, it tippled over and, as luck would have it, fell only 20 feet and there stuck. They waited for a landrover to come along, and asked for a pull. So the landrover got out the only rope it had — a piece of thin and very unsuitable rope. Then the two bods went and sat <u>in the car</u> while the landrover tried to pull it up. The rope, of course, broke, and the car fell many more feet and was quite smashed up. The bods, of course, were perfectly all right! If you had seen the road you would be staggered that the car didn't bounce to the bottom!

Jif has written me another letter!!! She said it would floor us, and it certainly did. The house sounds super, and I am so delighted. Can't wait to see it.

As luck would have it, there are two sordid cars down here in the crater. Do you remember, Mum, Norman Myers. The photographer? Well, he is here, and has to keep coming up to the hyenas. And this morning, was I livid. He went much too close to one of the scarey mums with a tiny black cub that we are trying to tame for Hugo's pictures. She and the cub were out as he drove up, and the cub, instead of rushing down the burrow, darted away into a hollow. Mum wanted to get it into the burrow so then and there, right in front of his camera, she picked it up and carried it back. Something I've only ever seen once before, and which Hugo had seen twice & got one <u>marvellous</u> picture. Anyway, Hugo had a nice chat with him, saying there were 500 hyenas in the Crater and as he, Hugo, was carefully not touching the lion Norman was photographing, could Norman find different hyenas. No, said Norman. So it's open warfare! The other car is a young scientist, working for his PhD, studying lion. He is sordid. Tell you anon. George is waiting to take this. More news anon.

Tons of love,
Jane

[Early December 1969]

Darling Family,

A very brief note. It is 10 at night, we've had supper, and are just going out soon for when the moon rises. We now have a fantastic bed in the car, made by Dov's son, and can all three sleep in blissful comfort when things are not happening. We've had superb nights so far with the "woops". Kills, clan clashes, mobbing lions. The things Grub has slept through so peacefully! In his padded cell! He has now witnessed kills. He is a little quiet, but not upset. He thinks about it, and then sees more wildebeeste and says they're not dead, and he's happy they're not dead. I've told him the hyenas have to eat meat, and he appreciates this, and does not hold it against the hyenas. . . .

We return to Nairobi in about 8 days to collect Simon, do a bit of writing, and finalize the photos for the book. Then we work Simon in at Seronera, then drive to Gombe for a week for Christmas — with Godi and Bobby which will be nice, and the lake and sand for Ub — how he loved and loved it this time. And to finalize the drawings (if Billy wants them) with David. Who goes on being nice — and who will be driving to Gombe with Godi and Bobby and Dov in about 5 days time. Dov is taking them in Hugo's car (quicker than his) and plans to do the trip in two days, rising at four in the morning and driving till late at night. He is staying a few days to help Godi sort out food problems — organize things in Kigoma, etc. Can you believe our good fortune? The only sordid thing is that we've still not heard from R, and it is now almost too late to send off to the Geographic. We are going to tell them it must have got lost in the post, if worst comes to worst, and send them a carbon copy. They will certainly give us enough money to keep going for Jan and Feb I'm sure. And, of course, we have SRC.* I do wish we KNEW what R was up to, don't you.

I really must end. The car is all ready, Ub is sleeping in it, and Hugo awaits me.

Tons of love,
Jane

Box 2818, Nairobi
8 January 1969 — no, 70!

Darling Family,

I do hope things are settling down after your somewhat disordered and hectic Christmas, and that the flue bugs have left you. It hasn't reached Nairobi yet — I almost feel I should stick all European letters in the oven before opening! We DREAD it getting to the chimps.

Well, are we hectic! It is quite unbelievable. Geographic has asked us to cut back considerably on our grant — and everything left on it was absolutely vital. They don't even say how much. They query not only my salary, but Hugo's — Hugo's is for 3 months during which time they asked him to go and make a film for them. I ask you. Do they expect Hugo to work for nothing just because of keeping Gombe running! So now we are compiling a huge report of the Gombe, past, present and future, all our plans, who we hope to have there and why, what studies we want and why, what buildings and improvements we are planning and why. We obviously need to

---

* Some grant money had been promised by the SRC (British Science Research Council); however, they were hoping that R[obert Hinde] would be able to help them locate more funding.

become affiliated with a university, even Louis said so. But rather than Carpenter we hope for Stanford, Dave Hamburg's.* So there is etiquette and problems, and offending Carpenter, or Dave who has after all wanted to finance us for so long, in some way or another. Letters about Neville Washington to get a grant for him from Leverhulme, deadline 15 January. Photos for Readers Digest world atlas, deadline 15 Jan. Letters to Robert about at least 7 different things, in 7 different envelopes. Finances. Letters to Wenner Gren, letters to a chap wanting to come from Canada, interviews with two people in Nairobi. James Malcolm lost and then found. Nicholas Owens† arriving — very lost, no one met him — serves him right. Chastened. Is due to come and stay with us in an hour, arrived with Simon who is still staying with his Christmas birds in Nairobi. Worst of all, I think, the airfreight parcel of photos, layouts, captions, drawings — almost 200 photos, 8 × 10 and some even 10 × 12. The parcel has not arrived. The dog chapter is getting so interrupted, the hyena chapter not started. The bibliography, glossary, index all to be done. The captions mostly to be done. Deadline — 13th January 1970!! And, on top of this, as though it were not enough, Hugo has the most terrible, horrible, awful malaria. Louis had us to supper, as he has written to you about, Mum. He was still the same charming and benign fellow. Whatever happened to him has happened permanently.

Anyway, Happy New Year to everyone. Your New Year starts hectically and somewhat depressingly. So does ours. So it must get better, I think, for both of us. Moeza's is as hectic, or more hectic. She even wrote to Hugo, which he didn't tell me for a long time, that she doesn't think she'll live much longer. Poor, poor Moeza. . . .

Oh yes, I knew there was more. Letter from Robert to say deadline for the toolusing paper is end February. Deadline for end of

---

* Two large American institutions, Stanford University and the Yerkes Regional Primate Research Center of Emory University, were competing to become associated with Gombe. David Hamburg, of the Stanford Medical School Department of Psychiatry, hoped to get Jane involved in their new Human Biology program; Ray Carpenter, chairman of the Yerkes Scientific Advisory Board, intended to make Jane and Hugo "staff members" on an "honorary" basis.

† Owens had come to study baboons with Tim Ransom and others.

Grub film is end February. Dian now has super photos of gorillas by Bob Campbell, though rather monotonous, they being gorillas. Do try and persuade her to agree to Billy publishing her popular book.* Because he can then so time it that it does not compete with the chimps book. I wish I knew if all her desperate tales were true. Hugo says that it is quite unthinkable that anyone could go around capturing anyone's son in a newly independent country. When even a man who ties an actual poacher to his tree gets strokes, prison, and deportation! . . . Tons and tons of love from us all, and I do hope things are better, and people are better, and everything.

Tons of love,<br>
Jane, Hugo & Grub

[March 1, 1970]

Being Sunday I can't buy a pen. The hotel can't lend me one. So I'm forced to use a pencil!

Darling Family,

Finally I went to Arusha. Judy Strong & Cherise had arrived and just as I'd decided I simply had to go & be checked because the fevers were getting worse, not better, Judy said she had to go because of a bladder infection. So we flew off together with Cherise — Grub, of course, stayed with Papa. The doctor here (Dove's) felt pretty sure it was malaria & gave me an injection. Dove was in town for a night between 2 short safaris so he came and chatted, with Mrs. Dove — Mibbs — as I lay covered in blankets in the hotel & shivering. But by next morning at 10 when I had to go to the Doctor (only 200 yards down the road) I was better. He still wanted to take serum tests but the labs are Government & so close down totally over the weekend. And I'd arrived on Friday.

Anyway, we were meant to fly straight back on Sat. but the pilot was sick so we are saving a very big amount of money & going by car to the Crater — where, I suspect, Hugo will meet us. Probably with Grub.

---

* Referring to Dian Fossey and her book, *Gorillas in the Mist.*

It is Sunday this morning. I'm still feeling so amazed and delighted to be better after those horrible ghastly 7 days of sweating huge wet drops. There wasn't even anyone to talk to all day long as, of course, Hugo was out with or talking to Billy. Sometimes Grub popped in but then he would clamber over me so it wasn't much help! And now I'm better, it's so super.

Ma. It has been bothering me for days. Did I forget your Birthday? If so — first time ever. I can't <u>believe</u> I did, yet I have no recollection of sending even a card. If so, you will realize how <u>horribly</u> overworked etc I have been & SORRY.

Anyway tons & tons of love from a recovered<br>Jane

[Postmarked March 14, 1970]

Darling Family,

I feel so repulsively neglectful. But I am not exaggerating when I say that I havn't had any time to write. I have been shut in the VW, day and evening, redoing the hyena chapter — which, as you know, I wrote when I had flue. And which, when I reread it, I simply couldn't bear. Anyway, I'm much more pleased with it now. Also there was an epilogue to do, which, although short, took some thinking. The legends for all the pictures. A new layout for the hyena chapter because Billy said I could have 4 more sides. The Bibliography. The list of Popular and Scientific names. Trying to think of titles for chapters — ugh. And frantically trying to get a few more photos of us for publicity. I could have written the first day I got back, but we went out most of the day, so there wasn't much chance, and George and Hugo conspired to say I wasn't to touch a typewriter, pen or paper. For 5 days they said, but of course that wasn't possible.

Anyway, after the injection and 4 pills I got quite better, instantly. Though I was still sweating like a pig even after I last saw the Doctor, and was quite worried lest I would arrive back and not be cured. Then I'd have been in hot water!

Please do give our love to Louis. We do hope he's getting better, but havn't heard anything from anyone for simply donkey ears. Tell Louis I'll write to him when I've finished Tool Using — which I have about one week to complete to meet Robert's dead line. And, on top of everything else, we have to charge off to Seronera today because we havn't done Immigration since we left Nairobi.

Anyway, how are all of you? Specially you, Danny? I really havn't had a letter since the one brought by Billy. Did I thank you, Mum, for the poem. I have incorporated it very nicely in the epilogue. It fits the wild dogs superbly.

There is an awful lot of news. Grub is simply thrilled with his new clothes — particularly the socks. He simply adores his socks! He looks very smart — they arrived just in time for the publicity pictures, most of which are to be in colour. He still calls us darling, but his speech gets better every day. The only letter he just can't say is R. So Gerald, — the polio chap* who is going to Gombe to do administration — is Uncle Jelly. It's a hoot!

Grub and Cherise had a splendid time together. . . . Cherise was here for Grub's birthday, and he had a simply super party. Two cakes — because I iced one, and Dove, who got back just in time, had had one iced too. Dove had brought him a whole bag of presents — quite crazy. About 12 gifts. Luckily Judy had bought some things for both Grub and Cherise. So she wasn't quite left out, but she was very good. Hugo got some nice pictures. I realize you havn't seen the Christmas ones, but they will have to wait until we next go to Nairobi. Hugo, actually, will have to go quite soon because he has [taken] some fabulous new wild dog pictures and wants to get them done quickly to change over with some already in the book. And also to get developed the publicity pictures. We are still not happy with the cover picture of Bushbaby and are frantically trying to get a substitute, but I don't suppose we'll manage. Grub is too self conscious. There is just a chance that Hugo may have a super one, but there wasn't much light, Grub was very close, and so we think that he or the giraffe, which was looking at him, will be too much out of focus. A pity.

---

* Gerald Rilling's legs had been paralyzed by childhood polio.

The migration is all around the lake, thickly. And, believe it or not, those stupid idiotic wildebeeste have been crossing the lake again, drowning and orphaning hundreds of calves again. Isn't it ridiculous of them. They crossed about 8 times in different groups. It wasn't as dramatic as last year because we are further away from the lake here, so we didn't hear that fantastic rushing water sound which I'm sure you well remember, Mum. . . .

Billy, I think, is very keen on the book now. He is crazy, as you said, about the wild dogs. He is financing Hugo to make a film on them. And, by fantastic luck, we found the Genghis pack just as the dominant female was in heat. So in 8 weeks, if all goes well, there should be pups. Hugo will get his film, and it can come out not too long after publication of the book.

How crazy life is. Remember last year, looking for the dogs? Remember the miles and miles they drove, the days of despair? This year hardly a day goes by without someone reporting a pack. Hugo rushes off to each one. We have pictures of 163 different dogs, and heaps of new information. Billy has pressed Hugo to keep on with studying the dogs. We have decided, for the next month whilst the migration is here and the grass too long at Seronera to start work on lions and leopards there, to take Simon and James off lions and cheetahs and put them full time on dogs — whilst the dogs are here.

It really is jolly nice being here. It is splendid for Grub. We are going to sack Thomas, who we are fed up with, and bring, for a while, dear old Mucharia here for Grub. With him and Moro and Dov, Grub's life will be constant paradise. He now has 2 paddling pools here — Judy got him one for his birthday, and Dov has mended his. He has car rides. He has so many toys he doesn't know how to play with them all, and a positively gigantic library of books — partly due to Billy. There is, in the Bright and Early books, a series of bears. He is wild on them. He has suddenly taken to 2 teddy bears, Wonk and Bina Wonk. They go to bed with him.

Simon and James are really doing very well. Dov is helping us to lick them into shape, as you can imagine. Simon is a little bit too jovial and hearty for me, but he gets on famously with George which is marvellous. And I do like him still, very much. James is quieter and more serious, but has a good sense of humour and a good brain. Hugo said that when he took James with him to watch the Genghis pack, he was absolutely staggered at how fast he learned the different dogs.

You should see the bar now.* The whole wall is completely filled up with Hugo's pictures, including some simply gigantic ones of chimps. We had them done for some museum that was doing a display, but as they didn't offer to pay, even for the enlargement, we decided to put them here. Next season we are going to do prints for sale. George reckons we could have made a lot of money out of them this year. Everyone remarks on them and says they are the best they have seen during their tour. . . .

Tons and tons and tons of love to all of you. I hope Rixy boy is still much better, Danny is better, Louis is better. I hope Mum and Grolly and Graud and Goo-goo and Od and Ob and Dido and the Naughty Pussy are still well. And hope to see all in 2 months' time.

Jane and Ub

[Postmarked September 4, 1970]

Darling Family,

I am drying my hair in the wind. Had to wash it because Hugo wants to film me & Solo & Grub. Now what has happened, you wonder. Well. What a story. Finally the pack of dogs moved off. And, of course, the tiny pup couldn't keep up. It struggled & struggled. Only 7 weeks old, smaller than Dido, a skeleton. One night the pack went 15 miles. James took the pup a few miles in the car — the last 1 1/2. Because the hyenas were rushing up. The next 3 nights Hugo & James followed. The pack hardly left the pup — pushed it along, carried it. But, every so often, it just gave up & lay down — in rushed the hyenas — & Hugo & James. So we took her, Solo, on the 5th night. The little thing had gone 40 miles in 5 nights. The plan is to make her strong & put her back with the pack in

---

* The main dining area of George Dove's Ndutu camp included a bar.

about 10 days from now — we've had her 5 days now. IF we can find the pack!!!

Many thanks for your letter, Mum. I got interrupted then & since then have flown to Nairobi — just for the day with this fellow Morris who has a twin-engine plane. We went to the house, saw the dogs — Yotta again any minute now! Grub thoroughly enjoyed his trip to see "HIS dogs" — as opposed to Daddy's.

Last night another letter from Um arrived for Grub which he was thrilled with. But one from Grolly never has arrived yet. In 3 days we are all off to Gombe in 2 planes! Because Dr. Bourliere from Paris & his girl ? friend want to come. So they plan to go down in one plane & us with Morris. James has been promised a trip to see the chimps. Trouble is, even with 2 planes, still not enough space — because David & Pat will be leaving! However, since I doubt we could get their luggage back <u>anyway</u> it can't be helped.

We are contemplating leaving Nairobi on 20th September — but havn't booked anything yet. Hugo will probably book on 6th Sept. — fly back to Nairobi when Bourliere returns.

Dove is sitting next to me — he says he wants you to come out for 2 years & run the camp, as he is tired!

Hugo & I have been summoned to Seronera today to see John Owen & Sandy.* I hate to think what it is all about! Hugo keeps telling me not to worry but of course I do! The Chalmers are having a baby! Arrives at Christmas. Can't help feeling it's all rather sordid. Tried to contact Louis in Nairobi — but of course it happened that he was at Olduvai. We had flown right over him!

Andrew arrived from Arusha last night with Dove. He apparently thought Lake Natron was Lake Rudolf! Which horrified Dove!!

Will write again soon. Do hope you are quite better Mum & everyone else.

Tons of love from all.

---

* Sandy Fields was one of two Serengeti park wardens.

Lake Legaja
16 September [1970]

Darling Family,

A brief note as Dove is off to Arusha and can post. We are trying to fix our arrival for 24th, i.e. the day before Louis. I hope I was right, Mum, that it would be nicer if we did not all arrive together? Louis seemed rather keen on the idea, and unfortunately we told him we were travelling on 25th before we knew he was. So we shall just say that Billy needed us a day earlier, and as he knows we are going just for Billy's publicity week, that will be O.K. with him. I just thought that Hugo me and Grub, plus Louis, all arriving together, would be utterly chaotic for you, Mum.

Have you seen Innocent Killers? Our copy has just arrived, and we think it has been produced really beautifully, and that the price, for the book, is amazingly cheap. Everyone who has seen it has said the same — even some Africans.

Am still tied to my typewriter all day, but have taken a few days off to go with Hugo dogging etc. But I still have Geographic accounts and report to type, editing on chimp book, and two of those foul abstracts for the Geographic. Isn't it all sordid. I was hoping for at least one week of holiday on the Serengeti before plunging into publicity, shopping for clothes, and going off to my fate in America, which I can't tell you how much I hate the idea of. Hey ho. Anyway, such is life, and the chimp book off my mind has lifted away some clouds that have hung for 6 years, so I don't really mind much about the rest any more. Just plod on.

Must end, or shall miss Dove.

Tons and tons of love to you all,
Jane, Hugo & Ub

# 6

# THE STANFORD YEARS
## 1971–1975

There was a spirit of cooperation among the students, a willing-
ness to share data, that was, I think, quite unusual.

— *Through a Window*

IN 1971 Jane Goodall was appointed Visiting Professor of Psychiatry and Human Biology at Stanford University in California.
Her mission was to add a primate studies dimension to a new undergraduate major called Human Biology. The program had been
drawn from more traditional disciplines and, in the words of one of
the initiators, focused on "the kind of biology uniquely related to
what it means to be human."* Human Biology's primate studies
component would include a twice-yearly series of lectures at Stanford, the opportunity for undergraduates to study a group of captive chimpanzees living in seminatural conditions, and the chance to
benefit from ongoing field studies at Gombe Stream National Park.

Thus, starting in the fall of 1971 and twice a year between 1972
and 1975, Jane flew to California, took up residence at the Faculty
Club on the Stanford campus or in a rented house in nearby Palo
Alto, gave lectures, and conferred with students. Also starting in
1971, Jane and others organized the acquisition of several captive
chimpanzees from laboratories and other locations in the United
States, then maintained them in quarters at the Delta Regional Primate Center in Louisiana and the Lion Country Safari in southern

---

* Donald Kennedy in "Interview," *Human Biology Newsletter,* 5(3): 3.

California, while they awaited completion of their new home: the Stanford Outdoor Primate Facility (sometimes known as SOPF or, more imaginatively, "Gombe West"), a very large fenced enclosure plus associated buildings in the hills directly behind the Stanford campus. Finally, in January 1972, the first Stanford students arrived in Africa and made their way by plane, train, and boat to "Gombe East." Many of the original plans for Jane's association with Stanford are described in the first letter of this chapter, written to Douglas Bond, president of the Grant Foundation, one of several funding organizations involved in the project.

Bond's visit to Gombe in September 1971 was anticipated as a "red carpet visit" in Jane's letter of August 19, 1971. He was followed by the Stanford biologist Paul Ehrlich and his family. Ehrlich, perhaps best known as a population biologist who wrote the best-selling environmental manifesto *The Population Bomb* (1968), had a strong interest in butterflies; some of his crew were already "madly collecting butterflies and caterpillars" by the time Jane returned to Gombe at the very end of the year (as noted in the letter of January 3, 1972). The first of many Human Biology undergraduates — Cay Craig and Dede Robbins — arrived soon after. Their arrival, in a chaotic series of hops and leaps from Nairobi to Ndutu to Kigoma to Gombe, accompanied by researcher Anne Pusey and the distinguished Dutch professor Baerends and his wife, is described in much of its complexity in the letter of January 16.

Jane's friend and ally at Stanford, professor of psychiatry David Hamburg, had also come out to Gombe that January. As one might gather from the three January letters, David was there primarily to lend aplomb to the "fateful meetings" taking place in Seronera and Dar es Salaam that focused on the practical problem of research clearances for foreigners. By then the immigration clearances for foreign researchers at Gombe and at the Serengeti Research Institute (SRI) had become stuck at a high level. Freeing them would require serious examination of the role of foreign research in Tanzania; and so it was (see the letter of January 16) that David and Jane participated in a high-powered meeting with key people from the Tanzanian government and the faculty of the University of Dar es Salaam, including Abdul Msangi, dean of the Faculty of Science.

Over time, Msangi became a friend of Jane's and of Gombe. He arranged for the translation into Kiswahili of *In the Shadow of Man*. And Jane, by the following year, was named Visiting Professor in Zoology at the University of Dar es Salaam, a position she continues to hold to this day. The new association with the University of Dar brought a small number of Tanzanian zoology students to Gombe during the Stanford years. Jane's increasing political and academic connections in Dar es Salaam more generally mark her increasing association with Tanzania and Tanzanians. Her fluency in Kiswahili had previously been merely functional; she now worked to improve it. And she began to encourage incoming researchers to learn the language before coming to Gombe. The Stanford undergraduates were in fact required to study Kiswahili, and as a result some of them were able, upon arrival, to communicate effectively with the Tanzanian field staff.

Jane also initiated a program to train the field staff in scientific data collection. During the 1960s very few of the Tanzanian workers at Gombe spoke any English. Most of them had little to no formal education of any sort, and with the exception of the men who had occasionally worked as trackers in the first years, the Tanzanian staff had little to do with chimpanzee observations. After the death of Ruth Davis in 1969, however, park regulations required that any researcher leaving camp to follow chimps had to be accompanied by a second person, who typically was a Tanzanian.

So began the field staff. Following chimpanzees across the rough terrain of Gombe is a very challenging occupation. The men who did it became physically tough, and as they came to know the individual chimpanzees and their family histories, they also turned into first-rate observers. The next step was to explain the logic of scientific data collection — in weekly seminars — and the step after that was to teach field staff members themselves to collect some of the general data. In addition to this gradual elevation in the status of the field staff, in 1973 Jane began to bring in Tanzanian park rangers from other national parks in the country and train them in the arts of chimpanzee and baboon observation and data collection; they would (letter of January 22, 1974) "set up their own research" back in their home parks. By the spring of 1974, Marietta (Etha)

Lohay had arrived. She was not only the first woman to be appointed a national parks warden in Tanzania, but also the first Tanzanian to become administrator of the Gombe Stream Research Center.

The Stanford years represent a major shift in Jane's attention. Geographically, the shift was away from the Serengeti and back to Gombe. Emotionally, the change included a gradual withdrawal from her marriage with Hugo, who becomes less and less a presence in these letters. Jane and Hugo were divorced in 1974; and in February 1975 Jane married Derek Bryceson, who was then director of Tanzanian national parks. In the first half of 1975, after their marriage, Jane and Derek commuted between her house facing Lake Tanganyika at Gombe and his home facing the Indian Ocean at 99 Old Bagamoyo Road in Dar es Salaam. Derek's place in Dar was enlivened by the presence of two dogs, Spider and Beetle.

In a domestic sense, Gombe seems to have been a comforting environment during those years. Jane and Hugo's friend from Ndutu, George Dove, volunteered his time and energy and made major improvements at Gombe. With some help from his son, Michael, George designed and built the lovely beach house that was nearly finished by the letter of March 30, 1972. That house was home to Jane and Grub for several months of every year during this period — and sometimes also a favored locale for the occasional scorpion, some pet rabbits, and a thieving baboon named Crease.

For Grub, Gombe provided a dramatic meeting of forest and water. A choice, actually, and Grub chose water. He loved to "swim like a fish" (January 23, 1972), catch fish, and play in the water with his African friends and playmates, the most regular of whom was the cook Juma's son, Sope or "Soapy," first mentioned in the letter of January 16, 1972. (Sope should not be confused with Grub's later friend Sufi, the son of Hilali Matama.) Grub kept an aquarium stocked with whatever he could pull out of the lake. He drew pictures of fish, and like a true fisherman, caught any number of fish "in his imagination" (August 16, 1972). Grub was extremely fond of his African babysitter, Mucharia, and his English one, Sarah. He had varying degrees of success with his teachers, who included Cricket Lyman, one of the Stanford students; Helen Goldman, the wife of a postdoctoral researcher; and Simon Petit, a volunteer who had worked with Hugo's wild dog study.

Socially, Gombe must have been wonderful during these years. The Stanford undergraduates arrived in a place already inhabited by first-rate graduate and postdoctoral researchers (including Helmut Albrecht, Harold Bauer, David Bygott, Larry Goldman, Stewart Halperin, Bill McGrew, Hetty and Frans Plooij, Anne Pusey, Mitzi Thorndahl, Caroline Tutin, and Richard Wrangham). Baboon research, at first administered by Hugo, was soon taken over by the unflappable Anthony Collins, who arrived from England late in 1972. From Holland, a passionate woman by the name of Emilie van Zinnicq Bergmann arrived to become general administrator in early 1972. Emilie also worked on chimpanzee research and by 1975 was on her way to Stanford. From the ranks of the field staff, Hilali Matama, Hamisi Mkono, and Eslom Mpongo distinguished themselves as chimpanzee experts; Apollinaire Sindimwo was fast becoming the resident authority on baboons.

If the field staff and the resident researchers and experts brought depth and academic seriousness to Gombe, perhaps the arriving Stanford students added sweetness and a measure of levity. The emotional tone of Jane's letters from this period makes the point clearly. The students were superb and fun to have around, and Gombe was a great place to be.

At any one time during those years, the student and professional research group at Gombe numbered from half a dozen to two dozen or more. For the most part, they lived in a rambling line of small prefabricated metal huts branching out from a path into the forest, leading away from the feeding area above the lake. Because the feeding area and several associated buildings (including the students' huts) were situated some distance above the lake, collectively they became "upstairs." "Downstairs," down by the lakefront, included some administrative buildings and a screened-in mess hall. Perhaps a hundred yards south of the mess hall was the African staff village, which included wives and children. A hundred yards north of the mess, still on the beach, was Jane's house. A typical day's end saw all the students and researchers from upstairs arriving down-stairs at the mess hall, to be joined by Jane for dinner and discus-sion, as well as other activities one might expect: gossip and shared observations about chimps and baboons; music, skits, and recita-tions, often on the same subjects; an occasional special event or party; and, starting in June 1972, a weekly movie. Jane's poem about a "new chimp tool" included in the letter of August 16, 1972, was recited one evening at the mess hall.

Jane sometimes talked about the "spirit of Gombe" as a cultural ideal. At its heart was the concept of sharing information. And here, during the Stanford years, students and researchers did freely and openly share their knowledge and observations. Chimpanzee (and baboon) research was a community effort, and information was a community resource.

Among the chimpanzee observations noted in these letters, per-haps three or four are worthy of further comment. As mentioned in the letter of February 8, 1973, the male political world among the Gombe chimps continued as it always had: the king and his plotting court. ("Figan is still challenging Humphrey, backed by Faben — sometimes backed by Evered. Sometimes Figan backs Humphrey against Evered. He's clever that one!") Flo, always one of Jane's fa-vorite females, was still the community matriarch. We have seen in earlier letters that, after the death of Flo's last infant, Flame, her son Flint — as he grew older and bigger — pathetically returned to his infantile ways. He tried to suckle, for instance, and continued to ride on his mother's back while she staggered under the weight. Flo now was ancient, forty to fifty years old, and approaching the end of her life. By August 16, 1972, "poor Flo" was "quite literally, a skeleton with some hairy flesh around it." And by September 15 of that year, Jane was writing to her friend Joan Travis about Flo's death, the "worst part" of which was that "Flint is taking it so terri-bly badly, and is unlikely to come through." Flint was still alive when Jane subsequently left for Stanford, but, as she wrote in her later book *Through a Window,* he was "hollow-eyed, gaunt and ut-terly depressed, huddled in the vegetation close to where Flo had died." Within a few weeks he too was dead.

One of the major events of this period was the division of the chimpanzee community into two separate, contiguous communities: one remaining in the area that included the feeding station, and a splinter group inhabiting a territory to the south. Because most of the chimps in the original study group were quite used to seeing people in their forest, the division allowed researchers to observe for the first time a set of interactions between two adjacent chimpanzee communities. What they watched, as it evolved over a period of many months, was disturbingly similar to a primitive version of human warfare. Male gangs from the northern community systematically raided the southern territory. Upon finding a lone and vulnerable southern male, they surrounded and then beat, stomped, bit, and pounded him to death. By the mid-1970s, then, war began to seem one more behavior shared by chimpanzees and their human cousins. So did cannibalism, observed as early as 1971 by one researcher following a group of community males into neighboring territory. Starting in 1975, though, a rogue female named Passion and her daughter Pom developed the habit of seizing, killing, and eating babies within their own community. Some of the letters addressing that emerging "dark side" of chimpanzee behavior — war and cannibalism — are assembled in the next chapter.

The degree of violence among chimpanzees was one astonishing piece of knowledge to emerge from Gombe during the decade of the 1970s. Human violence, on the other hand, should have been no surprise — but it was. The kidnapping of May 19, 1975, was perpetrated by a terrorist from Zaïre by the name of Laurent Kabila (later president of the Democratic Republic of Congo). Under cover of late-night darkness, a gang of forty armed men from Kabila's Marxist Parti de la Révolution Populaire (PRP) beached their boats on the gravel just below the Gombe staff village. They seized some of the African staff, beat them severely, and demanded to know where the *wazungu* (white people) were. The Tanzanian staff, especially Rashidi Kikwale and Etha Lohay, heroically risked their lives by refusing to give information, but the terrorists eventually wandered "upstairs," where they located some of the students' huts. They surrounded, beat, and bound the first four whites they found: Emilie Bergmann, the Dutch administrator and researcher, and three recently arrived Stanford students, Carrie Hunter, Barbara Smuts, and Steven Smith. Other students managed to hide in the forest. Jane, asleep with Grub in her house on the beach, well over a half-mile away from the worst of the commotion, heard nothing particularly alarming above the sound of the surf. She was alerted by some of the students soon after the terrorists had dumped their victims in boats and headed across Lake Tanganyika to Zaïre.

The four captives were threatened with death and subjected to Marxist "reeducation" sessions. Their minimum physical needs were attended to by slaves acquired by Kabila's soldiers through raiding lakeside Tanzanian villages. After a week, Barbara Smuts was freed and sent back across the lake with a list of the terrorists' demands: money, guns, and freedom for PRP guerillas held in Tanzanian jails.

Jane's letter of May 27, 1975, written after Barbara Smuts had returned with the list of demands, is surely the most complex of any in this chapter. It was clearly meant to provide reassurance to the three remaining captives by simultaneously acknowledging the seriousness of their situation and downplaying it. Of course, the letter would have been read by the terrorists as well, so while ostensibly addressed to Emilie, Carrie, and Steve, it appealed at the same time to their captors. ("We all feel that the most important thing for your captors is to gain world sympathy. Surely they must know that this is their chance.") It is a strained letter, written under one of the most stressful situations imaginable and suggesting the fatigue, panic, and desperation felt by everyone: Jane, Derek, and the students and researchers who by then were holed up in Dar es Salaam.

The letter is reproduced from a carbon copy that I found slowly disintegrating in a tattered folder in Jane Goodall's home in Dar es Salaam; the subsequent letter to Vanne suggests that the original of that carbon may not have made it across the lake. We can see from the June 13 letter to "Mum" and the rather distracted one of July 18 to "Darling Family" some of the difficulties brewing, including general tension and fatigue, and dissension among the parties working desperately to free the three captives. Both the Dutch and American ambassadors were involved. The fathers of the victims flew to Dar es Salaam and began to lobby determinedly on their children's behalf. American secretary of state Henry Kissinger reportedly sent instructions to the U.S. embassy that there were to be no negotiations with the terrorists, which was the official position also taken by the Tanzanian government led by President Nyerere. Jane's husband, Derek, as director of Tanzanian national parks and also as a friend and political ally of Nyerere's, was simultaneously expected to find a way out of the impasse and forbidden to negotiate openly with the terrorists. Derek, moreover, would have been entirely unable to assemble the ransom demanded: around half a million dollars. At the same time, Stanford's David Hamburg flew to Dar es Salaam to see if he could help. While the various governments and officials and embassies involved seemed largely paralyzed by their official positions and policies, Hamburg came as a private citizen and pragmatic problem solver; he met with representatives of the kidnappers and finally became convinced that paying the ransom was the best way to save the students' lives. One of the parents thus took out an emergency loan. The situation was complex and, as Jane declared in the letter of July 18, "so side-making." It became increasingly bitter when the ransom had been paid but only two of the victims released. Steven Smith was finally freed near the end of the month.

Like an earthquake jolting a seismograph, the late-night kidnapping of May 19 and the subsequent evacuation of all non-Tanzanians produced a one-day interruption in the otherwise continuous record of daily chimpanzee observations. Record taking was resumed the next day, in Kiswahili, taken over by the resilient field staff, while the administration continued steadily under senior warden Lohay and camp administrator Emmanuel Tsolo. For a time Adeline Mrema, a student from the University of Dar es Salaam, stayed on as well. Jane and Derek kept in touch, mostly from Dar es Salaam, via radiotelephone.

\* \* \* \*

Kastell Leuwenberg
Langbroek
Holland
1 June 1971

Dear Dr. Bond,

Thank you for your letter of 28 May. We are really delighted to hear that you will be able to visit us at Gombe this year, and please rest assured that it will cause absolutely no inconvenience. We shall all welcome the opportunity to show you at first hand the research of which you have so far approved on trust! Quite apart from any other considerations, the students at Gombe who are, as you know, quite isolated, benefit from and enjoy discussions with visiting scientists.

Early September is a very good time so far as we are concerned. Since it is far more efficient to try and communicate with you whilst we are still in Holland, perhaps you could let me know for how long you will be able to stay? It is likely that Hugo will still be studying African wild dogs at that time — would you be interested in seeing something of his work, and the Serengeti, as well as in visiting Gombe? Once we know the answers to these questions we can work out some kind of itinerary and send it off to you for your approval or disapproval!

I have very recently heard from Dave Hamburg that the Grant Foundation is prepared to consider our application for funds to establish the Stanford Outdoor Primate Facility — or Gombe West as we call it. This is wonderful news. I feel that perhaps it would be a good thing if, at this point, I let you and Mr. Sapir[*] know a little bit more about my own commitments to Gombe West — if it comes to be — and the ways in which I hope to combine my long term interests in the studies at Gombe with my equally strong interests in the proposed facility at Stanford.

As you know Dave and I plan that the research at Stanford be carried out in close collaboration with the ongoing studies at Gombe. In fact we view the research in these two locations as different facets

---

[*] Also associated with the Grant Foundation.

of one major goal — the better understanding of chimpanzee behaviour directed towards the better understanding of some aspects of human behaviour. For many years now I have wished that it were possible to do some work with chimpanzees in captivity, chimpanzees living in groups under conditions permitting some control over various social and physical features of their environment. Unfortunately most laboratory chimpanzees are maintained in such a way that they are unable to develop or exhibit normal patterns of social behaviour. Thus whilst such individuals are adequate for some kinds of experimentation they are not at all suitable for others. Our application has made clear some of the many ways in which research at the proposed Stanford facility could help to clear up problems which cannot be solved at Gombe.

At the end of this year I plan to be based permanently at Gombe and, from there, to make two visits to Stanford annually, one in the spring and one in the fall. One of these visits will be for about two months during which time I shall fulfill my teaching commitment to the Human Biology program as well as taking part in the chimpanzee research at the facility. During this period I shall also hope to work with Hugo on the making of scientific educational films from the materials shot by Hugo on the Gombe chimps. This footage (about 140,000 feet!) belongs to the National Geographic Society which has now agreed definitely for us to go ahead and make a series of films. Once we have obtained the necessary funds we shall send a work print of all this film to Stanford and hope to produce one film per year. In addition we hope to start work on analysing behavioural sequences from film, possibly with the help of some Stanford students.

There are other possibilities arising from our new affiliation with Stanford which I am currently investigating with Dave. The Human Biology program, as you have no doubt heard, has a large number of students deeply interested in primate behaviour in general and chimpanzee behaviour in particular. It occurred to us that such students might be only too willing to become personally involved with the chimpanzee research by helping me to analyse some of the vast quantity of back data from Gombe which still awaits attention. If this could be worked into their course requirements then these students would be doing an immensely worthwhile job and, in so doing, they would learn a great deal about the handling of data, which would be of great value to them. Quite apart from this idea it will obviously be most desirable to have a complete copy of the Gombe records at Stanford, if the chimp facility comes true, for the use of the group working there.

In short, my involvement with the proposed chimpanzee research at Stanford stems directly from, and is indeed an integral part of, my deep involvement with the work at the Gombe.

It is difficult to express strongly enough the very deep gratitude I feel to you for the part you have played in keeping the research at Gombe going. Sometimes I have the feeling that the Grant Foundation is like some kind angel that has swooped down out of the sky and scooped Gombe out of the financial mire! Otherwise we might not now be facing what I feel is an exciting new era of chimpanzee research — it is almost as though everything that has gone before has been some kind of preparation for what is to come. My own ultimate goal, as you know, has always been that out of a thorough understanding of chimpanzee behaviour should come a furthering of our understanding of our own behaviour. In this respect how fortunate it is for me to have the opportunity to collaborate with Dave. His outstanding ability to gather together first rate scientists from different disciplines and inspire them to work together as a cohesive and self-stimulating group will be our most valuable asset in the long run, for it is by pursuing this kind of multi-disciplinary approach that we shall, almost certainly, come up again and again with promising new lines of enquiry into problems of human behaviour.

I hope to hear from you soon about your plans for your African visit, and let me say, once again, how very much I look forward to seeing you again in September, and to meeting your wife.

Thank you for everything.

Yours sincerely,
Jane van Lawick-Goodall, Ph.D.

Ndutu
19 August 1971

Darling Family,

It is 7.30 a.m. and I am making use of writing to you first to un-stiffen my fingers! So exvuse all the m stakes. Mike is off to Arusha in about an hour, and I want to type a number of lettersmore before he goes. I already have 27 or so ready, having spent nearly all day yesterday typewriter bashing.

News. Thingsare well here. George in a most benign mood. We have just got rid of a huge and very well organized tour — a big American bird watching society, organized in 3 groups of 50 with a very nice tour leader who spent the time driving wildly from one group to another. They had lectures organized for them, so I was able to practise a couple which I will titivate for the States — it was thus quite useful and quite fun. Hugo spoke on dogs — and they said that our lectures, and Ndutu in general, were the high lights of their tour. All 3 groups said that.

We areplanning our house for Gombe. Will bring the plans to show you. It is going to be simply super. Then you will <u>have</u> to come back, Mum, and see the fruitsof George s labours of love. He and Mike, and some chaps, are going to Gombe mid-September — again, sadly, when we leave. . . .

Grub is very well and fit. I have had a bout of malaria, but that is over now. I am, as you can imagine, frantically busy, but Grub and I spend every afternoon together, collecting feathers, caterpillars and grasshoppers, and making feather books and red indian hats. He is chattier than ever and had great times when the big group was here autographing copies of the Grub book! Hugo lost him one lunch time, and peering round a corner saw him with two old ladies signing books for their grandchildren! Did I tell you about the crab Uncle David [Hamburg] caught for him at Gombe? Dominic, hopefully, is looking after it till we return on 1st September — with Douglas Bond, the President of the Grant Foundation. That will be a red carpet visit. Keep your fingers crossed for us for those 5 days. Then he and his family fly to Ndutu, the day Paul Ehrlich and wife arrive at Ndutu, and Hugo entertains them all here for three days — the dog den, Olduvai, and Seronera the back way, through the hills.

Then Paul Ehrlich flies to Gombe, where the plane waits one day, and then leaves him there and brings me and Grub back to Ndutu, thence all of us to Nairobi.

Now, thepart concerning you. We are (hopefully) booked on the evening of 14th September on a BOAC flight to arrive in London early morninggggggggggggggggggggggggggg (horrid g gggggggggggg ggggggg better now) of 15th. At least, Mike is m king reservations for us today in Arusha. Then I fly on to the States on Sunday 19th at mid-day. So that is better than we thought. I did wonder, Mum, whether it would be good if you and Grub set off ahead of me to Bournemouth. Thus he will be going to his beloved Bournemouth and Grolly's house, and the thxought of me going to America will not be very uppermost in his mind. . . .

I hope you'll forgive me for not writing the long letter I promised. I'm a bit frantic with far too much to do. Still have to finalize my Stanford teachinglectures, and the 27 letters are the middle, only, of the vast number awaiting me when I got here. There were recommendations for all thestudents and goodness knows what else. Then I have to organize thoughts for the application for Gombe West (the research, not the building now) which is the reason for my going to Washington) and thoughts for the paper I'm doing with Dave, and I've got a chapter of a book for Eibl,* and I have a paper to prepare on culture in chimps for the primate meeting in Oregon next August. And there is a chance I MIGHT get invited to the major America psychiatric meeting of the year to present the opening paper — the chimp film and a lecture. Dave has suggested it, and isnow wondering whether they can be un conservative enough to let a non-psychiatrist do it. If so it would be the first time in their history! What fun. Well — must end, as there are 6 more letters and time (as well aspaper) is running out. I do hope Danny's flowers did arrive for her birthday? No one has ever mentioned them.

Tons of love —<br>Jane & Ub

---

* Ethologist Irenaus Eibl-Eibesfeldt, professor at the University of Munich and director of the Research Unit for Human Ethology of the Max-Planck Institute, was a friend. He also contributed a chapter to Vanne's edited book, *The Quest for Man*.

In Flight!
Gombe/Seronera
3 Jan. 1972

Darling Family,

Well — Gombe is fine — a few problems between Harold and the Plooijs — but I think they are ironed out now. Dave's visit was as usual, very soothing for everyone.

Grub is fine. He has settled down well, has tadpoles and fish in a bowl (staying alive this time) and 2 baby mice he is watching. Paul Ehrlich's crew are madly collecting butterflies and caterpillars and Grub is very busy helping to get and raise caterpillars! He is developing into a fantastically good pelmanism* player — with those super cards from Moeza. He still plays constantly with his snakes and his soldiers — the sword is awaiting repairs!

Am dying to know how "Fifi" is working — but letters are taking so long to get here. The cards I posted about a week before Christmas only got here today!

The chimps rested right nearby 2 nights ago — Grub & Dave & I watched them make nests. It was fun & Grub was very excited. So excited that he set off along the beach to fetch Daddy. I called but he pretended not to hear. He had a head start of about 50 yards — do you know I couldn't catch him! We were about 300–500 yards from the buildings & he ran all the way, in bare feet, & was not even puffed at the end. I was absolutely exhausted! As I bore down on him he was calling Daddy frantically — Daddy was in the store at the back of his office & Grub couldn't find him — & wanted protection from his irate mother! It was all so funny! (I wasn't irate by the time I arrived, but I was as I plodded along the beach!) Will write again soon — after these <u>fateful meetings.</u>

Tons of love to you all —
Jane

---

* A card game similar to Concentration.

Gombe
16 Jan. [1972]

Darling Family,

Another sordid blue! I hope you have been getting a succession of my sordid blues! I can't remember now whether or not I wrote to you after Dar, or not. My mind is in such a muddle. If not — then our meetings couldn't have gone better except that we havn't actually got our clearances! But if anyone gets them, then I think we will. Silly typewriter, just back from Nairobi, still won't turn up properly. Sometimes only half. Msangi laid on a really super lunch with the vice-chancellor of the University, and lots of heads of departments and things, and it was in a sort of luxury beautiful hotel on the beach. Dave gave a really superb lecture — poor man, it took him about 5 hours to prepare as, of course, he hadn't got any of the relevant bits of paper with him. Anyway, he felt it was worth it. We have some really good friends in Dar now.

The journey back! It started off very well. I got E.A. Airways flight to Arusha, where [I met] a charter plane from Nairobi with Anne and the 2 Stanford students on it. We landed at Ndutu for coffee* but unfortunately George was on his way, driving, back from Arusha. Set off again, got to Kigoma. Paul Ehrlich and family should have gone straight off to Nairobi to catch a plane. We waited and waited at the airport — finally they came. Boat had broken down, and they had just made it in a water taxi which also broke down. So we set off. Had two VIPs from the Seronera meeting, Professor Baerends (sort of father of ethology from Holland) and wife. Boat broke down. They changed the broken bit — took about an hour. By now it was 5.30 ish. Then we chugged on for another hour. Same thing broke (shear pin). They had no other to spare, so they made one out of a nail. Took ages. At about 6.15 they started the engine — the home made pin instantly broke. I suggested we send Rashidi along the beach to see if our boat had been mended by Harold in the meantime. But this was not approved. So another 40 minutes went by and they tried to start the engine. This

---

* In other words, to share a cup of coffee with George Dove.

took 10 minutes. The new pin broke. Obviously. So we paddled ashore. Pitch dark by now. Hugo set off to the Parks Rangers' place, luckily only a few yards distant. We got out and wandered after him. Prof. B. lost his specs — pitch dark so couldn't find them. We got to Parks place, and at least could have some coffee. Anne and I were going to look, with a scout and a lamp, for Prof. B's specs. He elected to come. So we left Mrs. B and the 2 girls in the hut, and set off. It began to literally deluge. So we popped Prof. B. into a hut full of dagaa and 10 fishermen, and set off in the rain. The thunder! No specs. 30 mins later, soaked, we rejoined Prof. B. Poor man! We all sat in the hut on debes and sacks of dagaa* — because there was no raincoat, and we didn't see the point of Prof. B. getting soaked. Then Hugo and Harold arrived having had the most ghastly row over something — the lightning. No one was speaking to anyone. We got on the boat — the new engine Harold had got wouldn't start. When it did, our boat, which Harold was trying to tow from the water taxi (which we were still in, with all our luggage), bumped into us, and the engine stopped. Finally it went, and we got to the Parks place and picked up the other three who had been sleeping, with blankets. Anne and I were so shivering we could scarcely speak. But Hugo had brought a thermos of coffee and some bread. And we changed bits of clothing on the water taxi. 20 mins. later the engine started again, and finally we got home! They were waiting up for us (1.30) with hot supper. So all [was] well that ended well.

Grub is fine — he can swim like a little fish — but only under water! Hugo started that way too, apparently. He is so pleased with it — it's hard to keep him out of the water and he's fearfully sunburned. Oh well! Juma has a little boy called Sope (Soapy) and he and Grub play most superly every morning. Grub loves him — about the same age. He only had Papa's shirts to wear but I've put him into some of Grub's clothes, and he looks super now. (Soapy and Grubby!)

---

* Oil cans and sacks of sardine-like fish.

It is now fearfully late. Oh — the morning of the ghastly lake day, I'd had to get up at 4.30 to catch the 6.00 plane from Dar!

Lots and lots of love,<br>Jane

I had the <u>funniest</u> dream. Olly, all dressed up, was sitting with a pint sized chocolate liqueur taking huge swigs of drambuie out of a hole in the neck. Ma swept in in a chocolate brown trouser suit with <u>very</u> wide bell bottoms & trailing chiffon scarves — most outré — very high heels. <u>Frightfully</u> smart! She said "Olwen — you'll get quite drunk if you drink any more. Stop it." Olly said "It [would be a] pity to waste it — this hole will dry it up" & took another HUGE swig!!

Some English blues — no good to me!<br>Gombe<br>[Around 23] January 1972

Darling Um,

I <u>think,</u> to my chagrin, that it's the day before your birthday, but I can't remember what date it is, and nor can Hugo. If so, my plan of sending a cable when the next Kigoma boat goes, will be to no avail. Now that we have this store, you see, the boat doesn't have to go in very often — which is really super, of course. Anyway, please know we shall have thought of you on your birthday, and drunk a toast to you. This letter will be posted from England by Dennis Parnell, a very charming botanist (who knows BV)* who is doing a Sabbatical at Kew. He has been here for about a month, and is hoping to return. I tell you all this at this point, because he is going to ring up and give you some news from the horse's mouth, so to speak! He is a great fan of Grub's, and has spent a lot of time reading him Alice in Wonderland — which, surprisingly, Grub is much enjoying.

Do forgive me, really, for not getting a letter of birthday greetings to you in time. I feel most guilty — my excuse is that things have

---

* Bernard Verdcourt, Jane's botanist friend from the Coryndon Museum, now employed at Kew Gardens.

been difficult and trying, with many more late, late night sessions. The students have been a little problematical — the Plooijs and Harold. Not dear Anne, whose presence is the balm of my days! And things have now been sorted out well, and we've had a staff meeting which was good, and I feel in control of the situation. Hugo has really been working like a trojan on administration and building and things. Now the two fundis from Dove* have arrived, so the remaining staff blocks are going up, our house should be habitable in a couple of weeks, the shelves will go up for the library, Grub will have a little school chair and table made, etc, etc. Then you will simply HAVE to come and visit Gombe. . . .

The two Stanford Human Biology students are absolutely first class. Really good. They are already tackling "A" record (the record in camp) and going out with the mums and infants doing records for my long term family relationship study. What a relief, after the gap of the past 3 months since Richard and Mitzi left. One of them, Dede, actually did a Swahili course, speaks excellent Swahili, and is most helpful in translating the notes of the followers.

Our Tanzanian staff is really becoming quite an exciting project. We have 5 followers — field assistants now — who have got higher salaries, and go out following chimps (e.g. an adolescent for Anne, or a male for Harold) often all day. They are super at following. They also take accurate records — check sheets on very simple things, and written notes on fights and anything special. We are learning a lot in this way, and they are so proud. One little chap — Sadiki's son Moshi — speaks English and helps with translating — and is also quite a good assistant. We have a new English speaking one from Mwamgongo that Linda (Paul Ehrlich's student) is training to carry on the butterfly work after she leaves. And an old man, a friend of Dominic's, who also speaks good English, who comes tomorrow to do some of the simple Administration, hand out supplies, possibly do the radio telephone, and take over the translation of the field assistant's notes for Harold and Dede. He types quite well. He can do simple letters, and seems a nice chap. In fact, we now have a Gombe village over the stream.

---

* George Dove's two expert builders.

Grub's friendship with the little Soapy progresses. If Dave can really find a teacher, we could start a school tomorrow — I've never seen so many children as our staff have down here between them. I should think if they brought all their wives and children we'd have something like 20 children under 8! Anyway, they all seem happy and contented, and it marks the beginning of a new era for Gombe. I am longing to hear from the people in Dar.

I don't suppose YOU have any idea as to whether Billy was planning to provide the pictures, jacket and hard covers for the Swahili edition FREE — as a contribution — or if we need to pay. I don't suppose you could find out, could you? If we have to pay, I need to know what it will cost. Dar University — the Institute of Swahili — is going ahead with the translation — you've no idea how excited all the people in Dar were with the idea of the Swahili edition.

I've had a lot of flaps lately. A new deadline for the NIMH application for Gombe West — and the lengthy comments on our draft application arrived after Dave had gone, and so I had to stay up half of one night to make some comments and send them to poor Dave. Who was already going to be overworked, and was frantically worried about having left his family for the Franklin verdict.* Oh dear. Then there was a Wenner-Gren application deadline, and a Geographic research report deadline. We had a staff meeting and I had to do the agenda, and then the minutes which took a full afternoon. Detailed sessions with Harold (2), one of one morning all but an hour, and another with Frans. Afternoons with Grub, nights with problems. I'm quite exhausted!

Anyway, I'd better stop and try to get some more letters done from my pile. As I said to Hugo, my file marked urgent never gets smaller — never changes — because no sooner have I sent off one batch of stuff, than the things which come back to me, on mail day, turn out to be more urgent than what is in the file. So they have to be done for the next mail day — and then the same thing happens. Oh well! If only all communications could be cut off for 3 weeks I might get part caught up!

---

* H. Bruce Franklin, politically radical English professor at Stanford, was being fired from his job. David Hamburg had been involved in the process.

Did I tell you in the last letter that Grub can swim like a fish, only underwater though. We are going to get him a little child's mask, and flippers, when we are in Nairobi. He really does so love his swimming. Sarah is very good with him in the water.

Must end. I do hope you had a super birthday. I must tell you that I planned, right up to the last minute, to ask Dave to send you some flowers from me. But I just couldn't when the time came. He still looked as tired as when he arrived, we'd kept him so busy, given him so many new problems. I just couldn't burden him with a chore — though of course he'd have done it like a shot. So believe that the wish and the thought was there. I couldn't, believe it or not, find a card in Dar. Anyway, I'm sure the enclosed from Grub will make up. It's for Um's birthday — and, you'll be surprised to hear, not once did he say he wanted to keep it for Mummy!!

Now it's time for me to do Grub's egg.

Tons, and tons, and tons of love to all of you,
Jane


Gombe
30 March 1972

Darling Family —

Off to meet Hugo & the 2 new Human Biology students (for baboons). Our own engine has got stuck in Kigoma so we are on a Water Taxi together with an assortment of people and one goat. There are our two wagtails for a while too — they always come for the ride!

I'm sure, Mum, you know the details of my & Ub's arrival from Hugo. That is, amazingly, less than a fortnight away. How time does fly! At last Ub & I have managed to get into our new house — but it is nowhere near ready. No paint yet — no shelves or tables. But it is a beautiful house. We've had 2 nights in there & killed one scorpion! 2 nights ago I found Ub <u>wide</u> awake when I got back after supper. He lay like a mouse while I worked for 30 minutes — but was still wide awake. So we put on his slippers & sweater & he came & sat on the beach while I had a moonlight swim, & then we drank Milo, & finally went to bed about 11.45!! But next morning up as usual and still going strong at 7.00 p.m.! He has amazing vitality. He is actually quite keen to come to Bournemouth & not at all concerned about leaving Gombe for a while, in spite of his lake & his fish. He really does have the most fabulous fish tank. We just got a tiny cat fish — unfortunately it is so shy that, apart from seeing it in the jar it was brought in we've not seen it since.

The lake is flat as a millpond, & the engine working well — the only nuisance was that the boat didn't come till 9.00 — & there is a LOT to be done in the Market & elsewhere in Kigoma. Dominic is in disgrace again — he was supposed to bring back the engine & has some crazy cock & bull story as to why he didn't. Oh — the film show I did at the school in Kigoma might be described as a "howling, roaring" success. I've never heard an audience enjoy & identify with the film more. It was free. Again I was the only white person there. But if I hadn't had dear Ramji*. . . . The projector didn't work. If it had it would have ruined my film. But he helped me get another & arranged everything. I must try & see his son next time I have a few moments to spare in London. Have just done a draft of Model for Early Man — so it will be simple, Mum, to do the chapter for you.† Do hope it is all going well. Will not be writing again. Seeing you & ringing everyone else, Mum.

Tons of love,<br>Jane

16 May 1972

Dear Louis,

I'm so sorry about the mix up with the planes. And that you waited in vain, and that we were so late. It was pouring and thundering in Entebbe, and so the plane couldn't take off, and we just sat there, Grub getting malaria fast, and very miserable.

---

* Ramji Dharsi and his wife, Sudhadra, had a shop in Kigoma and were longtime, close friends.
† Jane wrote a chapter, "The Chimpanzee," for Vanne's book *The Quest for Man* (New York: Praeger, 1975).

Grub is simply thrilled with his presents — are they from you? It was all so mysterious.

Anyway, it was horrid to miss you. We got there safely — though, as I say, Grub had this horrid go of malaria. But he is quite over it now, and outside playing with Mucharia and his little African friend. I must make this brief, as a boat is just going in to collect John Savage, the Park Warden, since the Parks boat has broken down. That will be another friend for Grub to play with, since he brings his son, Jason. He is also bringing Grub a rabbit!

Things are well here at Gombe. Incidentally, I got the letter signed by you and Fleur,* but didn't manage to contact her during my couple of days in London since she was not there. But I shall, of course, be delighted to be on the new foundation in London if you feel this can be useful to you.

Must close, Louis. Do hope you are feeling O.K.

Love,
Jane

6 June 1972

Darling Family,

You'll never guess — we now have film shows at Gombe! And I mean <u>theatre films</u>!! Kigoma still gets one film a week from Dar — we pay a share, collect the film on Monday &, with the new fast boat, return it on Tuesday before 9.00 a.m. Really — what next! Hugo has bought this projector for his rushes, you see. The first one is tonight. We are letting all the Africans who want come in for 1/-. Since it is the first there may not be room for us! We pay 5/-.

The place is full of sadness at the moment — a poor baby baboon with a dislocated leg — he is protected, half the time, by an adult male. Another older, camp troop baboon who can't use one hand. And this morning a ghastly thing — a young civet sitting at the edge of the water with <u>more than</u> half its back eaten away by maggots,

---

* Fleur Meyer helped establish a London branch of the L. S. B. Leakey Foundation.

still just alive — a young baboon went up to it and actually took maggots from its back & ate them. When Hugo tried to catch it to kill it, it swam into the lake & mercifully drowned, very quickly. It was <u>terrible</u> — & the smell of rotten flesh in a living animal terrible.

Otherwise things are good. Grub is <u>very</u> healthy at the moment, brown as 20 berries, quite good about school. We have done all the writing, more than all the reading, & at this moment we are sticking little squares of paper on a card for his hard work.

The baboon study really is going very well indeed — the boys are all so keen, & that includes the 2 Dar students. They are great. So is the one working on chimps. The other, who was doing Kobi, the tame chimp,* went to Nairobi to see his family and missed the plane back — <u>certainly</u> not his fault — they changed the time of the plane & Hugo had no address or no. for him. Sad.

I have got the paper done for my Adolf Meyer Lecture — not typed finally, but written, & I will have it ready to send off next week. Then it's chimp culture. And we should be doing a newsletter. And there's the commentary on the dog film. And I'm desperately trying to read up on <u>other</u> primates for my lectures in the Fall — & there are so many meetings. Hey ho. Grub is fed up with his glueing & is whining like mad.

Tons & tons of love to all,<br>Jane & Ub

P.S. Cay Craig, my favourite Stanford student, would <u>very</u> much like a room in the flat† September–November. Can she? She really is a super girl — offered to caretake if Pen has gone. She is writing to you herself. Says she has, once — .

---

* Tourists had purchased Kobi, a baby chimpanzee, in Zaïre. He was probably orphaned by hunters who shot his mother for meat. When the tourists visited Gombe, Hugo agreed to keep Kobi temporarily until a better home could be found. The chimp eventually was taken by some Kigoma people who felt they could care for him.
† Vanne had rented a flat in London, which became a convenient and oft-used stopping point.

19 June 1972

Dearest All,

I feel I havn't heard from any of you for ages and ages and ages. I think it's because so much seems to be happening that, though the time appears to fly past, 3 days in retrospect (thinking of what has been accomplished) seems like a week. Anyway, I hope all goes well. Thank you very much, Uncle E, dear Rixy Boy, for your letter about my election to the AAAS.* I have written to find out to what it is equivalent in England, if anything. Judging from the people in the States who have written to congratulate me on the honour it must be quite prestigious.

Did I tell you, by the way, that I had an awfully nice letter from Robert about it? I'm sure I did. And did you get a letter asking if you could contact Anthony Collins and ask for his C.V.? We are having more problems in respect to students working here now — I won't go into them, as they may be rumours — but rumour has it that each student will have to buy a self-employment permit, irrespective of whether or not he has research clearance, and that this will cost Shs 600 each — and has to be renewed each month. But I can't believe that this can be true. That would be 7,200 Shs. per student a year — £360 a year. Surely not! We'll see.

The recent bad news is that we've had two boat engines stolen — almost for sure by the man who came and repaired them for us, since those two were taken, and the other two, whose parts he had cannibalised for the job but which <u>looked</u> perfectly O.K., were not taken. Too much of a co-incidence. So we have the police around again — this time they came with 2 soldiers with guns.

Has the British press been making much of the Burundi war?† It

---

* Jane had been elected an Honorary Foreign Member of the American Academy of Arts and Sciences.

† Hutu agriculturalists had been living in the region of Rwanda and Burundi since the eleventh century A.D. The taller, more martial Tutsis migrated in from the north during the sixteenth and seventeenth centuries and subjugated the Hutus. German, then Belgian, colonial rulers exacerbated the conflict and hostility between these two ethnic groups. Jane is here referring to a 1972 ethnic war when rebelling Hutus in Burundi killed more than a thousand Tutsis, and in response Tutsis slaughtered over two hundred thousand Hutus and drove half again that number out of the country. This, of course, was merely the start of the region's genocidal nightmare.

really seems to be ghastly, but we find it hard to believe it is all happening so close. Some of the tales from our staff are grisly in the extreme — and a number of them have relatives there, who have come plodding along the beaches of the lake to the safety of Kigoma. I only hope it will end soon.

I'm having problems in getting time to finish off Grub's school. Sarah spends most afternoons down here with Kobi, and so it's hard for me to resist the temptation of leaving Grub with her (he adores her now) so that I can get a bit extra done. After all, in another 2 weeks she will be gone. His reading is coming along very well, and I'll see if he'll write you a letter — or at least make a drawing — this afternoon. He is playing with Mucharia and the rabbits now. The rabbits are not handleable, but are a lot of fun, and he simply adores them. Oh dear — I have an appointment upstairs. Will finish anon. . . .

Yesterday afternoon I spent an hour solid bullying Grub and we got the last of his maths and story telling etc finished, so off goes that set, and we will try and do the last set of the term in double quick time. I tried to persuade him to do you a picture today, but he's not in a drawing kind of mood at the moment — just catching fish and collecting stones and sweeping the floor! And, of course, playing with his rabbits. The last two mornings Crease* got in. The first time I thought we'd not closed the door properly the night before — he came in just as I was dressing, got the bread, and finally left when Hugo approached him with a chair. Yesterday we realized that the latch on the door wasn't working properly. He got in and the door closed behind him, and strolled into the little kitchen where I was with Grub who got very scared indeed. Crease didn't actually threaten, or anything. But he did take the last of the bread, spilled the milk which I'd been mixing for 10 minutes, and also our last supply of water. So I got very cross. Especially as we don't have any of the chaps in to clean the house — which is big, really, so that I now have house work to do as well as letters, papers, administration and school. Never mind. It's not that much unless Crease spills

* One of the baboons.

muck all over the floor and Annie* and Grub arn't sick all over the floor!

Oh — I didn't tell you. Grub complained of a terrible pain the other evening, and couldn't eat his supper, and screamed and screamed — and I thought of appendix and was quite scared. Until I discovered that Sarah had permitted him to eat almost a whole pawpaw,† on top of his lunch, after which he had had a wild swim with me, and then had a huge mug of tea and thick slice of butter and jam. Anyway, he was sick 4 times, and this went on most of the night. And then he was fine! He still likes pawpaw! I told you we get the film from Kigoma Club once a week. Well, last week was a Walt Disney cartoon and, though we have it after supper, we felt Grub must see it. So I fetched him (still wide awake and chatting at 8.30) and, having seen it, he wanted to stay for the main film, which was Kidnapped, and super. Grub much preferred that to the cartoon, and stayed wide awake all through. He really did enjoy it very much, especially the fighting and the creeping about on the highlands and hiding in the bracken and behind water falls. The only decent film we've had so far. I missed the last one (luckily) as I was doing the commentary (my part of it) for the dog film. Which took me till 2 at night.

I'm sending the letter from the Secretary of the AAAS for you Ma. And I must again stop, do an agenda for tonight, and go and see how poor Sarah is getting on with her final tidying and filing and indexing before she goes. We are going to miss her so very much. No one to look after the little chimp when she's gone, either. Hey ho.

Tons and tons of love to all of you — how's Quest, Mum? Am still waiting for the new outline. You'll have to remind me what it was I was to do, when you send it. I guess I was going to write to Ehrlich and DeVore, and maybe Wilkie — was that it?‡ I gather Louis will be with you soon. And what is the news of the renewal of lease on the flat? Do let me know exactly how much money you

---

* Anne Vanderstroep, a student.
† A tropical fruit also known as papaya.
‡ Paul Ehrlich, Irven DeVore, and Leighton Wilkie — all potential contributors to Vanne's edited book.

want us to guarantee. And I think we should either all go to Stanford together, or you and Grub follow after a bit — only I must find out about his school.

Love —
Jane & Ub

16 August 1972

Darling Family,

There's nothing special to relate since I last wrote — except that I'm over this silly cold or whatever it was. But I had to write something to enclose with all these bits and pieces because it's always horrid — I think — to get an envelope with enclosures and no letter.

Sarah is back here, more or less on her way to England, and will be able to give you up to date news on life at Gombe. She is rather upset that she is not taking Kobi back — but it wasn't possible to get the export papers sorted out in time. And also, Molly Badham wasn't prepared just to look after Kobi until we could take him to Stanford — she wanted to keep him. And I wasn't prepared for that. Poor little Kobi. I'm still half hoping he may join this group in the Gambia and then when he is older, be released with them. It all depends on whether this first group [is] managing to adjust to life in the wild. Should be hearing any day now.

Poor Flo. She was here outside my window this morning. She is, quite literally, a skeleton with some hairy flesh around it. She spends most of the time lying on the ground. It is nice for her to have Fifi and Flint around, I suppose, only Flint is the most ghastly pest. He can't leave her to rest for more than 5 minutes without coming up to prod at her and poke her and whisper and whine till she grooms him. But if he loses her — my word, the tantrums. He's lost her now, and Mitzi is following him as he screams his way along the beach (so is Fifi). What will he do when she is gone? . . .

Since his two fish, Grub has only caught more in his imagination. He went fishing with Daddy last night, and came back to tell me that he had caught 3 dagaa, given them to the Africans, and they had cooked them and eaten them and told him how delicious they were, etc. All fabricated! He is a scream. He is in a constant state of misery because his line doesn't work any more — and a fish went away with the hook yesterday!

James is here, by the way, working on wild dog analysis. He is changed beyond recognition — the sort of change we saw in Nick. Blossomed and become much more adult, and nice too. I mean, he was always nice, but he used to have a superior manner, and doesn't any more.[*]

Must end. I see Sawa and Gwub coming along the beach, with Kobi. So I'll have to hear some more fishermen's tales. He even, this morning, "caught a huge one that got away"! Real fisherman. We havn't done school for a week — so this whole term is farcical, because we havn't completed the first 2 weeks, and we only have another 3 1/2 or so before we leave!

NEW CHIMP TOOL

<u>What led to the event.</u> It was almost dark when Craig and Anne[†] heard baboon screams and barks and a bushbuck call. They hurried down the slope and saw several baboons, with the dominant male carrying something. Figan and Mike were there. Figan began whimpering. He charged through the baboons who scattered. He followed, and charged again. Craig and Anne couldn't see what happened. He began screaming and screaming. When next seen he had the body of a small infant bushbuck. The baboons were harrying him — the dominant male had lost his object. When Mike climbed up to Figan, the baboons dispersed, and Figan stopped screaming. Mike begged, and got the larger half of the carcass. Figan and Mike took their meat to bed.

The next morning Mike came in to camp, still with lots of meat, and with the skin draped around his neck like a stole.

Only twice, in the annals of Gombe, has feces eating been seen — prior to this day. Both times the chimps were ill (once Faben, and once Pallas). Stewart says he is sure Mike was feeling ill too — when the following occurred:

---

[*] James Malcolm and Nicholas Pickford both assisted Hugo while he was following and photographing wild dogs.
[†] Stanford undergraduate Craig Packer and British graduate researcher Anne Pusey.

What a horrifying record to see Mike consume his dung —
The kind of horrid episode that never should be sung.
Yet we have to tell this incident, and pass the word around,
For he doesn't — no he doesn't — just munch it from the
   ground.
Feces on his lips is fine, it's okay on his tongue,
But culture's taught him "Never, Mike, never touch your dung
With any of your fingers, Mike — it simply isn't done".
He's watched the grown-ups wipe with leaves since he was
   with his Mum.
He feels much meat he ate last night is undigested still —
Young bushbuck is nutritious and he's keen to take his fill.
He knows his dung will shatter if he drops it to the ground
So thinks hard in his tree top seat, then quickly looks around
And picks the very largest leaves, the best that can be found.
He cups his hand and carefully he lines it with his leaves —
And Stewart has those pictures in case nobody believes.
Then he plops the half-digested snack into the waiting bowl
And with his lips picks out the meat, thus realizing his goal.

! ! !

Tons & tons of love to you all,
Jane

Nairobi
15 September [1972]

Dear Joan,

    A very hasty note en route to London — because although I'll see you soon, I must get things done as I come to them or go crazy!

    First — did I already tell you about Flo? I just can't remember whom I have and whom I have not told. I have written to Tita and told her a vague outline of what happened, and will tell you the details when I see or call you. The worst part is that Flint is taking it so terribly badly, and is unlikely to come through. We're trying to arrange a plane to take some medicines down to him, but it may be too late. He won't eat or do anything. Poor poor little Flint. . . .

I mustn't waffle on now. I want to save overweight by dealing with 2 bulging files of unanswered correspondence! Before leaving Nairobi, that is. We came early for cholera shots, and it is proving a useful thing to have done, including having been able to sort out these medicines for Flint.

Please give our love to Arnold, hope John Paul is still behaving himself.* We have lunch with Louis in 2 days, and leave for London on 20th.

Much love,
Jane

8 February 1973

Darling Family,

I wonder how you all are? I can't remember, Mum, if I answered your last nice long letter. I suppose I didn't. But I'm in a whirl of letters that is driving me mad. And I've just seen a quarter inch baby scorpion in a spider's web. Dead. Anyway, I've written 63 letters in the last two days — mornings and evenings, rather, since the afternoons are for Grub. Cricket came to me today, and offered to spend an hour each afternoon teaching Grub. That is very super of him, and should work far better than me. I eavesdropped, and Grub was reading fine. I had just thought of a new system — it works like a dream. We have a page, and he goes through it and gets a point for each word he knows. Any words left I get a point for — or Cricket, as the case may be. If Grub knows a lot, he does not leave many points for us, and therefore he wins. He's really trying now!

He's also really catching eating fish. So pleased and excited for hours on end. Still saving up for Charia's cow,† sweeping the floor, etc. He gets extra marks — I mean pennies — if he does very well with his school. He is fit as a fiddle, except that his lower right tooth suddenly keeps hurting. Did he have X-rays?

I get more and more pleased with Gombe. Bill McGrew and

---

* Arnold was Joan's husband; John Paul, their dog.
† Charia (Mucharia), Grub's beloved nanny, needed a cow for a feast or some other sort of ceremony.

Caroline are really great. You should see the library now, which Bill has organized. Our reprint library, which is presently stored in 3 tin trunks, will soon be transferred into a new file cupboard which Steven is making. Then we shall be in pretty good shape. Except that there are no more funds. Alan Grundman* was sure that funds would run out in June. I think this is true. But have just heard from Dave that, even if they do, we must, nevertheless, make them last till next April!! We are having emergency meetings, tightening our belts, cutting down on Kigoma trips, and so on. I have used every penny of my personal account for research — will hopefully get it back if money does come from Stanford. Everyone very cheerful about it. These new undergraduates are just absolutely great. David and Cricket — Chuck, Mark and Henry.† Wish you'd met Chuck, Mum. You did meet the other two — Mark, large and handsom and fair, who carried chairs about, had a pretty sister — she is here too. And Henry, who you said looked Geza-like, and who has an immensely wealthy father who is, I am pretty certain, about to be asked to get us out of our immediate financial difficulty. The difficulty, of course, is because of the drastic cuts in research, and science in general, imposed by dear Nixon. David thinks we might not get <u>any</u> of the money for Gombe West. Heaven only knows what we shall do then! . . .

Fifi's ghastly wound, got in a fight with Humphrey, is just about better. The poor thing — it went deep, and seemed to itch — I think there were maggots down there. Anyway, she kept moving to other chimps, head down, wanting them to groom it for her. But they were scared, especially Hugo, and hurried away making little hoo sounds. It was awful to watch. But we got her to take a massive dose of anti-biotics, and maybe that did the trick. Figan is still challenging Humphrey, backed by Faben — sometimes backed by Evered. Sometimes Figan backs Humphrey against Evered. He's clever that one! Magnificent Grinner, king of beach troop for 5 years, is faltering. Believe it or not, but Crease is challenging. Also a younger male who has cleverly formed a close bond with the dominant female ap-

---

* Jane and Hugo's accountant in England.
† Stanford undergraduates David Riss, Cricket Lyman, Chuck de Sieyes, Mark Leighton, and Henry Klein.

parently in order to have easy access to her black infant. When Grinner is near, Ebony takes the infant — he is thus safe from attack by Grinner and can take liberties.* It is amazing to watch.

I must close. The house, with its veranda, is really super, and you have to come, Mum, and see it. Emilie is really amazing — she wants to stay 1 1/2 years, and has everything in hand. Hugo was very cheerful when I last saw him, and have had a gay letter from him since. The hyenas are behaving themselves, and his equipment is more or less working.

Tons and tons of love to all,
Jane & Ub

FRIDAY THE THIRTEENTH!
APRIL [1973]
En route from East to West†

Dear All at Gombe,

I do not have a vast amount of news to report to you. I think the financial picture for Gombe is far better than I dared hope, but that we are going to have to be VERY careful between now [and] November when the renewal starts. (If we get it, which we almost certainly will.) Thank Goodness we are not running on Government funds. That scene is grim: I will be writing again as soon as I have talked with Hazel Eikworth who does the accounting.

So far as Gombe West is concerned the picture appears to be very grim. We have to fight very hard indeed on that front. However, it's worth fighting for. I'm actually on my way to see the chimps at the moment, before starting at Stanford on Monday. Of course, I have another shingle — suspect it's related to my small pox vaccination as the virus is supposed to be of the same family.

Do please write about anything of interest — everything will be of value to the fund-raising drive. Peggy Nichols is dying to get her material about Freud — someone was doing a photo/photos?

My return, I deeply regret, will be slightly delayed unless you get

---

* Grinner, Crease, and Ebony were baboons.
† Addressed to the students at Gombe as she is leaving for Stanford.

in a panic. I have booked plane for 22nd May. The girl from Gambia* will be coming with me for a few weeks. I suppose the Ehrlich contingent will arrive at the same time.

I rang your father, Caroline, & had a good talk. Your parents were out or away, Anthony — again on my return journey. And I had great talks with your parents, Chuck. Your father is very thrilled about Case Western. John Crock is going there too.† Take care, find out lots, write —

Yours —<br>Jane

2 July 1973

Dear Robert,

First, very many thanks for sending the cable about the baboon ecology fellowship girl (I've left it in the other building and her name slips my mind at present). Secondly, the good news. I've just got back from a really rather super trip to Dar. I showed the film to all the Members of Parliament — outside what they call the Bunge, which I think is a super name! It went down well. And then I had the most fabulous talk with the President. He is a truly incredible person — I mean, one knows this, and I'd met him before, but this time was very different. I last met him about 6 years ago and he looked lonely and ill. Now he radiates strength, together with an amazing quality of gentleness which makes his personality quite unique in my experience. He was quite adamant about no tourism for Gombe, which is the best news in years.

Now, about research clearance. There should be no major problems. There might be slight delays. It is January you want her to come? There are a couple of other points, which I'll mention to you now, but which maybe I should correspond directly with her about also — let me know what you think.

---

* Stella Brewer, who had been working on a rehabilitation project for orphaned chimps in West Africa.
† Stanford students Chuck de Sieyes and John Crocker were going to medical school at Case Western University.

(a) She should definitely get some working knowledge of Swahili. We are making this a requirement now, and students without it are finding themselves at a severe disadvantage since the field assistants are contributing more and more information, and it is not good not to be able to communicate. (This applies very much to the baboon work, incidentally.)

(b) There are certain requirements which I feel we should set out in a more formal way than before — types of data which we want collected for the long term records (such as the travel and group charts for the chimps, and the summaries which we also need for the baboons) copies of field data which must either be left here or guaranteed to be returned. (This is a requirement of S.R.I., with which we shall soon be affiliated, so that their rules will apply here.) Quarterly reports for government. Things of this sort. I should welcome your views on ways of doing this.

(c) I imagine you have found out that she is not any kind of hermit or difficult person in other ways. The group I have here now is quite superb. You thought it was good when you were here — so did I. You should just see this one! To have anyone come in and spoil it would be a disaster. Mitzi (who has arrived safely) can't get over what is going on here. It is the way I have always dreamed of it, without one single person being possessive or selfish, and with everyone helping everyone — chimp people help baboon people and vice versa, and learn each other's animals. Several chimp people know camp troop adult baboons. It is really super.*

[January 22, 1974]

Dear Jim,

The L.S.B. Leakey Foundation thought that it might be useful for people interested in the research at Gombe to know just exactly what were [our] needs. It was suggested that I write separately to everyone who attended the dinner in Chicago in the fall — but I feel

---

* This and a few other letters are typed but unsigned carbon copies.

a little diffident and prefer not to do this. Therefore I am sending to you a list of the projects for which we need support in the hopes that you might pass the information on to any of the guests who came under your auspices and whom you feel might in fact be at all helpful.

I have now been back at Gombe for a couple of weeks, and am really delighted at how very well things seem to be going. The team of students gets better and better — and this, of course, reflects the fact that their training and orientation to the work prior to coming is constantly improving. I am particularly delighted at how well our Tanzanian field assistants are doing. In a country such as this their participation is, of course, essential. But it is a fact that we could not operate Gombe efficiently without them. They provide the continuity so very necessary in a long term project such as this. They know the chimps and baboons, the mountains, the food plants and the behaviour patterns. Their own data collection becomes ever more sophisticated. They have a boundless enthusiasm for the work, and for learning more and more. So that we have weekly seminars with them. It's very exciting.

The ranger Training Scheme, which I talked to you about, is actually beginning to bear fruits. The first two, from Ruaha National Parks, have finished their 4 month training at Gombe, and returned to set up their own research at Ruaha. I visited there on the way back to Gombe, to get them started properly. It was nearly the last trip I ever made. The pilot made a crash landing, fearing fire because of a smell from the engine. Luckily the Director of National Parks, Mr. Bryceson, was with us and was himself a war pilot. It was he who switched off the engine and undoubtedly saved our lives. As it was we simply didn't know how (1) we survived at all and (2) were not even hurt. The plane was a complete write off. Lost its wheels, propeller, buckled a wing, damaged the tail. What an experience. Grub was really super and did exactly what he was told. I was proud of him. Anyway, that gave me an extra day with the Rangers, and I was proud of them too. I think this whole scheme is going to be very meaningful to Tanzania, to conservation, to the appreciation of animals by people themselves. I'm very enthusiastic. We start training the next two within the next couple of months.

It was really good seeing you again in Chicago, and I very much hope that I can see you again sometime this year.

10 Feb [1974]

Darling Mum,

So many thanks for the long letter, which <u>was</u> in the book Billy brought, but stuck. I just found it. But oh dear — you do sound <u>more</u> than frantic. . . .

Ub news. <u>SUPER</u> school with Helen. She is working VERY hard & he is reading like a dream. It's amazing. Helen is not <u>too</u> happy, but getting happier daily — & Grub is what is making her day. Thing is this — Hugo has a HOUSE, as I told you. I think it would be best, all round, if Helen takes Grub to Serengeti & goes on teaching him while I am those 3 weeks in USA. I <u>know</u> you will all miss Grub, but <u>you</u> are frantic, & for his sake I think it would be best. He loves his school, loves Helen — & has expressed the wish to "stay with Daddy because the America stay is short". I hope you will not all be too upset. I havn't suggested it to Hugo yet, but I know he will like it, & with Helen it will be really good. Then you will be less frantic. I hardly liked to suggest it, but when I got your last letter I felt it would be a good thing.

Gombe still great. All my students have taken to sleeping in chimp nests. John got "nest sick" last night! Late this month or early next dear John (Crocker) wants to dump a box of my data in the flat for a week. I'll give him all the numbers — I've said he can stay the night — he can have my room — our room. Hope that is okay. <u>So</u> glad Penny is still there — SUPER. Derek arrives unexpectedly on Sunday — in the new plane given to us by — GRZIMEK!! (in replacement of the smashed one). There is lots of news really — but anon.

Oh — most important. I read the 'rationale' of your chapter. I think it is SUPER. I'll read it again, more carefully. But from 1st reading — I have only favourable comments & no criticisms. I'll read it again tomorrow. I feel like you. But for less reason. I've been typing till 2 & 3 each night. First your chapter, 1–2 hours. Then letters when too tired for chapter! However, went with Helen & Ub to waterfall today — good for the soul. Climbed <u>vines.</u>

Loads love,<br>Jane

5 March 1974

Darling Family,

First — Mum. Have no idea whether the Fleur/Leakey volume has gone to press.* But I do hope this can catch it. Done in a bit of a rush. Please edit if you think. I didn't know where to send it, so am hoping you can pass it on for me. Hope you think it's okay. I'd forgotten all about it.

Grub. He's not having his proper birthday until 18th, as I think I told you. Then Derek will bring all kinds of things from Dar, which we can't get here. We're planning a super party for him, though we havn't quite got ideas yet — other than what I told you. Eating his fish, on the beach with a fire outside the house, and with pancakes (If Derek can get any flour. We certainly can't. Havn't had flour for months).

But he had a sort of birthday on his birthday. Sope came back, for one. He'd been back before, but had not been playing with Grub. Now, yesterday, he did. And Grub was thrilled. They climbed trees and had great fun, and he had the morning off school. For lunch he was to have worms, but they turned out to be snakes!† Anyway, luckily he loved the dish (though I was scared, when I saw it, he'd hate it — macaroni cheese). And I'd ordered him custard and banana. And Helen made him some super green peppermint sort of fondant things. Scrummy, anyway. In the afternoon we had a very long swim, with lots of tickling and fun. And I'd found one of his old kites, which I'd put away, and so I produced it, and that was great fun. And he had a special kind of fish for supper, and coconut

---

* Louis Leakey had died on October 1, 1972. Fleur Meyer, of the London chapter of the L. S. B. Leakey Foundation, was editing a memorial tribute to him.
† In other words, the hoped-for thin spaghetti turned out to be thicker macaroni.

pudding, and one of his green sweets. And some ginger wine! So he really had a jolly nice birthday. A bit of Gulliver's Travels thrown in somewhere along the line. I'm saving his cards and things — just as well, as two more trickled in today.

Had a simply ghastly time on Friday. Grub had this toothache. I think I didn't tell you, as I didn't want to worry you. Anyway, it flared up once before I did my lectures at Dar. I thought of taking him, but it was going to be a tough trip for him — night at Ruaha, 3 at Dar, Arusha, then night at Ndutu, then back. I thought it would be grim. Anyway, the tooth didn't hurt any more, and I thought a much better plan would have been for him to go with Billy and Pierre* to Dar, be met by Derek, go to the dentist, and then Steve was going to bring him straight back. Grub himself thought that was an excellent plan. Then, of course, Billy and Pierre cancelled. Well, the tooth came back one night about 9 nights ago, now. And the next day. But then completely went. I was working out ways of getting him to Dar, and then thought of this super mission hospital — Kabanga — where the fabulous Sister Margaret is — Irish, and always makes me think of Rixy and the nuns. Anyway, it turned out that there is a Sister Kate there, who is an excellent dentist. So Emilie made an appointment. Of course, by the Thursday, Grub's tooth had not hurt him for a week. I asked if he wanted to go, and he thought for a while, and then said that though he knew it would hurt, it would be worse to have it hurting again when he wasn't at a dentist. I thought that was marvellous!

Well, as usual, I funked the idea of going with him, and Emilie, who loves Kabanga and the sisters, was longing to take him. She had arranged for our great taxi man in Kigoma, Mikidadi, to drive there. About 60 miles. And Helen was going along as well. I consulted Grub about the arrangements. Said I was willing to go with him, but didn't like being there when he might be going to be hurt. He gave his little smile, and said he wouldn't like to watch me being hurt either, and he would like to go with Emilie.

Well, they set off, and he was very gay. It was raining, and he was

---

* Pierre was the wife of Billy Collins.

*The tool-using bird of the Serengeti.*

Jane and Grub inside "the Cage" at Gombe, 1967.

In the beach house at Gombe. Melissa is curious about the baby, 1967.

*Jane and Hugo playing kickball with Grub on the Serengeti, 1968.*

*On the Serengeti with Grub and George Dove, 1969.*

*Grub started fishing when he was two years old.*

*Portrait of Goliath.*

*Hugo and Figan.*

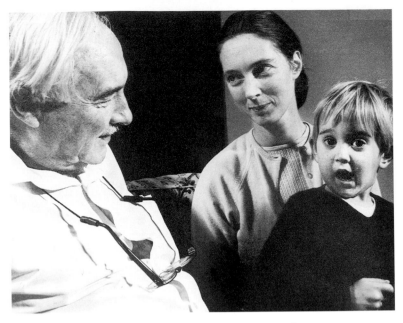

*Jane and Grub with Louis Leakey, London, 1970.*

*Students at Gombe. Top row (left to right): Curt Busse, Caroline Tutin, Grant Heidrich, Anthony Collins, Julie Johnson, Emilie Riss, Jane Goodall. Seated: Jim Moore, Lisa Nowell, John Crocker, 1974.*

*A chimp threatening a "stranger" in the mirror.*

*Charging males (J.B. and Humphrey).*

*Flo transports Fifi and a growing Flint.*

*Derek and Wilkie playing tug-of-war with a cap.*

*Grub and Derek relaxing at home in Dar es Salaam.*

*Grub playing with Wagga on the beach at Dar es Salaam.*

*Jane and Derek,*
*1976.*

*Derek with some of his constituents.*

*Jane and Grub outside the house at Gombe, 1980.*

*With Dian Fossey
at the Explorer's Club,
New York, 1982.*

*Jane ready for a day in the field with everything packed in her pockets, Gombe, 1987.*

*Receiving condolences from "Mwalimu" (Julius Nyerere, first president of Tanzania), after Derek's death, 1981.*

*With Professor Kinji Imanishi,
the "father of primatology," in Japan, 1982.*

*Jane with U.S. Secretary of State James Baker III (left) and Gilbert M.
Grosvenor, president of the National Geographic Society, 1992.*

*With Mikhail Gorbachev and Fred Matser at
the State of the World Forum, 1996.*

*Roots & Shoots members examine a wildflower, 1999.*

*Evening relaxation on the shore of Lake Tanganyika.*

draped in a black shiney plastic mac (mine) and lying in front of the boat looking down at the water and having great fun.

Don't worry if I'm not back until 8.00 had been Emilie's last words. Well, of course, I did worry when it got to 8.30. We all talked of everything under the sun until just after 9.00. Then we began going through all the things that could have happened. Finally I said I couldn't stand it any longer. So I planned to walk along to the ranger post where the Parks boat lies, borrow it, drive slowly to Kigoma looking out for a broken down boat, and see what was up. It was after 10 by the time we'd got petrol ready in case we had to come back here to get it — if Parks didn't have enough — and got a rope and a few tools, torches, etc. Tony was coming with me, and Grant. We set off — and had gone for literally not more than 10 minutes when we heard the boat. Whew!

Well, Grub was gay as a lark. He'd had TWO teeth out — an upper left molar (the one in front of the one which had the abscyss) and a lower right. Sister Kate wrote me a sweet letter, and had had a wonderful time because he was so good. Emilie said he was fantastic. He'd been eating away — still eating when he got into the dining room at 10.30. All the students were there, gathered round him, and he was showing everyone his teeth, saved in bandage, and having the time of his life. He could have had two more abscysses (or however you spell them). She says he will have trouble with his new teeth cos there isn't room. So I guess he'll have to have some out to make room. That will be no sweat for Grub!! He really is miraculous. He chatted away about having some more out later, to make way for new ones! He had led Sister Kate by the hand to help her develop the X-ray she took of his teeth! On the drive home he'd spied bamboo, and remembered that Jane needed bamboo for her curtain. So he and Emilie and Mikidadi cut three poles — well, they were 9 feet long, about 6 inches in diameter — (I needed a 5 foot long 1/2 inch diameter rod for a curtain!) So I have to think of something to do with them, he's so proud of them. The reason they were late, by the way, was that Sister Kate got held up and sent word she couldn't get to the hospital till 4.00. Emilie, rightly, felt she must stay there, having driven 60 miles, and get it done! So.

What an adventure — and what a relief for me. There was an incredible storm that night, and after the worrying I couldn't sleep so I sat on the beach at 3.00 and watched this amazing lightning.

Many, many thanks for your super letter, Olly. What a surprise! Do hope you're all okay. Havn't heard about the election yet! We feel very remote. Me, Juliet and Tony are the only British here, and none of us seem to care, d'you know! Tony goes to Edinburgh in April. Comes back here after the summer. We shall miss him. Luckily Robert's Juliet is charming, and Larry and Helen are doing fine, and with Dave Riss and Anne Pusey coming back we'll have a super team. Grant and Curt and deep voiced Kitt all still doing just fine.*

Must end — still lots of letters. Now have the radio telephone to Dar working, which is super. We can get messages through every morning. Makes a difference, to be in contact with the outside world like that. Keep forgetting, though, to ask about the election result!

Tons of love —

Jane

P.S. Mum — hope the <u>end</u> of the chapter arrived safely. Cable if it didn't.

29th March [1974]

Dear Emilie,

A hundred million million apologies for my leaving things behind. I do hope you found that manuscript for Glyn Isaac's chapter, poor wretched man. It should have been with Feb's monthly report. If you havn't found the latter, could you look — it's in one of those cardboard folders with monthly report written on it!

Here it is cold, grey — snowing in the morning. I miss you all so much. I ACHE for Grub. I'm off to try & find him some cards — I know he doesn't like letters.

---

* Recent arrivals included Juliet Oliver from Cambridge, as well as Grant Heidrick, Curt Busse, and Kitt Morris from Stanford.

Hope things are okay. It was lucky I caught Hugo — or he caught me! But unfortunate that, because of that, things got in a muddle. Please write often & tell me about Grub. Tell Helen to write and tell me ALL about him. I'll write myself & ask her too.

I'm still scatty. I left 2 vital things in London. And I did buy Grub a few cards this morning & left them in the shop. So now I must be on the way, into the cold, to go & see if they are still there, in their little paper bag! Poor me. In a bad way!

David, Molly & Cathy will have arrived by the time you get this.* Give them, as well as everyone, my love. I had, by the way, 2 very good plane trips, especially the EA airways Nairobi–London. I had 3 seats all to myself — stretched out & actually slept! Did have a 3 hour sit in Frankfurt. But that was OK. I got 15 letters written on the flight, and 12 on the London–USA flight. Flo's bones are safely here.† I was greeted by the airport manager who said was I Dr Goodall & could he help me. What luck! So I explained, & was seen through customs in a private room in a few moments. Smashing.

Much much love,
HEAPS & HEAPS FOR GRUB
Jane

Good Friday [April 12, 1974]‡

Hello Everyone,

I'm afraid the typing will be terrible — not quite sure why, but anyway, hope you'll be able to read. I had to go out to a fund raising dinner last night and was not brought home until terribly late — it's awful not having a car — you make noises about going, but can't exactly get up and leave when your host is driving you! Oh well, I'll recover soon!

Well — first the best news. The first group of chimps is moving in, for sure (well, things still can go wrong I suppose!) on Friday week — next Friday. They will be knocked out on Wednesday and

---

* Stanford students David Riss, Molly Brecht, and Cathy Clark.

† Flo's skeleton went to Mary Ellen Morbeck at the University of Arizona.

‡ Written from Stanford, addressed to "everyone" at Gombe.

taken, in cages, to the inside cages at Gombe West. And then, after recovering inside for 2 days, they will be let out at about 7.00 a.m. in the morning on the Friday. It is a super group now, for Zippy has been added to Bashful, Topsy, Willy and Babu. Zippy is about 1 year older than Babu, and a super little fellow. They all started grooming his eyes (that is a characteristic of the group, eye grooming) until they ran, and the more they ran, the more the others groomed them, until, by the second day, he had such swollen eyes he almost couldn't see. Dr. Pinneo almost took him out, but he suddenly asserted himself, and so all was well. It will be so super to see them out in that great enclosure.

Unfortunately, I shall have to leave after lunch, as I'm going down to poor forgotten Pal* at Lion Country, to see him and the chimps — especially Palita. (Who is now bald!) Bido is probably pregnant too! Hope she has a little boy. A very nice girl I met at Oklahoma is working on mother-infant, and feeling very depressed because she says the conditions are not good there, and her data are therefore invalid. So I've invited her to Stanford to meet our group — they are doing such marvellous things. I'm really excited about it all — David, you will have told them all about everything, so I'll not need to repeat. But let me just say — first, thank you (still talking to David) for all that you did, and second, that I think your sleeping paper is super, and ready for publication (Dr. Hamburg is reading it over the weekend), and the Figan document is going to be excellent. I'm much looking forward to discussing it with you when I get back to Gombe. . . .

Well — love to you all — Larry, Kitt, Curt, Dave, Molly, Tony, Juliet, Grant, Jim, Kathy — am assuming that Helen and Lisa have left. Carry on the good work, write to me — and see you soon. Quite soon, really, by the time you get this letter, I should think.

Love,<br>Jane

---

* Pal Midget was a devoted caretaker who worked with a group of the chimpanzees going to SOPF.

[Postmarked January 19, 1975]

Darling Family — Darling Grub —

How are you all I wonder — and especially Happy Birthday Um. We shall be thinking of you on your Birthday. Derek arrives that day & we'll drink you a toast.

I'm very lonely here without you, Grub. The fish are fine — they've grown & grown. Spotted Jane is quite big now. Both the eels are fine — they seem to like one another very much. It is raining & raining and raining. All night and morning yesterday — & very dull seeming today. I hope this gets posted — Dominic is taking it into Kigoma — he's off on leave. Did I give you a picture of Dominic in his new hat? I'm sure I had one done for him, but it's not here. Too bad! If it's in that collection of slides I left — with you, Um, or Olly — could you get a print made & send it here with all due speed. Many thanks.

Well — it seems so long since I left — so much has happened. Things really are <u>fine</u> here at Gombe. A very happy & quite different Emilie — Gombe has cured her. She is off to Stanford for the summer! Doing her own study now — I always thought she would. Don't mention to <u>ANYONE</u> who might know the people — but she & Dave Riss are <u>very</u> fond of one another.

Grub — I'm so longing for you to come. It all seems strange & peculiar without you. I keep whispering in the evening — thinking you're asleep. And sort of <u>looking</u> for you everywhere. Waiting for you to come into my bed to wake me in the morning. The wagtails are very busy chasing other wagtails away — probably the grown baby, for one. Then perhaps they'll make another nest.

Lots of love to all — Dan, Olly, Aud, Rix.
Happy B. Um —
Happy sausages Grub,*
Jane — Mum

---

\* Jane sometimes closed her letters with this expression, which originated with Grub. While staying overnight at the home of some friends, he had once caused great amusement by saying, at bedtime, "Happy Sausages," instead of the usual "Happy Dreams."

5 March 1975

Darling Family,

Was glad to have your letter full of news, Mum. I gather the package missed Barnes — will have to come with Jo!* The birthday cards all arrived in time — & he had a <u>fantastic</u> birthday. It was actually really nice that he forgot his rod in Dar — since it arrived, all new, for his birthday. And the evening before his birthday, the evening after D & the rod arrived, he caught a really big fish with it! (He celebrated his birthday on the Saturday because all the students have the afternoon off then).

Well — the day, amazingly, was bright & sunny. He fished all morning & caught a few, too. Had his big fish for lunch — enough for me & D also. He was very pleased about that. After lunch he did things with Simon & various students while D & I finished off his things. I'd drawn his birthday card most of the morning — a sequence of fishing, 5 pages long! At 3.00 the party began. 1st — not apple bobbing, but strychnos ball bobbing.† We got absolutely <u>hysterical</u> — hope the pics Simon & I took come out! Grub won his heat <u>and</u> the finals. Then a scavenger hunt — Ub & Juliet were partners & <u>easily</u> won that! Then "stick the fish". I'd drawn 4 super big fish on a board — blindfold, you had to stick in a pin — the board having been twirled. 10 for the shark, 8 for the swordfish, 6 for the Moorish idol, 4 for the eel. Anne & Craig won that. Finally, before tea, a sack race. Simon won that — but Ub won his heat (neatly tripping me up!) Prizes — squares of choc (brought by Simon, forgotten, along with the rod, in Dar!) Then — what a cake. A super, Sadiki-made, choc. one. Iced (with runny chocolate sauce) by Anne. D had brought some Tanzanian whiskey to try — it was super over the cake! (Grub didn't partake, Danny & Aud!)

Then we 3 wandered home, had a swim. Lovely, warm, calm water. Sat on the steps & consumed apple pie — Grub's other birthday treat. He had his presents — net, fisherman's knife (Finnish), pen knife, <u>huge</u> set of Lego, nylon fishing line, little cars — just before tea. We even had birthday wrapping paper! After apple pie Grub

---

* Richard Barnes and Jo Richard were recent arrivals at Gombe.

† *Strychnos* fruits, a favorite chimpanzee food though with hard rinds, were the size and shape of tennis balls.

tucked into the regular supper, we talked, & he went off to bed. D & I felt absolutely <u>whacked</u> — a lot of organization went into it all. Anyway, we had some coffee, some brandy, & soon followed Grub to bed!

Simon came to discuss Ub's schooling with us yesterday. We have worked out a system whereby, if he works well consistently, & gets so many stars in the required subjects, he will get a reward in May — an evening dagaa fishing. Anyway, since we had a talk with him he has been working <u>very</u> hard & <u>very</u> well, and <u>very</u> cheerfully. In fact, all is very good on the Grub front.

D had been here for a week — he should have left today, but the aircraft company went wrong. Thus he must follow the railway line back to Dar, cannot get to the meeting he should have been at tomorrow in Serengeti, so has an extra day — if you follow my meaning!

We have got the house looking even more super — D brought a heap of things from Dar — super big tray, curtain material, shells & coral, baskets, <u>and</u> the posters, mounted & now hung. They look fantastic. Also, guess what he got for me? A <u>real</u> typing chair. <u>What</u> a difference that makes. My office is fantastic now. Fit for kings & queens.

Since Ub's birthday it has rained & rained & rained. Floods in the mess, waterfall(s) by the house, leaks in the roof, drenched people, drenched chimps, drenched baboons. Guess what — after a cold wet day Figan & Faben made a double-nest & slept in contact!! Amazing. Both brothers have mated their sister who is, at present, pink!

My front teeth. It won't be sensible to come & have them done before autumn. Do you suppose Mary's hubby can do them at <u>end</u> September? Something like 31st. Or even 1st or 2nd October. Stanford will have to adjust!

Emilie is about to go off to Stanford. Isn't that amazing! End of May, she leaves. <u>So</u> excited. I'll miss her, but still. She is now doing a lot of chimp work as well as helping Etha a bit with administration. She is a <u>really</u> good egg. She follows & follows. It was she who saw Figan & Faben nest together. Having got back, soaked, from one follow, she went out again. After my own heart! . . .

Saw such a marvellous white tailed mongoose outside the window. Put food out each evening & have him, civet & genet all coming. The toast is now ready. I must help carry in the tea. Onto your Xmas present cloth, Mum. With the last year's birthday present tea cosy — all very elegant.

Tons & tons & tons of Love to you all,
Jane, Ub, Derek

Dar es Salaam
27 May 1975

Dear Em, dear Carrie, dear Steve,

We are all thinking of you, we are all praying for you, all over the world. Everyone, everywhere, all sending love and prayers and hoping and hoping that you are still well in mind and body. We have spoken with your parents and they send so much love and hope.

We are all so pleased that you have been treated considerately and kindly, that you can speak with Mulele's men,* that you can listen to the news. We all feel that the most important thing for your captors is to gain world sympathy. Surely they must know that this is their chance — that by treating you well and by returning you safely to your families, the world will be most impressed in their favour. On the other hand, if they harm you, the world will be shocked and the whole operation could bring them to a much worse position than they were in before they started it.

We were surprised that your captors didn't seem to know that their comrades who were arrested in Tanzania had all been released at least two weeks <u>before</u> you were captured. In fact, their leader, Monsieur Yumbu, has left the country — presumably to rejoin his friends.†

Please try not to worry about your future. Everything is going to

---

* Possibly an error caused by some uncertainty about the identity of the kidnappers. Pierre Mulele led a Marxist-Leninist guerrilla movement against Zaïre's Mobutu during the 1960s, but he was no longer alive when this letter was written.
† Some of the guerrillas had been arrested earlier. One of the kidnappers' demands was that they be released.

be all right. All the world feels certain that your captors are humane people. We are doing all that we can do. Please believe us and try to have faith.

Let me tell you some news you will not have heard on the radio. We have, of course, had to evacuate all non-Tanzanian staff from Gombe. Etha and Tsolo are in charge, and Adie is there with them. We could not keep all the domestic staff, but have kept Sadiki and Rashidi and Bofu. The field assistants are all doing their records on the chimps and baboons. Tony and Juliet are doing fine in Ruaha, braving elephants and buffalos! and they send you their love. Barbara arrived in Dar yesterday (and was "kidnapped" again by the American embassy, where she still is). Her mother is here now, and your fathers, Carrie and Steve, and your Uncle, Em, arrive tomorrow. Almost everyone else is here with us in Dar, in the guest house, or with various friends in town.

We send all, all our love. And we're telling you not to worry. It's all going to be okay.

With so <u>much</u> love,
Jane–Derek

P.S. 2 telegrams just arrived: (1) Our love and prayers go to Emilie, Carrie, Steve and all of you. Much love. Curt, Dave and everybody. (2) For Bergmann, upon return: Em, so very, very sorry. Hope you are OK in every way. Phone as soon as possible. I love you much — David.

P.P.S. We have spoken to your Mum, Em. We have seen your fathers, Carrie & Steve. They are all okay, all strong, all firmly believe you will soon be home. Everyone is together, waiting, in Dar es Salaam.

[Postmarked 13 June 1975]

Darling Mum,

Am absolutely shocked and horrified to hear, from Olly, about your poor mouth — and you never said a word to me in your letter. You say I should tell you such things, so then you should tell us! Anyway, Derek and Ub and I are shocked and so sorry, and do hope that it will clear up without your having to go to the Dental Hospital in London. Please let us know. And hope it's feeling much better. Note Olly says it doesn't affect your talking or your drinking! There was one time on the telephone you sounded most peculiar, and I thought you were angry about something — maybe it was your jaw. . . .

Things plod along here. I didn't ring about the messenger we sent over because he never went! The son got ill again, and they didn't set off. We got very, very depressed. It began to seem as though someone was paying everyone <u>not</u> to go. But now it looks up again — the son was genuinely ill — his hernia played up. He's been to the doctor, is now fit, and they are setting off on Saturday. Relationship with the American Ambassador is now good, they have a new and reasonable man in Kigoma, and he is in radio contact with Dar. So he is going to radio back as soon as he knows the old man has set off. With all the packages. In the mean-time the Dutch and U.S.A. ambassadors have received letters, reiterating the demands, and asking that we send over someone to negotiate in a boat with a white flag. So we have added, to the old man's letter, that we suggest the middle of the lake, or somewhere on this side. (And we have also suggested walkie talkies of course. No one thinks it would be wise for anyone to go over there.) Anyway, provided they set out, they will be back on Monday, they say. Again, if there is any exciting news we'll ring. . . .

What else? Nothing much. Michelle* is helping with the fathers, Dave is helping everyone. The poor USA Ambassador is going crazy with the fathers sort of pressuring him to do things all the time, when he is. No one blaming those poor fathers — just that it does make things so difficult for everyone, them being here, everyone feeling so sorry for them — awful for them, nothing to do. We're having them to lunch in a couple of days. Must go into town and post this.

Tons and tons of love to everyone,
Jane

---

* Stanford student Michelle Trudeau.

[Postmarked July 18, 1975]

Darling Family,

Super to hear your voices, Um & Danny, the other night. Sorry you couldn't hear me, Dan! At the moment Grub & I are in the house in Arusha (it used to be John Owens' & now belongs to Parks). It is lonely & cold. While Derek was at the office yesterday afternoon Grub & I walked around town searching for <u>INCENCE</u> sticks for him!! And a few other bits. Then we walked home & made the house look a bit like home — flowers, rearrange chairs — then we collected lots of wood for the fire & lit a super fire. So we had a super cosy evening (ending with D & I having Irish coffee when Ub was in bed). Now D is finishing off his things in the office & Ub and I have lit the fire again. The Rangers have been practicing "Parade" outside. Now they have gone. We have Mendelssohn's violin concerto playing & a huge super alsatian lying on the floor & Grub is V. excited about a drawing of aeroplanes bombing ships etc.

The whole kidnapping business is so side-making. The Americans don't really tell us what they're doing — we just found out that Mr. Hunter is going to Kigoma today. Why? The students said things were looking optimistic — but we're not in the picture. Perhaps he's taking some more money. Who knows. I'm feeling V. relieved to be out of it. Utterly tied up with Em being peculiar & all the tensions going on. Poor Dave, he was coming to lunch on Monday, but was sick again. He's been sick all the time. He sounded in the very <u>depths</u> of gloom — thinking things might drag on another month. Perhaps Hunter & co. feel that Steve may appear soon because the original 60 days will be up on 18th July. Hope, I <u>hope</u> so. Then they can all go home. Jo arrives in Arusha today & will get somehow to Seronera. (Only 4 seats in our little plane.) I gather the roses for Dan didn't work?

Now have Bruch's violin — super. Did I tell you about the party Ub went to? Of David-next-door? He had a good time except that when they were finding hidden money he didn't find enough! And he would have preferred a choc. cake to a hamburger! Unfortunately they are off on leave — so when Ub gets back from Serengeti his friend — as well as his teacher — will have gone. Damn the

PRP(!) How can they demand <u>publicity</u> in exchange for Steve. I'll give them some publicity if I get the chance when Steve is back! I bet Spider is missing us! But Ann Pierce is there and Richard. If you have a chance to send a few sea-sick pills back with Tony — or even in an envelope to 727 — for Grub who gets a tummy-ache in a little plane. If you send a couple by return we'll have them for when we go & collect Ub after his holiday with Hugo.

Tons & tons & tons of love,

Jane

Love from Grub

# 7

# THE DARK SIDE

## 1975–1979

Then, suddenly, we found that chimpanzees could be brutal —
that they, like us, had a dark side to their nature.

— *Reason for Hope*

A PERSON ENTERING the forest of a chimpanzee community
for the first time will be astonished by the clearly recognizable gestures of affection, comradeship, and good will
among those wild apes: embraces, kisses, mutual grooming, handholding, play, chasing and tickling, and even laughter. The social life
of chimpanzees is remarkable for its positive emotional tenor.

From the first observations at Gombe, it was evident also that the
chimpanzees could be aggressive and sometimes violent, albeit in a
seemingly controlled or comprehensible fashion. Males regularly
bluffed and threatened, and they sometimes fought one another seriously, even viciously, during the politically unstable periods when
the male dominance hierarchy was uncertain or shifting. The males
also regularly threatened and sometimes attacked females, once
again in a pattern and style that might be recognized as the expression or establishment of dominance. Yet those forms of violence —
though impressively earnest, sometimes damaging, and potentially
lethal — ordinarily ended once the loser acknowledged defeat by
gestures of submission to the winner. As distressing as such attacks
might seem, they never appeared to be killers' attacks. They never
seemed comparable to the worst sorts of human violence.

Human violence can be so disturbing and unexpected that we

sometimes prefer to deny its potential and significance, to imagine it as somehow alien, as separate from our true selves. Human violence in its more extreme forms, we tell ourselves, is "unnatural," meaning that it is beyond or beneath "human nature." Having simplified our analysis of human character into the false disjunction of *nature* versus *nurture,* we then assign the better aspects of ourselves to nature and the worse to nurture. The most extreme human violence, we sometimes say, really must be a consequence of culture.

The cultural theory of human violence is at once convenient and hopeful, since it allows us to assign blame simply and imagine solutions quickly. Indeed, specific cultural or legal or social changes in specific societies around the world will certainly reduce the appearance and alter the style of human violence. But a culture-only theory requires us to ignore deeper, more disturbing and fundamental truths about individuals and societies, and so it dims our understanding and limits our ability to change. In her recent book *Reason for Hope,* Jane Goodall tells of participating in a UNESCO conference in Paris during the 1970s in which the analysis of human behavior was already distressingly politicized. No one wanted to hear that violence might be partly an aspect of human biology. "I was amazed to hear scientists whom I greatly respected solemnly declare that all aggression, in their opinion, was learned."* By the late 1980s, an international forum of twenty distinguished scientists had signed a formal declaration on behalf of UNESCO pronouncing, with all their learned authority, that war was certainly a "peculiarly human phenomenon [that] does not occur in other animals" since, after all (and fortunately), it is "a product of culture."†

As with war, so with cannibalism. Discoveries inside the Baume Moula-Guercy cave on the Rhone River seem to indicate that Neanderthals butchered and ate one another 100,000 years ago, leading some researchers to conclude that Neanderthals must have been capable of "very elaborate intellectual behavior." After all, there was no indication that the Neanderthals were starving; thus, declared the French paleontologist Alban Defleur, they must have been eat-

---

* *Reason for Hope,* p. 119.
† Quoted in Richard Wrangham and Dale Peterson, *Demonic Males: Apes and the Origins of Human Violence* (Boston: Houghton Mifflin, 1996), p. 176.

ing their fellows for symbolic or ritualistic purposes — as humans would.* In short, even some otherwise sophisticated scientific observers presume that cannibalism requires the presence of a humanlike symbolic culture.

And yet cannibalism has been observed among a number of nonhuman species: lions, leopards, and hyenas, for example, as well as redtail monkeys and baboons. The first sign of cannibalism among the chimpanzees of Gombe occurred on September 15, 1971, when researcher David Bygott witnessed a group of males from the study community who happened upon a "stranger" female (from a neighboring community) with her infant. The males, led by alpha male Humphrey, attacked the stranger wildly, seized her baby, and three of the group ate pieces of the baby.†

The incident was deeply disturbing, but the ringleader Humphrey was already known as a particularly brutal fellow "with a history of vicious attacks on females of his own community." Jane and others at camp therefore speculated hopefully that perhaps Humphrey was simply the chimpanzee equivalent of a "psychopath."‡ By that time, moreover, it was obvious that chimpanzees treated non-community members very differently, much more aggressively, than they did members of their own community. So the researchers concluded that this instance of cannibalism was probably the more or less accidental by-product of generalized vicious aggression by Kasakela community males on an outsider adult female.

Nearly four years later, in August of 1975, a Kasakela adult female, Passion, was observed seizing the three-week-old infant of Gilka, another female in the community. As Jane noted in her letters of September 24 and October 14, Passion killed Gilka's baby with a bite to the forehead and then, joined by her daughter Pom, ate the infant. The event took place after all non-Tanzanian researchers had been removed from Gombe as a consequence of the May 19

---

* *Discover* magazine, December 1999, p. 24.
† Mentioned in *Reason for Hope*, p. 112. For a fuller description, see *The Chimpanzees of Gombe*, p. 298: "Only a few of the individuals present ate, or tried to eat, any of the flesh, and only Mike and Humphrey ate for more than a few minutes."
‡ *Reason for Hope*, p. 112.

kidnapping, and the research station was guarded by a Tanzanian army field force. Jane and Derek were only occasionally allowed to visit the research site from their home in Dar es Salaam during that period; the Tanzanians who had taken over day-to-day research and observations reported the gruesome events to them by radio.

Passion's cannibalism was shocking in part because it seemed so different from the 1971 attack and cannibalism reported by David Bygott. First, the attack was perpetrated by an individual adult female. Second, it had been against a member of the community, not a stranger. And third, Passion, instead of focusing her violence on the mother, had seized and then quite methodically consumed the infant. It appeared to be a deliberate act of cannibalism for the purpose of acquiring food.

In the summer of 1976, Gilka gave birth again. Her male infant was named Orion, and, as Jane reported in the letter written around August 26, 1976, Gilka and Orion were being followed by a team of observers for a month: "At least if it [the infant] must get eaten, we had better know the facts, horrible as it all is." But the subsequent two letters of October 4 tell us that Gilka lost Orion as well. This time the murderous mother and daughter, Passion and Pom, together seized the newborn. "I just cried and cried when I heard that over the radio," Jane wrote of Gilka's loss. Gilka was "such a sad chimp" with an "utterly pathetic" history, including a chronic fungus infection disfiguring her face.

A revealing related event is recounted in the second of the October 4 letters. While Passion and Pom were joined in their cannibal feast by two others (Passion's elder son, Prof, and the orphan Skosha), a third chimp, Sparrow, "picked up a bit of meat, after staring and staring, sniffed it" and then, in an act of apparent disgust and powerful aversion, "flung it down and vigorously wiped her fingers on the tree trunk." Cannibalism within the community, it might seem, was not merely a rare and anomalous behavior. Like incest and intracommunity killing, cannibalism may have been for the ordinary ape citizens of Gombe a terrible violation of something like a chimpanzee "moral code."

About a year earlier, a community female named Melissa lost her baby. Observers had been alerted by the sounds of a fierce fight a couple of miles away from the provisioning area; by the time they reached the scene, they found the baby dead, bitten through the forehead in the killing style of Passion and Pom, with Melissa surrounded by a party of Kasakela males and appearing to shrink away from the two cannibalistic females. Perhaps, the Gombe staff concluded, the males had intervened after an attack by Passion and Pom, though not quickly enough to save the baby's life. Now, as we read in the first October 4 letter, Melissa was pregnant once again and due to give birth at any moment. Indeed, though Jane has not written about it in the letters, by November 1976 Passion and Pom had struck once again, seizing and eating Melissa's three-week-old infant.

There were other episodes. Less than a year later, Passion and Pom made a serious attempt to steal the newborn of Little Bee. Fortunately, Jane witnessed their approach, and she and Gombe administrator Emmanuel Tsolo made a commotion that may have helped Little Bee escape (August 1977 letter). And as we see in the letter of November 8, 1977, Melissa gave birth again, this time to twins (subsequently named Gyre and Gimble). Although Passion, Pom, and Prof attempted to seize one of the twins, the field assistants closed in and "prepared for the battle," while Melissa "shot down the tree," bit Prof in the neck, and threatened Pom. Pom meanwhile was recovering from injuries of her own, while Passion may have been "too pregnant to bother" any further.

Passion gave birth late in 1977, and since Jane had hoped a new baby might somehow end the mother's cannibalistic attacks and thus usher in a peaceful era, she named him Pax. Alas, in June 1978, Passion made "a very serious attempt at grabbing Mo from Miff." Later that year, Pom gave birth to her own son, Pan; and (October/November 1978 letter) Pom, upon seeing her baby-killing mother, ran away with the newborn. Passion followed her fleeing daughter, slowly and patiently, and eventually Pom relaxed. "I wonder — " Jane wrote hopefully, "maybe this will be the end of infant killing for a while." It was. Passion died of an unidentified disease in 1982, orphaning her then four-year-old son, Pax, who was raised by his sister, Pom, and his brother, Prof. A strong gust of wind swept Pom's son, Pan, out of a tree to his death in 1981. Pom disappeared in 1983 and was eventually seen within another chimp community to the north.

During this terrible period of baby-snatching and cannibalism, a second dark drama was unfolding. In her letters from this period, Jane regularly referred to the "murders" taking place, and frequently they were indeed deliberate killings of chimpanzees she knew well and often regarded as friends. If those same killings had taken place in a human context, however, their circumstances might lead us to describe them not as simple murders but as war atrocities.

During the early 1970s, as alluded to briefly at the start of the previous chapter, Gombe researchers had a unique opportunity to observe social interactions at the edges of a chimpanzee community. The community that had been under observation around the provisioning area — a social group of several adult males and females, along with their dependent young — divided into two subcommunities. This split occurred gradually, over many months, and it was most clearly defined by the actions of the adult males. They began to arrive at the banana feeding areas from two different directions, north and south, and were organized in two increasingly distinctive groups, each with its own set of leaders: Humphrey as the alpha male of the northern group, and the brothers Hugh and Charlie as leaders of the southern, breakaway community.

In 1971, individuals alone or in groups from both subcommunities were still approaching the provisioning area. If they happened to reach it at the same time, there might be tension or a noisy commotion of dramatic and hostile displays, followed by segregated groups of chimpanzees sitting and calming one another with mutual grooming. The northern subgroup, known as the Kasakela community since its territory centered on the Kasakela Valley, consisted of eight adult males: Humphrey with Evered, Faben, Figan, Hugo, Jomeo, Mike, and Satan. Six adult males had taken up separate residence to the south, around the Kahama Valley: Charlie and Hugh with Dé, Godi, Willy Wally, and Goliath. Sniff, an adolescent at the time of the division, had also joined the splinter group. In addition, three adult females — Madam Bee, Mandy, and Wanda — and their dependent young came to be identified with the Kahama chimps.

Those fifteen males, previously members of the same community, had until the early 1970s been friends, companions, and often allies. They had known one another and lived together relatively peacefully, inhabiting the same territory, often feeding in the same places, sharing many of the same experiences. But by 1972, although they most certainly would have still remembered and recognized each other, they were increasingly divided: almost never moving together, behaving aggressively when they occasionally did meet, and in general avoiding their former companions. Only the two oldest males of the two groups, long-time friends Goliath and Hugo, still maintained some contact across the social and geographic divide. By 1973 even that association had ended. The Kasakela and Kahama chimpanzees had become two separate communities inhabiting mutually exclusive territories with a contiguous border area. The males of each community formed temporary parties that regularly patrolled their borders and sometimes made stealthy incursions into the territory of their neighbors. When a raiding patrol found neighboring chimpanzees grouped together and therefore capable of defending themselves, the intruders fled. But when the patrol happened to find solitary individuals unable to protect themselves against superior numbers, the invaders would attack wildly, brutally, and with a persistence that seemed to signify lethal intent.

From the breakaway group of Kahama males, Hugh disappeared soon after the final division, as early as 1973. In January 1974 a Gombe observer, Hilali Matama, witnessed the ten-minute attack of six Kasakela adult males on a lone Kahama male. Godi, feeding in a tree, had been caught by surprise. Humphrey pulled him to the ground and pinned him down, while the other Kasakela males stomped and beat and bit him. Godi apparently died of his injuries.

Two months later, three Kasakela males and a female, Gigi, located another Kahama male, Dé, who happened to be alone. The three males struck and kicked and bit Dé. Gigi eventually joined in, and all four of the Kasakela group pummeled and pounded their victim, dragged him on the ground, and with their teeth tore the skin away from his legs. Dé also disappeared; he probably died within a few days.

A year later, one adolescent and five adult males from Kasakela found Goliath in a clump of undergrowth, perhaps trying to hide. Goliath was quite old by that time — his hair sparse, his teeth worn to the gums — certainly not a threat to anyone. But the Kasakela males pinned down, stomped on, beat, dragged, and lifted then slammed the old male to the ground. One of the attackers sat on Goliath's back and tried to twist his leg around as if intending to break it off. Camp manager and researcher Emilie Bergmann witnessed the attack, as Jane notes in the first letter of this chapter.

Two of the three Kahama females also disappeared during this period. The third, Madam Bee, was attacked several times in 1975 and finally left to die of her injuries (letter of September 24). Her two daughters, Little Bee and Honey Bee, were recruited and mated by the Kasakela males.

A fifth male, Willy Wally, disappeared in 1976. Charlie, the sixth, was killed by a Kasakela gang in May of 1977 (June 1977 letter). And, finally, Sniff, the last of the Kahama males, was attacked and killed on November 11 of that year (December 1977 letter), thus ending forever the rebel community.

To summarize, over a period of four to five years, in a series of lethal gang raids against typically solitary and virtually defenseless victims, the Kasakela males exterminated their Kahama neighbors. Ultimately, the victorious northern males were able to expand their territory into the area previously occupied by the Kahama community and to recruit two young females formerly from Kahama. The nature and dynamics of this intercommunity warfare became better defined over time; and eventually comparable episodes at other research sites in Africa confirmed that this style of intercommunity conflict — male border patrols, male raids into enemy territory, male gang attacks on lone victims — is part of the ordinary repertoire of chimpanzee social behavior. For Jane, it was a painful discovery; and the "dark side" of chimpanzee behavior may have seemed darker than ever during those years, perhaps colored by such difficult personal events as Jane's divorce from Hugo in the summer of 1974 and, of course, the terror of the kidnapping in 1975.

Grub had tutors at Gombe, but by 1976 he was old enough to begin attending school in England. Thus, several of Jane's letters home during the second half of the decade include poignant comments to and about Grub from his mother. Still, Grub was in capable hands in Bournemouth, and his holidays in Africa must have been glorious: fossil hunting with Hugo in the Serengeti, fishing in the Indian Ocean with Derek and "a marvellous old fisherman" named Ndugu (around August 26, 1976), and then "happy as a king" (August 1977) fishing with the Gombe fisherman Maulidi and playing with his favored playmate, Sufi.

The chapter ends on a cheerful note, with the February 9, 1979, announcement that a Gombe observer ("just about the best man on the spot") was able to climb into a tree and watch the chimpanzee Winkle give birth: the first such observation in the wild. Aside from the wondrous arrival of Wunda, Winkle's female infant, other births had recently taken place or were about to: "Baby after baby after baby!!" The cannibalistic females Passion and Pom, moreover, were showing "absolutely <u>no</u> predatory interest at all." And finally, of course, the horrific war between Kasakela and Kahama was over.

*　　*　　*　　*

[February 11, 1975]

Darling Family,

A quick scrawl — to say we are all arrived safely at Gombe.* The house was virtually finished & it is <u>SUPER</u> now. We've knocked down all the walls between the rooms & the passage — so they are all bigger. I have a <u>super</u> office now. Grub has a bigger bedroom and, where the rabbits were (<u>all</u> dead) a place for a museum — which he has elected to call The Pit!! (Don't know why but I think thoughts of the Tar Pit were in his mind.)

---

* Written, of course, more than three months before the kidnapping.

He's well into school. We arrived after the slight delay late Sunday. Well — latish. He had short school on Monday, & full school today. Larry had got him a super chameleon. Everyone is fine — Michelle sends her love, Mum. She is quite settled in. There is a ghastly story about Goliath — he was murdered, in cold blood, by Faben & Satan, helped a little by Figan & Jomeo. Goblin joining in but not knowing what to do. Emilie saw it all & was in tears. It lasted 20 mins. The chimps were wild, wild, wild. It was lucky Emilie wasn't hurt herself. No sign of Goliath since. There is no chance he can be alive, though. Another major search goes out tomorrow. Horrible. And old chimp Hugo died last week. Only Mike of the old timers. He's okay.

Must fly as Derek is off tomorrow, & it's supper time. Must get Ub — who's fishing — a Milo & put him to bed. In the new bedroom he has a little desk at which I'm writing now. It has a stand, made today, with 4 beautiful quill pens in it! Looks smashing.

Hope all is well at the Birches. Glad you are gay, Ol. Hope your rheumatics will soon be feeling better in the spring, Danny. Will write longer soon.

Tons of love,
Jane
Ub
Derek

24 September 1975

Dear Joan,

Sorry to send you this. Almost certainly this Honorary Degree thing won't fit into the Washington etc schedule at the beginning of November. I thought I'd made it clear to him, but I've now packed up everything, and I can't remember the dates, and I think it will save time if you could possibly write to him, a nice letter! and tell him it won't work. . . .

Must end — shall post this at the airport at London. I'm sure there are things I should add into it, but I can't think what they are right now! Hope things are OK with you over there? All sorts of ghastly things happening at Gombe — the Kasakela chimps have killed Madam Bee, by repeatedly attacking her. And I expect you heard about Passion seizing killing and eating Gilka's adorable little infant? Oh dear. Also the Fisheries boat, which was giving a lift to our new Senior Park Assistant and one of the Field Force stationed at Gombe, protecting it, sank — and the Field Force man drowned. Poor Gombe — it seems fated just now.

But I had a super 5 days there with Derek, and the work is going very very well — even if they have to record unpleasant, gruesome, behaviour! And have just finished training 2 bright young Tanzanians who hopefully arrive at Gombe tomorrow, provided the train doesn't derail or their water taxi sink!

> Love to Arnold, and to Tita and Hugh,
> And to you — and to Lulu of course,
> Jane

October 14, 1975

Mr. Edwin W. Snider
National Geographic Society
Committee for Research and Exploration
Washington, DC 20036
Dear Ed,

Thank you for your letter of 4 September about video equipment. It is an oversight on our part that we did not inform you about its usefulness. I think I need say little here since I have talked to Harold Bauer and he is writing a full report. However, he probably will not tell you that, for as many months as it worked, he was the happiest field worker I've known! Just like a little boy with a long coveted toy train. He got a lot out of it and so did we, for he would play back complex behavior sequences for us all to see.

Yes — it's been the worst summer ever — and the trouble is that things are not yet sorted out, as you may have heard. There seem to have been some tragic misunderstandings and I certainly hope we can all sort things out soon. The world is too full of hatred and violence just now. Even the chimp world. For instance — did you hear that little chimp Gilka lost her three-week old daughter to old female Passion — who seized it, bit into its brain and partially ate the carcass which she shared with her daughter, Pom? Ugh! We have documented four adult "murders" and three child "murders" now.

Hope I see you soon.

Yours sincerely,
Jane Goodall

P.O. Box 727
Dar es Salaam
[Around August 26, 1976]

Dear Joan,

Am feeling so guilty, oh dear oh dear. Oh deary me as Louis would have said. What with Gombe AND Grub and flu, I am vastly behind hand with everything. Mail, reports, requests, and anything else it's possible to be behind hand with. And this typing will probably be extra bad as I've just been helping Grub with his net in the cold water (it is freezing this time of year!). We spent Sunday at the island looking for shells, and the water was so cold that Grub, without a wet suit, couldn't swim at all, but he pottered on the reef and got some super things. It will be his last trip shelling as we go to Gombe day after tomorrow (his second trip) and soon after we get back — school. That will be awful, but I shall be able to catch up perhaps!

Our last trip to Gombe was simply super. They sent 8 extra field force to guard us, because of Grub being there. Jolly nice of them, and I must say, I felt a lot safer at night knowing they were constantly patrolling! If I were there on my own there is no way I'd stay in a house at night — I'd just be sleeping in the mountains with my little blanket! Anyway, as I was saying, it was a super trip. Super for Grub because he caught lots of fish, and super for me because we saw just about every chimp there was to be seen. All the habituated ones except two mothers with infants who very rarely visit camp. I managed to follow chimps too, and had some wonderful times. Fifi's son is absolutely gorgeous — Frodo. Fifi had two encounters with high ranking females (the only 2 higher ranking than herself, in fact, Gigi and Passion). It was Passion who killed Gilka's last infant. And then, coming as a surprise, about a month before I'd estimated (just as Fifi's came 2 months later!) a radio message two days ago — Gilka has another baby. Orion. (Because of being Olly's grandson.)* And so we're following Gilka for a month, just as Fifi was followed for a month. At least if it must get eaten, we had better know the facts, horrible as it all is.

What I mainly wanted to write about was the lectures in the spring. Over the phone I said the role of the female in chimpanzee society for one, and something had to do with aggression for the other. As you know, I am always wary of specifying too many details so far ahead. As you appreciate, a lot can happen between now and next spring, and I shall, of course, want to use the most recent information. However, the female one will be very interesting anyway — it will serve, just as the inter-community one did — or rather, that was aggression and intercommunity, for the most part — to show how much we yet have to learn. However, I do realize that I make things difficult for you by being so vague. If you really would like a paragraph about each of these two topics I'll send it — and I suppose I can always announce something different at the lecture! (I've done that many times without — so far as I know? — anyone objecting).

a. The role of the female in chimpanzee society. This will discuss the female in her role as a mother, the tremendous expenditure of effort which she puts into the raising of each child, and why this is important. It will discuss her reproductive cycle and the various factors which can influence the kind and frequency of her sexual relationships. The effect on her social status of i) the kind of mother she has had, ii) the kind of family she has. The complexity of the female hierarchy and female social relationships one with another. And, finally, the role of the female in preventing inbreeding, and the possible consequences of her wandering between communities.

---

* That is, the "O" of Orion follows the "O" of Olly.

b. Aggression and hierarchy. (I am not so keen on this, and would like to do the female one in as many places as possible, because it's new — and anything I want to say about males can be said in contrast to the way it is in females, if you see what I mean!) Anyway, as I see it, this lecture on aggression will deal mainly with the male hierarchy, especially the alpha status. This will include some discussion on adolescence. The aggressive behaviour of the male (in contrast to that of the female). His methods of perpetuating his genes in competition with other males, and how beneficial for the evolution of chimp intelligence this unique system could be (i.e. when almost any male can reproduce even with low status). His role in food finding and protection for the females of his society, which includes savage attacks on neighbours. (I see that what I have done, as I think and type, is the opposite of the female role — the role of the male in chimp society with emphasis on the importance of aggression. This would be quite a good second title.)

I'm not sure if all this has helped you, or made it worse? If you need a swanky sort of lecture, I'd rather like to put together one on chimp intellect. This would have been a good one for Caltech (wasn't that the one you called about?). It would have been so new for them. But perhaps we should save it for next time. As soon as you can send me just a very rough list of places and the order of going to them, I'd much appreciate, even if it changes a bit between now and then. . . .

In the meantime, please keep your fingers crossed for Gilka's baby. It's (or he's) her fourth go. This is the reason for Orion — on the 4th day God created the lights of the firmament — rather cunning, and coming back to O again. Gilka is such a lonely little soul that I really pray she can keep this child to be a companion. She'll be such a super mother.

Grub sends his love. He is sorry not to be coming back to America any more just now. So is Vanne, I know. She'll miss it much more than Grub. Poor little Grub is just off to his brand new, much bigger and more terrifying school, with the 3/4 hour bus journey each morning and evening. He's had to have a tutor this holiday — actually, a rather smashing tutoress! He is still behind, but thank goodness we found her. He's just come back from two weeks fossil hunting on the Serengeti, complete with 2 chameleons, 1000s of fossils, and a box of seeds to plant, which, it turned out today, are all full of beetles — they've hatched in the box! His major occupation here has been fishing a) from the shore with his rod, b) with a net and c) Derek (I'm getting tired and making millions of mistakes) found him a marvellous old fisherman, and they go out, he, Grub, and a helper, in a little motor boat into the open sea. Everyone says that old Ndugu is the best fisherman in the village (which is about half a mile along the beach from us). When Hugo came here, he wanted to take Grub fishing, so they both went with Ndugu and came back with quite a haul. Now he's off to do some more Lake fishing at Gombe. My word, what a fisherman he is. I wish he devoted 1/4 of the energy he devotes to it to his books!

Anyway, please give lots of love to Tita and Hugh,
And much love to you and Arnold.


Dar es Salaam
Monday
[Possibly October 4, 1976]

Darling Family and especially darling Nibs,*

The telephone call was not much success, was it? Rix sending Grub away to fetch Um, so that wasted half a minute, then Grub shouting about the television not to be turned off, and then the sad news that Danny was still very ill. And your veiled hints, Um, about discipline, which left me wondering what on earth was going on. However — Ub, you like the school now, which is the most super news. That made me very, very happy.

I think about you all so much these days, with Eric and Grub. But most of all I think about Danny. I wish, so much, I could spirit myself over, but I don't suppose it would be much use if I did. However,

---

* This is the first time Grub is addressed by his new nickname, Nibs, which later becomes Nibbs.

if you would like me to come, or need me to come, I always could, you know.

The news from here is not so good either. Heaven only knows what will happen about Rhodesia. It all sounded to be going O.K., but when we heard the details of the interim government, with all the important posts white, then we felt that the other Presidents wouldn't be too happy. On the other hand, I doubt if there are any black ones in Rhodesia who could cope. The same old vicious circle. Oh well. Luckily it's not that close to Tanzania. But very unsettling, altogether. With Amin, dormant for a while, but one never knows what on earth he'll be up to next. He's been quiet just a bit too long I think.

Then there is Gilka's baby. I just cried and cried when I heard that over the radio. Poor little thing. She [Gilka] is such a sad chimp. That whole history of hers is utterly pathetic. I very much wonder whether the fungus hasn't slightly affected her brain. Because it is so stupid of her to hang around camp. She doesn't get many extra bananas — just occasionally an extra one with medicine in it. Anyway, next time (and she does seem to conceive very easily) I shall stop giving her the medicine, and give her even less bananas than anyone else. It might help. But Melissa's baby, you see, was killed miles away from camp. I havn't heard the details yet, but I suspect [Gilka's] baby was killed in camp. The radio has been rather bad recently, so we have no details except that it seems to be Pom rather than Passion who was the villainess this time. Melissa will have her infant any time now, so let us hope that she keeps this one.

Well, Ub, more than ever do I want to hear about school, games and the other boys there. Do you have a special friend? If so, is he one you go on the bus with? And how many of you go on the bus, and how far do some of the others go? Oh, I have so many questions. There was no point embarking on them on the phone, because it would just have taken too long. I only rang just to hear everything was O.K. — and you told me it was. So that was fine. I'd have liked to go on talking for ages longer, only the trouble is that the phone bill is paid by National Parks, in Arusha, so it all gets a bit tricky! We can all talk a _bit_ longer when the phone calls come through the other way round — when you and Um ring me, instead of me ringing you! . . .

Oh dear, I do wish phoning wasn't so expensive so we could ring up every day, so I could hear how things were, with Danny, and with Grub, and with all of you. I shall write you a blue of your own, Grub, this evening. But wanted to get this off now. It comes with all love, and all thoughts.

Tons & tons of love, lots of thoughts, wishing I was with you all,
Jane — Mummy

Dar — Monday
[Probably October 4, 1976]

Darling Family, one and all,

Many thanks for your letter, Um. I was delighted to hear about Ub and school. I'll bet he would love being a weekly boarder. But it's a bit soon to choose, probably! . . .

Heard the details of Gilka's baby's barbarous murder now. Passion attacked Gilka, Pom helped for a bit, and then while Passion continued, Pom seized the baby, went off with him, and — just as Passion did before — deliberately killed him, biting into his forehead. Then the cannibalistic family fed on his remains for 5 hours, Passion taking charge of the body, Pom and Prof begging. The weird thing was that orphan Skosha was there — again. Yet so far as we know this was the only time since last Gilka's baby was eaten, that she has been with Passion! All other times with Pallas or males. Still, we don't know, of course. But it does seem strange. Sparrow (the female I think is really Beattle — you remember Beattle and Bumble, Um?) came alone, picked up a bit of meat, after staring and staring, sniffed it, flung it down and vigorously wiped her fingers on the tree trunk. Her daugher, Sandi, did exactly the same. Poor Gilka. She was badly hurt this time, and couldn't use her hand the rest of the day — maybe longer. Don't know.

Grub. Two things to tell you. First of all, we saw, out of the drawing room window, one of those big cuckoo like birds — coucals they're called — pecking and pecking at something down at the bottom of a bunch of bougainvillea blossoms. Finally I went close to the window (it was a bunch hanging down near the tap) — it was the smaller of your two chameleons!! So I quickly rushed out and rescued him. He wasn't pecked at all, luckily — I mean, no wounds. So he has spent the night in the drawing room. I'll put him back in a higher, safer spot later on, when he's recovered! Isn't that super! The second thing to tell you is that I have also found one of your toads. And guess what? — every evening, when I say goodnight to the dogs, he is sitting comfortably and fatly in the dogs' drinking water! His own private bath!! Well, the other evening, out went Wagga. She felt thirsty, so trotted to her bowl, put down her nose — horrors! The toad saw danger coming and leapt out of the bowl, narrowly missing Wagga's nose, but she avoided him only by herself leaping into the air in surprise! I laughed so much! And so did Emmanuel when I told him. Emmanuel sends his salaams to you, and so do the little girls. Oh yes — I have another thing to tell you also. I found the most amazing, fantastic olive* you can ever imagine. Shiney as anything, and a glorious, bright ORANGE. Just the colour of an orange. It is quite super, and I'll try to remember to bring it home for Christmas to show you. Oh yes — I should also tell you that on Saturday our shell cabinet arrived. I did wish you had been here. It was exciting, 'cos it's a super cabinet, and it was such fun putting the shells in. Your dark zigzag has pride of place in the cowrie cabinet. Carol† was so jealous when she came round yesterday evening. We had a cowrie for her, and she came in to collect it — we planned to surprise her because she ordered one at the same time as we did — the same week that all you boys came out for the holidays. She really was surprised!

Well, family, I don't have much news. I hope you all are O.K. and that the rain will continue but gently, in Bournemouth, no awful floods or other disasters. I'll write again tomorrow, but after that you won't have a letter for a week cos we'll be at Gombe. I'll write there, and post it the day we get back, at the airport. I'll end now so

---

\* A shell.
† Possibly Carol Ganiaris, a friend in Dar es Salaam.

that Derek can post this bit today, and he's just finishing his business on the radio and then off into town. . . .

Tons and tons of love to all of you, to you Danny, and Olly and Um and Rix. And lots of special Jane love to you, Ub. How is cuckoo clock? Happy sausages, Ub, happy school, happy dreams.

Love,

Jane

[Around June 1977]

<u>Welcome to USA!</u>

Darling Um,

Well, I trust you hada reasonable journey, withoutjars of marmalade falling onto your head? Though, no doubt, you neverslept a wink! But it was a daylight flight, soyou shouldn'thave, of course. Isn'tthemachine a bore joining up all its words. Makes itlook like German, or something!

Said I'd tell you more about Gombe. The circumstantial evidence concerning Charlie's death was overwhelming insuggesting that he, too, wasa victim of our Kasakela males. Hilaliwas downthere in thesouth. The fishermen said they had heard a terrific noise of screaming andcalling from chimps. Soon after (or before, I forget which) they had encountered 5 large males whowere not afraid of them at all. Hilali and Sadiki then went to see if they could find anything. They heardthis about 2 days after it happened, by theway (i.e. they happened to see the fishermen). Anyway, then they foundCharlie's body, lyingin the stream. He had innumerable wounds all over his back, his hands and feet. Quite clearly he had been murdered just like De, and Godi and Goliath and Madam Bee. I often suspectthat, probably, Faben was murdered by Sniff and Charlie. Anyway, now it's onlySniff left. They say that henever is answered, whenhe p.hoots,* so presumably WillyWallyhas gone too. I wouldsuspect that.

---

* Pant-hoots, the most common element in the vocal repertoire of chimpanzees, are given in a variety of situations; they are individually distinctive, often used to communicate in a call-and-response style between separated groups and individuals, and probably identify who is making the vocalization.

It is now early inthe morning, which is why the machine is joining up more words than it did for Joanne.* Also my hands are cold. It is very chilly here now, which isa relief. Maybe I told you about Gigiand Patti playing? It started in the evening, when Patti so badly wanted Fifi to play withher, and kept reaching outa hand and tickling Fifi inher neck or groin. Butall Fifi did was to present for grooming. Then Patti tooklittle Aphro away, and began playingwith her. Then Freud and Atlas began a realwild rough and tumble — and before you could say jack robinson Patti was in the thick of it, tumbling, somersaulting, laughing. Like thegood old days. Poor little Aphro did her best to join in, but it was much too rough, so she just ran back andplayed with Frodo.

Well, the next daythe same kindof thing happened, only Gigiwas there, and Gigi joined in, andafter a while it was just Gigi andPatti. Patti hasthe same large build as Gigi, and theywere quite hilarious! We got the giggles watching them. There was also the wildest play session, onanother occasion, between Prof and Freud, which ended in Prof getting hurt, banging hishead, and crying. And between Freudand Frodo, the two brothers, with orphan Skosha, who laughed and laughed and laughed. Butshe is funny — so often she would show a fear face, forno obvious reason, and clutch little Frodo tightly to her for a moment, then she was O.K.again.

One of the most super things was Gilka and Evered. They came together. Evered was aboutto lead the way, and we opened a box to give them bananas. Gilka got there first. Evered came galloping across, haira bit out, and just stood and watched as Gilka quite calmly finished taking her bs. Then Evered got his. He moved over to a comfy placeto eatthem, and Gi lka followed, having much difficulty and constantly dropping one or more. Then, thestrange thing was that with one hand and arm and thigh she held onto this pile of bs, with the other she groomed Ev. Not until he had finished his very last banana did she begin hers. He watched her,so she turned her back on him, but occasionally turned, when he wouldgently take a finished skin! Suddenly he charged off after the sounds of pant

---

* Joanne Hess, who had recently visited for National Geographic purposes.

hootsand screamsup the valley. He ran fast. Kipuyo followed him, and I stayedwith Gilka who looked after him, then followed, much more sedately. Evered went wildup the valley, with a huge group, mostlyfemales. He displayedfor about 15 mins almost non-stop, up and down the stream bed, hurling boulders, crashing through the undergrowth. Gilka just climbed a tree and ate figs — which wasall that was going on anyway. And I met Freud, watching Evered intently, and went with him to Fifi and Frodo. So it was all rather super. . . .

Tons of love —
Jane

[August 1977]

Darling All,

Hope you are all fine. We are well. What's the matter with me? — well, I get this way sometimes, you know. Was light headed the night before last, but luckily there was a mechanism in my head that pinged, twice, after turning over, and turned off something so that I could sleep. It was so funny. I tried so hard in the morning to remember exactly what it had all been about — but it was gone, like a dream goes. I just know there had been this super mechanism, which, every time I turned over, I had thought how lucky I was to have it. But, contrary to impressions, I am not light headed anymore. This morning Andrew Cummings is coming to spend the morning and have lunch. Grub is most keen on the idea. If only I'd thought he was this keen I could have arranged it before. There was going to be an invasion of 6 little boys on Monday, but it rained, so Carol and I decided to put it off, and have just Andrew. Andrew is the older of the two, and he and Grub got on very well when they all came to tea. Unfortunately the tide will be back in by the time he gets here, and the tide pools were their main interest before, but they can go along and help the fishermen pull in their nets, and I should think that will be a fun occupation for Andrew. I hope it's all a success. Also, Maulidi arrived yesterday, so Grub is less keen on Andrew than he was before. I can't type very well cos my bones still ache and my fingers are weak!

Well — Gombe. Grub was happy as a king (in a fairy tale, mind) from dawn to dusk. Catching fish after fish. They have become magnified considerably during the days since we left! But he did, certainly, catch enough fish for us to live on every single day. Mostly with his rod, when he and Sufi and Maulidi went out in the canoe. What bliss! Yes, Sufi was there. By luck he had an infected thorn in his foot, and hadn't been able to go back to school, so they had a super week together. And we cured Sufi's foot into the bargain, and saved him from having his father cut open the whole thing! Luckily we had some anti-biotic medicine which was super.

We saw just about all the chimps. I had a fantastic follow of Fifi when she and her family travelled with Figan. Freud was watching Figan, and when Figan did a display, so did Freud. They came to a little tiny stream — a mere trickle. Fifi sat there on a rock, and Frodo dabbled his lips in the water, and played, and Freud did a grown up stream bed display. He planned to end this in a most intimidating (to me!) way by climbing a sapling on the bank close to me, swaying it around, and then (probably) leaping off it, between me and Figan, stamping, and sitting so we all could see him. Well, up the sapling he shot. Unfortunately for him it was a kind of plantain, and when he got to the top and began the swaying part, it snapped in the middle and Freud, clinging to the top, crashed down onto his head (about 6 feet). For about 1/4 minute there was absolute stillness and silence. Then a small rather shamefaced head appeared from amongst the leaves and peeked round. And a small deflated little chimp crept out from the fallen vegetation and climbed right out of our way into a tall fig tree where he ate figs. Fifi went and sat close to Figan, who was in a very relaxed mood, and little Frodo went to him, and Figan very gently groomed his head. If my pictures (on the new little camera) come out, they will be super. But I have problems with the exposure on it. But it fits into my pocket and is super to carry around.

Of course, the real drama was the Passion incident. How fantastic that I had chosen to follow her! How fortunate that it was so near camp, so that Tsolo heard my hoo calls (the sound the followers make when they are separated and trying to join up again). It was Derek who said to Tsolo that he'd better go and see what I wanted. He found me with a huge stick, shivering. Pom and Prof were up in this tiny palm with LB [Little Bee], and Pom, who had touched the baby and then sniffed her finger, was looking from the baby to Passion. When Passion moved to the base of the palm Little Bee began to get scared. She gave squeaks, and climbed higher up the frond, and then Pom moved after her. I tapped Pom on the arm with my stick. I kept saying, "No, don't you dare" and silly things like that. When I tapped her she took the stick and sniffed it and pushed it away and went on after LB. Then LB screamed and leapt to the next tree and Pom leapt after, and I think Passion went straight up that second tree, only it was too horrifying for me to objectively record. Tsolo and I threw sticks and stones and yelled. And I honestly think that but for us they would have got the baby. I can't be sure. But LB leapt down and in all the confusion (me and Tsolo making a noise and the sound of the river) she managed to hide. For an hour Passion and Pom looked for her but didn't find her. The PS PM [Passion-Pom] follow started then, and so far as I know is still going on. We havn't had a report for three days.

Anyway, after the incident Pom was scared of me — she ran off, like a stranger, screaming! So let's hope she got the message. PS didn't care much, but even she gave a fear grin when Tsolo or Rugema (her first followers) got close suddenly. Super. I thought maybe LB would be scared too, but not a bit of it. We had no idea of the sex of the baby — but she'd been seen only 3 days before without a baby, so knew the age pretty well. Casually, later in the day, Maulidi had said to Grub (sorry, the <u>following</u> day) that he had seen the female chimp with the bad foot and a tiny baby at the kitchen at 7.30. If only he'd told me! I could have gone and watched her! Anyway, 4 days later we heard over the radio that she'd been to camp, the baby was a male (we won't name babies any more until they're a month old). Passion had come, with Pom, Little Bee had screamed and gone. Passion and Pom had NOT followed her! Could it be that they KNOW in some way that their behaviour is wrong? Wouldn't it be interesting? I'm so looking forward to the next report from Gombe. Well — I hope I am!

What else? Grub's work. We have come to a little better under-standing over it. There is slightly less temper etc etc when I suggest the maths, but not much. I have not sent anything to Mrs. Beard be-cause there really is nothing to send. I will send off the mess he is producing at the end of the week. The whole thing is a fiasco. BUT he is learning poems VERY well. Despite the disappearance of the French teacher, I think we are doing very well. Derek's French is pretty good, and we are making meal times French. Grub after much thought decided that he would agree to learn words each day, from us, and cooperate, if we did not find the French girl. It could well be that we will teach him more. The accent won't be so good, but now that he has agreed to do this, he is doing it. And his mem-ory is really very good now. His diary is almost up to date. His maths he is actually doing now, most days. His stories — he thinks of super ones, and gets all excited, but can't be bothered to write them down. Still, he is doing something, and that, I hope, is better than nothing!

Gilka, now that her nose is so much better, has got some horrid disease. She has chronic diarrhoea, and since the last baby has not had a swelling. We are getting the right stuff for preserving the dung so that it can be analysed here in Dar. In the meantime we have sent some Lomotils* and hope that these will help a little, as a sort of temporary measure (they won't cure anything). She is as thin as a skeleton. . . .

Anyway, tons of love to you all, thank you for all your letters Um, and your letter Ol. Dying to hear all the American saga. Will end now and D can post this on his way into town. Grub yells out his love.

Tons of love,
Jane

---

* Antidiarrhea pills.

P.O. Box 727
Dar
8 November [1977]

Darling Um,

I think it's your turn for a letter! Well — we're trying again to get to Gombe tomorrow. The awful thing is that for the past five days we have not been able to talk to Gombe on the radio. I think their machine must have packed up, or the battery gone into Kigoma to be charged, or something. So, because the disappointment would be too terrible otherwise, I have made up my mind that a twin must have died. In actual fact I don't see how poor old Melissa really could cope. Anyway, I've had the first batch of reports, which I've just finished typing, and so I'll tell you some of the gems.

First, the first record. I thought how casual Rugema sounded about the whole thing. Followed ML [Melissa] for nearly an hour, raining, up in high tree, they couldn't see much. (Rugema is the one who is best on ma-inf.)* Then ML returned to camp. Eslom had told Rugema he thought the baby was a male. Rugema saw that ML was at last in a good position for observation, so he went up to check on the sex. He looked — he looked again. He rubbed his eyes. He looked once more. Could it be true? He went inside to fetch out the people there to ask them if they saw what he saw. They said yes — it was true! They were all struck wordless by enormous amazement! This is almost word for word — I thought it was marvellous how he sent the record just as he had seen it! He is really good, that chap. Anyway, off he went, following ML, who has to pause every few steps to sit and cradle the babies.

The next morning was a gem. ML stayed long in bed. Then she stood up to leave — immediately both babies squawked their protest loudly. ML looked down at them, sat down, looked again, seemed to think, and decided to lie down again! She lay for 30 more minutes. Then decided to try again. This time she first gathered them properly, then stood bipedally and clutched them tightly to her breast. But obviously pinched them — there were very loud vo-

---

* Meaning that he (Rugema Bambanganya) was the expert on mother-infant relationships.

cal protests from both babies, who screamed. What was she to do? She sat down again. Then seemed to decide that speed was the thing, so very fast she gathered them, got up, shot down the tree — and made it to the ground with hardly a protest!

When she walks without supporting them, one falls off. And, added to these problems, she had the most appalling cold and cough. And every time she coughed the babies squealed in protest at the disturbance, and she had to quieten them. And when she bent to drink they both screamed, and she had to stop drinking. Oh dear — what terrible problems. No wonder I doubt they can survive. But I want to write you all this now, because it would be too sad to write about if I KNEW they were no longer there, together. And it really is fascinating.

Finally, the miraculous escape — well, probably. ML was in a nest. Gremlin (who is now 7) was grooming her. GM [Gremlin] suddenly saw that the Passions* had arrived. She grinned in fear, and reached to touch ML. ML sat up, stared, squeaked, and shot down the tree. PF [Prof] came up, and ML instantly pressed him to the ground and bit his neck. He ran screaming back to Passion. Then Pom approached, the field assistants prepared for the battle. But Pom did little when ML threatened her: Pom merely jumped up and down a little in front of ML and then sat. Suddenly they noticed that Pom was COVERED in wounds. Face, ears, head, arms, legs, hands, palms, fingers, feet, soles, toes. Only her chest and tummy were unmarked. She was lame, and it gave her much trouble. What a fantastically lucky thing for Melissa! And I think Passion is now too pregnant to bother — anyway, she never even went up to ML, then, with either PM [Pom] or PF. ML had made a lot of noise, during all this, including some very, very loud pant hoots (you remember Mum, the jolly hockey sticks type). Anyway, soon some other chimps came, and all was well.

Well, that's it to date. For good or bad I'll let you know when we get back. Will you ring next time? On Thursday or Friday or Saturday evening. If you ring after 7 your time it will only be us that an-

---

* Meaning the Passion family: Passion, Pom, and Prof.

swers — Emmanuel has always gone by 8.30. If they are alive, I think I'll send a black and white roll to you in Bournemouth. . . . Must leave some space for Grub.

Tons & tons of love,
Jane


[Probably December 1977]

Dear Joan,

The letter you wrote before telephoning arrived last week when we were at Gombe. But I think we cleared up all the points on the telephone. I do hope that the various members of your family are doing all right, especially, of course, your mother and father. What a real bad time you have been having with illness recently. Let us hope that 1978 will be much better.

Well — we're just back from Gombe. The Twins were alive — but one not very well at all. Bad, bad skin trouble & a wound on one foot which makes him scream every time he grips Melissa's hair — which he does every time she sets off. She gets very worried by the screaming — she is supporting him as well as she is able & doesn't know what to do — except to make a nest & lie in it. When she does this he is quiet. But <u>she</u> doesn't spend enough time feeding — for one chimp let alone three. So we are giving her a bit of extra food — and keeping our fingers crossed.

You know Alice Through the Looking Glass — the Jumbling song = "They did gyre & gimble in the wabe"? Well, they are Gyre and Gimble. Gyre is the sick one. . . .

All else here is well otherwise. And at Gombe too. Fifi's two absolutely tip-top form. Passion very, very pregnant. She must have had her baby by now. Only we can't get the news as there was a theft and they took a) the radio and b) the Ranger's rifle. The first is absolutely maddening — the second quite serious. And so it goes. So I can't give you the most up to date news. One poor little chap (4 years) has dislocated his leg — he'll be lame for life. And our "gang" has just killed the last remaining male down in the south. They broke his leg — we wanted to shoot him to put him out of his misery but he hid too well. He could not have survived, though. Leg smashed at the hip and his face torn. Horrible creatures. Did not mean to end on this note as I want to wish you a happy holiday.

Love to you & Arnold —

Jane

[Around June 19, 1978]

Dear Joanne,

A hasty note to try & thank you, though it will be inadequately, for ALL that you did for us while we were in Washington, and other places too. We certainly could not possibly manage without you. Many, many thanks.

We have just got back from a fabulous visit to Gombe. Unbelievable though it may seem, the twins are <u>still</u> O.K. But they are like 3 month old babies (though they are 7 months). Even to their <u>teeth</u> — Gyre <u>just</u> has his first 2 lower incisors (which normally appear at 3 mo) and is the more advanced. Gimble has <u>no</u> teeth yet. They have not yet broken contact.

Worst news — Miff has another baby — Passion, despite new baby Pax, made a very serious attempt at grabbing Mo from Miff. The field assistants threw things — they said it was as though Passion was drunk — she did not notice. However, Miff was able to beat her off. <u>Fortunately</u> Pom <u>was</u> scared off — she did not join in the attack. And this, clearly, saved little Mo. Who is now 1 month & should be safe. But I had <u>so</u> hoped that Pax would, indeed, bring about a Pax. Now he is inappropriately named.

There is cholera in Kigoma. Very, very bad. The worst yet. Very close to Gombe. I'm frantically trying to find out if chimps can get cholera. I'm told not.

The News Service girl — Brenda? — she told me she rang Geoffrey Bourne at Yerkes (He'd probably know about cholera — but he's not pleased with me — 'cos I don't like the way he keeps his chimps at Yerkes! — so I can't ask him) to ask him about the incidence of twinning in captive chimps. He quoted her a figure, which I would like to use. Could you ask her (without letting her know I've forgotten her name!!) and let me know sometime.

Derek is telling me I have to stop as we are hoping Rob McIll-
vaine can bring this to Washington on Monday. He sends loads of
love and thanks. (Derek, not Rob!)

Spider has cut her pad open, poor thing. . . . (Yes; Spider is a dog.)
I'm flustered. I'll have to write again as I had lots more to say.

For now, just love and THANKS,

Jane

[Late October or early November 1978]

Darling Family,

Sitting in the Science Research Council waiting for Addie (who
was at Gombe, remember?)* because I must get Research Clearance
now for Rosie — and also another girl, Vickie Leslie, who is one of
Jeff Short's† protegees & who is staying with us now, & off to
Arusha, we hope, tomorrow (with Alan Root who is going to be
coming in & out of the Serengeti filming).

Super to hear Ub so gay and full of beans on the phone last night.
No way of getting a word in edgeways! Sounds as though the school
has really done the right thing by him in a real big way. His math,
French, his "colours", new friend and all the rest.

Olly — when I got back from Gombe I thought Emmanuel must
have not properly looked after my precious parsley. 5 out of about
10 or 11 plants were sort of broken off at ground level. I really
couldn't understand, as it had been <u>perfect</u> when I left. Do you
know who the culprit — or rather, plural. Ub's <u>TOADS!</u> They jump
in the pots and sort of dig hollows so they can nestle in the lovely
damp earth. If a stem is in the way — well, bad luck to it! I've raised
them all now. We've just sowed a 2nd batch of tomatoes.

Gombe was <u>super</u> this time. All grass etc flattened so <u>perfect</u> for
following. Pom had "disappeared" when we arrived, and Passion
was being followed daily so as to see the reunion. Which took place
on fifth day there, so I was able to see quite a bit of the new baby —

---

* Adeline Mrema had been an undergraduate at Gombe from the University of Dar es
Salaam; now she was working at the Tanzania Science Research Council.
† Jeffrey Short was an American friend and a trustee of the newly formed Jane
Goodall Institute.

a ♂ PAN. As I said on the phone, Pom is a surprising mother. When she met PS she ran! PS followed v slowly, and after an hour Pom came back. She soon relaxed with Passion — it took longer for her to allow Prof anywhere near her precious baby! Pax is allowed to crawl all over her. I wonder — maybe this <u>will</u> be the end of infant killing for a while. I hope so! Winkle is any minute now. She's HUGE. We've decided to call the baby Winston or Winnie! Seki was making a new check sheet & wanted to know what initials to put, so we chose names that had the same — WN! They have found <u>no</u> trace of Alfons* — his canoe, his nets, his body — NOTHING. It's a mystery. Means no more fish for us at Gombe. Till we go with Nibs of course. Melissa is looking much better — Gimble still tiny, but much, much more strong, and beginning to do all the things he should. Gremlin loves him. So does Moeza love Mo. Mo is a funny child — she is now 5-1/2 months & still has no lower incisors — though she has some molars.

Have now vaguely caught up back log of work. Letters — translations etc & end of September. So, after today, should be able to get back to the old monograph. How is Silver,† Um? No chapters ever arrived. I suppose you never sent them?

I'll have to go out now, & see if Rosie and Vickie are waiting — they were going to do Embassy & Driving License & Bank — but I've been here so long.

Thanks tons for all your letters, Um. . . .

Heaps of love —

Jane

<u>Burundi</u>

Friday

[February] 9th, maybe [1979]

Darling Family,

We are at Burundi airport, waiting to return to Dar. Have just had a week at Gombe. Super, of course, but not as super as it could

---

* A local fisherman.
† *Silver* was Vanne's story for children.

have been! A lot of rain and <u>very</u> few chimps around as they are all wandering about in small groups eating milk apples.

One <u>fantastic</u> thing. Truly incredible. You remember that Winkle was pregnant? Well — they actually SAW HER GIVING BIRTH!!! Almost in camp, at 9.30 a.m. And just about the best man on the spot to record. [illegible] climbed a tree & so saw into her nest. Saw the first son, Wilkie, watching — and opening her bottom & peering up a few times to see what was inside! Took her 2 hours. Then she moved a bit, climbed into another tree, made a very big nest, and stayed there for the night. Since that, they followed her daily for a month. She met Passion & Pom 3 times when they were on their own (no males present) and there was absolutely <u>no</u> predatory interest at all.

Anyway, we saw the baby — a ♀ "Wunda." And, while we were there, yet <u>another</u> baby was seen for the first time — Athena's. Don't know sex yet. She was glimpsed during another follow. Baby after baby after baby!! Now comes Patti and then Nope.

Anyway, I had a rather splendid follow of Passion, Pom and co in the rain. Pom lost Passion & cried till she found her. And a terrible follow of Fifi. She stopped on a narrow track. I thought she looked pleased with herself & suddenly found she had neatly placed me in the midst of 1000s of safari ants!! By then they were all over me & Fifi, with a last leer (the Witch, remember?)! streaked off when I was nakedly picking them off the insides of all my clothes!!! (I caught her up later)! Little Bee traveled me up a mountain rather fast, sat there 10 mins, and hurried all the way down again! And Pallas did more or less the same! So they had fun with me.

Despite the rain, everything was going well. No complaints, no one was ill, everyone cheerful. One request. From dear old Rashidi. Mum, do you think you could somehow get a little bottle of those eye drops which wet lips gave me (Dr Birch also prescribed some, in ointment form). It is called BETNASOL & is on prescription. Rashidi says it's the only thing that really cures his eyes. Perhaps James would oblige? If you <u>could,</u> then I'll let you know a way to send it to us. His eyes look awful.

We have just taken off. Due to rain everywhere we are flying straight to Dar, not stopping anywhere else, which is nice. And Rosie should be there to meet us. I wonder if Emmanuel will be back? We're taking steps to replace him if he doesn't return soon!

When we set off & got <u>almost</u> to the airport I suddenly realized we'd left our box of food in the hall! No time for Rosie to fetch it! But as it turned out we had plenty of fish, Toni* lent us some milk, and all was fine. Just a pity there were not a few more chimps coming to camp.

Tons of love to you all —

Jane

---

\* Toni Brescia, a friend in Kigoma.

# 8

◆ ◆ ◆

# THE BRYCESON YEARS
## 1973–1980

> It was just before my world turned upside-down that I met the man who would, for a few short years, be my new partner — in love and in endeavor — Derek Bryceson.
>
> — *Reason for Hope*

DEREK BRYCESON significantly entered Jane Goodall's life in 1973. They fell in love, married in 1975, and parted upon his death in 1980.

The love affair took them both by surprise, and it happened quickly. Both were married to other people at the time, although in Jane's case at least, the first marriage had rather clearly run its course by 1973. Jane had briefly met yet hardly noticed the crippled Englishman when he visited Gombe as Tanzanian minister of agriculture in 1967. But by the time she met Bryceson again in 1973, he was, as the new director of Tanzanian national parks, both more directly important to the research at Gombe and more personally attentive to Jane. She noticed him.

Derek was tall, slender, and white-haired. He was physically awkward, walking with a great, rolling labor and the assistance of a cane. But he was dignified and, as one might discern from a sweet, youthful, rather puckish smile that could illuminate his face in a moment of repose, inwardly graceful and self-assured. He could be tendentious, too sure of himself, authoritarian. He "was honest to the point of brutality," Jane has written, with "a strong and forceful character" — but "he had a wonderful sense of humor."*

---

* *Reason for Hope*, p. 97.

Born in China on December 31, 1922, Derek Bryceson was educated in England, leaving school in 1939 to fight in the war as a Royal Air Force pilot. Shot down by enemy fire, at nineteen years of age Derek was so severely injured that he was told he would never walk again. He taught himself to walk anyway, studied agricultural science at Cambridge University, and in 1946 moved to Kenya, started a farm, and married Bobbie Littleton. In 1952 the Brycesons moved to Tanganyika and began farming a 1,200-acre rectangle at the foot of Mount Kilimanjaro. Within three years Derek met Julius Nyerere, one of the leaders of the Tanganyikan independence movement then, later to be revered as the founding father of modern Tanzania. It was a critical meeting, for Derek soon became among the earliest white supporters of Nyerere's political vision for a democratic, multiracial African society. He remained for the rest of his life a personal friend to Nyerere — or "Mwalimu" (teacher), as he was later affectionately called. After Derek quit farming in favor of politics, he moved to Dar es Salaam and built a simple but charming, light-filled house on the beach. Nyerere loved Derek's house and indeed decided to make his own home next door. Derek accompanied his friend to the bank when Nyerere applied for a building loan.

Aside from that personal friendship, Derek distinguished himself as one of the few influential whites in Julius Nyerere's political party, the Tanganyikan African National Union. He was the only white member of Prime Minister Nyerere's first cabinet; and, as a Member of Parliament representing the Kinondoni constituency in Dar es Salaam, he was for many years the only freely elected white person in all of postcolonial Africa.

Derek Bryceson was a hero to Jane Goodall, both personally — as someone who had overcome great adversity — and in a public sense — as one of the few politically powerful Europeans from the colonial era who had gracefully and honorably made the transition into the new Africa. He was a man of genuine idealism, who shared with Jane a love of classical music, poetry, and nature, and a positive vision for the future of Tanzania. "He is identified completely with Tanzania," so she wrote enthusiastically on May 27, 1973, to

Joan Travis and Tita Caldwell of the Leakey Foundation, "and, more importantly (and it is rare), with Tanzanians."

The opening letter in this sequence details Jane's first meeting with Derek in Dar es Salaam. At the time, she was very anxious about the future of Gombe. Even though the connections with Stanford University may have seemed to promise a better chance at reliable funding, she had recently learned that the Nixon administration in the United States was drastically cutting federal grants for basic research in the sciences. Additionally, the Tanzanian bureaucracy had for mysterious reasons continued to delay necessary clearances for incoming American and European students and researchers.

Thus, after a brief visit with Hugo and Grub in the Serengeti, Jane flew from Arusha to Tanzania's capital city, Dar es Salaam, on February 28, intending to be "battling away for Gombe." She established herself in a room at the Kilimanjaro Hotel. After an informal lunch with Derek Bryceson at his house and, later, a "dainty tea" with Bryceson, Tumaina Mcharo (the new Tanzanian director of the Serengeti Research Institute), and Myles Turner (recently retired park warden for the Serengeti), she returned to the hotel. Dar was, as usual for that time of the year, oppressively hot, and the air conditioning of the Kilimanjaro offered a tolerable environment for her to work on her contribution to "the dog book" (Hugo's *Solo: The Story of an African Wild Dog*).

The next evening, March 1, she had dinner with Derek, Mcharo, and Professor Abdul Msangi, who, as dean of the Faculty of Science at the University of Dar es Salaam, soon invited Jane to join the faculty as a visiting professor.

In short, Jane's visit to Dar es Salaam seemed a tremendous success. Derek Bryceson appeared to be especially won over. He visited Gombe late in May, accompanied by the Canadian high commissioner, and was rewarded by seeing "more chimps in camp together . . . than there have been in the past FIVE months!" Jane concluded that he could not have been "more impressed and delighted" (as noted in her letter of May 27, 1973).

Derek made increasingly regular visits to Gombe; and Jane, in turn, found reasons to fly back to Dar es Salaam. There seems to have been a mutual attraction from the start. Their affair began sometime during the summer of 1973, possibly during the early August visit referred to in the letter home of August 8. Jane's first love letter to Derek was written on August 15 — dozens of similar messages were exchanged during the next two years, when circumstances kept the pair apart more often than not. The circumstances that separated them included Jane's visits to Stanford University in the fall and spring of each year until her tenure ended in 1975, Derek's responsibilities as a politician and as the director of national parks, and Jane's continuing responsibilities at Gombe.

For the first six months at least, their separation was complicated by feelings of guilt and agonized uncertainties. The uncertainties, at least, were ended by a dramatic plane crash (described in the letter of early January 1974) that took place soon after Jane returned to Africa from her term at Stanford. Jane, Derek, and Grub were being flown out in a four-seater Cessna to the Ruaha National Park for an official visit combined with a small holiday. As the pilot made a sudden decision to crash-land, Jane believed with some certainty that she was about to die, and the experience of facing death proved enlightening. As she wrote home, "Lots of things seem to have fallen into shape after nearly being dead." Included among them was the decision to make their private lives public. Jane and Derek decided to marry as soon as possible.

By early February, Hugo had come to Gombe to discuss the situation. It was, as Jane declared in the letter home probably written on February 10, an "upsetting talk," even though Hugo seemed "quite cheerful" — perhaps partly because he was feeling "so enthusiastic about Stella & all her family." (Stella Brewer had visited Gombe for two and a half months the year before; she was running an orphanage in the Gambia, West Africa, for chimpanzees confiscated from an illegal trade.) Jane felt, as she noted in the letter, "sure something is up" regarding Hugo and Stella. If something *was* up, nothing overt came of it. In any case, Jane and Hugo divorced simply and amicably in August 1974. Derek was given a divorce later that year. By February 1975 Jane and Derek were married but still somewhat frantically commuting between Derek's home in Dar and Jane's in Gombe.

After the kidnapping of May 19, 1975, Jane's visits to Gombe were severely curtailed for many months. When she did go, Derek often accompanied her, and they were usually trailed by an armed guard. After May of 1975, then, Jane and Derek were together much more regularly than they had been in the past, so they had much less reason to exchange letters. The written record of their relationship attenuates after that crisis, and the character of their relationship may have slowly become more quietly domestic.

Certainly the letters home between the middle of 1975 and the start of 1980 tend to forward the occasional bulletin from Gombe and the domestic news from Dar. Of course, some of Jane's correspondence during this period was addressed to Grub, who was attending school in England, and focused on matters of particular interest to him, such as fish and dogs. Derek collected seashells and kept aquarium fish in their home in Dar es Salaam; and the dogs — first Beetle, then a "miniature golden retriever" named Spider, followed a year later by her daughter, Wagga — were always very important members of that household. Derek employed a housekeeper and cook named Emmanuel, who was eventually replaced by Zano. And Jane developed a wide circle of friends in Dar es Salaam, including the few briefly mentioned here: Dick and Marina Viets, Heta Bomanpatell, Prashant Pandit, and Chris Liundi.

The domestic years from 1976 to 1979 were quietly punctuated by Jane Goodall's ongoing research and writing. But the termination of her position at Stanford undermined her ability to count on traditional grants. Indeed, funding had always seemed problematic, as we can see from the earliest letters in this chapter. Major research grants finally came through in 1973, as well as the helpful emergency grant of $6,000 from the Leakey Foundation, acknowledged in the letter of May 27, 1973. After the kidnapping, a very large grant from the W. T. Grant Foundation was not renewed, purportedly because Gombe had no resident Ph.D.

In desperation, Jane raised money by lecturing in the United States, at first under the auspices of the Leakey Foundation, which helped to organize and publicize the lectures and continued to support her work financially after the kidnapping. By 1976 two close friends in the States, Prince Ranieri and Princess Genevieve di san Faustino, had established a tax-exempt, nonprofit entity called the Jane Goodall Institute for Wildlife Research, Education and Conservation that eventually would become Jane's primary vehicle for financing her work. The letter of July 6, 1978, to Ned Harrison, president of the Leakey Foundation, formally describes some of the history of Jane's relationship with that organization and, in addition, announces the start of the Jane Goodall Institute as a way to achieve "a little security for the future" of Gombe.

Danny died in 1976, as we note in the sad letter home of October 28 of that year, and both Spider and Wagga succumbed to a canine virus epidemic in May 1980. But nothing would prepare Jane for the illness that struck Derek so suddenly. He had been suffering from severe stomach pains and in early June saw a doctor. Derek's "revolting barium meal" (letter of June 8) and the X-rays took place on June 9, 1980, and he returned home with the bleak information that a "mass" had been discovered. Within the week, Jane and Derek flew to England and consulted a high-powered London specialist, who at first seemed quite hopeful. In fact, the cancer had already spread. After surgery the same specialist took Jane aside and declared bluntly that (early July 1980) "he'd removed the primary tumour — he could do no more. There was <u>no</u> treatment that would help."

Jane's response — characteristic, I think — was to fight the gloomy prognosis in every way imaginable, with every ounce of energy she could summon. She visited nontraditional healers in London, persuaded a friend in Dar to look for African medicinal herbs, asked an "old Indian nanny" to help locate a "wonderful root" found in a "remote village in India." And with Vanne's help she contacted Hepzibah Menuhin, pianist and sister of the renowned violinist Yehudi Menuhin, who was herself a cancer patient. Hepzibah's experience gave hope. She told of a wonderful physician, Dr. Hans Nieper, who at his clinic in Hanover, West Germany, treated cancer successfully with a controversial substance known as laetrile.

Jane has written extensively in *Reason for Hope* about the wrenching summer of 1980, which she identifies as "the hardest time, the cruelest time, of my life." Still, it was also a time of great intimacy: "Derek and I became very close in this strange new world." He was able to start work on his autobiography. Jane typed it. Friends visited from England and Tanzania. There were long, consoling conversations with Hepzibah and her husband, Richard. But in spite of all the hope and the encouraging news and the positive messages, Derek's condition worsened. He died on October 12. After a brief respite at the Birches Jane returned to the house in Dar es Salaam. Accompanied by Ian Bryceson, Derek's son, and sharing an umbrella with Derek's stalwart friend, Chief Adam Sapi Mkwawa, Jane endured the ceremony in "a little building by the quay" (late November 1980). Then the mourners set off in three boats, headed out to a favorite spot where she and he had so often swum and snorkeled and "marveled at the magic world of the coral reef,"* and there Jane Goodall saw her beloved partner's ashes cast onto the waters.

*   *   *   *

1 March — fancy that! [1973]

Darling Family —

At last, a proper typed letter. Here I am, at the Kilimanjaro, and funnily enough, Hugo and Grub are in Nairobi. So I am battling away for Gombe, and, believe it or not, it is all going very well indeed. I have worked out the undergraduate business with a very nice man in the Prime Minister's office called Mr. Chambo. Derek Bryceson, the new Director of Parks, says he is pretty sure he can work the clearance for graduate students. And they are all being so nice.

So far I have got here free. I don't remember when I last wrote — oh yes I do. I sent you two blues from Kigoma, when we stayed the night there with Ramji. We had dinner with the pilot that night, and Grub didn't go to bed till 10 because he was so excited by the kittens and by Samir — Ramji's little boy. He and I were sharing a large

---

* *Reason for Hope*, pp. 154, 158, 161.

bed — when I joined him, after a nice supper with Ramji, he was like a dead lump, so tired was he. Nor did he wake till morning.

Well, we had a good flight to Ndutu, where Hugo was worried because of course he was expecting us the evening before. We drove out with Grub to look for nearby fossils in the afternoon, and the next day took him to Olduvai where he had a super time and a nice picnic. Charia came too, of course. Grub found lots of bits of bone, and we dug out a little piece of elephant tusk for him. Dove was in a pleasant and relaxed mood and Mike, now that he is about to get married, has relaxed so much, and is really a super person.

Well, a message came through that my life ! = lift to Dar was departing on Wednesday morning at 6.30 from Arusha. It didn't leave much time, but in the end Mike flew me to Arusha in his tiny little plane, and it was a rather nice flight. The next morning Hugo and Grub were going to Arusha for Hugo to ring England about his contract. Anyway, I stayed with Mibbs (Dove's wife). . . . Well, we had quite a nice gossipy evening, and she woke me at 5.30 a.m. and we had some coffee, and she drove me to the airfield. There was nice Don,* and we had a really good flight to Dar. He is a really interesting man and has great hope for Tanzania. We arrived in Dar, got a cab to the Kilimanjaro (where most of the air conditioning is broken) and I installed myself. Since when I have been writing dog book and seeing people.

Later

I have just this minute got back from having dinner with Derek Bryceson, Msangi, Mcharo (the new Tanzanian Director of SRI) — and who? — oh yes, myself! We had dinner at a neighbouring hotel which has amazingly good food. I treated them all! We had a fun dinner, and I've never seen Msangi so relaxed. Have I ever described to you the view from the Kili window, if you get the sea side? It is so utterly glorious. You look right out onto the harbour, and the sea is almost directly below the window. There are always a number of big ships riding at anchor, and at night, when they are all lit up, and especially if there is a moon (which there isn't now) it is absolutely

---

* The pilot.

exquisite. Air conditioning or not I really like the hotel. It is rather expensive, but if one has to write a book it's worth it. I've got a lot of the dog book done, in between times.

I also had lunch at Derek Bryceson's house. (He's the one with polio in one leg, but he walks with a stick.)* Their house is out on the bay, right next to the President's, right on the white white sand under coconut trees. It is glorious. He has a boat, and a huge aquarium. And a poor wife, who arrived back the day I was there with hepatitis. She went to Arusha where it is cooler than Dar (which really is terribly hot) in order to get her arms better. She broke one wrist and the other forearm. And just as they were getting better (not swelling under the plaster) she got hepatitis. After the journey in the little plane she looked far more dead than alive. Quite awful. I felt awful being there at all, but it didn't seem to matter. . . .

I think I must stop for tonight as it is 12.30 and I'm sure there will be complaints soon about the noise of the typewriter. The coolest place is in the middle of the room, so I have the typewriter on the little coffee table and am sitting on the two big cushions from the arm chair. It's just write — right. My legs tend to get slightly stiff after a bit, but there are various positions I can arrange them in. Oh, one funny thing. Yesterday, after lunch at Derek's house, he and I went to have a talk with Mcharo. Mcharo was with Myles Turner (the Park Warden who is Tanzania's chief anti-poaching chap). Well, we were all sitting having dainty tea, when two drunks arrived. One knew Derek, from the time when he was a Minister. He kept saying Derek was his minister, and the other, much more drunk, kept saying yes, but he wasn't now. And then one began to talk about how he had managed to poach in a game reserve, and I was watching Myles, who has absolutely NO sense of humour. He just pretended he wasn't there. Finally Derek, who was twinkling, introduced Myles, saying about his anti-poaching work. And so the man immediately told Myles the story all over again, and Myles couldn't pretend he wasn't there. I was feeling hysterical. Suddenly we heard

---

* Obviously, Jane was mistaken here; she had not yet learned that Derek was crippled in an RAF plane crash.

a bang, and there was the other man, who had again announced Derek was, after all, not a minister any more, and fallen to the ground. Looking up, he said "Well, that is the first time I've been pushed out by a chair"! Oh never mind, said the other, patting him consolingly, things round here do move by themselves. Derek was being so attentive to them, Myles still solemn, Mcharo and I trying to talk business, as we didn't have long. Every 5 minutes or so, one or other of the drunk men would offer us a drink, we would refuse, and he would march up to the bar and order a drink. But no drinks ever came. It was totally Alice and Wonderlandy. This evening we were telling Msangi (we hadn't had a chance to discuss it amongst ourselves). And of course, reminiscing, it seemed funnier than ever and we were quite weak with laughter, including Msangi. Mcharo said Myles had come up to him afterwards and said "Wasn't that simply awful" with a solemn and pained face! It really was a fun evening.

It's morning now. I've decided to have some breakfast up here, to look out over this lovely morning ocean for the last time (it will be quite dark tomorrow when I leave, as the plane departs at 6.10). Even now, if I open the door to the veranda — and they are huge plate glass sliding doors — it must be 90% outside. It really is a very, very hot place this time of year. Between the hotel and the sea there is a road, and also a belt of green. Somewhere in that belt must be fresh water, cos I've never heard anything like the frogs last night!

Well, I'll just write this page, and then go down and post this letter, read the latest news (believe it or not, they have a Telex here!), send a cable to Ramji saying when returning, and maybe get a bite to eat.

Had a super afternoon. Went out to the University, and had a good talk with Professor Msangi (who's Abdul now). And, imagine — he has invited me to be a Visiting Professor at Dar — just imagine. It has to be approved by [the] Senate, but he reckons it will. I shall be rather proud of that one. Undoubtedly Tanzania's first lady professor! He is becoming a Scientific Advisor to Gombe. . . .

The frogs are at it again, the ocean is still so beautiful with more boats in tonight so that it looks like fairy land out there, with the water shining and rippling, and the almost unreal, illuminated cargo boats and one passenger liner. And, occasionally, an Arab dhow slips past silently. Or a little tug chugs busily on its errands. Or a tiny speed boat races by, the engine quite lost below the chorus of frogs.

I ought to do some more of the dog book now, but somehow I don't think I shall. Somehow I don't feel like it. The seminar this afternoon wasn't taxing, but yet in a way it was more important to do well in that tiny little group (all the poor students doing exams and most of the poor faculty marking, and in all that terrible heat) than for many of the huge audiences in the States. So they got my best, and we had a good discussion afterwards, and Msangi was delighted. He told me, after, that many people and students have commented on how much they enjoy my lectures and the way I talk to them. So I will be spending probably about a week every so often (maybe twice a year) teaching here, and that will really be a challenge, and I shall really enjoy it. I really do like Msangi very much indeed.

Well, look after all yourselves. I hope, Rixy, you are better — I heard you were under the weather. And I do hope Jif has got some help by now, and the news about the shop and things all seemed very good. So glad the baby is a beautiful one — I have written to Jif.*

Tons and tons of love to all of you,<br>Jane

27 May 1973

My dear Joan and Tita —

I simply can't believe it! How simply fantastic, and marvelous and wonderful — and SUPER! A million thanks to you both from all of us here, and most especially, a hundred fold more thanks from me. The others havn't had to worry the way I have worried for the past few months. It was fine for me to say "We'll get the money

---

* Sister Judy had just given birth to her second daughter, Claire, nicknamed Pippit.

somehow" — but there were times when I had to face up to what it would mean if we didn't, and that was pretty horrifying. . . .

An amazing thing was that all the good things came within a week. The cable last night capped a week of celebrations. First the Emmys.* Then we had the new Director of National Parks here, and that visit went off so very, very well that I have virtually NO worry about research clearances for the next few years. That was a huge weight off my mind, as you can imagine. And the very next night — last night — your cable. Oh — and, of course, there were cables from Dave about 2 grants which are for Gombe West, I think, or part West part East, or something, and your letter, Tita, about [the grant of] $6,000. What a week. It's hard to imagine. . . .

I havn't even begun to catch up on anything yet. I came here with George Dove who is putting up a house, and will be doing more. He is FANTASTIC. Gombe would be very, very different without him and his buildings. When are you both coming to see Gombe? It's disgraceful. Anyway, I have had to spend quite a bit of time with him, choosing places for houses, etc. We are, at last, getting pull and push choos and running water for hand and dish-washing. I think it's going to make all the difference in the world to health at Gombe. It will be great.† And, re health hazards for the chimps, most vital. We've had money for this, but never actually got around to organizing it till now. Gombe is paradise. Then, 2 days after our arrival, was this visit from the Director, Bryceson. This, of course, meant real VIP treatment, and I went in to meet him — with him, the Canadian High Commissioner, a very nice chap. I was desperately hoping they would see good chimp things. Bryceson was shot down in the war and walks with a stick and will power. He managed to actually walk up to top camp, though we had a stretcher planned. He is a marvelous person, and will do more than any other single person in Tanzania could do, at this point in history, to save our wild

---

* These are American television awards given out by the National Academy of Television Arts and Sciences. Over his career as a filmmaker and producer, Hugo van Lawick won a total of six Emmy awards. The two referred to here were for his production and direction of *Jane Goodall's World of Animal Behavior: The Wild Dogs of Africa.*
† Alas, the anticipated plumbing was never installed.

life. Anyway, believe it or not, but while he was up there (one morning) there were more chimps in camp together (and all the time there were some) than there have been in the past FIVE months! Since he left, just one or two. The chimps' God Pan was watching over us indeed this month! Bryceson couldn't have been more impressed and delighted — and delightful, for that matter. He is identified completely with Tanzania, and, more importantly (and it is rare) with Tanzanians. A really super people. Oh yes — Figan has made it as alpha male! Isn't that super. He soundly thrashed Humphrey and Evered when they were in bed in their nests in the evening!

Well — unlike you, Tita, I don't have the outside [of the envelope] to write on (and the job I had trying to open it so as to still be able to read it!!) Can't <u>ever</u> thank you both enough for all you have done for me & Gombe.

With much love,
Jane

8th August 1973

Darling Family,

Yesterday was a funny kind of Kigoma day and I planned to send you a letter from there but never got there. Went in with Derek for some meetings about the Kigoma National Park. . . . Anyway, since several meeting people were not there after all, & since there were 2 boats, Derek & I decided to leave early. An excellent idea in <u>theory.</u> In practice it didn't work out too well. One thing promised were some inner tubes for Grub. To make a raft so that he can paddle his net out deep — it's too heavy for him to pull with all the stones attached. Derek found a place where they agreed to patch up too-old inner tubes. So we sat & chatted — & chatted — and sat. One by one all the people who had been helping left on various missions & still we waited. We waited over 1 1/2 hours for Grub's tubes! And you remember, Ma, how one feels after a Kigoma day. Luckily I had spotted some <u>ginger wine</u> in Kigoma & bought 2 bottles, so when we finally got onto the lake we decided to revive ourselves with ginger wine & tomatoes! Super ginger wine — & we both could think back to Christmas times with Stone's ginger wine — & how we both thought it was called 'Stones' because it came in stone bottles! Anyway, to see Grub in the water with his tubes made the wait worth the while.

Have you heard that the rabbits have had babies! 4 — she ate one — so now 3. They are super little things. Ma had them in the middle of the floor so we have been able to watch how they grew hair after 3 days & are just beginning to open their eyes after 5 days. Grub was up most of the night when they were born — you <u>never</u> heard such a noise. Papa was performing 'that certain behaviour' with fanatical zeal — head, tail — <u>anywhere</u> — & she, of course, was objecting equally vigorously! Eventually I got him out & left her to cope with her babies.

In the morning he said how strange he thought it was that she had laid her babies at night. I said lots of animals did. Long pause, after expressing his surprise. Then he said "Did you lay me at night?" I had such a job keeping my face straight as I told him I had, indeed, "laid" him at night.

It is quite wonderful having Derek come to Gombe — & Kigoma. He's going to make more difference that I can quite imagine now to the ultimate success of Gombe in Tanzania. The students are so much more prepared to listen to him when it comes to questions of relationships with the local people than to listen to me. So many things which are necessary for the successful running of a place as big as Gombe depend on discipline — which, suggested by me, is interpreted by some as "Colonialism"! We are having a meeting on some of these things tonight. And Derek not only knows and understands the Tanzanians, but he has great wisdom, and all the students love him. So do the staff. He gave a super speech at our 13th anniversary. We all sat on the sand, by a fire, eating goat and rice off communal plates. Dominic was in fantastic form and made a nice speech — lots about you, Mum! And I endeavoured to say something which would have been OK if only my Swahili was better — well, it's almost non-existent!*

---

* Soon Derek would be encouraging her to work on her Kiswahili.

Grub is at present mending his net on the veranda with Charia, ready for his raft. It is past lunch time & I must take him along. Derek has a meeting with the Rangers & some of our people — sorting out some problems for me. And Gombe is almost back to normal, with the huge influx of visitors just about over. Pal is still here — everyone loves Pal. He really is a wonderful person. We also have a girl who works in a lab with monkeys — <u>hates</u> lab conditions but has remained in a lab in order to work to <u>improve</u> conditions. She is a good person too.

I'm looking forward to Grub's visit to Dar. He will adore the sand & the sea and things. We shall have 3 days — going on the Park's plane & returning E. A. Airways. This is for my lecture at the University. I have some lovely Beethoven going & really am not in a mood to go for lunch, but I'd better take Grub along. His appetite, by the way, is <u>excellent.</u>

Hope you'll see Hugo soon Mum. He is very cheerful about things at present and seems to be in excellent spirits. So he should after 2 Emmys! Oh — <u>Thank</u> you for your letter Danny. What <u>amazing</u> writing you have — <u>you</u> apologized for a scribble, illegible it isn't — it's super! I'm so glad the flowers were beautiful & arrived in time.

Tons & tons of love to you all from<br>Jane & Grub

P.S. Writing this from Dar where Grub is having the time of his life. He is on the search, in the tide pools, from morning to night. He has his little friends following him around, he is catching tiny fish to feed to the fish in Derek's tank, playing with crabs, finding shells. It is so super for him to be on a beach where he doesn't have to watch for baboons or chimps! Tomorrow we are going on the boat to the coral reef. . . .

on flight to Kigoma<br>[August 15, 1973]

Dearest Derek,

So many, many, many thank yous for such a wonderful time at Gombe and Dar, both. For all you did for me and especially all that you said to me. For the super, super pen, and the book, and for being so super to Grub. I know you don't need 'thanking' for that — maybe I'm thanking something else that has brought it all about.

It was sad to say goodbye, but luckily it nearly is early September, and luckily there will be an awful lot to do in between, for both of us. The time after next to goodbye will be much worse, so it's good to practice.

You know, I would 100 times prefer to go on the sea in bad weather than not to go on the sea at all. It was much worse for you — you always have the sea & you can pick & choose. But just to see the corals again, & the fishes — just to smell that glorious tidal smell — to see the octopus & the worms & urchins & brittle stars. For me it was fantastic. And who cares for a few bumps. The only part that bothered me about the journey back was the stiff engine & you having to battle with it. Otherwise I really quite enjoyed facing the elements. Of course, a smooth hot day would have suited us better — but it was still glorious for me and a glimpse back at the world which haunted my imagination when I was a child.

Last night was sad, but it was happy too. I hated it when you had to go off out into the cold — of course, it wasn't cold, but you know what I mean. It was so good to wake up & find you there so close and strong.

I shan't actually write more letters like this — there is no point. You know it all, and there is always a risk. We don't want to spoil something that is beautiful & so ultimately good. We both would hate it. But this one will get to you soon, & should be fairly safe, & you will destroy it — or bring it to Gombe so we can destroy it together.

You know — it is easier to think things than to carry them out, but it helps to think them through — helps a bit. And if the happiness of being together can make miserable the times when we cannot be together, the essence of the love will be contaminated. It is possible to miss someone yet feel the warm glow of their being & their love of you. And I feel that warm glow now, so strongly, and the strength & joy of your love. It would be easy to wish away the days because they did not contain you — much better to feel I can perform better & even enjoy them more because of knowing your love.

I knew that was rambling & waffling. But you will know what I am trying to say. Grub is chattering away to me about fishes & Sufi. And I am thinking of you in Arusha, & hoping you are not too tired. I had a cat-nap and feel good at the moment.

Derek, beloved — my thank yous again, and my love, & many kisses & much strength until we meet again.

Jane

P.S. Mwalimu's book — when I put it in that box, I thought quite hard about asking you if you thought he might write in it for me. You know, only I didn't ask you, I expect.

[Early January 1974]

Darling Mum,

I do hope that you havn't received reports of a crash before you get this letter. At the time I thought I couldn't tell you because you'd all worry — I thought I'd tell you later. But now I find that the crash has been in the papers and on the radio — and it was STUPID of me to think you wouldn't hear about it from someone else. I just felt it would be less shocking if I told you about it later on when it was less fresh — but, of course, that was stupid thinking. It would only be less fresh to ME!

Anyway, I'm sorry I didn't tell you straight away. (Maybe, though, you havn't heard, in which case you won't know what I'm talking about!) We crash landed at Ruaha and the plane was a write off. To this day we don't know how we ended up not only alive, but even unhurt — except that Derek got a bruised (probably cracked) rib. It would be him, wouldn't it. Anyway, I'll tell you the details later. But it was a silly thing, we landed only 1/2 minute from the landing strip because the pilot thought we might burst into flames. And he never warned us we were crash landing — pure luck my belt was tight. And then he leapt out of the plane and vanished. Grub was simply wonderful. I got Derek's and my door open before we finally ground to a halt, undid Grub's belt, told him to get quickly out of his door and run from the plane. He did it. Derek was pretty stuck — his chair wouldn't go back because luggage had fallen there, which I frantically removed, and the door that side only opened about 2 feet because there was no wheel that side and we were right down on a buckled wing. However, since Derek had quickly turned off the engine just before landing we did not burst into flames and I joined Grub and he crawled out head first. Then people came running over the river and we decided to go back that way, with all our luggage carried, and Grub swam and had the time of his life. (It would have taken an hour to get the car round by the ford.) I am glad, now that it's over, to have had that experience. I was quite calm and collected, I did not even have time to feel frightened. I only remember, as we raced down at 80 mph onto this tiny space where it was obvious we'd hit a tree (which we did) that soon I'd be dead. So I held Grub tighter. He wasn't scared at all — he had no idea what was going on — nor did I till the last minute. Derek had been watching the instruments, not the ground. Suddenly he said "You're not going to try to land here!" in a horrified voice. "Yes" said the pilot. "Well, DON'T" said Derek. That's when I looked, saw the situation, and hung on.

Derek is now going to get his licence again. Then he can fly himself around which will be much, much better. Anyway — since so few people ever crash at all, and certainly so few survive the kind of ruined plane that we got out of — we feel confident that we are now safe. The people here have been telling me that God wanted us to finish our work to help them in Tanzania. It is like an omen, and I feel quite strange about it. For me, Africa has always been the ruling force of my life, I suppose. Now it is even more than that. Lots of things seem to have fallen into shape after nearly being dead — you know, you suddenly realize that it could happen (death, I mean) at any moment. So [you do] what is best to do with the life entrusted to you.

It would have gladdened — and still would — your heart to see the sunny, happy, non-whining, super mood Grub's been in ever since we got back. Like he is when I'm not around in Bournemouth.

Really nice. And his reading is leaping ahead. We're having torrential rains, he has a new net, the students are wonderful, your chapter's coming along, good new baboon things — maybe there was a reason we were spared! The field assistants have a new office upstairs, and I bought them chairs as a present. They're working on reports for the newstype monthly reports. And when are you coming out to see Gombe?

Lots & lots of love,
Jane & Ub

[Probably February 10, 1974]

Darling Mum,

I was going to make this a long letter, but it's so late — 12:45 — & I'm half dead. Thank you for your last letter. . . .

Had a visit from Hugo who said we had to make up our minds about the future. Would I leave Gombe for him. Or more or less. He seemed quite cheerful about it, but it was an upsetting talk. We covered everything & decided, quite calmly, how it wasn't any good. He said he needed someone on safari with him. He was so cheerful, & so enthusiastic about Stella & all her family, that I feel sure something is up. Which could be super. Only he wouldn't say. Grub knows all about it. He suggested to me that since I couldn't look after things properly, it would be a good idea if he [Hugo] got another wife & then she would have a holiday if I went to Ndutu & another if Hugo came here! (He's grown up with people who have several wives!) He is very happy about things — you've no idea what a super & calm mood he's been in since we got back to Gombe. He only wondered if Hugo could still go to Bournemouth — & I said of course. He wasn't sure if he wanted Hugo to have another baby, but thought it might be fun — so long as I didn't!! Hugo was so calm about things — we talked of Grub having time on the Serengeti with him — but later, when Grub could enjoy it all. . . .

Other than that, things are going so splendidly for Gombe, but I'll write to you anon. Got the goggles & book from Billy — hoped there'd be a letter from you in it! (Maybe hidden in the book which comes from Kigoma tomorrow — no room for luggage this evening). The lectures at Dar were fine — I did 2 & the 2nd, I know, was one of my best ever. Goodness. Wish I'd taped it! Billy & Pierre didn't get to Gombe — Pierre ill.

Lots of Love,
Jane

8 days gone
17 days to wait
1/3 over
[Around March 1, 1974]

Darling beloved Derek,

Tomorrow that beastly radio again. I still hate it. But I suppose it is better than nothing. Though I don't know. It so filled me with haunting fears last time that they have not gone. Not at all. Perhaps tomorrow will calm them. Perhaps confirm them. Anyway, I'll hear your voice, distorted as usual. And you'll hear mine, clearly I hope. Every time I say 'Over' I'll be meaning "I love you". Think back on the conversation with that in mind. Over — and Over — and Over — again. Just as we tell each other we have to, somehow.

Soon I'll get a letter from you. Then I'll know. Emilie couldn't get on the plane, and I doubt my letter caught the plane either. They started late as usual. Tomorrow they'll start early because Grub is off to [the clinic at] Kabanga to see Sister Kate and have his tooth out. I've funked going — like I always do! So he's going with Emilie and Helen.

Strange how the act of writing makes you feel even closer than if I was just sitting thinking to you. Maybe the idea of you reading the words, touching the same piece of paper. I just kissed the 'Derek' at the top!

Today it has rained. And rained. All morning it teemed down. My office was like a piece of the outside — rain just pouring in under the eaves and through the veranda window. So I went to the kitchen — oh — dining room! But no sooner settled there with my typewriter than — lo! the wind changed. It poured in there. In the sitting room it came under the bottom of the curtain & the floor was an inch deep, and a slow stream of drops cascaded onto the table, where I placed a washingup bowl. Leaks all over. In the end I climbed onto my bed & wrote letters & outlined the baboon booklet there! It rained till 1. The waterfall is racing down, & water seeping from the mountain itself is running down & streaming along the back passage. It turns the corner and gurgles merrily to the lake. So I'm virtually on an island!

My darling, goodnight. I shall blow out the light and imagine your strength is close beside me, and imagine your strong arms around me and we can take comfort from one another — until next time.

All my love is with you,<br>
Your Jane

[Postmarked October 8, 1974]

My darling darling Derek,

Today, unless the lines don't work or there is some kind of earthquake, I shall hear your voice.* That is such a wonderful thought I leapt out of bed — it was still more or less dark. It rained all night — thunder & lightning. I was reminded of Gombe. (Left my car windows open again!) But it had just stopped and the birds were singing when I came out into the wet garden with my tea and cheese. The humming bird has found his feeder and comes so close — he has just been here, a tiny, quivering scrap of feather, his wings vibrating. And now he's flown onto a little branch, and is singing his funny whirring song — which might be pretty, if you could slow it down. So I just had to write to you — because I want too much to share the things I love with the man I love. I so much wish you were here to share the humming bird, my darling, for I love you so very much. For always. For ever. Sometimes when I'm looking at something beautiful, or listening, I imagine you are right beside me, & see your face, or your voice saying something, and then a big smile

---

* Writing from Stanford, California, she refers to a planned long-distance phone call.

comes over my face, & I sit like a Cheshire cat! Oh — how super. It is a pair of humming birds — I thought there were 2. They just came together! It is raining again. I love the rain.

Last night Genie rang — di san Faustino. She immediately asked all about you so we had a glorious talk. Ranieri is miles better, she says. They have just got back from Italy where she — I quote her letter to me, waiting when I arrived — "passed the beaches staring over the blueness of the sea towards Africa". They are driving all the way here to see me on Saturday — bringing some supper!! Gordon Getty is visiting Gombe West tomorrow, so various old acquaintances are being renewed, I have been mainly working on my lectures, sorting slides, and thinking about you. These things have occupied just about all my time. It's really great having Julie, Curt & Nancy as my T.A.'s (that's teaching assistants).* They do an enormous amount to help — although they do perhaps more than I would care for if I were one of the undergrads! (The 3 have all graduated now.) I briefly saw Dave Riss who is working hard at Med. School. Soon, soon — I'll hear your voice, my beloved, my own darling, dearest Derek. I need 2 more pages — but I'll wait till I've talked with you. I must gather my things & myself together now.

All my love, dearest, all of it,
for always & for ever & ever —
your Jane

[Around April 1, 1975]

Darling Family,

Sorry no word for so long — but as you'll have gathered I was laid fairly low with a sordid go of malaria. It really was a lousy time — bit like the go I had at Ndutu. Just lay, sweated, shivered, couldn't eat. Just orange juice (till we ran out of oranges!) and dear Michelle found some soup. It was really super when Derek arrived & could make the orange juice and soup. He read to me & generally helped me to recover. Think I'd still be lying unable to eat otherwise. Very depressing.

---

* Stanford students Julie Johnson, Curt Busse, and Nancy Nicolson.

Anyway, he decided I'd get better much quicker if I went to Dar with him. As he was going just for 5 days, to do various things before coming to Gombe for Easter, it seemed sensible. When he 1st proposed it, I couldn't stand the thought of 5 hours flying — but by the Sunday I decided to go. So we left on Monday & returned on Saturday. Grub stayed to do school, and Etha slept with him & gave him breakfast & supper. With the group here now, plus the × 2 daily radio contact with Dar, I don't mind him staying here for a short time. Anyway, got better rapidly in Dar. Had a tide pool morning, and on Friday, a coral reef morning & got super fish for the aquarium. But, best of all, we got Spider. Don't know if you knew we were looking for Spider — but did I tell you about Baggins? Anyway, we wanted a friend for Beetle. So have been visiting the dog pound since before last fall. Baggins was exactly the most unsuitable dog — large, boisterous & long haired. We felt he had to be rescued, & went to collect him, with Grub. But by enormous good fortune, because we were late, owing to the late arrival of Grub & Simon, someone else had taken him & paid for him. Huge relief really. Anyway, this time — there was Spider. Exactly the dog we have been looking for. Small, pale yellowish-white, short haired, about 9 months. She smiles, talks (incredibly talkative). If I were to give her a breed, I'd call her a miniature golden retriever! She's pretty. Anyway, carried her home — just like that, in the car. (Paid 70 for her). Took her out to the kitchen. Gave her some food. Put on the spare flea collar. She barked like anything when Beetle 1st appeared — dog smell — but hardly dog appearance! Since she'd never seen a peke! Anyway, Beetle was very crusty to start with, but she is so friendly — he began to melt. She goes & kisses him. When he appears. And no sooner arrived in the house — at home. Absolutely. It was simply super. And Beetle is rejuvenated already. With her there, he came down to the sea edge to see us off in the boat. And they lay together. We tied her the 1st night. She whined for about 30 mins. Then settled. We did not tie her again. Emmanuel likes her. She's thin — but the dog pound man likes dogs. She doesn't flinch or cringe. Yet she'd been there 2 months and spotlessly clean. Very good. So Spider is now part of the family.

Well — got back safely. Awful long journey when you do it

straight through without spending the night en route. We didn't get to Kigoma till after 4. Then home James. To find a very perky Grub — lots of 5 stars. House very spic & span & ship shape. Such a super house now. . . .

Happy Sausages to all. Much love,<br>Jane

P.S. Could you thread a decent needle into your next letter, please!

[September 24, 1976]

Darling Ub,

Well — the pen wouldn't write, and so now I am upstairs tapping away and you will be able to read this letter — I hope.

I'm so glad you enjoy football — I thought you would. I am very anxious to hear all about the school, the lessons, the masters, the boys, the games, the gym — and the bus journey! Who fetches you in the morning? What time do you have to get up? And everything about everything.

Spider has just come wandering into the room, shaking. She must have stolen some food yesterday — she got a very fat tummy and made disgusting poops all day — first in my office where I was working, then while we had lunch, then in the hall where we were trying to do some telephoning — and then we had a long walk and she was much better after that! We found 17 shiney olives yesterday evening, Derek and I. This morning I found about 10 more. So it is a good time for olives right now. Derek got a super black one, but I only got greys.

Nowadays I am getting up at 6.00 in the morning again, and going a long way with the dogs. Then again in the evening — I go some of the way with Derek, and then leave him looking for shells and run with them along to where we found all the shells. (No shells there any more now, though.) Wagga is fantastic, running in the water and chasing birds. She gets the most fantastic exercise! . . .

Tomorrow is Saturday, and we are going to go to the Island, and Derek is going to catch some more fish. We have returned the big puffer to the sea because he was trying to kill the toady. So I hope you would approve of that? Also the remaining barbels — 2 more died, with those bites in them, and one looked ill — so we put them in a lovely tide pool and maybe the ill one recovered. The butterfly is doing superly. Both the cones in the tank are fine, and the other shells we put in there. And the nudibranchs. The feathery one still goes flying around. Also the little pipe fishes — red and grey. Doing fine.

But funny things happening in the Gombe tank. The spotted Jane suddenly died!* The other fish is quite fine — loving his sand hoppers. But poor old Spotty — she suddenly appeared, lying in the middle of the tank, all her skin sort of shredding off. Like a sort of mucous layer. I took her out, and within half an hour she was dead. It may be because of the coral we put in. It is very rough on their skins. Luckily Henrietta, or Harriet, or Horace — I vary these names! — doesn't lurk in the coral. He is getting very tame now, and knows that the approach of a red bucket means feeding time. Up comes his dorsal fin, and that disagreeable mouth gets all ready for the feast. He's very quick at chasing and catching the hoppers — and he's learned that when they are close to the glass he must be careful or else he will bump his nose! Misha† came while I was in the middle of this letter — I had just typed "But funn ..." at the top of this paragraph. He's brought some special gravel and funnels so that we can make 2 filters for the Gombe tank, and some medicine for the water so that Horace won't catch the skin disease, if that's what it was, that Sp.J. died of. He is going to bring 4 other fish who eat bits of dead fish — then Horace, competing with them, will learn to eat dead food. Because I can't see Emmanuel catching sand hoppers when we're away! What I do is to put about 1/2 inch sea water in the bottom of the big red bucket, pick up a handful of the rubbish along the tide line — especially where there is seaweed half covered by sand, and hold it some way down inside the bucket. Then the hoppers jump out of their hidey holes and land in the

---

* A catfish.
† An acquaintance.

bucket. As they crawl up the side of the bucket from the water, so I put my finger on one and bring my finger up the side of the bucket, and catch the hopper between that finger and my thumb when I get to the rim. It's very tedious and takes too much time.

Well, Ub. Apart from the fact that it rained a lot yesterday, I think there is nothing else I can tell you. Do please dictate a nice long, long letter to Um for me, telling me all sorts of things. Remember you promised to dictate something every weekend? Because I miss you very much, and think about you all the time, and I want lots of letters to read so I know exactly how you are getting on, how you are feeling, and what you are doing. OK? Anyway — give my love to all of the family, and to Jiff and Rod and Emma and Pippit. Happy everything in all the whole wide, wide world — happy sausages, happy dreams, happy swimming — even happy maths!

Derek sends lots and lots of love and happy everything too and will write.

Lots & lots & lots of love,<br>Jane

Thursday [October 28, 1976]

Darling, darling family —

Oh dear, it is really the end of an era, the old things ending — but the old things were so much better and stronger than the new. It is all so sad. I feel awful about our telephone — I had a feeling you were trying to ring — but they kept promising to re-connect our phone and then it was not done. The bill HAD been paid. Anyway, that cannot be undone. Derek didn't tell me he'd seen the cable until the evening because I was teaching all afternoon at the university. Of course it was a very, very tearful evening. I didn't think I'd be able to speak to you at all. And of course I wish I'd been back, and seen Danny again, and that made it so much worse. And sleep was impossible.

But eventually I had the strangest — well, I don't know if it was a dream, or a half dream — or what it was. But there was Danny. The little figure of recent years, sitting up in her bed and saying "Oh I am a silly old thing. No use to anyone. Don't think of me like that, oh dear me no". And she went on talking — only I don't know what she said — lots about "Daddy" and her "blessings" but all mixed up with things about Monica and the Twins and Tetenhall.* And I found that she looked quite different from the Danny I remember & very young with black hair. I didn't even know that it was Danny. And then suddenly she was "my" Danny again and she had that twinkle in her eye and she said "I've found him, you know". I wasn't talking to her — somehow just listening. But I <u>thought</u> "Do you mean 'Daddy' or Jesus?" And she twinkled even more and said "Wouldn't you like to know!" I knew there was lots more — I can't think of it. It means I am freed to think of the Danny of my childhood again — croquet — tea in the garden with Percy Bysh† mating — Goering on the bread in treacle — puddings with everything in them. Instead of the brave little figure in its bed that has been in my thoughts almost all the time. I just feel so sorry for all of you — in the house — the kitchen — the drawing room. I WISH I could help. But we do know that she is happy now — with part of her she's wanted it, even for some time. I'll write again.

LOVE,
Jane

Box 727
Dar es Salaam
6 July 1978

Dear Ned,

I am writing to inform you of a new development in our plans for long-term support for the research at Gombe. As you know, the problem of funding the research by means of grants from U.S. Foundations became more difficult after the 1975 kidnapping. This was for two reasons: (a) no longer was it possible for American students to work at Gombe for security reasons and (b) there were no

---

* Monica was a cousin; Jane's favorite teacher from her first school, Phyllis or Auntie Philly, had an identical twin; and Tetenhall was the name of Danny's first house before she acquired the Birches.
† A pet tortoise.

scientifically qualified personnel on the spot. At that time (fall of 1975) I was hopeful that the L.S.B. Leakey Foundation (which had already risen magnificently to help Gombe out of a tight spot a couple of years before) might grant funds to fill in gaps in the budget. My hopes were well justified. However, as you will remember, many members of the Science and Grants Committee, at that time, were concerned by the lack of qualified people collecting the data. So that my concern, for long term funding of Gombe, was not assuaged.

Friends in San Francisco shared our concern. They felt that one solution, in the long term, might be to set up an institute for the collection of donations to Gombe. The appeal would be broad-based and aimed specifically at smaller ($10 to $100) gifts.

We discussed the idea with many people including a number of Leakey Foundation Officers and Trustees. Although some felt that an institute of this sort would have major drawbacks (such as tax difficulties, much extra work for little gain and endangering my relationship with the Leakey Foundation), others felt that it was a good idea. A main argument on the positive side was that it was against the principles of most foundations to provide support for the same project year after year and that we should not expect the Leakey Foundation to be different in this respect.

Because many people in whom we had great confidence felt that this was a good avenue to explore, our friends in San Francisco went ahead with their efforts. The institute was to be called The Jane Goodall Institute, although I would be neither an officer nor a trustee. The Institute would also aim to raise money for conservation and research projects of Tanzania national parks. This Institute has now been registered and, last week, received final tax exempt status from Federal and State authorities.

I am sure you have already heard most of the above. The object of writing to you now, as President of the L.S.B. Leakey Foundation, is to let you know that I do not wish to interfere with the good relationship that now exists between the Leakey Foundation and myself. I do not see this Institute as being, in any way, competitive with the Foundation. It is not an organization with members, but simply a vehicle for the collection and disbursal of funds. As you said in your letter of 16 January 1978, the Leakey Foundation and myself have enjoyed a mutually beneficial relationship in the past — and I hope this will continue into the future. Our hope is to slowly build up a fund which may provide a little security for the future of the long term work at Gombe. While this is going on, the need for finance to keep up the on-going operations will continue.

Before closing let me add that the Twins are still alive. They are extraordinarily backward in their development: when I saw them at seven months, they were exactly like normal three month old babies! Even to tooth development. The more advanced of the pair, Gyre, had just got his first two lower incisors! The same with regard to behaviour.

Must now get on with the monograph, which progresses — slowly.

Yours sincerely,
Jane Goodall, Ph.D.

[September 17, 1979]

Darling Um, Darling Olly,

Ah — super. Last time I used the typewriter my hand still hurt and made me type all the wrong letters! Now it does not hurt at all! The next time I tried to type, actually, the machine was broken, as I think I told you in my early morning missives yesterday..... Yesterday — was it only 24 hours ago that we trailed out to the airport with one small Nibbs? It seems, already, like a week ago. Zano has been gathering up all the little bits and pieces and putting them in his room. Rods, hooks, reels, lures, wires used for catching geckos, nooses for rats, lead weights, squids, bits of line, bits of fossil, guns, knives — on and on. Sad little reminders. But I do think it was the best holiday we've had together yet. Of course there were some bad times — but they were very quickly over, very minor, nothing like last summer when I sometimes wondered what on earth I had produced! It was good having the two weeks at Gombe, but it would have been nice if Derek had been there for one of them. In fact, Grub hardly saw Derek the whole holiday. One of the weeks he was here in Dar Derek was ill, and the last 5 days Derek was working almost all the time.

It was a pity about Grub and the chimps at Gombe. The first time he came upstairs was the first day — he was FAR too excited about his fishing to want to look at the chimps — and there were about 10 in camp! He only wanted to eat his lunch in a "comfortable chair". He came up one other time, one little family came in, he had forgotten his camera (brought it the first time, but with no film!) However, he did not come to Gombe to see chimps, so it didn't matter really! One of the "tiffs" at Gombe was when I asked him to help me wash up the supper things. Oh, why not leave them till tomorrow. (Sadiki was going to do chimp work the next day.) It was so lovely in the bright moonlight with the lake a few yards away, I couldn't believe he wouldn't come. But he pottered about, doing all sorts of other silly things, until I had nearly finished. (I was doing the fishy plates and the pan, anyway, and had given him the cups and knives and glasses — no more!) Very, very begrudgingly he finally came and was then so nasty and rude that I really got livid! But it was over after a bit. I can't remember the other two, except that in one he retired to his bed — oh yes, because there were only vegetables for supper!! In fact, Sadiki has a way of doing veg which is absolutely delicious. And I had made soup, and there were fried bananas for pud! I really was angry that evening, and tore the bedclothes off him! The following day he sheepishly admitted that the supper had been delicious! — oh yes, there were peanuts too, to start with!

When I could really tell how much more grown up an adult he is, was this last little time in Dar. All our plans for him to fish fell through — no petrol tank for our little boat, other people's boats out of the water or the people away, or the boats broken down. But he was absolutely O.K., as I would have been, just "messing about". I was really, really thrilled with this. He played with the dogs, shot things off trees with his catapult, chased rats with Zano, fixed up his lures, changed line from one reel to another — and so on. It was super. Enjoyed his meals — I wonder if he told you? About 4 of the meals I cooked him were greeted with "just like a restaurant" — high praise! And he simply loved his last evening

with Annie and Steve* — filleting the fish for supper, shelling peanuts, long walk with me first, for your birthday shells, Olly (oh yes,
and earlier a trip to the market for the fruit with Spider and Wagga
in the car, his great joy). And ending up with his Africoco and a cup
of tea with the dogs in his bedroom!

Well, there must be lots more to tell about him, but perhaps he'll
tell you some of it. I don't think the fishing trips with the two little
Dutch boys were a very great success, but I'm not sure. He did like
them at the time, but less in retrospect. Derek is really going to lay
on the trip to Tanga at Christmas time, where there is this friend of
his who has a really super duper fishing boat (chap has huge sisal es-
tates, and Derek has known him 10 years or more, and I met him at
the airport once, and liked him). Derek has various projects in
Tanga which he should visit, so it can be a combined trip, business
for Derek and fishing for Grub. We've not made a big thing of it to
Grub, because it may fall through — the man may be on leave or
something. But we really shall try. That and Gombe will take all the
time, because we will DEFINITELY give you and him a MINIMUM
of 3 complete days at the end of the holiday!! Not much time for
Spider and Wagga!

Just 3 Gombe things to talk about. First, Fifi and family. Fabulous
to follow. Freud, at just over 8 years, already can totally dominate 4
females — Sparrow, Patti, Little Bee and Dove. While I was there
with them I saw him display and display at Dove until she was
screaming. Finally she rushed up into a tree and "hid" in an old
nest, lying flat and peeping down! Of course, he rushed up after her,
and displayed above her, until she leapt down and, screaming, ran
away! And little Frodo was up there "helping" Freud — absolutely
as excited as anything! He threw 4 rocks at Patti another time —
she was less fearful though, especially now she has her infant. And
he actually <u>attacked</u> Little Bee — she did turn on him, but she
screamed first! By contrast, he spent 25 minutes vainly courting
Gigi, shaking little, then bigger branches at her, harder and harder,
staring and staring at her semi-swollen bottom. And she didn't even

---

* Visiting friends.

<u>look</u> at him once. So he gave up and lay down. But how history is repeating itself. Fifi is becoming really aggressive now — she flew at and quite badly attacked Melissa — who was livid and screamed and screamed and, in about 5 minutes, Goblin displayed into camp from the valley, and this put paid to Fifi's little schemes! And Fifi also attacked Little Bee for daring to do a drumming display close by when they travelled together! Soon, with Freud getting bigger and stronger all the time, and Frodo who is HUGE for his age, Fifi will certainly become top female, I should think. As Gigi gets older. Though I don't know about the Passions — thing is — Passion and Pom just stick together, and very, very rarely meet any other chimps at all now. Very interesting. But I must finish the Fifi thing. It was an afternoon follow. Warm, lazy. Frodo picked himself a strychnos ball — opened it on his own with 45 bangs! (First time he's been recorded doing that.) Then Freud got 2. He opened and ate one, then played with the other. First he just put it on his head and picked it up as it rolled down his back, and did it again. Then he threw it up a little so it landed on his head and rolled down. THEN, to my absolute amazement, he threw it about 2 feet in the air with his left hand — and CAUGHT IT! He did this 4 times. Once, before catching it, he hit it up with his right hand as it came down, then caught it with his left hand. I simply couldn't believe it. A child playing with a ball. What a lucky thing to see! Then he lay on his back and, using his toes, managed to balance his ball on a tiny little forked twig that was just about level with his feet. Spent a long time playing thus, balancing, then tipping it off, putting it back, etc. Ended up with Fifi taking it from him and eating it! That family — honestly, how much one learns from them. Even when, for the first time, this time, I myself saw a real proper waterfall display, it was, of course, Figan who did it. I'd only seen rain, wind and streambed displays before. The waterfall display really is fabulous to watch — my little notebook that day is a hoot — as I followed Figan and Humphrey and Goblin up the valley, I began to hear the roar of the falls — wrote in my little book "Please, please, Figan, do a waterfall display". And as we slowly got closer, my pleas were written with bigger and more desperate writing. And, of course, they were answered!

Goblin is the second chimp to mention. Only 15 years old (this

September) — yet he has even intimidated Figan! I think, by the end of the year, Figan will no longer be alpha. I don't think there will be one. Goblin will finally emerge as the next alpha, but perhaps not for as long as a year. Very interesting! The third thing, Patti and her baby. You remember she handled the first one so badly that it died? Well, she simply adores this one, Tappit — No, I suppose it must be Tapit, with one "p". But she really is not all that competent! It is so amusing to watch. She lets him do far too much, far too soon. He is already climbing and walking, at only 4 months — and she just watches benignly. He keeps falling, getting lost — all kinds of mishaps — great dramas for such a minute person. Eventually she gets upset also, and retrieves him and kisses him! When they play, which is often, often, often, they kiss one another all the time. It's not <u>really</u> kissing, it's touching, nibbling and licking each other's lips!

Well. Quite a lot of news. The house seems so odd without Grub in it. So silent. The dogs don't know what to do with themselves — no rats to hunt, no sunny walks, no one to sit and stroke them for hours on end. Spider's wounds are slowly healing — she's as aggressive as Fifi, but bad luck for her, Wagga is no Freud! She's just a coward! And now, for me — back to the Monograph. I wonder how much of it I can get down before the Christmas holidays? I am aiming to get 3 chapters done — Feeding, Hunting, Ranging, social organization which includes hierarchy. Oh — that's 4 chapters. Well, I hope I can. . . .


Dar
Monday, 26 May [1980]

Darling Um & Olly,

Sorry I havn't written before. But there was — is — such horrid news to write that I have kept putting it off. Both the dogs are dead. That dog flue. <u>Both</u> of them. And Simba & Tim. And the dog next door, that <u>super</u> Whiskey, has nerve problems, after living through the disease, and her lower jaw snaps up and down all the time. The house is so bleak and empty — and it just seems impossible to believe — yet it is, of course, true.

I don't know how to tell Grub about Spider. Shall I leave it till the end of term? What do you think? Certainly not before Common Entrance.

He sounded sort of peculiar yesterday on the phone. Was everything OK? After Hugo's visit perhaps. He just didn't sound himself at all & I felt quite miserable afterward.

Well, let me now turn to more positive things. Thank you both for giving me such a super time in the Birches, all those lovely fattening meals. I have run to one stew & one curry since getting back. Each of which did us 3 meals — now, today, I must embark on a new one! We have had problems because our last lot of eggs all tasted of very strong disinfectant! Bit better off food-wise these days! Can get sugar, rice, bread, milk. Maize meal is short, still no margarine. . . .

Another sad thing — the Viets will be away <u>all</u> the time you are here, Um. Oh dear. She is very upset. Tried to persuade Dick not to go — but he has an 82 year old mother, at present in very good order, longing to see her grandchildren. And he feels that he must spend time with her this summer. So I don't know, now, when Marina will do the Diplomats' fund raising dinner. They came round yesterday for a late tea, wanting to hear all the news. Marina was thrilled with her violet, which traveled very well. I planted the lilies of the valley, in 2 spots. One lot has been <u>totally</u> devoured!! The other lot is droopy. I think that is an experiment which cannot work, sadly — Olly — <u>why,</u> if they <u>ARE</u> lilies do they not have corms? Or bulbs, or whatever lilies have. Why only roots? R.S.V.P.

Well, thanks again 100 times over for everything — that spider is meant to be 100!! Zano and our garden in good order, at least. And the fish are OK! Some v. interesting Gombe things in the reports — will tell you later.

Must end off & give this to D.

Tons & tons of love,<br>Jane & Janey Wayne

P.S. <u>Please</u> could you give Ub some ADDRESSED stamped envelopes. We just got another, <u>months</u> after he posted it, from a wrong Box No!!! So could you send him some urgently!!!

Dar

8 June 1980

Darling Um, Ol et al,

Half a year has just about gone. I HATE writing "June". Oh well! I just remembered, after talking to you Um, that it was <u>GRUB</u> I wrote to about the fact that I would only stay at Gombe one week. D goes off to his revolting barium meal tomorrow. We <u>can't</u> believe there is anything much wrong because he still looks so well. If there is anything awful I will ring you up.

Gombe was a disappointment — <u>very</u> few chimps. It <u>ALWAYS</u> seems to be the way when D comes. I am <u>REALLY</u> going to make a sort of sedan chair for him. You can use it too, then, Um! Still, saw FF PS PM ML and families. And Patti, at the very last moment — Tapit has been very, very sick, but was OK when I saw them, the usual flu pneumonia. Saw the males, too. Goblin <u>very</u> subdued! . . .

Heta & I will be going to Gombe either the end of this month or early July. And I hope Marina will come for a few days before she goes on leave — she can help more with fund raising then.

Dar is breezy — nice for us, bad for the garden! But most of our new plants are doing well & blooming, and the new drive is made — just needs a load of gravel on the top. And then some rain, so that grass will begin to cover the present road.

I have almost caught up Gombe to end April, & am about to finish off the paper — the long demography one. Did you throw away the little metal egg containers from your <u>old</u> poacher? If not, do you need them anymore, & can we have them?

Tons of love to you all —

Jane, Janey Wayne

Krankenhaus am Silbersee
Room 513
Langenhagen
Hanover, W. Germany
[Early July 1980]

Dear Joanne:

I know you will have heard from Mary about Derek's operation and all that went before. Our fear, then our hope that those fears were groundless.

Derek got back to the ward after the op at 8.00 p.m. (having left at 1.30). You can imagine what a horrid time I had waiting!

The surgeon came up at 9.00 p.m. Took me to a next door room and said it was cancer, he'd removed the primary tumour — he could do no more. There was <u>no</u> treatment that would help. He hoped I was staying with a relative or friend, he felt I should take a taxi, goodnight.

Joanne, I don't know <u>how</u> I got back. I decided to do battle with the underground — that at least was forced contact with the outside world, keeping me sane — just!

Fortunately, I <u>was</u> staying with someone — Derek's sister-in-law. His brother's widow. Whiskey and a sleeping pill. Through the next day, <u>somehow.</u> D. was told that it <u>was</u> cancer & that the "part that mattered" came out. So I knew and he didn't.

That evening Mum arrived. After a weep & a whiskey we started to talk. Right from the first scare I had prepared myself for this, to some extent.

O.K. In Africa, there are witch doctors, herbs. I rang my best friend in Dar & she got going on that. In a remote village in India is a wonderful root. An old Indian nanny got going on <u>that.</u>

The next day we found out about Hepzibah, Yehudi Menuhin's sister. She was given 3 months to live — <u>5 1/2</u> years ago. I went to meet her & her super husband. She told me about laetrile and Dr. Hans Nieper. She gave me books. She <u>proved</u> that what I knew was right — that "<u>nothing</u> to be done" was WRONG.

Well, the days went by. Mum tackled the awful surgeon (because I <u>KNEW</u> he would tell me this approach was no use and I didn't want to <u>hear</u> it. I was right!) But Mum got the proper prognosis out of him. Then the Hepzibahs went away for the weekend. Then they thought I should try a Dr. in England first, so I went off to him. No good. Finally they managed to ring & speak to Dr. Nieper. He has a waiting list a mile long — but said he'd better take D at once. So I told D the truth, got him out of the hospital, into the flat, booked seats to Hanover, & here we are.

The surgeon (who, fabulously, was <u>away</u> when I whisked D out of the hospital) made a point of ringing up that night. He did so wish he could have told Derek <u>himself.</u> (Can't you imagine!) What was I doing? Oh — Nieper — never heard of him (everyone else has — he's been there 15 years & gave a lecture to a <u>packed</u> auditorium to the British Med. Assoc. last year). You are wasting your time. Laetrile, of course, will be <u>absolutely</u> useless. Derek should be allowed to spend the last few weeks of active life in Dar tidying up his affairs. Charming!

The first day here — tests — second day, lots of pills & more tests. 3rd day — laetrile derivative all day in intra-venous drip. 4th day — same. 5th day — today. Dr. Nieper in as usual (5 mins. ago). The cells are inactive. D feels <u>no</u> pain at all. We are <u>so</u> excited. Still another few weeks here. Diet terribly important. But the great <u>hurdle</u> is crossed. The path lab report indicated a <u>FAST</u> growing type of cancer. This seldom responds to Laetrile. But the blood tests indicate that, in fact, it was a slow growing kind. Which is <u>SUPER.</u>

So — a long way to go, as Dr N says, but the end is good. So I wanted to write to say what had happened — we need your sympathy (of course!) and good <u>positive</u> thoughts.

Could you please share this with all our friends at the Geographic. The message being that we want to share the happiness of proving the London chap wrong.

We will keep in touch.

Lots of love,
Jane & Derek

Krankenhaus

22 August 1980

Dear Mary,

Well, here we are, back in the boring old hospital. It is pouring with rain, so a bit dismal. However, after one scare (D. developed what Nieper called a "nodule" — one of the metastases, I suppose, on the colon and we were terrified of an obstruction. That night I know there was a miracle of healing. Because I felt it. And next morning Nieper said "Oh, your nodule has regressed." Phew!) Derek is doing very well. Yesterday Nieper said that quite soon he hoped to have the cancer stabilized so that he could work out a "Do-it-yourself" regime and we could return to the big, wide world. He is looking very fine, and feeling better all the time.

We had a very nice letter from Andy Brown* — do tell him it ar-rived and I'll write to him soon. I'm planning to write an account of our experiences and send a copy to all our super friends.

We have one favour to ask, Mary. There is one kind of alcoholic beverage which D. is allowed to drink. A Mosel type wine, sour, white. It has to have a very low sugar content, and low alcohol. Dr. Nieper said the best in the world, that he knew of, was from the Napa (Napper?) Valley in California. We have asked Genie di San Faustino if she can find some. And I wondered if it would be OK if she sent it to you. And then, if someone is going to England without much luggage, if a couple of bottles could go with them. Would that be an awful bore? It makes a big psychological difference if he can join in a social "tot"! . . .

Did I tell you he was writing a book? It's coming on jolly well. First two chapters done, and I'm typing them. The publisher is very keen. Wants second consultation after reading these two chapters. It gives D. something to do, so he doesn't fret about inactivity. D. himself is very keen too! It all helps in these difficult days.

Of course, much love from Derek to you and Tom.

Love,

Jane

---

* An editor at *National Geographic* magazine.

[Late November 1980]

Darling Family,

Oh dear — coming back to the house is even <u>worse</u> than I dreaded. I am still with the Viets, coming to the house to work every day. Ian is being super and somehow we have got through all the ceremonies. The ashes part was helped along by <u>everything</u> going wrong. It POURED with rain. (I shared an umbrella with dear Chief Adam.) While we waited for a pause, we went into a little building by the quay & there was a very moving statement read out about Derek from Kinondoni. I'll get it translated. Then we set off. 3 boats. . . . Well — too wet to see where we were, not enough petrol to get to the island (discovered <u>after</u> we started out!), they couldn't unscrew the box for ages (not prepared ahead of time, of course), no rope to tie the rock to the box (after Ian put out the ashes, they wanted to sink the box & wreath), no one had a knife. I'm sure Derek was laughing. Ian & I agreed that had all gone well, clear day, fishes on the reef in the sun, we'd never have got through it. Yesterday was the final ceremony when Chris & 18 others came & presented a huge "Condolences" book with about 200 names, Mwalimu's first & [a gift of] 3000/- from Kinondoni. Ian replied for me to the speech. . . .

I have spent this morning, with Zano, in making Grub's room into a sort of bed-sitter for me. It's one of the coolest rooms in the house and, like my office, has no connotations of Derek. Which is a help. It's beginning to look nice. I'll bring back some more bits & pieces for it from England after Christmas.

Heta will be returning in 3 weeks, so if you want to send a letter via her it will be sure to arrive safely. Then she's off to India for Christmas. She's going to work a few weeks without salary when she gets back! Prashant has a new job & is v. pleased.

Have no more news — it is still quite cool, amazingly. I'll hope to speak to you today or tomorrow — tomorrow, Sunday, I expect.

Tons of love,
Jane

# 9

❧ ❧ ❧

# MOVING ON
## 1981–1986

During the first six months or so after Derek's death I often felt his presence. . . . And then, after a while, as though he knew that I was all right, that my days had, indeed, brought sufficient strength, I felt his presence less and less often. I knew it was time for him to move on and I did not try to call him back.

— *Reason for Hope*

JANE GRIEVED QUIETLY during the months that followed Derek's death, seldom or only obliquely recalling her loss even in the more personal letters to family and close friends. As ever, she turned to the forests of Gombe for consolation.

Her first brief visit back, in late 1980, was, she later recalled, "awful," while a second short excursion in early February of 1981 was "still very sad." Nevertheless, "the forest was cool, greens blending with each other, all through to the yellows, oranges & browns. With splashes of red. Restful to the mind" (February 15, 1981). At the end of May, she returned to her research site and found it "lousy" in terms of finding chimps, as she noted in the letter of June 5, but otherwise "as beautiful and peaceful as ever." After Grub arrived for his summer holidays, the two of them went back to Gombe for an extended and seemingly very satisfying time. Among the more notable events of that summer were the severe illness of Pom and the startling death of her two-year-old offspring, Pan, who fell out of a tree. Pom's eventual disappearance* is not re-

---

* Male chimpanzees stay in their birth communities; females sometimes emigrate, particularly during early adolescence. Pom was later sighted in a neighboring community.

ferred to in these pages, but Passion's extended and mortal illness is (February 12, 1982).

As we can gather from the first note (a fragment) in this sequence, the crisis of Derek's death was unexpectedly compounded by emergency surgery for Vanne, whose weak heart valve was replaced by a comparable part taken from a pig. Jane was reluctant to visit her mother in hospital (though she finally did), mainly because "my associations with cut open people recently have been so horrid." Still, the operation was successful, and the daughter determined to celebrate by pasting together for her mother an elaborate Christmas present, *An Anthology of the Pig*, which, as Jane wrote a year later, "ended up as a great volume!"

A second project begun after Derek's death was the Bryceson scholarship, referred to in several letters in this chapter, including the early one addressed to Dr. Maletnlema of February 9, 1981. Derek had been named chairman of the Tanzania Food and Nutrition Centre a few months before his death, and the staff and board members very generously made a contribution to Jane of 6,000 Tanzanian shillings (at that time equivalent to more than $700) as a spontaneous gesture of sympathy. She decided to use the money to memorialize Derek in a way he would have approved: as a contribution to the future of his adopted country. The Bryceson scholarship fund, seeded with that gift, grew during the early 1980s through fund-raising lectures and individual appeals (such as the one dated September 6, 1981) and was administered by Cornell University in the United States. Godwin Ndossi, described by Jane as "hard working, talented — and utterly charming" (January 23, 1985), was the first Bryceson Scholar.

In 1984 Jane started work on a third significant project, called ChimpanZoo. The idea originated during one of her American lecture tours when she visited a zoo; it may have been discussed with Ann Pierce, a former Gombe student, who showed up at Gombe in late January 1982. Two years later Jane was supporting Ann in a plan that was at first "deliberately vague": "to go round, get the feel of the groups of chimps and people, talk about the ideas . . . get ideas . . . and make a report" (letter of October 28). Ann was to survey U.S. zoos and, ideally, create an organization that would coordinate and standardize a major long-term study of the behavior of zoo chimpanzees, compare that with the behavior of wild chimpanzees, and more generally try to improve the psychological health of zoo chimps through enriching their physical and social environments. Within a year, the Jane Goodall Institute had begun paying a modest salary to Pierce — who, driving around the United States in a donated VW bus, had set up data-collection sites at more than a half-dozen zoos, had developed affiliations with about the same number of colleges and universities that were ready to send in behavioral science students as volunteers, and was beginning to establish a common data-collection system that could be centrally computerized. ChimpanZoo turned out to be a great success, with annual conferences comparing research and data on the lives of some 130 chimpanzees at a dozen zoos. It is, in fact, still supported by the Jane Goodall Institute.

A fourth major project was the ongoing research at Gombe. Altogether, 1981 to 1986 were positive years for Gombe. Jane continued to visit regularly and to direct the monitoring and record keeping done by a steady, professional Tanzanian staff, of whom several are mentioned in these pages: Rashidi Kikwale, Sadiki Rukumata, and Hilali Matama (February 15, 1981), as well as Apolly (Apollinaire Sindimwo, head of the baboon study), Eslom Mpongo, and "the new chap" Bruno Helmani (February 1983). Eventually several of the Tanzanian staff had begun videotaping chimpanzee behavior as part of their monitoring work, including Yahaya Alamasi, Eslom Mpongo, Hilali Matama, Yusufu Mvruganyi, and Hamisi Mkono.

A number of Europeans and Americans dropped in for various periods during these years, including most obviously Christopher Boehm. An anthropologist from the University of Northern Kentucky, he visited Gombe to study vocal communication among the chimpanzees and visited Jane in Dar es Salaam several times during the decade starting in 1984. He is the "Chris" mentioned in the letters of August and November 1985. Other visitors referred to in this chapter were Irenaus ("Renke") Eibl-Eibesfeldt of the Max Planck Institute, who came near the end of 1984 to "start on a long term filming project" (October 28, 1984); Richard Wrangham, a former Gombe student who was by then assistant professor of anthropology at the University of Michigan and writing a paper on chimpanzees and medicinal plants (letter of November 30, 1984); cameraman Warren Garst from the *Wild Kingdom* television show (in November 1985); and three people referred to in passing: former Gombe researchers Tony Collins, Bill McGrew, and David Bygott.

Hans Kummer, professor of ethology at the University of Zurich, spent time at Gombe in the second half of 1982, and Jane regularly stopped to visit him and his colleagues and students in Switzerland. She attended a seminar for Kummer's students in 1983, and in February 1985, at his invitation, gave a lecture that "was <u>packed,</u> and worked well" (letter of February 11, 1985). Goodall and Kummer coauthored a paper on "Conditions of Innovative Behaviour in Primates" in 1984.

During this same period, Jane was also developing ties with Japanese primatologists. She was later (in 1990) awarded Japan's most prestigious scientific honor, the Kyoto Prize for Basic Science; her first trip to Japan took place in November 1982 (described in the letter of December 1, 1982). After attending a symposium on "Parent-child Bonding," she traveled "into the mountains" with the distinguished pioneer of Japanese primatology, Junichero Itani, and some of his "chimp students."

Anthony Collins (mentioned above), who studied baboons at Gombe before the kidnapping and eventually returned as a senior scientist and administrator, should not be confused with Antonio Brescia — whose shortened name Jane conveniently spells "Toni." Nor should Christopher Boehm, mentioned above, be mistaken for Christopher Liundi. This second "Chris," an important friend of Jane's who lived in Kigoma, was a regional commissioner of Kigoma and, later, Tanzania's ambassador to France. Toni and Blanche Brescia, also living in Kigoma, had a slightly more formalized relationship with Jane and other research people passing through. They sometimes provided transportation or gave stranded Gombeites a place to stay overnight while waiting for a late plane or a recalcitrant train. The Brescias left town in the summer of 1985 and were replaced by Asgar Remtulla, and Kirit and Jayant Vaitha (who exported tropical fish from Kigoma).

I have not yet mentioned the most consuming project of all during this period: The Book. *The Chimpanzees of Gombe: Patterns of Behavior* began in the late 1970s when Jane imagined she could rather simply expand and update her original scientific monograph of 1968 ("The Behaviour of Free-living Chimpanzees in the Gombe Stream Reserve"). This new "monograph" would merely summarize, for a scientific audience, everything she had learned from that time on.

Since 1968, however, the research center had acquired a small mountain of data. In the first years, only Jane or a temporary substitute had been watching chimps and taking notes; but during the late 1960s and throughout the 1970s several people had been observing and recording their observations, and because the data-acquisition system had been standardized, all these observations were theoretically comparable and collective. If we guess that between 1960 and 1980 a rough average of four people were collecting daily observations on the chimpanzees at Gombe, then by 1980 Jane had amassed some 80 years' worth of data, which was bursting out of filing cabinets and cartons and boxes in the Dar es Salaam house and still growing: a vast, messy heap of potentially integrable information. The task of synthesizing all that new knowledge — the steady, quantitative data so patiently gathered, the great stack of written reports and summaries, and Jane's embracing sense of the significance of it all — was enormous.

Jane had help, and from among her several research assistants four appear briefly in these pages: Heta, Trusha, Jenny Gould, and Judy Taylor. Heta Pandit is referred to in a couple of early letters. She actually lived for a while in Jane's guest cottage at 99 Old Bagamoyo Road; and for a time her estranged husband, Prashant Pandit, lived there as well. Heta left in 1981, and Prashant remarried. His new wife, Trusha, began assisting with the monograph and is referred to in some of the later correspondence. Other people appearing in the Dar es Salaam context include Ian and Yenan

(Derek's son and young grandson), Zano (Jane's housekeeper and cook), Anskari (occasional gardener), Dick and Marina Viets (friends), Ramji Dharsi (who had recently moved from Kigoma to Dar), as well as Tony Avigon, Dimitri Mantheakis, and Dino (friends).

In the note of June 17, 1983, Jane deplored the "initial labour process" in writing, "which is absolutely inevitable and absolutely hideous. Everything I have read and thought goes grinding and crashing about in my head, and I sit all day and end up with one page and tear up 100s more." Aside from the usual mental numbness most people experience when trying to write a book, as well as regular bouts of malaria, there were other problems. Tanzania's official experiment with socialism had proven disastrous, and by the 1980s the economy was collapsing: with shortages, inflation, severe unemployment, rampant corruption, political repression, and lots of crime — such as the break-in at Jane's house mentioned on June 13, 1982. The economic failure of Nyerere's radical socialism was probably compounded by an idealism that led to the support of several African liberation movements on the one hand and, on the other, the granting of asylum to Ugandan exiles during Idi Amin's monstrous regime.

In 1971, for instance, the former Ugandan prime minister, Milton Obote, found himself cooled by breezes from the Indian Ocean just five houses down the beach from Derek (and later, of course, Jane). Obote's presence in Tanzania eventually provided Amin with an excuse to invade Tanzania — on October 30, 1978. In response, President Nyerere sent a hastily trained, inadequately equipped force of fifty thousand young Tanzanians into Uganda where, after combining with Ugandan rebels, they drove Idi Amin, along with his several wives and few dozen children, into premature retirement. The war was a great victory for Tanzania, but it cost half a billion dollars and returned a large population of unemployed soldiers with time and guns on their hands. Milton Obote eventually went back to Uganda, leaving behind only one pathetic, skulking dog. The dog was "habituated," named Cinderella (nicely described on September 1, 1981), and joined Jane's ever-changing pack of well-loved beach mutts.

With Cinderella at her feet, Jane continued laboring on The Book. By September 26, 1983, she could declare, in a note to fellow primate researcher Alison Jolly, that "I really have broken more than the back of it by now." By October 6, 1984, Jane believed she could at last say that "I have, to all intents and purposes, got the book DONE."

Not quite.

The book was enormous and enormously complex: a compact encyclopedia in undersized print spread across 650 oversized pages, color coded, with dozens of intricate maps and charts and graphs, a couple of hundred photographs, nineteen chapters, five appendixes, twenty pages of references, and two indexes touching on virtually every aspect of chimpanzee behavior anyone had ever considered. The complexities of publication (and communication with the publisher)* were such that, finally, Jane's manuscript editor at Harvard University Press, Vivian Wheeler, got her shots for cholera, typhoid, and yellow fever, and flew 8,200 miles to sort things out. We find Vivian being missed in a snowstorm in Switzerland (letter of February 11, 1985), where author and editor had agreed to rendezvous before moving on to Dar es Salaam.

Still, a monumental *Chimpanzees of Gombe* finally rolled off the presses in the summer of 1986, and Jane was able to write glowingly back to Vivian and the rest of the publisher's staff: "I gaze & gaze at the finished product. The dream that I believed would come true one day — that kept me going through the worst times."

*The Chimpanzees of Gombe,* a summation of approximately half of Jane Goodall's lifework as a behavioral scientist,† appeared on bookstore shelves in September 1986. It went through several printings, received stellar reviews, and was awarded the R. R. Hawkins Award for the Most Outstanding Technical, Scientific or Medical Book of 1986. Most impressively, the book's publication

---

* Not to mention the complexity of attempting to produce it all with a run-down manual typewriter, tediously stamping characters onto flimsy blue tissue (the only paper available in Dar at the time).

† She has not yet written the second volume, which would include mother-infant relations, infant and adolescent development, family dynamics over a life cycle, and so on.

became the focal occasion for a major international conference of chimpanzee experts sponsored by the Chicago Academy of Sciences, held in November 1986. As Jane described the concept in a letter written the year before: "Oh — did you hear about the conference they are putting on in Chicago to 'celebrate' the publication of the HUP book? A full 3 days, sponsored by Chicago Academy of Sciences — with chimp people from all over the world. Japanese, West African people — sign language and, of course, Chimp Zoo people. Exciting." Although, alas, I have not found anything written during or immediately after the conference, it was nevertheless a crowning moment in Jane Goodall's career, a great public acknowledgment of her pioneering role, seminal position, and breakthrough achievement in the study of humankind's closest relative.

*　　*　　*　　*

[January 1981]

Darling Um,

Will leave this for you to read when you are feeling much better. I have been thinking about you lying there cut apart all the time. I half wanted to be with you and half not. My associations with cut open people recently have been so horrid that even though your op is — thank <u>heavens</u> — quite different — I might have allowed some of the bad feelings to creep into you & that would have been no good. You are supposed to be more susceptible to telepathic communication when you are doped! Anyway, in thoughts I have been with you. It was even less possible to settle down to work! So I didn't even quite finish August!! I shall have a lot of catching up to do.

<u>So</u> many people rang up about you. . . . Pam arrived — only got a bit lost. Olly cooked me one of her best chicken lunches and it was a SUPER chicken from the △ butcher (I think you should use him, he is so nice). We had the wine Olly got (the day Joan M came & brought wine) and drank toasts to your speedy recovery.* . . .

---

\* Sympathetic visitors included Pam Bryceson, Derek's sister-in-law, and Joan Moseley, the mother of Grub's friend at school.

P.O. Box 727
Dar es Salaam
9 February 1981

Dear Dr. Maletnlema,

Firstly I should like to take this opportunity to thank the staff and Board members of TFNC for the very generous contribution. Ian Bryceson and I are both very grateful.

In fact, what we both want to do is to use this money to start a local fund for the Bryceson Scholars of the future. Therefore, as we agreed yesterday, I have started an account, in my name as a Trust fund for this purpose. (Jane Bryceson — Scholarship A/C No. 2059, Bank House Branch). This was how the bank manager advised me to proceed. This account now stands at Shs 6,500 (they require a deposit of Shs 500 cash before they open an account these days!). As we agreed, this account will be formally handed over to the TFNC at some future date.

I have written today to Professor Michael Latham, and hope he will be able to see me during my visit to the United States. I have also contacted some other people there who may be useful. Incidentally, I shall also be in Zurich, and possibly Geneva, in case there is anyone there you feel I should try to see?

I hope to see you upon your return from Japan and mine from Gombe.

Yours sincerely,
Jane Bryceson

Sunday
Gombe
[February 15, 1981]

Darling Um & Olly,

Well — I just wanted to tell you about our trip to Kigoma. I am hoping this will get posted tomorrow so it may fill the gap between my leaving & returning to Dar.

We set off — minor disaster — thought we'd left the eggs behind, so turned in the drive — & got stuck! Zano & Anskari had to be fetched by Heta to push me out! Anyway, we got to Marina in time.

Then the Vietses' car & driver took H & me & Marcus Borner to the airport. H & I were not confirmed, but got on easily. We arrived at airport at 7.20 — got on the plane at 10.30. The usual!

Anyway, Toni met us & took us back for lunch. Poor Blanche is ill — sounds bad. She's off to Dar for a checkup. Borrowed [a] boat & engine. V slow journey, but made it by 6.35. So unpacked in the light, & just caught the sunset with a drink.

My first day was hopeless. No proper follows at all. But today I had a lovely follow of Pallas, Kristal & Skosha a.m., & in the rain I was able to keep quite dry under a palm. Then, just as I got back at 1.00 — PS & [illegible]. I followed them until 5.00. And now our supper is cooked — cooking — we have had a swim. No terrible problems with the men. <u>Very</u> wet, but we were quite lucky today as the rain wasn't too <u>hard.</u> In fact the forest was cool, greens blending with each other, all through to the yellows, oranges & browns. With splashes of red. Restful to the mind. Not such an awful trip as the last one, though still very sad. We are all thinking about you, Um. I DO hope you are feeling much better now.

Tons of love —

J

Many salaams & good wishes from Rashidi, Sadiki, Hilali — &, of course, Heta.

P.S. If Ub comes out again soon there is an interim Birthday pres for him in the bottom drawer of white chest of drawers (with mirror).*

*In my room. A small THERMOS.

As from Box 727
Dar es Salaam
5 June 1981

Dear Mary,

Am writing this from Gombe — just like the old days, paraffin lamp & all! Except that when this paraffin is finished we may not be able to get any more, & even if we can — wow! The <u>PRICE</u> of everything in Tanzania! It is <u>really</u> scary.

It was so nice having the time together in Sweet Briar.* I really enjoyed that. And thank you for the lunch at the Geographic too.

This is in lots of ways a lousy trip to Gombe — as far as the <u>chimps</u> go. The place itself is as beautiful and peaceful as ever. But the chimps are far away, and in nearly 2 weeks have seen <u>very</u> few. <u>No</u> Fifi yet. And only 3 1/2 more days.

I'm writing to know what you really think about a baboon article? There's a lot of fascinating material. Troop splits, male transfer, infanticides (rarely reported in baboons), ♂ ♂ carrying infants, etc, etc. I was not thinking of a long article — a short(ish)! one. We should already have quite good picture coverage if we include Hugo's original pictures, my 1972 stuff, and various others that I could put together & bring next spring. However, if it is not the time or place, then I won't! Let me know.

I'll be sending off a quick batch of film — mostly baboons actually, as we've hardly seen any chimps to photo. Unfortunately there still seems something wrong with the light meter of that famous camera! It seems to show 4 or 5 stops <u>over</u>exposing. Anyway, you'll see, & I'll mark the first roll, before I realized, & subsequent rolls from that camera when I adjusted the setting. Naturally, I'm anxious for the results before I come back for 3 weeks with Grub.

Do you think you could send me a package of Ektachrome 200? And black & white Tri-X film. It's perfect for Gombe lighting. Could you mark the package "Dr Jane Bryceson — FILM for Scientific Research in Gombe National Park".

As usual, I'm running out of space. Anyway, my very best to Tom, thanks again for everything.

Love,<br>Jane

Later

P.S. I realize that this is virtually illegible. Really was dark!! Will be writing again — I'll use the typewriter!

---

* Jane had joined Leakey's two other ape researchers, Dian Fossey and Biruté Galdikas, for a symposium at Sweet Briar College in Virginia on April 28 and 29.

Dar

29 August 1981

Darling Um and Olly,

I'm sitting in my office, Cindarella (no, it must be Cinderella, of course!) curled up on the carpet. Outside the rain is pouring down in a grey drizzle. Old Nibbs is out on the high seas on a mammoth fishing trip (which almost didn't come off). I'm afraid that it will be a total disaster unless he catches a big fish! He was to have gone, as you remember, with Ian, Yenan and Tony Avigon. Well, Tony rang me and said that he'd got a friend coming from Somalia, who was a fishing fanatic, and that he'd be going the far side of Zanzibar, and it was no trip for Grub. Waves coming over the boat, cold, quite horrible, so he'd arranged for Grub to go with Dino. This Sunday. Neither of them could do Saturday. Grub — distraught. He wanted to go to Zanzibar, where the big fish were. I talked to Ian — he said that he was sure Tony would take Grub if he realized what a keen fisherman he was. But Tony had been "had" by people who said yes, they wanted to go all day, but then began to moan about 11.30 that it was awful and they wanted to go home. Well, I talked to Dino. He got the boat in the water on Friday, and was all set for Sunday morning fishing. This was especially for Grub, and Grub knows Dino, so after a lot of talking this way and that, he made up his mind that Dino was best after all. Whereas I, though at first I plumped for Dino, woke in the middle of the night and thought — how stupid — he MUST go with Tony. Even if he hates it, it is a REAL fishing trip. However, his mind was set. He was going to enjoy Dino. And he didn't want to go with Tony because Ian was not going — too much for Yenan.

Well, yesterday p.m. (about 7.30) Dino rang. He'd been working on the boat with his engineer — mechanic or what have you — since 2.30 and he couldn't get the engine going. He would ring Tony and ask if he'd take Grub. I thought — well, if that isn't fate! But Tony was out. Deep gloom descended. It looked as though there would be no fishing. And anyway, what would be the fun — he didn't KNOW Tony — what would he say to him — how would he say hello? How did he offer food? Etc, etc. Finally I got Tony at 9.45

p.m. Grub already in bed, deep despair. Yes — of course he'd take Grub. Meet us at the Club at 6.30 a.m. Back 6.30 p.m. Mind — no complaints! I told Grub. Elation — but "Now I'm really scared". Anyway, peacefully to sleep. I had to drag him out of bed at 5.15 — to make sure he had a good breakfast. I don't think he'll be warm once all day — he wouldn't take any more clothes. Maybe he'll be O.K. with his waterproof. Track suit, etc. Oh well — I used to get frozen to the marrow riding at his age, and still wanted more! . . .

Next day. Well — fishing trip over. I got so agitated because it was such a terrible and rough and wild day, that I couldn't go on typing! Rang Dino to ask if the bad weather here meant that the Zanzibar weather would be worse — he had gone off to the hospital with his brother, who had just been flown back from a safari with a probably fractured skull. Which must be one of the worst things to have here. Anyway, Grub's boat got safely back, and I'll leave him to relate his fishy news. I went to meet them (despite not having a permit to drive on Sunday afternoons!). Went the back way, through the village. No policemen around, so all was well.

It is an awful thought, him off tomorrow.* I'm finishing this off while he does his final sorting of lures and traces. One day "I'm not going to take any of my fishing things back. I'll buy a whole lot of new reels, etc, etc." Then he was going to take everything, rods and the lot. Now he has come to a reasonable compromise (I hope!). . . .

He will tell you all about Gombe. . . . The very first day I went out was very, very cold and windy. I followed Figan and Evered, and they greeted Pom who was up in a palm tree with little 2 year old Pan. I couldn't see them up there, 40 feet up, just occasionally a face looked round, or Pan moved from one frond to another. Suddenly — and it was like a nightmare and I couldn't believe it — I saw a tiny body, on its back, spreadeagled, coming down through the air. There was a sickening thud, then total silence except for the wind in the trees. Then as, with shaking legs, I moved to the spot, I heard a tiny, high pitched sort of squeak, long drawn out. Then another. Then silence. I saw the little body, still spreadeagled on its back, ab-

---

* Grub was about to leave for England and school.

solutely motionless. It took Pom about a minute to realize what had happened. Then she climbed down, slowly approached, picked up what I thought was a dead body, and to my amazement he gripped with hands and feet. For the next three hours he stayed curled up beside her (she rested a lot of the time, or ate on the ground) and then he opened his eyes. Then she climbed a tree and moved away from him, moved about, slowly, even ate a little. 2 days later he was seen, clinging to her tummy, not moving about. 4 days after that Pom appeared without him. He must have damaged himself internally — like a little boy of the cook next door who fell from a coconut palm and split his liver. He had an operation, walked about and ate for a week, then died. Poor little Pan. Pom is like a skeleton. (Before Pan died — rather like Gilka. Must be a disease. I think she will die as well. That will virtually eliminate the risk of the cannibalism being perpetuated. Perhaps she caught whatever disease Gilka had from eating the flesh of her infants.)

I have been giving Grub some real cordon bleu cooking. At least, I think so. Not sure about him! I'll try some of my recipes out at Christmas, and save you two some cooking! Though some of it is fish, and that won't be possible. Anyway, Grub has not starved, and I've put on about half a pound as a result. Now Cinderella must put on some weight! . . .

Do hope all is well at the Birches. It's nice Grub will have about a week. He's looking forward to it. Oh — there was a friend of Hugo's, going to set up a fishing thing from Dar, fishing off the best place on the coast here. He promised to take Grub on at least one trip while he was here, between 19 and 28 August, if Grub rang up. Grub forgot to ask Hugo for his name and address!! So I didn't feel as bad about some of my things falling through. Grub met this bloke, liked him, and said, oh yes, he was quite, quite sure the man meant it. He is a hoot when taxed — gets all blustery, then has to break into a sheepish grin. Says when at Gombe he can't get keen on sea fishing. Now is not keen on Gombe fishing! Am just going in to chivy up the last bit of packing, and see what has been left all over the room.

Tons and tons of love,
Jane

P.O. Box 727
Dar es Salaam
1 September 1981

Dear Mary,

Collected the slides and contact sheet today. Am quite pleased with some of the pictures. Anyway, thank you very much.

I have enclosed, in the parcel with the latest rolls of film, a few slides from those you have just returned. I couldn't resist it after your comment (couldn't see anything wrong with my meter). These are the ones I took with the meter reading set for 400 ASA. After taking these I suddenly realized that in sunlight on the beach it could not possibly be as dark as the meter indicated. So I changed the setting, and for future rolls I set the camera for 100 ASA (film speed actually 400 ASA) etc. Anyway, that new setting clearly worked out OK. . . .

Many, many thanks for the copies of the pig article. I have not got on very fast with the Pig Anthology but now that Grub has gone (this morning) I will tackle it on Sundays! The house feels very empty and sad without him. However, I have at last acquired a dog. Bitch actually. I "discovered" her 6 weeks ago. She had been abandoned when Milton Obote and family left for Uganda (he used to be 5 houses away along the beach). They took their other 5 dogs with them, but this one was left alone for some reason. Only the odd servant remains in the house, and this dog must have been hiding in the vegetation like a wild animal. It just happened that she had ventured out onto the beach one evening as I was walking along. As her colouring is exactly the same as Spider's (my dog that died), I approached her. I've seldom seen a dog more terrified of a human than she was. With tail tucked tightly between her legs, cringing in a terrible way, she crept into the sea. She had beat marks on her. Well, first I found out whether anyone wanted her. No. Then I set out to "habituate" her. Grub arrived after a week of this, and I had JUST had my first direct look from her. The day Grub came with me (we took the odd bit of crust, cheese rind, etc) we got our first wag. Still, we could not touch her for another week. Even if she made the move, and touched an outstretched hand with her nose, she leapt away as though we had electrocuted her. Then, overnight, she obviously decided to accept us. And we could pat and stroke her. (She stank and was full of fleas.) 3 days later she came home. I defy anyone at all to think that she had a history like that. She is confident, has filled out (let me give her a flea bath the very first day), is gay, wags her tail, follows me like a shadow. Unfortunately she went and came on heat while we were in Gombe, and I'm afraid she is now pregnant, which is a dead bore! Oh well. I've called her Cinderella. She is close beside me as I type, so I am not totally alone in the house any more. (Dear me, what a lot of space she has taken up!)

Gombe was fabulous so far as chimps were concerned. Bit funny with Hugo there, but he is getting some super material — especially on Fifi and the new baby, Fanni. Had another deliberate baboon infanticide. There were thousands of chimps all the time, and I did so much work. I did not take too many pictures as I was too busy with doing records. But shall be returning to Gombe in 3 weeks for another 2 to 3 weeks. . . .

Must close — please give my best to all my friends.

> All best wishes,
> Love,
> Jane

P.S. Someone is going to bring the film to Washington so I'll send this now.

P.P.S. Could you bear to send another packet of Tri-X black & white film? I meant to ask for it before, but obviously forgot. The other arrived safely & I am most grateful.

> 6 September 1981

Dear Mr. B — ,

We have never met, but my late husband, Derek, often spoke of you to me. I am writing to you now at the suggestion of S — M — and I do hope you do not mind my doing so.

I'm not even sure whether you heard about Derek's tragic death? Every year, from 1975 onwards, he and I went round the States on a fund raising lecture tour — for my work with the chimps and for Tanzania National Parks when Derek was Director. The tour of 1980 went off as usual — and, strangely in retrospect, many people commented on how well Derek was looking. Then, when we got back to Tanzania in mid-May he had some pain — and by July he had been operated on, in London, for cancer. We were told there was no hope and that he had 3 months to live. This turned out to be true but we found a marvellous doctor in Germany who gave us great hope and took Derek into his hospital near Hanover. I don't think we could have got through that 3 months without hope.

Just before Derek became sick he was appointed Chairman of the Tanzania Food and Nutrition Centre. He was really pleased about this appointment as he had helped to get the Centre going originally. The current Director, Dr. Maletnlema, is a really splendid person. He and Derek did a lot together in the 6 months that they worked as a team. While we were in Germany, Derek and I learnt a lot about food and nutrition (in a personal way) and Derek was always saying "I must tell Maletnlema that when we get home" and so on.

Now (at last) I come to the point of this letter. When I was trying to think of a really good way of honouring Derek's name, it suddenly came to me that I should try to establish a Scholarship, in his name, in Food and Nutrition, for the training of Tanzanians abroad. Maletnlema was enthusiastic and got his Board to agree. He advised me to contact the head of International Nutrition, Dr. Michael Latham, who knows Tanzania well, who was a friend of Derek's, and who is now at the Division of Nutritional Sciences at Cornell University.

Dr. Latham was marvellous. I went over to the States this year a few days early in order to visit the Cornell people. The outcome was the establishment of the Scholarship, with Cornell agreeing to sponsor the students, to administer the Bryceson Scholarship Fund (even if a student trained elsewhere) and to get their Endowments Committee interested in helping. We have arranged a big lecture for me at Cornell in April next year (I shall talk about feeding, hunting, etc. in the chimps!), all profits of which will go to the Fund. And a dinner in New York with some of the wealthy trustees, alumni, etc. Everyone at Cornell was so helpful and wonderful: it made it possible for me to carry on with the lecture tour — I could be doing something that I knew would please Derek as well as my own fund raising.

I thought you might be interested to hear about this plan. If you can help in any way, I should be so grateful. Maybe you can think of people who might be willing to make donations? (All of which, of course, would be tax deductible.)

All particulars about the Scholarship can be obtained from Dr. M. C. Nesheim, Director of the Division of Nutritional Sciences, Savage Hall, Cornell University, Ithaca, NY 14853.

I do hope you don't mind my writing to you like this? I also hope, very much, that we might be able to meet sometime when I am over in the States. It is very helpful to me to be able to talk about Derek with people who knew him well.

Yours very sincerely,
Jane Goodall Bryceson

The Birches
10 Durley Chine Road
Bournemouth
1 January 1982

Dear David,

I'm afraid Em will have left with the children for Holland by the time this arrives.* I've somewhat neglected letters. Have been very busy on a new project — An Anthology of the Pig — for Mum's Xmas present. It started off as a lighthearted little collection of pics and anecdotes — ended up as a great volume! Absolutely fascinating — pig history and behaviour and intelligence; pig in myth, legend, folklore, art and literature; pig personalities etc and etc! I did it in Dar as relaxation in the evening, after chimps all day. Then, when I got to Bournemouth, late because I was snowed up in Geneva (at

---

* David Riss and Emilie Bergmann, both former Gombe students, had married.

the airport!) for 15 hours on the way back, I had to work every night till 3.30 or so to get the thing finished, as people had sent lots of material for me here — and, of course, it would not have been nice to hide myself away all day, and there were presents to buy also — so I had to do it at night! Anyway, I'm really delighted with it, and have learned so much, and become really fascinated. (All because of the pig valve in her heart, of course!)

Shall be with the Geographic on 15th Jan. Possibly also on 16th. If you drop a line to me, c/o Joanne Hess (Miss) "To await arrival" with instructions when and how to reach you on the phone, we can have a chat. They have a cheap line, and I'm sure I'll have a chance to get a bit of time. I must call Pal, as well.

I won't give you any more news now. Have so much to do to get ready — including getting some chapters ready for my prospective publisher — Harvard University Press.

So — hope 1982 will be a really good year for you and the family — most especially hope to see you near the start of it. I don't think there will be time for me to come to you, but I havn't heard recent plans. You may know more than I do!

Love — & to Curt,

Jane

PS If you see any pig things, please save or send — the book is continuing to be added to! May publish it, in fact!


[Postmarked February 12, 1982]

Darling Um & Olly —

Well — I'm on the way back from a super week at Gombe — no problems. When I arrived I found Ann Pierce was there, which was nice. . . . Anyway, I followed Melissa & family, Pallas & Patti & Tapit, Little Bee & Tubi, Winkle & FF, and the Passions. I know Passion is foul & all that, but it is PATHETIC to see her now. And after all, she didn't KNOW what she was doing. She is only skin & bone, can't climb tall trees — suddenly crouches down as though in pain. Moves VERY slowly. And has something obviously causing intense pain in one eye. She moves her eyes very, very slowly, as you do when something hurts, and each time she moves them, she touches the bad one with her hand. Sometimes she gently rubs the closed eye with one finger. It's odd, 'cos in 1971 she lay, with a hand over her eyes, for hours on end, for over a week. The eye watered & watered, she often dabbed at it. Her nose watered too. At the end a small, white opaque patch could be seen on the iris. And ever since then she has had a runny nose — on that side only. And a funny ear. Any ideas? It is the same eye now.

I <u>saw</u> Fifi, but not to follow. She & the boys, with Fanni dorsal, were walking along the beach. The boys were playing, Frodo was rolling about in the sand, then chasing Freud. Fanni wanted to play with the sand, so after a bit she dangled down, trailing one hand in it, and ignored all Fifi's attempts to shove her back into a more comfortable (for Fifi) position! Wished I'd had a camera.

Pallas was a hoot. When Kristal went on suckling too long, she began to laugh. On & on & on, louder & louder. Just sitting there, splitting her sides! Suddenly she bent over & play bit KR's face — so KR stopped suckling & laughed too. A very good way of weaning without stress!! And Patti did much the same. She grabbed Tapit from a game he was enjoying 'cos she wanted to go. Tapit tried to go back, & when Patti kept hold of his arm he began to scream, struggle, hit his Ma, & bite her fingers — obviously as hard as he could. And what did Patti do? The more he yelled and bit, the crosser he got, the more she laughed! Yes — she just sat & laughed! It must have been infuriating! They are a hoot.

The boat worked, going & coming back. The planes left almost on time! I have 4 super fish for my tank, from the Indian fish man in Kigoma. When I got back to Kigoma I found it was Blanche's birthday, so the three of us went to dinner at the hotel. Not very nice — but nice for B — who <u>never</u> goes out anywhere.

Well — this is just a letter en route. I'll write again soon with news from Dar. We are just about to land. I did lots of Ma/Inf check sheets on the journey — till I ran out of them.

Tons & tons of love —

Jane & Janey Wayne

P.O. Box 727
Dar es Salaam
13 June 1982

Dear Mary,

I'm afraid this letter is going to be rather full of problems! So let me start off by saying that I hope all is well at your end. And thank you for arranging for me to have those prints made. They arrived just before I left Bournemouth for Dar, and they'd done a really super job. I wrote to Neva,* and sent a cheque, along with slides for black and white negatives — I hope all arrived safely?

Now the problems: First (and probably I should write to Neva about this one, but perhaps this will be O.K.). One of the things we discussed, during my visit in April, was to have some contacts and negatives (of Tony Collins' Gombe baboon pictures) sent to me in England. At the same time as I handed over those rolls (to Neva) — and I think there were three of them — I also handed over a couple of colour films. Well — the problem is that none of that stuff has arrived anywhere! Either England or here. . . .

The next problem is that camera! It quite clearly should be thrown out. You remember I brought it over in 1981, and found that, despite assurances as to its correct functioning, I had to make massive adjustments to the exposure? Well, believe it or not, the same thing is STILL wrong. The main trouble is that, stupidly, I assumed that this time it would be O.K. I trailed it around to try to get pictures of Gremlin's brand new baby — and only when I was about to leave Gombe (where, incidentally, I had a fabulous 10 days) did I discover that the misfunctioning of the exposure metre seemed to be the same as ever. I shall give all the information when I send in the sad little rolls I took. I am hoping some of the pictures can be salvaged, to some extent. The baby is called Getty, after Gordon Getty (who has given Gombe $50,000 in the last two years) and I badly want to be able to send him a picture! However, that is not relevant here.

While I was away, there was a break-in here in Dar. Among other things (such as my electric typewriter) they took my only well func-

---

* Neva Folk, a good friend who worked at the *National Geographic*.

tioning camera. (I think I already told you this in my last letter). This all means that I am virtually without a camera. And so I come to the point of all this long rigamarole. Do you think I could make an application to the Society for a camera? Preferably a light one, and with normal, wide-angle, 105 lenses. What is your reaction to this? And, if favourable, what steps should I take?

Well, that's enough of problems. The weather at Gombe was absolutely perfect for following — bright and sunny with cool winds. I was expecting a June greenhouse — but no, not at all. I had some of the most lovely days out in the forests. In a strange way, I felt free as I have not felt free since Hugo arrived to film in 1963. There was him, then for many years I didn't follow at all because of Grub (not enough time to do all the administration, and be a good mother AND follow chimps), and then, when I was there with Derek after the kidnapping, when Grub was in England I felt really guilty if I stayed out too long, when poor Derek was virtually a prisoner in camp. And then, for the first visits after he died, I hated it. I really felt miserable, and bitter about everything. But quite suddenly, this last time, there was the incredible sense of freedom — wandering about and feeling 23 again!

Pax is still fine, still spending more time with Prof than with Pom. Gremlin is a super mother     incredibly young, as she's only 11 1/2 and most mothers at Gombe are at least 13 before they give birth. The southern, unhabituated community has come right to the southern edge of Kakombe Valley — where camp is!

Love,
Jane

As from: The Birches
10 Durley Chine Road
Bournemouth
Dorset BH2 5JZ
1 December 1982

Dear Mary,

I was so sorry you were not in when I rang from Anchorage — I'd have loved a brief chat with you. Mainly to say how totally and utterly captivated I was by Japan, and the Japanese — the scenery, the empathy with nature, the temples, the monkeys — I can't put it all in a letter. But it was one of the really meaningful experiences. I went with Dr. Itani and his chimp students (after the symposium on Parent-child Bonding, which was why I went) up into the mountains. We stayed at a little Japanese inn which, translated literally (I mean, of course, the <u>name of</u> which) means "Sleep to the sound of running water". Have you been to Japan? If not, I'll fill you in when I come over in the spring. A Geographic article on the snow monkeys, other monkeys, mountains and temples where they live, would be FABULOUS. You should ask Itani to do one. I know the perfect translator — a young woman who lived 10 years in New York, so has perfect English (well, as perfect as one can expect from a mere American......!) as well as perfect Japanese, loves monkeys and chimps, translated my papers at the symposium, and was the only one who made sense of the Japanese papers. It could be a lovely article — every spring Itani goes with his family (and he has a super mother, who still wears the traditional kimono, and a father, now dead, who was a famous painter, especially of mountains, as well as a niece in South America!) into the mountains and collects wild plants, for eating. He has climbed EVERY one of the mountains in the north of Kyoto. He is a fantastic person.

Heavens — what on earth made me dive off on that tangent. The idea only came to me as I began to write to you! Still — it IS a good idea, for all that.

Thank you very much for the slides and contact sheets sent to England. I have now looked at them, and have a list of prints I would be most grateful for. I will put it on the other side of this. It's a bit long, but then this represents most of my photos for the whole year. I'm not really happy with the pictures from the little camera, and would love to talk about "using" a camera from the Society next year. I'll give a ring from England as you suggested.

One misery — I got back last night from my trip. Well, in the morning. A bit tired. It's a long long trip. Rang Kigoma to say I was all set for going there this Friday. BOTH BOAT ENGINES STOLEN — including the lovely new little one that I adored and have only used 4 times. DAMN!

Will end for now, and hope to have a chat over Christmas. I'll be in England until about 10 January.

Love,
Jane

P.S. Happy Christmas.


[February 1983]

Darling Um and Olly — and Grub — for you will all be together.

This will not be a very long letter, but longer as it is to all of you together, instead of two letters. Because very soon now Bill McGrew, who will post this, will be coming to supper with David Bygott, with whom he is staying. . . .

I told you, on the phone, about the Gombe trip. I went on my own, in the end. It was Adrian's birthday, and Judy didn't want to leave him.* It was SUPER being on my own, actually. I really enjoyed it. The plane trip worked fine, and got to Kigoma early — 10.30. Toni there to meet me. Blanche in Nairobi with an ulcer of some sort. Toni very gay. I rushed to find out if there was a water taxi — the one and only day of the week (as it transpired) that there was not one. And I couldn't get a lift with Jayant because there was NO petrol — people just had bits left in their tanks. So, next morning — after being lunched and wined, and dined and wined, by a VERY gay (and rather above himself!) Toni, I trudged to the water taxi with Apolly (who happened to be in town, sick) and Toni's Ramadhani carrying my bags and traps.

Got onto boat at 9.30. At 10.30 (thank goodness) the little Park Warden (Eli) joined me. Gradually it filled up. By 11.30 there was not an inch of wood on the floor to be seen. Everyone very gay — dipping a tin on a string over the side for drinks of (dirty) water, chewing sugar cane, bread, chapati, peanuts, popcorn, and pineapples. Babies and chickens (one actually flying about) galore. At 11.45 the customs man got on. For a long time only his buttocks were visible as he sort of dived under the bodies and bundles, look-

---

* Referring to Adrian and Judy Taylor; Judy was working as Jane's assistant at the time.

ing for — well, goodness knows what, really. It is a crying shame they treat people that way. He vanished under some matresses for ages, and I began to hope he had suffocated! No such luck. At 12.30 he seized a suitcase and took it off the boat, followed by the protesting owner. I believe money changed hands, and case and owner got back on.

Finally, at 12.45, we set off. Went round the first headland, stopped at village. How more people got on, I don't know (our final load had been about 50 debes of paraffin). But they did. We chugged 5 minutes to the next village — really people could have walked! MORE people got on. And then the engine wouldn't start! For one hour and 10 minutes we bobbed about on the lake. After 30 minutes I said to Eli "You know, it could be much worse. It could be really rough" (it was actually very calm). He agreed that it could. After a bit I said "You know, it might have been pouring with rain, and windy — we'd be so wet and cold by now". He agreed that that was so. More minutes passed and I said "You know, it could have been scorchingly hot — we'd have roasted, especially all those bodies out on the prow". Eli agreed. Finally, 10 minutes later I said "You know, we might have had this boat filled with sacks of stinking dagaa — how horrible that would have been". He agreed. So then I said "Eli — aren't we really most terribly lucky!" He roared with laughter, and it cheered us up for the rest of the trip!

Well — we got to Gombe (no more engine trouble, but stopping at every village where more people always got on — as many as 15 into the boat where there really was no room at all! — and no one ever got off!) at 4.00 p.m. No key. Rashidi had it. However, Eslom said he would send someone to Mwamgongo — meanwhile some chaps cleared up the old Guest House, and I sort of camped there. I had everything I needed in the way of food, and the house had pots and pans, and Eslom got wood, and the new chap, Bruno(!) got water. So it was quite pleasant, and I sat outside in the sunset. But there were lots of rats, and so I took the matress and my sheets (which I had brought from Kigoma, of course) to the veranda of my house, and slept there. Though I hardly seem ever to sleep these days. I didn't sleep at all the night before going to Gombe, so it made me tired enough to sleep at Toni's. But only ONE of my 5 nights at Gombe did I sleep before 3.00. And last night, after talking to you, and despite feeling <u>really</u> tired, I didn't sleep till after 3.00 either. I despair. It's so STUPID.

The chimps were all hiding when I first arrived, as the southern lot had come to the top of Sleeping Buff and the northern lot to Linda. Which means ours really only have Kasakela left. However, the southerners retreated again three days later, and I did, anyway, manage to follow someone every day. And it was lovely and green and damp, and mostly cool. So I did have a good time, though MUCH too short. Once followed Evered from camp straight up to almost top of Sleep. Buff almost without stopping — only for 1/4 minute at a time, 4 times. I was drenched in sweat when he finally stopped. He then sat listening for 45 minutes. Then he raced back down to the bottom and only then did he dare start feeding on the fruits there. Because, of course, down near the stream he couldn't hear others coming, so he had to make quite quite sure first. Very interesting.

Nope has a baby — another daughter. I've called her Noota, after Nancy Nooter. She is a good friend, and writes to me a lot. She'll be tickled pink! Toni sends lots of love and so does everyone else.

Nibbs — hope to hear a report soon about the term — this weekend hopefully. Hope you got my letter of congratulations about the English. Do you still take the other English, this term?

Tons of love to you all.

Box 727<br>
Dar es Salaam<br>
17 June 1983

Dear Mary,

Am not sure if these will be hand delivered or posted. But at least they will go by hand as far as Washington (or New York).

Just got back from a simply fantastic trip to Gombe. Usually in June the chimps are going round in small scattered groups — but they were all in big noisy gatherings. I got super data on all but one mother-infant pair. Little Getty is doing fine — in fact more than fine — he is an outstanding little chap, full of fun, and starting what promises to be a delightful relationship not only with Uncle Gimble, but also with Grandma Melissa! Gremlin and Melissa are never apart.

Not only were all the chimps around, but the plane went without a hitch both to Kigoma and back. The engine to replace the stolen one had arrived and worked supremely well — and there was petrol!

Tanzania certainly is in a bad state but it's really only the Asians who have panicked, and some of the really crooked Africans. Mostly what is being done is all for the good — the short term effects are terrible, because all the people who kept the economy going have got nervous and simply don't work any more. Also some injustices were, for sure, perpetrated. And victims still languish in prison.

However, the worst problem is food. And that doesn't really affect me. Just finding food for one is not too difficult and I have good friends who help me with the dogs and with my servant Zano.

Am not getting on too fast with the Monograph, but that is because I am going through the initial labour process, which is absolutely inevitable and absolutely hideous. Everything I have read and thought goes grinding and crashing about in my head, and I sit all day and end up with one page and tear up 100s more. But in the long run the chapter gets born! Right now it's "Social Structure" — which is unbelievably complex, and all too easy to oversimplify in a glib way. That is what most people seem to do. And if you don't oversimplify, then it is really difficult to write. Oh well.....

Will close, and take the dogs for a walk since the light is fading and I need a pause. Please give my love to everyone.

Love,
Jane

P.S. Hope all is well with posters? I don't remember if you were going to let <u>ME</u> know the actual price, or Dick Slottow? He is our Treasurer & contactable at the Institute address.

1 August 1983

Darling Um & Olly,

This will be rather a scribble as I must not use up much oil. It is
<u>not</u> available! Things basically go well. Having Lane is great — he
is splendid on a follow — one of the few people I don't mind having. He gets on well with Grub.* And is, of course, enjoying himself!
Grub has actually been with me on a follow. And is now <u>NOT</u>
scared of chimps anymore. He has even said he will come on another! He & Lane are going to have a picnic up on the Rift in a couple of days. And they will walk to Mwamgongo next Friday or
Sunday & buy meat. They both <u>crave</u> it — & I didn't know before
that it could be bought there. Every Market day. We discovered because a really nice French couple came for 5 days — filming fish. It
has been nice for Grub. (They will post this letter from Burundi.)
Fishing not too good — but he is good with his harpoon, & is having fun. Enough fish for a meal <u>almost</u> every day. Oh — to finish
about the meat. The French couple went there to get food on Sunday & brought it back. They couldn't cook it, so brought it to the
house & I cooked it. It lasted 2 days — a real good stew today. She
is a vegetarian so I made her a vegetarian dish. I am quite exhausted
by cooking! Also, we left some food behind — because of the lights
going that last evening & because of leaving Wed. instead of Friday!
However, we are getting more rice, & sugar. And I think the 2 big
packets of porridge we <u>did</u> bring will last. We had bread for <u>more</u>
than a week. It lasted <u>well.</u> And those packets are so great. And the
soup — super soup!

Little Kristal <u>is</u> dead. But all others <u>well.</u> Frodo a ghastly bore —
he kicked Grub on our follow (which was one of the nicest ever).
A few displays, but mostly just sitting <u>absolutely</u> surrounded by
chimps, in a shady glade, with them resting. It really was <u>super.</u>

The things we left in Dar have arrived. Tony is due back from
leave at the end of this week. Didn't see Chris, who had a meet-

---

* Lane Batol was a friend of Grub's from England who came out for the summer
holiday.

ing, but delivered his aquarium & had delicious lunch with Mama Chris.

Do hope all is well at the Birches. <u>Wish</u> you were with us.

Tons & tons of love —

Jane & Janey Wayne


September 26, '83

Dear Alison,

This is just a very quick note to thank you so much for the generous contribution to the Institute and for returning the photographs.

I do hope that all goes well with your book — if only my book were far enough ahead that I could be thinking of final photographs! However I really have broken more than the back of it by now. I only have three Chapters left to go — and all the analysis on those is virtually done. Certainly the worst chapters are behind me. Of course there is all the ghastly job of references, tables and figures to number and sort out, etc. etc. etc.....

etc etc etc!

Love,
Jane


November 18th, 1983

Dear Prince Bernhard,

I so enjoyed being with you again last month and the opportunity that we had to talk about and discuss various subjects. In fact, I shall soon begin to look forward to your visits to Tanzania as a chance for an annual get-together!

Since you left Tanzania I have made a two week visit to Gombe where I found the work progressing very well although somewhat hampered by heavy rain. It is always so fantastic to actually get back into the field and be with the chimps for a while after spending so much time poring over the data and writing up the results. The termite fishing season was in full swing and it was fascinating to watch the techniques of the different infants and juveniles as they tried to capture the termites. There is quite a marked individual difference in age at which they start to concentrate and are able to manipulate the grasses and stems in a satisfactory and productive manner.

Almost as soon as I got back from Gombe I fell victim to a singularly unpleasant bout of malaria which has only just left me. This is why I have not written before, enclosing the information on the financial needs of the Research programme at Gombe. I am so sorry to have been so slow — but there is nothing much one can do when laid low by this horrible bug. I bitterly resent the wasting of valuable time as this means I'm even more frantic about writing my monograph than I was before.

If you do have any ideas about fund-raising for Gombe I should be most awfully grateful. If it was necessary I could always stop off in Holland — or almost anywhere else for that matter — on my way to England and the United States from Tanzania and back again. This journey I do every spring. And in addition I go to England at Christmas time. I am determined, if I possibly can, to match Gordon Getty's challenge gift of $250,000. If I can do this, it means that the basic needs of Gombe can be met from income from a $500,000 endowment. This would make such a difference to me and relieve so much of the pressure of the hand to mouth way of living which I have been struggling with for so many years. Any suggestions that you might have will be very gratefully received. I have simply enclosed a package of relevant information of various types, but I could quite easily, of course, put together a more specific set of material if this was necessary for some specific purpose.

I just heard an hour ago that the boundary between Tanzania and Kenya has finally opened — this should make the most incredible difference to all sorts of things in Tanzania. I find it difficult to believe it's really true after all this time! I keep thinking that something is bound to go wrong and in one or two weeks or a month we shall be back where we've been all this time.

Once again, it was a very real pleasure to have the opportunity to be with you and talk to you at that very pleasant evening last month. May I wish you and your family a very happy Christmas and that 1984 will be successful and healthy for all of you.

Yours very sincerely.

Box 727
Dar es Salaam
6 October 1984

Dear Neva:

Is it a <u>terrible</u> imposition to ask if you could post these for me? I just don't have stamps for so many. Keep an account and I'll pay in the spring. In fact, I think I'd better leave you with a little pile of cash!

I should have addressed them to the Institute to do. But somehow — they are arriving in Washington in the pouch, and you are in Washington, and I don't yet know the new person at the Institute. So, I do hope you don't mind. . . .

No electricity. Am writing by candle light (1.45). Cinderella (dog) snoring. Full moon. I'm going out walking on the beach in a minute. This is my last letter tonight. I got out my pile of correspondence when I couldn't use the typewriter (for going on with my book). The pile was about 2 feet high!! We have no water, either. Nor can I get to Gombe. Why? No planes to Kigoma. Why? The fire engine at the airport had an accident — and caught fire!! Waiting list for train — 2 months!!

So — I have, to all intents and purposes, got the book DONE. Just typing the chapter that has hung over my head almost since I began the book — way back in the distant past!

Don't suppose you'll be able to read this. I'm too tired. Arm aches. Eyes wuzzy. Fingers sore and stiff. My coil has gone out and the mosquitos are after me. The real reason for my giving up!

Thank you, Neva. Love to all.

Yours ever,
Love,
Jane

28 October 1984

Dear Adrienne and Jerry,

First, the good news — my book is — FINISHED!!!!!! I have not really taken it in yet. Nor can I afford to relax, even for a second, since everything has piled up while I finished it. Since I was in the States in September (meeting the poor wretched Harvard University Press editor ostensibly to hand over the final pages), I have written two new chapters! Honestly! Anyway, apart from being a bit at a loss as to how to cope with 25 years of acknowledgments, it really is all done. Really and truly, all 21 chapters of it. If I don't get around to writing a long newsy letter, which I should after being such a bad correspondent, you can imagine me, over the next week, writing two papers, one article and 56 — 55 letters now, when this is done!

Well, there is a point in writing this hasty letter, in addition to the good news. I am terribly anxious that nothing else happens to delay my poor plans for ChimpanZoo. The reason it went wrong before was only partly my fault (the fault being not enough communication, because I was trying to do too much at once). I am still not clear how it went wrong, but I want to make quite sure that this time I do communicate. So this is really to you, Adrienne, as Chairman — or Secretary, isn't it, of the advisory board.*

The proposal I submitted was supposed to cover Ann Pierce's trip. Knowing that her duties were somewhat vague, I was a bit scared that what in fact DID happen, might happen. i.e. that she would be required to submit more details. With this in mind, I rang Bruce and told him that the money for Ann's trip was guaranteed. That it would be forthcoming from me. . . . The plan for Ann was deliberately vague. I just wanted her to go round, get the feel of the groups of chimps and people, talk about the ideas I sent to her, re checksheets and things, get the ideas from the various people, keepers, etc involved, and then sit down and make a report. . . .

Well, enough. The book is finished, muddles of this sort due to my own inefficiency will not happen again, I hope. And maybe, after all, I can put something together before the spring. Otherwise a whole year will probably go by and I shall lose the goodwill of all the zoo people (if I havn't already!)

---

* Probably referring to the advisory board of ChimpanZoo. Anthropologist Adrienne Zihlman first came to Gombe to help with cleaning and labeling skeletons; her husband was a board member of the Jane Goodall Institute.

I cannot get to Gombe, another cause for depression. There are no planes running, and the waiting list for the train is about 2 months. To charter a plane, now, costs Shs. 80,000!!! The worst of it is that I had Eibl-Eibesfeldt coming out to start on a long term filming project, and now I almost think I must put him off — unless there is good news soon. The problem — no planes can land because the airport fire engine caught fire!! I did have most of the summer there, but had to force myself to do the book. I think I told you, Adrienne, all this. And my stupid bouts of malaria which accounted for half of Grub's summer holiday? It is such a draining thing.

Guess I should end, and start on letter no. 54 from the end! Oh — before I end, are you in the picture about the Chimpanzee project — I can't type chimpanzOO without great concentration — my fingers are schooled for the zee! Anyway, about the meeting at San Jose in the spring? I guess for the West Coast zoos taking part — Portland, Fouts,* San Francisco, maybe, though I've not actually heard from them. Possibly Colorado Springs. . . .

Must end. There are millions of mosquitos, and it has quite suddenly got really hot so that sweat is trickling down as I type. (Unless, heaven forbid, I'm getting a fever again!! Don't actually think so.)

Love to you both — see you soon.

Gombe<br>Sunday<br>[November 25, 1984]

Darling <u>Everyone</u> — Um, Ol, Ub, Aud, Cida —

Must write <u>one</u> letter from Gombe. Sitting here on Sunday evening, 6.00 p.m. Lake the hottest and calmest I have <u>ever</u> known it. Sun, watery, sinking towards the Congo hills. A lone canoe slowly paddling past, going through the diffused light from the sun's reflection. Crickets. A few tree frogs. Dragon flies dashing past on

---

* Roger Fouts, researcher teaching American Sign Language to apes in captivity, was probably included in this list of "West Coast zoos" because he maintained a socially coherent community of several chimpanzees in the Northwest.

brilliant sorties after flies. Rain smell in the air. Green — utterly beautiful.

Renke — i.e. Eibl — sitting in his track suit reading a fat book on Austrian history in Italian. Meat, brought by Rashidi and prepared (what <u>delight</u>) by Renke — simmering on its fire. Peanuts and brandy consumed. And imagine — a baboon horde just north of camp yesterday and the kill, made by Goblin, brought by Goblin <u>INTO</u> camp! And earlier almost in camp. All beautifully (we hope!) filmed. Also nice Ma/inf. material — Gremlin & Getty, GR in a tree, in a nest, while Getty showed all his inventiveness all round her — for 2 hours! Fifi and Fanni being weaned and throwing tantrums. Winkle and Wunda — WK <u>must</u> be having <u>TWINS</u> — MF & Mel. Little Bee and Tubi. I hope it all comes out.

We had a fine train journey. The only <u>really</u> bad part — the smell of the loos. But with the door shut, OK. But at times one <u>had</u> to have the door open. Not many cockroaches at all. Godwin came to see us off, and Ramji with bread, lemon juice that keeps. The new friend, Jack Calvert, drove us and <u>ALL</u> our baggage to the station, with his young adorable little boy African friend. With gift of crackers, cheese, corned beef, peanut butter and chocolate!! Renke brought so many good things —

So a little hymn of thanksgiving from Gombe. Wish you were here, Nibbs. We've talked of you <u>such</u> a lot. And Um — <u>all</u> the men hope you will come in the summer.* Hope your tooth is fine, Olly. And you had a super birthday, Aud.

Love,
Jane

As from P.O. Box 727
Dar es Salaam
[Possibly November 30, 1984]

Dear Richard,

Apologies for the delay in replying. Your letter came as I was just off to Gombe with Eibl-Eibesfeldt — no sooner did I get back than I

---

* That is, all the field staff.

was again laid low by malaria. This is getting beyond a joke. It was Gombe again, what's more. And, worst of all, poor Eibl went down with it immediately upon his return (to chair a conference organized by himself) and had to go into intensive care — where he still is. I don't know what we're going to do. The Kigoma people say that it is becoming quite devastating there — utterly different from anything they have known in the past.

Well — very good news on the Aspilia front. First of all, I think your project sounds exciting and eminently feasible.* I would, myself, like to become involved with the Gombe part of it — in a supervisory way, of course, but it is important to keep not only Eslom but the other men interested. (Winkle, a few days after birth, ate practically nothing during one whole day except these leaves.)

The best news of all concerns research clearance. The other day (with the monograph finished I am, suddenly, free to do things, and it's a fabulous feeling!) I went to talk to Dr. T. N. Maletnlema, Director of Tanzania Food and Nutrition Centre, about the Bryceson Scholarship. He is a very go ahead, energetic, and thoroughly articulate person, with imagination. A man of action. Anyway, it suddenly occurred to me that a link up with the TFNC might be an ideal sort of arrangement. I therefore described your project, the properties of aspilia and so on. He was immediately delighted. The great asset here is that if TFNC takes the project under its umbrella NO RESEARCH CLEARANCE IS NEEDED!!!

I can't tell you how this relieves me. Not only this, but the tie in is very logical. Maletnlema might like a Tanzanian involved — this would mean a person who could stay much longer at Gombe — as long as was wanted. (I am not advocating this, but it remains a possibility.) Anyway, Dr. M is interested himself in the medicinal prop-

---

* When they were apparently ill, some of the Gombe chimpanzees were carefully selecting and swallowing whole the very rough, "hairy" leaves of *Aspilia* plants — not an ordinary item of their diets. Richard Wrangham was developing a theory that the apes were treating their own ailments with these leaves, perhaps swallowing them as roughage or, alternatively, as a source of some pharmacologically active compound. Wrangham had been corresponding with pharmacologists Eloy Rodriguez and Neil Towers, mentioned later in this letter.

erties of plants, and he told me that just the previous week he had been driving to Dodoma and seen a whole lot of healthy looking baboons by the side of the road in a semi-desert and drought stricken area. He had actually stopped the car to look at them and started to wonder about what <u>they</u> were eating, and how more knowledge might help rural communities in arid areas.

I would suggest that the proposal be slanted towards this angle — primate food studies helpful to indigenous people. Dr. M is in a key position here, and would be able to help in a number of ways. Quite a number of laboratory facilities are available and this might be helpful for some aspects of the project. I can foresee all manner of interesting possibilities. (Do you remember how keen I was to have those little nodules on the grass roots at Gombe analysed — the ones the baboons eat?/and that it turned out they were full of nitrogen and that all kinds of people do, in fact, eat them as well?)

There are many people interested. At TFNC there are also people from all over the world coming in on projects, so there is a good feeling of being part of the larger scene — a feeling which one does not get, I fear, at the University.

I would appreciate it if no formal letters or discussions were held about students remaining for periods of longer than 2 weeks at Gombe. In fact, periods of one or two months would probably be quite OK, but we just should not TALK about it. The main reason for this is that I am even more scared, than when I saw you, of problems being made at Gombe. Firstly, the tourist business has really become absolutely appalling, and I'm actually trying to do something about it from the top. Which puts me in a danger spot for a while! Secondly, and rather more to the point (and please do not spread this around, I beg of you, but treat as confidential among yourselves) . . . the kidnappers have become active again. Maybe you heard? They organized a large scale armed raid in the south, but were repulsed by the Tanzanians. They have threatened a kidnapping at Mahale. Any talk of expats at Gombe right now, therefore, could be disastrous! And the beauty of the TFNC deal is that precise stipulations of who spends how long where just won't come into it.

I shall be in Bournemouth from Christmas until about 15 January. If I don't get back in time to see Towers and Rodriguez (to whom I have written), they should go to see Dr. Maletnlema. The address TFNC, P.O. Box 977, Phone 28951 (his direct line). It is not far from State House — 22 Ocean Road. They might find it useful to contact Godwin Ndossi, the first of the Bryceson Scholars. He just got back from Cornell — he is utterly charming, and very helpful, and, of course, knows TFNC and all the people there frightfully well (far better than I). He is, at present, teaching at the Azania Secondary School (right next door to Muhambili Hospital) and can be reached either by dropping a note there and waiting while someone finds him, or leaving a message for him to phone: their number is 21587. (I am thrilled because I've worked it so he can return to Cornell to do his Ph.D.) He himself is interested in what you are doing and I hope you can meet him. And Richard, please, with all these new contacts you are making, do keep an ear for where I can apply for a contribution to the endowment at Cornell.

As from P.O. Box 727
Dar es Salaam
23 January 1985

Dear Mr. Rodale,

I do want to thank you for your letter, and for sending me the very interesting information about what you are doing in Tanzania. I had, of course, heard something about some of this from Mollie Miller. And, in fact, it was she who had given me your name, as a possibility for help with the Bryceson Scholarship, early last year. But somehow we never connected! I had not realized, until Dr. Carter pointed it out, that you were the editor of Prevention! (It's a small world).

I must tell you that our first Bryceson Scholar, Godwin Ndossi (who was selected from among 200 applications when first we advertised the opportunity in the local press) turned out to be a super choice. Hard working, talented — and utterly charming. A perfect "ambassador" — and that is so important. Anyway, I've persuaded everyone concerned that, having completed his first year's training (he's back in Tanzania, as he just went for the one year course) he should go back to the States and work for his Ph.D. So he will be starting that in September this year.

In fact there's not enough money in the fund for him to complete the course!! But we have enough for the first two years, which gives me plenty of time to find the shortfall (about $8,000). Of course my ultimate goal is an endowment (around $150,000) so that there can be one student a Bryceson Scholar at all times.

So, to end — if you have any suggestion of anyone to whom I could write, or whom I could talk to when I'm in the States in the spring. I'm not after that much money, but it means a lot to me. Even very tiny donations are very, very much appreciated.

Once again, I thank you so much for your letter — perhaps we may be able to meet some time. I certainly hope so. And that 1985 will be a good year for you and your Tanzanian projects.

Yours very sincerely,
Jane Goodall, Ph.D.

<u>Monday</u>
[February 11, 1985]

Darling Um, Olly, Nibbs & all —

Well, am <u>finally</u> on train. Instead of being on the way to <u>Geneva,</u> am off to <u>Zurich</u>! SNOW!! They told us the Geneva train would be 50 min late. But then we found they had made a mistake. It was only <u>10</u> [minutes] late. So — missed! But <u>then</u> we found the roads from station to airport in Geneva were closed. And <u>then</u> we found the plane was diverted to Zurich!! So — the lady who made the 1st mistake gave me an extra 2 hours of peaceful discussion at the Gunterns' apartment (with all the furniture that came for the conference weekend being carried out around us — 'cos it's a new apartment & the people making their new furniture agreed to let them use couches, tables & chairs for free!) So — it was a GOOD mistake! So we sat and ate bits of party food, & broke a sugar bowl, and made plans to meet again. They are really super people — she's an artist & does all the graphics for his work. A very splendid team.*

Zurich was fun. I saw Hans' mongoose colony, & jackdaw colony. The lecture was <u>packed,</u> and worked well. Hans was pleased with it, which was good. I saw so many friends — including my little Swiss Air (he IS little!) steward. The only sad part was that there was a dinner after the lecture & I had to leave people after just saying hello. Very sad. But the dinner was nice once that break had been accomplished. So — I have just seen a man riding a black horse across a white snow field. The scenery is <u>breath</u>-<u>taking.</u> I also just ate an incredibly good chocolate from the box pressed upon me by Greta. She also gave me large pieces of cake and apples. I am <u>so</u> well looked after.

We hope that poor Vivian Wheeler will find me! We are trying to page her at Geneva! Well, they are.

Well — that was a super weekend in B'mth, and even the London bit was fun — though a bit chaotic. These trees are <u>so</u> fabulous. I wish you could see them.

You will see photos of the conference. I'll bring them in March. We're high in the mountains & most of the scenery is now in cloud. I went to see the little 300 year old wooden house (TINY, on stilts) where Gottlieb was born. After that it snowed so we couldn't see anything! Now we're in a tunnel, under part of the mountain. Out — a small brown bird lands on a tree and snow falls. How on <u>earth</u> do they live? . . . We have now come to a complete stand-still in the middle of a cloud! I shall write all my other letters and perhaps add to this when I know if I'll get to Zurich on time. Luckily, if it fouls up, I have lots of friends in Zurich but it would be sad if Vivian Wheeler arrives in Dar without me!! Ah — we move and I find the other end of the train was in a station. So there was a reason for stopping!! Adieu.

Could you scout around and see if you can locate a book by

---

* Jane had attended a symposium in Brigg, Switzerland, organized by Gottlieb Guntern and his wife, Greta, on the subject of "autoorganization," that was attended mainly by psychologists and psychotherapists. In addition to Jane, the speakers included Gottlieb Guntern and Fritjof Capra.

Fritjof Capra called <u>something</u> like Tao Physics.* If in paperback — I'd like it. Shan't understand, but am fascinated and want to read.

You know — it is very flattering to be invited to all these places. Paris (two separate people), Amsterdam, Antwerp, Spain, Basel and Bern.

<u>Later.</u> Well — Swiss railways & Swiss efficiency are a myth! I got off a reasonably fast train (was told to!) and am on a <u>very</u> slow one that stops at every stop. I <u>very</u> much doubt I shall catch my plane. But you will know if I did not 'cos I shall have rung.

I send this as is — in case I <u>JUST</u> catch my flight I want to stick this up so I can throw it at someone to post.

Utter <u>chaos</u> — so I put some of my plane brandy in my coffee, got out my MS — and I DON'T CARE. I just <u>HOPE</u> Vivian Wheeler doesn't get on the plane if I am not on it!! Mama — mia!!

Tons of love,<br>Jane<br>Janey Wayne

[August 1985]

Darling Um and Olly,

Just a "hello" note to send with Grub. Who, as I write, is struggling to pull all his instruments of fishy torture apart prior to oiling them for next year. He — and Chris, I may say — have just eaten <u>ENORMOUS</u> meals — Grub ate 3/4 of a chicken (small one, admittedly) and Chris enough tuna to last one of us mere women for a week! And followed by chocolate pud — Nibbs — and fried banana — Chris. Then Swiss chocolate. The veranda is nearly finished. Chris has persuaded me to have mosquito screening put up over the "dining room" doorway — so I have a mosquito free room. Simon popped in the other day and will be driving to Nairobi

---

* *The Tao of Physics: An Exploration of the Parallels Between Modern Physics and Eastern Mysticism.*

and Gombe so he will bring the screening. Also a huge cupboard in which I can keep <u>all</u> my equipment — DRY. All the news will probably emerge, in time — from Grub or, failing that (since you may get rather a one-sided (fishy!) picture of the summer) from me.

I have sent a suitcase of mine inside Grub's. With 2 dresses and a pair of shoes that I <u>might</u> need in Washington. And some photos, most of which I want to take to USA — to send people. I'll arrange them, so you know, Um, which to bring. Returning the pig leash. And the girl on a swing — Olly — you wanted to read. . . .

Jenny and I come Club Class on Swiss Air — I leave her in Zurich. I'll be with you on Tuesday evening — my book STILL incomplete. All news later.

Tons of love,
Jane

[August 1985]

Darling Um and Olly,

A quick note to send with someone who is going to Cambridge. Here is the reprint of the chapter I wrote for Japan. I think it came out nicely with its photos. Havn't read to see if they've made mistakes — but anyway, have sent me and Robert.

Gombe was super — but it was horrid to have to spend so much time working on the book instead of with the chimps. However, I got to follow all of them. Little Mel is splendid — so is Tita. Thank goodness they're both OK! Getty goes from strength to strength and the relationship between him and Melissa is <u>FABULOUS.</u> She plays with him <u>MUCH</u> more than she ever did with her own youngsters!

Chris was fortunate in seeing lots of things near camp — even a hunt! (Not successful.) But he saw meat eating — Goblin with the carcass of a monkey sparrow killed the day before. But his <u>poor</u> back! He has to lie flat every possible moment. As soon as it seems better he forgets, does something he shouldn't and it goes back to the beginning. I can't see how it will ever get better just doing these exercises. Oh well. Anyway, it was <u>really</u> good for the monograph that he came. We have discussed it endlessly and he has had some excellent comments. The main thing, of course, is the vocalization thing. Today I shall tackle typing out my notes. The new baby typewriter is <u>SUPER</u> to use — but its <u>RIBBONS</u> are so expensive. They are the kind you can use once only. We spent <u>hours</u> rewinding — but unless I find a way to rewind better, it still doesn't work. . . .

On Tuesday Toni and Blanche leave for good. Well — Wednesday. On Tuesday they come here for a farewell party — so shall ask Ramji, and Dimitri is bringing a pig! D. goes to USA at the weekend cos one of his sons, who is our age, is getting married. Anyway, sad though it is to lose Toni and Blanche, they have fixed us up very well with Jayant and the other Asians. We have a room there, at the fish place. Done up <u>really</u> nicely, curtains, beds and chairs (from Toni) and shower and loo, and store. Warm invitations to have meals with them. Nice.

Saw Chris Liundi in Dar <u>before</u> I went to Gombe. He came out in a taxi, had a drink, then <u>walked</u> home! He is a super person. He was not in Kigoma when I arrived, or when I left.

Zano has gone home for a few days, as his father is sick. And Anskari is sick himself. So we are all fending for ourselves! Prashant and Trusha will be having a holiday in England in September — so maybe you will see the little pair? Trusha had a bad ovary infection, but is more or less over it now.

Must end and get on with vocalization.

Tons and tons of love to you all,<br>Jane and Janey-Wayne

2 November 1985

Dear Barbara and Jeff —

What a lousy correspondent I have been. <u>Yesterday, finally,</u> I sent off the very <u>last</u> re-writes, omissions, alterations, reorderings, lost bibliography references, etc, of my book. This was the <u>galley</u> proof stage. Phew! It's practically DONE. I can scarcely believe it. 600 pages it will be. Maybe more. 200 photos. More, I think. (Odd to think it's only the <u>first</u> half of the writing up. Now I want to update "Shadow" while, at the same time, starting analysis to the 2nd part of the more scientific publication. (2nd part is what I really <u>want</u> to get going on — infant development, change over the life cycle, the family.)*

Now I set to on mounds of correspondence, piles of untranslated reports in Swahili from Gombe, articles awaiting me — oh, so, so much. I just left everything in order to get this awful book done.

Jeff — thank you for sending me cuttings and news. I really do appreciate it, and I really do apologize for my silence. I really have been <u>frantic</u> — to the point of almost giving up sleep in order to try to get things done! Never, ever, shall I let myself get into such a frantic rush again. Because a book like that <u>cannot</u> be done in a hurry. Well — I'm off to Gombe in two days for what I feel is a well earned two weeks of peace. Unfortunately the planes are not working — because the fire-fighting equipment at Kigoma doesn't function & they can't get spares! So — 2 nights and all but two days on the train. Heat — dirt — stink! However, when the reward is Gombe, it's well worth it. I just pray the plane will be working for the return journey!

Must close. This is the 6th letter I have penned today. That leaves approx. 50 more!! Oh for a secretary!! I keep finding letters all over the house, in weird drawers. Where I shoved them so that they were out of sight and I felt less guilty during those past hectic months!

Much love to you both,

Jane

<u>Gombe</u>

[November 1985]

Darling Family,

As I write this, in the first light of day, munching a banana, two adolescent baboons are chasing each other in the sloth position along the rafters of the veranda. They look so funny! So — obviously I am at Gombe! This will (hopefully) be posted from Dar by two Dutch students. Don't mind these tourists — they are the only

---

* Her planned second volume *The Chimpanzees of Gombe* was to be titled: *Patterns of Development*.

two to have shown up in the past two months!! This is because of the Park fees being so high that people don't come!

Anyway. Lots of news. Where should I start? Well — the train journey was one of the nicest ever. You know, Nibbs, how I take a cloth & disinfect & clean the compartment? Well, I did, as usual — and practically <u>no</u> dirt came off on it. I.e., the compartment had been <u>cleaned!</u> The fan worked. The loo floor was <u>dry!</u>

However, when we got to Tabora we remained shunting back and forth, for ever longer than usual — like 5 hours! Then we got to Uvinza, the salt-mine village. And there we came to a grinding halt. After 3 hours, I went to find someone who would <u>know</u> what was happening. Oh — it was a derailment on the line ahead. But, I was answered, we <u>would</u> go that day. By this time it was about 11.00 a.m. — and we should have got to Kigoma at 9.00 or 10.00 a.m.!! Well — we made out as best we could. . . . All this time, as I have quite forgotten to mention(!), Warren Garst of Wild Kingdom was semi-buried amongst his <u>30</u> boxes of equipment in the adjoining compartment. He couldn't see out of his window!!

Anyway, the time passed. We shopped for Mangoes under a shady tree. Soon the grassy station was filled by opportunistic vendors selling plates of food, tin cans' worths of water — and the inevitable mangoes, since it is the mango season. And eventually we set off — about 4.00 p.m. Stopped another hour in the middle of nowhere. And eventually crept past the derailment in the sunset. What a sight! It was a goods train. A soldier, complete with machine gun, mounted guard over a whole bogey of sugar, some spilling out over the green grassy slope.

They had made an excellent job of repairing the line. In fact, they had made a whole new section, going around the derailment — which had derailed because the line eventually broke under it! Finally we got to Kigoma.

No one was expecting us by then. But my friend the Chief Booking Clerke let me use his phone. I got Asgar. Jayant was out but would come as soon as he could. And yes — he would drive his landrover onto the platform with all Warren's stuff. We decided to get porters to unload everything & make a pile on the platform.

They had to carry it quite a ways & get into the light of one of the few lamps. One part was pitch dark & we had to get everything out with torches!

When Jayant arrived, some 30 mins later, the gates were closed and so we had to get everything carried along the 200 yards of platform, up the steps, and to the road. Two journeys for each porter. My, what a <u>ghastly</u> thing to be a Warren — or a Hugo — and have a trade that makes you have to travel with all that luggage. What a worry, what a responsibility! How super, by contrast, to be a writer and have to carry just a few personal belongings, a pen & paper. (Even if one moves with the times & composes on a word processor, there are super little ones these days, no heavier than a typewriter. Warren has one.)

We couldn't get Warren in at the hotel, so Jayant and I, leaving Warren & Chris sitting forlornly on the second pile of luggage (we took one lot) went & asked Maurice Marrow if he could take pity on Warren. Which he did. So we collected the remnants, dropped Chris & luggage at Jayant's, and took W over to the Marrows'. Had to pay for the lodging by stopping to have a cup of coffee!

Then back to Jayant's. A hot Indian supper at 10.10 p.m. — and, finally, to bed. What a trip! <u>But</u> what we found out was that that train was the <u>very</u> <u>first</u> to get through, past Uvinza, for 10 days. Previous trains had disgorged their hundreds of passengers at Uvinza, into buses. Can you imagine us, Chris's back, Warren & his luggage, in a BUS — a <u>Tanzanian</u> bus!! Phew — in retrospect it was a <u>wonderful</u> trip!!

Got to Gombe — me & Chris in our boat, Jayant's big boat bringing the luggage & Warren. (Jayant & co very glad of the opportunity to make money because, as no planes, no fish export! <u>Poor</u> things.)

The filming is hard work. It is raining a lot. Warren's camera is even heavier than Hugo's. And though my bit in the film is small, & most of the filming is of chimps & Field Assistants, I have to be there for the filming of the men. Because Warren knows no Swahili, and I know it will be <u>better</u> — and probably essential actually — for me to be there.

However, I have got in a few <u>super</u> follows. One on Little Bee & her family, when Chris came to observe the behavior of Mustard who was with us, took me to the top of Sleeping Buffalo. All sorts of super things happened. Then I did a fabulous follow of Winkle & her two youngest. Little Woolfi — that looks odd! — Wolfi — wants to be with Wunda <u>all</u> the time. He whimpers & follows her whenever she moves off! She almost <u>always</u> comes for him! That follow took me through really trampled vines, way up above the house.

The best follow of all was almost a day — started with Melissa & new Groucho. Then she vanished into tall trees so I did Gremlin. We joined a huge group. We went up Sleeping Buffalo and there I met Gigi & Patti, so switched [letter torn]. Gigi <u>adores</u> Tita & vice versa. We met [letter torn] & Melissa so I ended up with them — they left the group & wandered on their own. A fabulous day. Then it poured with rain & I arrived home soaked.

The men are now very enthusiastic about the film. We have <u>no</u> good uniforms. The ones Warren got, along with 100 metres of material, we left with the Customs in Dar. <u>Oh dear.</u> So we've had patches sewn on. And made them look as good as possible. Piles of to-be-used clothes are neatly folded upstairs, ready for use. We still have a long way to go!

I should stop now. Just time for a mandazi* & cup of coffee before the next day's work. Trying for a mother-infant group & two of the men. We have <u>done</u> Hilali doing a B record with one other.

Rashidi sends his salaams to Um & Nibbs. Maulidi is off. Sufi sends many salaams, Nibbs. He has dysentery. Oh dear.

Tons & tons of love —

Jane & Janey Wayne

P.S. — I have <u>No Book</u>.

---

* A small, slightly sweet square of pastry, the African equivalent of a small doughnut.

Dar es Salaam
Tanzania
28 November 1985

Dear Mary —

First of all I'm hoping that Tom is continuing to do well, and that life is treating you both properly for a change. You surely deserve it and I continue to think of you often.

Just back from three weeks at Gombe. Once again — <u>no</u> planes can land in Kigoma owing to the fact that there is no fire engine in good working order. (Because the fire brigade have been using their equipment to drive all over the region selling water, using the pumps until they wore them out. Six weeks ago the last plane landed there! Still waiting for spare parts!)

This meant a struggle for train seats. Coincided with Wild Kingdom. Got Warren Garst and 35 pieces of equipment into one compartment. Fortunately his wife decided to return to the States. He, alone, was barely visible beneath the boxes and bags!! (He is rather <u>fat</u> but despite this took with him 5 huge boxes of dried food for 3 weeks filming at Gombe!!) Discovered, on arrival in Kigoma, 14 hours late, that it was the <u>first</u> train to get through in 10 days. . . .

The derailment had been "staged" (so we were assured in Kigoma) because a Kigoma Indian had got permission to import 1 1/2 million shillings worth of foreign goods. When he heard of the crash, he rushed to the scene in his truck — too late. All his stuff had vanished. The derailment itself was real enough. We <u>crept</u> past the overturned bogeys, containers — whatever you call the cars of a freight train. A solitary soldier and machine gun stood guard over a huge mountain of glutinous sugar. Clearly doing a brisk trade in selling bagfuls to whoever turned up at the site! The corruption in Tanzania has reached truly horrifying magnitude in the past few years. I wonder what will happen now with the new president.

The filming went well, but took up a <u>lot</u> of my time as I had to be on hand to supervise just about <u>all</u> of the filming of the assistants (who speak no English). I mean — it was in my own interest to see that all was done properly.

Now back in Dar — galley proofs done . . . and just a few odd bits and pieces [left to do]. Which brings me to enclosed package of film. Result of summer's shooting at Gombe. We still have no <u>cover</u> [jacket] for the book. If you — or someone — are planning to look through the slides before sending them to me, could you possibly put to one side <u>anything</u> that is even <u>remotely</u> possible. Title — "The Chimpanzees of Gombe". Needs a <u>group,</u> which <u>must</u> include the range of apes and sexes — i.e. an adult male and female, a youngster and an infant.

This pile is <u>frantically</u> needed by Harvard University Press. Mrs. Vivian Wheeler, HUP, 79 Garden Street, Cambridge, Mass. 02138. An alternative is to send <u>everything</u> to her.

There are also some rolls which were taken of <u>me</u> on my <u>own</u> for a <u>back</u> cover. Me, trees and a bit of sky was what they wanted. Could you send her all that/those rolls too!

Actually, as I shall be going to Boston for a couple of days after Xmas, perhaps you could send <u>all</u> slides and contact sheets to Vivian to await my arrival. That way, even if you do make a pile of any possible cover pics, she can plough through all the rest if she wants to. Some will probably be awful — they include quite a number of experimental ones by the men, and with an automatic focus Nikon which turns out <u>not</u> to be able to focus on just a few things — including "black hair"!!

Both HUP and myself will be tremendously grateful for anything you can do to hasten the arrival of slides in Cambridge!

Well — I've gone on long enough. Oh — did you hear about the conference they are putting on in Chicago to "celebrate" the publication of the HUP book? A full 3 days, sponsored by Chicago Academy of Sciences — with chimp people from <u>all</u> over the world. Japanese, West African people — sign language and, of course, Chimp Zoo people. Exciting. I'm supposed to be organizing it, but they do all the arrangements including funds.

Well — my very, very warmest wishes for you and Tom to have a wonderful Christmas.

And with much love,
Jane

[Early August 1986]

Dear Vivian and <u>Everyone,</u>

It is <u>SUPER.</u> What a book! I actually had stopped believing in it, after that delay. People kept arriving at Gombe, one after the other. Would they have the book? No ———— .

Then, last night after a weary day getting back, THERE it lay! I gaze & gaze at the finished product. The dream that I believed would come true one day — that kept me going through the worst times. When I would say "Trusha, <u>one</u> day it will be bound, with pictures. Won't it?"

Well — all my thanks, millions, to all. . . .

Do you need me in Boston on 18th Nov? I <u>COULD</u> come, if desperately needed. Anyway, talk with Sue.*

Am frantic — getting all ready for Chris's departure. The men at Gombe — Yahaya, Eslom, Hilali, Yusufu and Mkono — are <u>FILMING</u> — 8mm video!! <u>Fabulous</u>.

Much love — millions of thanks —

Jane

TRUSHA sends love.

---

* Sue Engel was director of the Jane Goodall Institute at the time.

# 10

❧ ❧ ❧

# THE LABORATORY NIGHTMARE
## 1987–1990

The first laboratory I ever visited was just outside America's capital, in Rockville, Maryland. I had seen a videotape taken during an illicit entry, but even so I was not prepared for the nightmare world into which I was ushered by smiling, white-coated men.

— *Through a Window*

"UNDERSTANDING CHIMPANZEES," the November 1986 conference organized by Paul Heltne of the Chicago Academy of Sciences to celebrate publication of Jane Goodall's *Chimpanzees of Gombe,* assembled an international community of chimpanzee experts: people who knew one another by reputation and through scholarly reading and networks, who had often met at an intellectual remove but in many cases never in person. Flying into Chicago from Great Britain, the Netherlands, Africa, Japan, and from other parts of the United States, the attendees included some of Jane's contemporaries and peers, former Gombe students and research associates, and representatives from other research sites, including several Japanese primatologists who had been studying chimps and bonobos (also known as pygmy chimps) in Tanzania, Zaïre, and Guinea. In addition, a number of important representatives came from zoos (including those associated with Jane Goodall's ChimpanZoo project) and from laboratories. Laboratory scientists were invited if their research was "noninvasive"; so in attendance were distinguished pioneers such as Sue Savage-Rumbaugh and Duane Rumbaugh (who were teaching chimps and bonobos at Georgia State University and the Yerkes Primate Center to communicate via computer-based symbols) and Roger and Deborah Fouts (using sign language with a group of chimpanzees in Ellensburg, Washington).

The Chicago conference yielded many interesting expressions of the latest research findings. At the same time, it hummed with a collective whisper, a communal background noise, an underlying concern that divided roughly into two parts and was openly discussed during the two final-day sessions. First, nearly every field researcher agreed that wild chimpanzees in Africa were seriously threatened by a looming, continent-wide degradation of environments as well as, in many places, by hunting for meat and the collection of live infants for the captive trade. Second, other experts expressed alarm about the quality of care for chimps in captivity: in zoos and labs, as pets, and in the entertainment industry.

The conference concluded with the founding, by thirty top chimpanzee experts, of an organization to improve the situation for wild chimpanzees and the standards of care for those in captivity. Someone with a penchant for alliteration named the new entity the Committee for the Conservation and Care of Chimpanzees. Jane agreed to fund it via her Jane Goodall Institute, but the CCCC would function independently, with strategic ends to be determined collectively by the scientists backing it and tactical means to be organized by an elected chairman. The CCCC was potentially a formidable voice indeed on behalf of the voiceless chimpanzees. The chairman, Geza Teleki, a Hungarian-born American of strong personality and engaged political instincts, was a former Gombe student who had gone on to receive a doctorate in anthropology before conducting a survey of chimpanzees in Sierra Leone, West Africa, and then helping that country set up its first national park.

For Jane, that three-day conference had a galvanizing effect. It was like "Paul . . . on the road to Tarsus," she later wrote, comparing the depth of her personal transformation to the Apostle Paul's dramatic conversion to Christianity.* She entered the Chicago conference as a chimpanzee researcher, having completed the big first

---

* *Reason for Hope*, p. 206.

volume of her research summary, intent on moving on to the second. She left the conference an activist, a committed reformer.

Her life before had been active. But after the conference, the professional aspect of being Jane Goodall was transformed into a Sisyphean progression of lectures, conferences, meetings, fund-raising galas, solicitations, lobbying, arm-twisting, and back-scratching. Of course, now she was not alone. With the CCCC, she could count on broad support from a large and distinguished international community of chimpanzee researchers; and under the tenacious leadership of Geza Teleki, the CCCC was gathering filing cabinets full of critical information and advising Jane on the intricacies of American politics. Geza happened to live in Washington, D.C., and so (as mentioned, for instance, in the letter of July 5, 1988) his home and office became a convenient resting and meeting place whenever Jane was in town for lobbying or other purposes.

The first two letters in this chapter, written in the aftermath of the 1986 Chicago conference, addressed to language researchers Sue Savage-Rumbaugh and Duane Rumbaugh and to Japanese primatologist Toshisada Nishida, identify some of the aspects of Jane's new mission. Nishida ("Toshi") was a professor of zoology at Kyoto University and also directed a major field research station in Tanzania's Mahale Mountains National Park. As we can conclude from the January 15, 1987, note, he had also agreed to help prepare a "master plan" for surveys and new research projects in Central and West Africa.* The chimpanzee situation in Africa was desperate in large part because of an unprecedented expansion in human populations, a continent-wide doubling of numbers every twenty-seven years. As Jane noted, perhaps in the face of such "human pressures on the land," any attempts to protect chimpanzees would be doomed to failure "in the long run." Still, "we cannot sit back and allow chimps to vanish all over the country." New research projects might define significant areas to preserve. And new surveys of chimpanzee distribution in Africa were important both to create a functional map of conservation needs and to provide support for a

---

* East African chimps are limited in distribution and were already comparatively well studied.

move then afoot in the United States to shift chimpanzees from the *threatened* to the *endangered* category maintained by the U.S. Endangered Species Act (about which more will be said shortly).

Another conservation approach considered in this letter was to develop ecotourism — for example, to arrange a grand viewing package for wealthy tourists to compare chimpanzee cultural differences in tool use between Jane's site at Gombe (where the chimps were fishing for termites in mounds using deliberately modified twigs), Nishida's site in the Mahale Mountains (the fishing was for ants in trees), and a third site maintained by Christophe Boesch in Ivory Coast (where chimps were cracking open hard nuts with hammers and anvils made of stone or wood).

In the meanwhile, as Jane noted in her conclusion to the letter of January 15, 1987, she had become "horribly involved in the lab chimp issue."

Jane had never visited a biomedical research laboratory before 1987. She was, however, almost universally recognized as the world's foremost authority on wild chimpanzees and since 1972, first through work associated with the Stanford Outdoor Primate Facility and then through ChimpanZoo, she had developed an expertise on chimpanzees in captivity. But her real education in the special world of biomedical research laboratories began at the end of December 1986.

On a late Friday night earlier that month, an underground group of animal rights radicals had secretly eased themselves into an ordinary-looking building in suburban Maryland. Inside that structure a company called Sema, Inc. maintained around five hundred primates (monkeys mostly, along with a few dozen chimpanzees) for studies such as experimental vaccine testing. The chimps would be shipped in from special breeding colonies maintained by a massive federal bureaucracy called the National Institutes of Health (or NIH), and they were kept by Sema while undergoing various research protocols, such as being injected with an experimental vaccine and then being "challenged" by a virus. Even though the building was officially closed to the public, the operations inside were in fact entirely underwritten by U.S. taxpayers to the tune of about

$1.5 million a year, which came out of an NIH multibillion-dollar budget.

The radicals photocopied records, stole two cages as well as four chimpanzees, and made some rough videotapes as documentation. The videotapes and paper records were then sent to an animal rights organization called People for the Ethical Treatment of Animals (PETA), which edited the tapes and produced an eighteen-minute sequence entitled *Breaking Barriers*. PETA then sent that tape, plus written information, to a number of people they believed might be interested. Jane received a copy while she was in England visiting her family for Christmas, and a short while after that holiday she sat down with the family and watched *Breaking Barriers*. Particularly for someone who had known wild chimpanzees — with all their clearly expressed humanlike emotions and obvious intelligence, their loving family bonds, their individual personalities — the tape conjured up a Dantean sort of world, a nightmare vision that was disturbing indeed.

She mailed copies of the videotape to anyone she thought might be sympathetic or might possibly be able to influence the situation. Thus, a copy of *Breaking Barriers* landed in the mailbox of Jane's friend and colleague Alison Jolly, accompanied by the letter reproduced here as third in the chapter and dated January 18, 1987.

Jane requested permission to visit Sema, and in late March of 1987 she was given a full tour. The records showed that Sema, Inc. had an unusually high rate of mortality: seventy-eight primates lost in five years, including twenty-six monkeys steamed to death when a heating pipe broke. During the previous two years, inspectors from the U.S. Department of Agriculture (USDA) had regularly reported serious violations of federal standards for animal care, including, it was noted in every report, cages that were too small.

But the most chilling abuse, made clear both by the videotape and by the personal tour, had to do with the housing of their apes. Sema was taking chimpanzees from the breeding colony when they were eighteen months old and keeping them in pairs for their first six months in the lab, inside cages scarcely big enough for them to move. Once these creatures were injected with the research viruses — including respiratory and hepatitis viruses, and HIV —

they were separated from their companions and each was placed inside a closed steel box with a window on one side, 31 inches deep, 26 inches wide, and 40 inches high. The apes were kept in their boxes in total isolation for the duration of the study, typically two and a half to three years. It might be argued that subjecting almost any animal to such extreme isolation and sensory deprivation would amount to simple cruelty, but to treat a chimpanzee that way seemed cruel to the point of perversity.*

Jane went on to visit other labs in the United States and Europe, and in the process discovered a wide spectrum of physical situations and perhaps an even broader variety of management styles or corporate cultures. The Yerkes Primate Center, for instance (referred to briefly in the first letter), remained closed to public scrutiny, while the director, Frederick King, took a strikingly hostile public stance toward any hint of reform. The Southwest Foundation for Biomedical Research, with a very large chimp operation outside San Antonio, Texas, is obliquely mentioned in the letter of July 10, 1988 ("one of the big labs in Texas"). Jane actually visited Southwest more than once, and she was favorably impressed by the physical setup and quality of care, and the management's genuine openness to discussion and change. In Europe, she stopped at the Netherlands TNO Primate Centre, which likewise seemed responsive and open to discussion. And Jane toured the Immuno A.G. laboratories in Vienna, where, dressed in a spacesuit, she was escorted into an underground area to see some chimpanzees caged in concrete and steel. Immuno had indeed become "infamous" by the time she applied that adjective (letter of July 28, 1988), but mostly for reasons other than laboratory conditions. And back in the United States, she was given entrance into the big chimpanzee laboratory known as LEMSIP (Laboratory for Experimental Medicine and Surgery in Primates), maintained by the New York University Medical Center

---

* Under the leadership of CEO John Landon, possibly in response to Jane's criticisms and bad publicity more generally, Sema eventually changed its name to Diagnon — and then changed its entire physical layout in order to provide a vastly improved primate environment. The new enclosures at Diagnon are large plexiglass cubicles that enable the chimps to live in pairs and see their labmates in the other enclosures. Landon also introduced toys and enrichment devices, and he arranged for human volunteers to visit and play with the young apes.

and directed by Jan Moor-Jankowski, with veterinary care under the hand of James Mahoney.

As we can discern from the letter of July 10, 1988, LEMSIP was a study in contrasts: with an exemplary nursery for infants and youngsters not yet old enough to be injected with viruses and then, for the big boys and girls over two years old and ready for research, "bleak, barren rooms, windowless" containing "the traditional 5 foot × 5 foot, 7-ft-high cages." Suspended as they were from the ceiling, these looked rather like gigantic steel canary cages. They dangled a few inches off the floor, so that urine and feces would drop onto plastic sheeting below that could regularly be drawn away and incinerated. The system was designed with modern sanitation in mind, but the overall effect was rather medieval. Still, the chimpanzees were able to socialize with one another through the bars and sometimes visit through cage interconnections, and veterinarian Jim Mahoney seemed genuinely committed to improving things. The dynamic, Polish-born director, Jan Moor-Jankowski, appeared willing to discuss possible improvements as well — and, commendably, as a matter of policy the laboratory remained always open to scrutiny from the public and the media.

LEMSIP's chimps came from a variety of sources, so the 200-plus apes suspended in those cages included some ex-performers, a few formerly pampered pets who had become too big for pethood, and several apes who, before the funding dried up, had experimentally been taught to communicate using American Sign Language — and thus might awkwardly try to bum a cigarette from Mahoney, who was a smoker but did not know sign language. Chimpanzee language expert Roger Fouts accompanied Jane on the tour of LEMSIP described in this letter, and he was able to chat with some of the chimps, including an old friend who remembered Fouts from ten years earlier. He finally arranged for a graduate student to instigate various means of enriching the chimpanzee environment in the laboratory for a while.

Although Jane only obscurely alluded to it in her letter, that visit was marked by a traumatic incident. It was an extremely difficult day, largely because the AIDS virus was being injected into LEMSIP chimpanzees for the first time; veterinarian Mahoney was sufficiently upset for some of the chimpanzees to notice. Apparently caught up in the emotions engendered by a noisy mixture of unfamiliar visitors and Jim Mahoney's visible tension, at one point the veterinarian's favorite chimpanzee reached through the bars, grabbed Jane's hand, and in an instant had bitten off the tip of her right thumb. Jane wrapped a piece of cloth around the bleeding digit, continued the tour, and later had her injury attended to by a doctor. However, it became infected and very painful, and would trouble her for several months.

Soon after her March 1987 visit to Sema, Jane had begun to mention that laboratory's appalling conditions quite specifically in her public lectures. In addition, she wrote a forceful opinion piece that was published on May 17, 1987, in the *New York Times Magazine*. "The chimpanzee is more like us, genetically, than any other animal," she began. She went on to expose the conditions at Sema and to express, in her own way, the following paradox. Since chimpanzees are genetically almost 99 percent human, they make very interesting models for medical research; but since they are not 100 percent human, many laboratories were treating them like oversized rats. It is important to emphasize that Jane, in that article and elsewhere, always chose to take a moderate position. While she would have preferred to empty the cages and somehow find alternative situations for the approximately three thousand laboratory chimps around the world, she refused to engage in impossible arguments that might have seemed to weigh chimpanzee welfare against human welfare. So the campaign to better the status of chimpanzees in laboratories never called for removing them, but rather focused on improving their treatment.

Jane Goodall had also, around this same time, begun discussions with various potentates at the NIH, including Thomas Wolflie (letter of April 28, 1987) and deputy director William F. Raub (June 30, 1987). She proposed that the NIH sponsor a conference of specialists from all sides of the issue to see if they could create a consensus about how to improve the physical environment of chimpanzees in laboratories and therefore, ideally, define environments for the "psychological well-being" of the caged primates. In spite of the hopeful tone of these early letters, in the end the NIH leadership chose not to support that conference, which took place anyway, paid for by the Jane Goodall Institute and the Humane Society of the United States (HSUS), in early December of 1987. And the NIH decided more generally not to get very deeply involved in continuing discussions, which included a second conference that took place in the Netherlands and a third hosted in the Boston area by the Tufts University Center for Animals and Public Policy. The July 28, 1988, letter to Frank Loew, dean of the Tufts School of Veterinary Medicine, refers to some of the planning for that event.

Other than the two most obvious ways of improving the psychological well-being of chimpanzees in labs — bigger cages and more interesting things to do (or "enrichment") — a third way was perhaps at once least obvious and most important: allowing caged chimpanzees some social interaction. The management of Sema, as anyone might have predicted, defended its use of ovenlike "isolettes" by declaring the solitary confinement of infected apes to be strictly necessary for scientific and safety reasons.

Jane moved to have some of the best experts address that issue. The result was a correspondence with such virology luminaries as Huub Schellekens of the Netherlands TNO Primate Center (letter of July 13, 1987), and Luc Montagnier of the Pasteur Institute in Paris (January 2, 1988). In the note to Montagnier, Jane mentioned a "paper prepared for publication by Dr Alfred Prince" on the issue of whether infected chimpanzees could be caged together. (Prince was a well-known virologist associated with the New York Blood Center in New York; from there he directed, with the assistance of Betsy Brotman, a very large chimpanzee laboratory in Liberia, West Africa.) The article alluded to stated very directly that laboratory chimpanzees did not have to be enclosed individually inside "solid-walled isolator boxes" during the usual studies involving hepatitis viruses and HIV. Moreover, such unnecessary isolation, the authors declared, would "cause sensory and psychosocial deprivation, which contravenes their psychological well-being."*

---

* Prince, Goodall, Brotman, Dienske, Schellekens, and Eichberg, "Appropriate Conditions for Maintenance of Chimpanzees in Studies with Blood-borne Viruses: An Epidemiologic and Psychosocial Perspective," *Journal of Medical Primatology* 18: 27–42 (1989).

That publication was a "real breakthrough" (as Jane noted in her letter of December 10, 1988, to a supporter), but it was counterbalanced by a major defeat. The phrase "psychological well-being" was crucial partly because it had been inserted into a 1985 amendment to the U.S. Animal Welfare Act, which required federally funded laboratories to provide "a physical environment adequate to support the psychological well-being of primates." The man who had added those words was Senator John Melcher, a Democrat from Montana, the only member of Congress who had been a veterinarian before turning to politics. Melcher became an important friend during Jane's efforts to have the 1985 amendment enforced by the responsible agency, the U.S. Department of Agriculture (or USDA). Republican Senator Orrin Hatch likewise proved a strong ally during that time (letter to him of December 31, 1987).

As a matter of fact, by March 1987 the USDA had actually proposed a set of regulations designed to specify how federally funded laboratories might ensure primates' psychological well-being. Then the department solicited opinions from anyone concerned, and the battle began. Under the guidance and coordination of a lobbying organization supported by the biomedical research industry, several laboratory managers and researchers stepped forward and delivered their opinions: primates are "extraordinarily adapted to surviving radical environmental change" and therefore can easily tolerate many styles of treatment and confinement; "the reality of psychological similiarities between humans and other primates has not been . . . established" and so we should not concern ourselves with their psychological well-being; primates are unable to "contemplate their condition" anyhow, so why worry? The resistance to change was powerful and, in a strictly fiscal sense, reasonable. After all, reshaping laboratory environments to account for the psychological well-being of laboratory primates (up to eighteen hundred chimpanzees and perhaps as many as sixty thousand monkeys) could become very expensive and might introduce new ethical precedents.

Ultimately, the whole debate over regulations migrated to the White House Office of Management and Budget (OMB), a special bureaucracy with some legal authority to influence proposed regulations in the light of budgetary constraints. Aided by the official wisdom of James Wyngaarden (who had recently left his post as director of the NIH to become the top biomedical expert within the Office of Science and Technology Policy for the White House), the OMB essentially scrapped the proposed improvements by declaring that regulations to support primates' psychological well-being should focus on "performance" rather than "engineering" standards. In other words, almost any changes would be fine, so long as laboratories could then show that they had improved their own "performance" in considering the psychological well-being of primates.

During this same period, Jane was also pressing for a simple but important change in the U.S. Endangered Species Act. Under the leadership of Geza Teleki, the Committee for the Conservation and Care of Chimpanzees was gathering data and promoting surveys on chimpanzee distribution across the African continent. With that information in hand, Teleki and the CCCC prepared a report. Finally on November 4, 1987, it submitted a petition to the U.S. Fish and Wildlife Service that formally requested an upgrading of the status of chimpanzees from *threatened* to *endangered,* in the words of the U.S. Endangered Species Act.

This act was the legal mechanism for enforcing a treaty signed by the United States in 1975, the Convention on International Trade in Endangered Species (or CITES), aimed at reducing the destructive effects of international trade in live and dead animals and animal parts. CITES identifies traded animals and animal parts by category, and assigns special protection to species considered to be seriously under threat of extinction. CITES officially placed chimpanzees and all the other great apes in its category of highest protection: Appendix I status.

Of course, CITES is a treaty, not a law. All the signatory nations agree to enforce it with their own internal laws and, allowing for a number of special and sometimes peculiar exemptions, their own styles. The United States law for enforcing CITES, for instance, as a response to pressure from various interested parties, gave chimpanzees only its second-highest level of protection by defining them as *threatened* rather than *endangered*. The *threatened* status of chimpanzees in the Endangered Species Act had little effect on the comings and goings of chimps within national borders;* it did inhibit the international trade of chimpanzees directly out of Africa with a single clause declaring that any federal or federally funded agency applying to U.S. Fish and Wildlife for a permit to import chimpanzees would have to demonstrate that the importation was "not likely to jeopardize the continued existence" of the species.

Before the United States and other major importers signed CITES and moved to enforce it with their various laws, the live-animal trade in chimpanzees may have had a significant impact on African wild chimpanzee populations within certain localized areas. When American laboratories ordered new chimpanzees, they usually bought babies. Older chimps were, and are, simply too powerful and intractable to deal with easily. Typically, the babies arrived in a wooden box, with the papers and return address naming an official U.S. importer. The importer, in turn, would have bought the babies from an export station in Africa. Occasionally, buyers in the United States tried to determine how their baby chimps were actually acquired in Africa, and the usual answer that came back was designed to soothe sensitive consciences. A live-animal dealer by the name of Dr. Franz Sitter, for example, who in the 1970s and 1980s controlled the chimpanzee export business out of Sierra Leone, would say that his workers captured chimps by luring them into traps with bananas or chasing groups of females with dogs until the mothers were so tuckered out that they set their babies down and took off. The babies could then be gathered.

The reality of capturing baby chimpanzees, as people who investigated the situation knew (and as anyone studying wild chimps might imagine), was different. These apes are too smart and alert for simple traps. Netting them is possible but expensive, difficult,

---

* An uncontrolled domestic trade could make the international trade harder to monitor and enforce.

and dangerous for the netter — liable, in any case, to result in chimp deaths. Chasing the mothers until they set down their babies? Chimpanzee mothers would no more abandon their babies in a moment of exhaustion or panic than human mothers would. No, the easiest and most common way to acquire a baby chimpanzee in Africa was to shoot the mother and then pull off the clinging infant. Often the baby was accidentally killed or injured as well — and perhaps an aggressive second or third adult in the group might have to be shot. The captured baby would be bound, sacked, and hauled off to a local agent or the central collection headquarters.

Considering the primary killing of the mother, probable secondary killings, and the high likelihood that the captured baby would die of injuries or trauma or disease before or during export, some experts believed that approximately ten chimpanzees died for every baby who made it whole and healthy to a U.S. laboratory in a wooden box. Thus, a trade that supplied some six thousand chimpanzees to the United States from a single point of exit in Africa — Freetown, Sierra Leone — during the twentieth century might have accounted for the destruction of as many as sixty thousand chimps from a single region of the continent; and by the 1970s, the best survey available indicated that only about two thousand wild chimpanzees remained in all of Sierra Leone. Whether one preferred the stories of Dr. Sitter (tired mothers set down their babies and run away) or the claims of his critics (mothers and other adults are shot, resulting in high levels of mortality) became significant after 1976, as the United States started enforcing the CITES treaty by means of its U.S. Endangered Species Act.

The last person to import African chimpanzees into the United States legally was Jan Moor-Jankowski of LEMSIP in New York, who in 1976, a few months before the Endangered Species Act went into effect, purchased seventy-two babies from Dr. Sitter. In 1977, the year after the act was operative, two other U.S. labs applied to buy almost three hundred baby chimps from Dr. Sitter. Even though the dealer had supplied the applicants with his own personal assurance that no wild animals would be killed as a result of the deal, the applications were turned down by U.S. Fish and Wildlife because the applicants had failed to present a compelling enough argument that such an exchange was "not likely to jeopardize the continued existence" of the species.

So it would be possible to imagine that the lower protection offered to chimpanzees by a *threatened* category in the U.S. Endangered Species Act, in concert with the CITES treaty, effectively protected African chimps from any further damaging effects of the international wildlife trade. There were, however, reasons for concern.

Consider, for example, the case of Austria. That nation had signed the CITES agreement in April 1982, but at about the same time, Immuno A. G., a major Austrian pharmaceutical company, decided that it wanted some chimps. By March 1982, when the firm's ongoing attempts to buy a load of dealer Franz Sitter's babies seemed increasingly futile, Immuno started to consider an alternative approach. In talks taking place in Freetown, the capital city of Sierra Leone, on April 18, 1983 (a year after Austria had signed CITES), Immuno executives proposed simply to move part of their operation into Sierra Leone "precisely because they would not otherwise be able to import chimpanzees into Austria" (so a Sierra Leonean government minister characterized the logic). Where would the apes come from to begin this ambitious operation? Dr. Franz Sitter was named as a logical source. Where might the breeding operation be situated? Dr. Sitter's farm just outside Freetown was identified as an appropriate locale.

The plan was questionable from a number of angles, including the most obvious point that it seemed to violate the spirit if not the letter of Austria's CITES agreement, supposed to curtail the trade in endangered species. Dr. Sitter's secret past (as a thief, an ex-convict, a former Hitler Youth leader in occupied Czechoslovakia, and possibly a former member of Hitler's Schutzstaffel — the dreaded SS) was perhaps irrelevant, except for undermining the truthfulness of his claims about how all those baby chimps were acquired. In any case, the big lawsuit came when a woman from South Carolina, Shirley McGreal (head of a small group known as the International Primate Protection League), typed out her own set of objections to Immuno's plan and mailed them to the editor of an obscure journal with a circulation of approximately three hundred. The editor published McGreal's letter, and soon she was dealing with a $4 million lawsuit. Immuno A. G., which regularly confused its legal with its public relations departments, went on to sue the publisher and distributor of the journal, a writer for another periodical who quoted the journal, the publisher of that other periodical, and also the editor of the *Journal of Medical Primatology* himself, who happened to be Jan Moor-Jankowski, director of LEMSIP in New York.

As the litigation proceeded through the American courts, it quickly became so expensive that every party but one gave up and settled. (Shirley McGreal's insurance company settled over her objections and paid Immuno $100,000.) The only holdout was Moor-Jankowski. Starting in December 1984, while he was trying to run his laboratory and still edit his journal and keep his personal life in order, Moor-Jankowski was also conferring with his lawyer, assembling legal documents, responding to whatever further requests and challenges Immuno's staff could come up with, migrating from the lowest civil court in New York to the New York Court of Appeals and eventually up to the United States Supreme Court, which instructed the New York Court of Appeals to consider the case once again. This the court did and finally, though Immuno was still filing various torts and writs and motions to continue, the court dropped the case without comment on June 1, 1991. That was about six and a half years of litigation for Jan Moor-Jankowski over the case of a letter he had not written.

None of Immuno's proposals to establish its own chimpanzee operation inside Sierra Leone worked out. Meanwhile, however, the Austrian firm was working hard on another approach. Immuno executives had been trying to buy babies from Sitter since at least 1982, and finally in 1986 they succeeded. Just after midnight on July 30 of that year, a chartered plane carrying twenty baby chimpanzees from Sitter's farm in Sierra Leone landed at Vienna's Schwechat airport. The apes were quickly passed through customs and trucked out to the protection of a complex of buildings behind high walls, barbed wire, and armed security guards: the headquarters of Immuno A. G.

The importation was contested. There seemed to be irregularities. For example, the expert who ordinarily would have scratched her opinion on the import papers only heard about these chimpanzees after they had arrived. The person who actually gave an opinion was a beetle expert from the state of Lower Austria and, as it eventually turned out, a former business partner of Franz Sitter's. So the Austrian World Wildlife Fund protested. Immuno sued the secretary general of that group. The Austrian division of TRAFFIC (which monitors international wildlife trade) protested. Immuno sued the director of that group. Various newspapers and magazines protested. Immuno sued the responsible journalists and editors. Immuno sued and sued and sued again, until the Austrian pharmaceutical giant was simultaneously processing some five dozen separate sets of legal papers.

Given the hullabaloo about their new baby chimps, executives from Immuno agreed to an open public meeting at the Vienna Town Hall on August 21, 1987, during which all of the unfortunate misunderstandings would be addressed. The meeting was contentious, but Immuno was able to argue its case effectively with the assistance of a star witness from the United States. Dr. Robert Gallo, at the time considered a discoverer of the AIDS virus, was enjoying a public reputation as the most brilliant research scientist in the entire NIH system. Geza Teleki attended that Town Hall meeting, where he wrote down a paraphrase of what Robert Gallo said: that "chimpanzees can be justifiably obtained by his laboratory at any time for the purpose of AIDS research, regardless [of] what import limitations had been set until now by the U.S. government." Or, as Gallo later phrased the concept to an Austrian journalist, "I will put anyone who prevents us from importing apes into a mental institution or a prison."

What was Robert Gallo doing in Vienna? The nature of his relationship with Immuno was never openly clarified; but a later Freedom of Information request uncovered an agreement signed on July 23, 1986 (one week before the shipment of Sitter's twenty baby chimps to Vienna), by representatives of the NIH and representatives of Immuno A. G. to share recombinant viral material, possibly as part of a larger collaboration.

By 1987 Robert Gallo was publicly describing the drastic shortage of U.S. laboratory chimpanzees necessary for the fight against AIDS. At one point he told a reporter from the *American Medical News* that he needed seventy-five chimpanzees in the next two years to continue his work but that he would be "lucky to get two or three." At approximately the same time, James Wyngaarden, then director of the NIH, was declaring to reporters that "we clearly don't want to get into an international fracas over seeming to subvert the rules that apply in this country," but "we're taking lots of looks at Africa."

Was there a desperate shortage of chimpanzees needed for AIDS research at that time? Were the research needs of the biomedical community then so compelling that the United States would have been justified in scrapping its already tenuous commitment to the protections of the CITES treaty? Several well-informed and highly respected experts — including Alfred Prince of the New York Blood Center and Vilab II in Liberia, Jan Moor-Jankowski of LEMSIP, Jorg Eichberg of the Southwest Foundation, Huub Schellekens of the TNO Primate Center in Holland, and Marc Girard of the Pasteur Institute in Paris — thought not. They expressed that point of view jointly in a statement for *Nature* magazine that Jane (who was a coauthor) referred to in her letter of December 10, 1988: "Best news — the big shots in the AIDS research world have finally come out with the fact that chimps are NOT useful for AIDS research. A few are likely to be needed to test batches of vaccine." And was it true that Dr. Robert Gallo, the star of the NIH system, would be "lucky to get two or three" chimps for his own critically significant work? An official registry listed at that time some twelve hundred chimpanzees in U.S. laboratories, and an NIH chimpanzee breeding program was producing at that time around fifty new chimps yearly, while the more than two hundred apes sitting in cages at Moor-Jankowski's laboratory in New York were, for unclear reasons, never used by NIH researchers or even included in the official tally of U.S. laboratory chimpanzees.

The full story of the U.S. biomedical research industry and its eccentric pursuit of chimpanzees is longer and more complicated than can be told in these pages, but perhaps enough has been said for the reader to appreciate why Jane Goodall expressed alarm about the activities of the NIH in her letter of May 30, 1990, to the U.S. secretary of state, James Baker, and why she, with the support of Geza Teleki and the Committee for the Conservation and Care of Chimpanzees, was pressing so actively to strengthen CITES enforcement in the United States by upgrading the status of chimpanzees within the wording of the U.S. Endangered Species Act.

The petition for that upgrade was formally submitted in late 1987 to the U.S. Fish and Wildlife Service and accompanied by a thorough, sober, and detailed report compiled by Geza Teleki, Toshisada Nishida, and other members of the CCCC. Fish and Wildlife, in turn, examined the petition and then solicited public responses between March 23 and July 21, 1988. During the period of public commentary, some fifty-four thousand postcards and letters and other messages arrived at the offices of Fish and Wildlife in support of the petition, including around forty informed comments from members of African governments and relevant organizations and from experts who had studied chimpanzees in the field. Six letters opposed to it also arrived at U.S. Fish and Wildlife during that period. One of the opposing letters was written by a representative of a circus. The other five were written by well-placed officials associated with biomedical research, including Frederick King (director of the Yerkes Primate Center), James Wyngaarden (director of the NIH), and the recently named CEO of a newly established American firm called Immuno U.S., which was the little-sister subsidiary of a much bigger entity with headquarters in Vienna, Austria, known as Immuno A. G.

In the end, U.S. Fish and Wildlife, moved apparently by the strength of arguments on both sides, declared a compromise that defined chimpanzees as *endangered* if they happen to live inside a forest in Africa but *threatened* if they happen to be sitting in a cage outside Africa.*

\*    \*    \*    \*

---

* Unless otherwise noted, all quotations, stated facts, and other information in this section were taken from chapters 6 and 11 of *Visions of Caliban: On Chimpanzees and People,* by Dale Peterson and Jane Goodall (Boston: Houghton Mifflin, 1993).

PO Box 727
Dar es Salaam
Tanzania
January 8, 1987

Dear Sue and Duane,

Just back in Tanzania after my hectic rush-around in America and Germany. Just want to write very quickly and thank you for your letters and card and the super pictures of Panzee and Panban[isha].* The Conference in Chicago was a really fantastic occasion I thought — seeing together so many of the people whose names I have referred to in publications over the years, some of whom I had never even met before. I thought it was particularly lovely having the Japanese team over. I managed to arrange a dinner party with all of them except Sugiyama† (who seems not to get on with the rest!) on the last evening, together with Mum and Paul Heltne. I was so glad to have that opportunity because they had come such a long way. That was the one problem for me at the Conference — there were so many people I wanted to talk to and so desperately little time in which to do so.

I really hope that the new moves we have set in motion will result in doing something both for the wild chimps that remain in Africa and for the chimps that are captive in the United States. I know that there will always be a little tension between us because of your association with Yerkes. However, as you know, for me the chimpanzees must always come first. It is even seeming to me now that my efforts in these two directions (i.e. conservation and captive welfare) should, at least for the present, come before Gombe. That is quite a thing to say, but I feel strongly that I am one in a position, thanks to being able to work with such wonderful creatures, to be able to reach out a hand towards them. If I fail to do that, for any reason whatsoever, it would be a betrayal of all that I have learnt during my years of working with them. . . .

---

* Jane had visited Sue Savage-Rumbaugh and Duane Rumbaugh in 1986 at their language laboratory in Atlanta and met these two appealing infants. Panzee was a chimpanzee, Panbanisha a bonobo.

† Yukimaru Sugiyama of the Primate Research Institute in Kyoto, who ran a chimpanzee study site in Guinea.

Let us hope that 1987 will be a good year for all of us, for the Gombe chimps, for your chimps, for chimpanzees everywhere. Goodness gracious me — I almost forgot to send congratulations to Lana on the birth of her infant. How absolutely super that is and the development of that baby will be fascinating to watch. I hope the baby will stay with his mother.

Must end now.

Love,
Jane

P.O. Box 727
Dar es Salaam
15 January 1987

Dear Toshi — Happy New Year!

It seems so long ago, the conference in Chicago. I do hope that it was a good experience for all you wonderful primatologists from Japan? It was, I think, a simply fabulous conference — if only the Boesches and Tutin could have been there, it would have been perfect.[*] And it would have been super if Jun could have come, also. It was a difficult time for me — there were so many people I wanted to talk to, and so little time. . . . However, I was SO pleased that we had the chance to have that last dinner together, and that you had a chance to meet my amazing mother. It was a lovely evening, I thought, and I was so pleased that all of you were able to come.

I am writing now about the surveys/researches in Central and West Africa. I know that you are preparing a master plan for this. And I have been in touch with Geza. I wish you were a little closer! Anyway, after USA, I went on to West Germany. There I found a very great deal of interest in trying to conserve the chimpanzees. I want to "strike while the iron is hot" — in other words, they committed some money and said they would find a student, and I want to follow this up QUICKLY. . . .

You know, Toshi, way back in 1965 Hugo and I tried to persuade

---

[*] Christophe and Hedwige Boesch were studying the stone-tool–using chimpanzees of Ivory Coast's Taï Forest; Caroline Tutin, a former Gombe student, was conducting ape and ecological studies in the Lopé-Okanda Forest Reserve of Gabon.

WWF to help us with a plan to set up a series of reserved areas for chimps spread out across their range. So that we could preserve not only chimps, but all the different, as yet unknown, cultures. It might have been quite easy then. But they felt that chimps were not endangered, and so did not help. And without some overall organization, we couldn't cope.

Well, now we have an organization! CCCC! We need money, but I think we should be able to do fairly well. Perhaps many countries would volunteer money and one or two students. It's up to us to tell them <u>where those people should go.</u>

I must tell you one other thing. I meet many people who say "It's all very well. You plan to do a survey, and to start research in a place that seems to promise well. But surely you understand that human pressures on the land will mean that even if you do establish a reserve or park, the edges will get nibbled away, the government will give in to timber companies, for money. In the <u>long run,</u> you will fail." My answer to them is (a) we cannot sit back and allow chimps to vanish all over the country. We must TRY to save them. And (b) while we try, we have the opportunity to learn something. We begin to document all the different cultures. We collect film, video film, wherever we can. We all use the same ethogram, or at least understand each other's (i.e. community = unit-group, unit group – community!!).* We find out much before it is too late, before the chimps and their unique behaviours are gone forever. And there is NO ONE I have talked to who has not, immediately, seen the point. And become positive instead of negative. So I thought I should share that with you, since you are co-ordinating this whole conservation part of CCCC.

I have also been talking to tour operators — because of my concern over the damage that tourists are causing by being allowed to wander about among the Kasakela chimps, and my urgent need to establish a place for tourists in the north or south. So it occurred to me that we should get the tour operators involved in conservation. I enclose a memo which I jotted down, as to how this might

---

* Jane had introduced the description of chimpanzees as belonging to a "community"; the Japanese preferred (and still prefer) to speak of a "unit-group."

work. I have a feeling that you, in Japan, could help a very great deal in plans of this sort? What are your views?

The last time I talked with the Boesches they were in despair over poaching and government attitude. I told them I thought that tourism was the ONLY answer for conservation in a situation like theirs. I had just been talking to Lars Lindblad, a very big tour operator from USA (who takes very "exclusive" tours, very wealthy people). So the Boesches and I put together a tourist package — they could go to Tai, come across to Tanzania and see chimps perhaps at Mahale (for ant eating in trees) and Gombe (for termiting) — as they will hopefully have seen nut-cracking in Tai. And then they could end up with gorillas. Well — this sounded great to Lindblad, and he sent out a representative to Tai. That man — Nigel Sitwell — came to see me in England (he is English) — just after he got back. He is very enthusiastic. He is coming to Gombe next month.

So, Toshi — that's about it. I have got horribly involved in the lab chimp issue — IMMUNO in Vienna, and the new horrors uncovered at the SEMA/Meloy lab in USA. It's taking up a LOT of time. But one must try to help. I suppose there are some bad things going on with chimps in Japan now, re AIDS? Are you involved in that at all? I feel that I MUST try to do whatever I can, even if, as a result, Gombe comes second for a while.

Well — let us hope this will truly be a year of the chimp, even if unofficially! Please do let me know how things are going, if you have any plans, how I can be helpful. Are you coming to Tanzania this summer? I hope so.

Please give my salaams to any of my primatology friends who are around. I wonder if Mariko got her scholarship.* I must write to her. So hard to find time to get everything done.

Once again — Happy New Year.

Yours,
Jane

P.S. Forgive awful typing.

---

* Mariko Hiraiwa-Hasegawa, of the Department of Anthropology, University of Tokyo, had been part of the Japanese group attending the conference.

18 January 1987

Dear Alison,

Enclosed is a copy of an 18 minute film, "Breaking Barriers" — available thru PETA in Wash. D.C. It shows the kind of things going on in our labs all over the world. The kind of things that we have all heard about, and intellectually "know" about, but which do not seem real until we see them with our eyes. It is hard to believe that such inhumanity is for real.

This particular facility, the SEMA/Meloy Inc. facility at Rockville, Maryland, is particularly bad, and many of their cages do not measure up even to the minimum size required by federal US laws. The same is true for the standard of caretaking at this facility.

But all over the world, where non-human animals are used to further human knowledge, there are labs where the conditions are similar. There are places where the conditions are worse. And even in countries where laws exist regarding sizes of cages and standards of care for laboratory animals, they almost always fall far short of the real physical and psychological needs of the animals concerned. Switzerland is one of the exceptions.

I feel that as many people as possible should see this tape. It was taken by brave people who raided the lab over the weekend — when, as in many labs, the animals are left largely to themselves. I suspect that, after you have watched the film, you will be as relieved as I was to hear that four of those little chimps were "stolen" by the raiders.

If you feel as I do about this horrifying inhumanity practised in the name of science, I beg that you will show this tape to as many people as you can, scientist and non-scientist alike. So that more and more people understand just what it is that is meant when we talk about unacceptable conditions (ethically speaking) in the labs. You are free to make copies and send them to anyone you wish.

If you have any ideas as to how we, who care about preserving and encouraging a humanitarian ethic in the world today, can work together to change existing laws, and make our laboratories places where decent human beings need not be ashamed to work, then please let me know.

Love,
Jane

You may have seen this? I want people to become <u>AWARE</u> of what goes on. Then, when we try to change laws, people will know WHY it is necessary. Not <u>only</u> to protect animals from such abuse. But to prevent <u>HUMANS</u> from being given free rein to behave in this INHUMANE way. It is a black mark against our humanity if we allow this to continue — once we know it does. Show it in class. And to anyone you can. Please, Alison. See you in spring.

April 28, 1987

Dr. Thomas Wolflie
National Institutes of Health
Bethesda, MD 20205
Dear Tom:

I'm sorry that it has taken longer than we hoped for Roger and me to get back to you regarding the December conference on the welfare of laboratory chimpanzees. The issue is such a desperately important one, and the results will be so far reaching, that we both felt that it was absolutely essential that we should get together to talk things through. The telephone simply does not allow for the free exchange of ideas and back and forth discussion. If you saw my schedule, you will realize why it was difficult to find time when I could get to Ellensburg! However, we finally managed a late night session and a good part of the next day. I hope you will agree that the results were fruitful.

However, I should start out by saying that Roger and I both feel that the format of a Consensus Development Conference might not be quite the right one for the soul-searching discussions we have in mind. For one thing we feel that the central issue — the need for change in the housing and care of lab chimps — is <u>not</u> controversial. Presumably all those attending will realize that there must be changes, even those who might be happy to continue the way things are, because of the "psychological wellbeing" clause in the new amendment to the Animal Welfare Act. Thus, our goals will be: firstly to come to some agreement as to what these changes should be, and secondly to work out how best they can be implemented in the various facilities, taking into account the differing types of biomedical experimentation to which the chimpanzees are subjected.

Some of the changes that we are proposing are so major that, without doubt, there will be strong resistance from many of the participants. But hopefully we can all agree on some things, and thoroughly thrash out the rest, giving representatives of the different interest groups — those actually doing the research, facility administrators, care-takers and animal technicians, veterinarians, field biologists and individuals concerned with animal welfare — a chance to express and defend their various points of view. Provided those who are invited are all reasonable, honest, and caring people, a conference which covers the topics suggested should accomplish a great deal. We would certainly hope for a consensus of opinion on a great many of the issues that will be raised.

We believe that the December conference is timely not only with regard to the psychological wellbeing issue, but also with regard to the controversy over the chimpanzee breeding program. Hopefully the conference will make substantial contributions in both areas.

If NIH agrees to a conference of the sort outlined, Roger and I are prepared to submit specific names and topics for speakers. And, of course, we expect similar input from your end.

Tom — I hope this can be worked out. I had closed my eyes for too long with regard to the issue of chimpanzees in the laboratory. Now they have been opened so wide that it is hard for me to sleep at night.

Thank you for your help, and for caring.

Very sincerely,
Jane Goodall, Ph.D.

June 30, 1987

William F. Raub, Ph.D.
Deputy Director
National Institutes of Health
Building 1, Room 132
Bethesda, Maryland 20205
Dear Dr. Raub:

Enclosed are five (5) copies of our proposal for an International Conference on Methods of Enriching the Environment for Captive Chimpanzees. The proposal basically follows the outline which we presented at our meeting with you on June 22, although there have been some minor modifications in the proposed dates for the Conference and in the budget.

We appreciated the opportunity to discuss our plans for the Conference with you and were most pleased with the supportiveness of your comments and suggestions. Hopefully, we have successfully incorporated those ideas in the final proposal. If there are questions and/or if additional information is required, please do not hesitate to contact Dr. Judy Johnson at the Institute office.

On a more personal note, I certainly appreciated the amount of time you and your colleagues were able to give us on such short notice. I shall be looking forward to your response to our proposal.

Sincerely,
Jane Goodall, Ph.D.


P.O. Box 727
Dar es Salaam
13 July 1987

Dear Dr. Schellekens,

Three days ago I returned from my visit to the United States, and now make haste to write to you.

First of all, I should like to thank you so much for the time you took to talk with me and answer my questions about the conditions of your chimpanzees during testing of hepatitis. In particular, I am really grateful to you for the letter you wrote me indicating that, in your view, it is not necessary to isolate the chimpanzees for testing of vaccines.

I was very impressed by my visit to the TNO Primate Center and the care and consideration that is given to the chimpanzees. Of course there is room for some improvements (there always will be!) but everyone I talked to there was willing to try new things to make life even better for the chimpanzees.

I mentioned to you the conference that my institute in America is planning for this coming December. We should hear by the end of this week whether NIH agrees to fund it. So far the results of my conversations with NIH staff lead me to believe that they will go ahead with the idea.

As soon as we get confirmation of this, you will receive an official letter of invitation from my institute. The date will be the first week in December. I truly hope that you will be able to attend, as I think you could make a truly significant contribution to the welfare of laboratory chimps.

Again, thank you so very much for your time and help.

Yours sincerely,
Dr. Jane Goodall, Director

December 8, 1987

Senator John Melcher
730 Hart Senate Office Bldg
Washington, DC 20510
Dear Senator Melcher:

The recommendations set forth in the enclosed document represent the results of a professional workshop held in Washington during December 1–3, 1987, with the aim of providing an expert forum to determine what improvements are needed to ensure the psychological well-being of chimpanzees held at laboratories and other facilities.

These recommendations are based on the collective expertise of scientists and other professionals familiar with the behavior, psychology and biology of chimpanzees in both wild and captive settings, and can be supported by experience and empirical evidence. Everything that we have recommended is, in fact, standard practice in at least one biomedical laboratory. The recommendations are therefore not based simply on humanitarian ideals.

Additional information can be supplied, as needed, to counter any criticisms or opposition that might be expressed when the implementation of these recommendations is considered by federal authorities.

Sincerely and respectfully yours,
Dr. Jane Goodall

31 December 1987

Dear Senator Hatch,

Just a short note to thank you so very much for taking the time from your busy schedule — and at such short notice — to talk with me. I really appreciated that generosity — and I also immensely enjoyed meeting you.

I have just got to Gombe, after spending Christmas with my family in England. Right now it is <u>pouring</u> with rain and so I am taking the opportunity at catching up on some paper work. I <u>dread</u> the mound of mail that always awaits me on my return from a visit to the States.

This morning I followed Fifi and her two daughters, 8 year old Fanni and 3 year old Flossi. The forest is green, lush and very beautiful. Crawling after chimps through very dense wet-season underbrush, a tangle of thorny vines in places, was less beautiful! But well worth it for the delightful observations I was able to make. Once, for example, Flossi got stuck up a tall, thick-trunked tree. When she began to whimper in distress it was Fanni who hurried up the tree to help her young sister. The family encountered a large python and the two girls were absolutely fascinated. Fifi threatened it a few times, then wanted to leave. But Fanni and Flossi refused to follow: for 25 minutes they peered at the snake, shook branches and stamped their feet. For much of the time Fanni had one arm protectively around Flossi.

I cannot be with these chimps, so magnificent in their freedom, without feeling heart ache for the prisoners in our labs. We <u>must</u> give them something better. I know you understand why I feel this way.

Once again, I thank you most sincerely for your time. I hope that 1988 will be healthy, productive and successful for you and yours.

Yours very sincerely,
Jane Goodall

P.S. I hope the pictures (for my closet!!)* have come out okay?

As from: The Birches
10 Durley Chine Road South
Bournemouth
Dorset BH2 5JZ
2 January 1988

Dear Dr. Montagnier —

Thank you so much for sending me a copy of your 17 August letter. The original must have gone astray in the France-Tanzania postal system!

Yet I still should like to pester you a little more! In your 25 November letter you say "separation is required when the animal is getting big for the available cages".

The whole thing I am fighting for is better living conditions, which include bigger cages. Thus my question to you is the following: If the cages are big enough, could you carry out all your research/vaccine testing procedures on PAIRS of chimps?

I enclose a paper prepared for publication by Dr Alfred Prince on this issue. I would be extraordinarily grateful for your view.

I'm sorry to bother you — but I think you understand why it is necessary — for the chimps, who cannot ask you themselves.

Thank you so much for being interested.

Yours sincerely,
Jane Goodall

Oh — and I hope 1988 will be successful — a vaccine for AIDS!

---

* When Jane had asked to have her photograph taken with Senator Hatch, he modestly wondered why she would want a picture of *him*. What would she do with it — put it in her closet?

[Postmarked July 5, 1988]

Dear Neva —

From the Clipper Club — where I just met a wildlife artist who is going to donate a couple of chimp bronzes for us!! (I was on same plane on way over as he & ?wife — we sat in the Clipper Club in London. Such a coincidence!)

Anyway, I had a cab driver on way back from my last lobbying. I gave a sigh. He asked what was up. Said exhausted lobbying. "Oh — what you lobbying about?" I told him.

He turned to look at me and his round black face broke into an amazed grin. "My Gawd! You're Jane Goodall in my cab!!" I thought the cab would leave the road! He insisted on driving with his head turned over his shoulder — so I made him draw up & I got in the front seat. We talked all the way to Geza's.

Anyway — he has a video machine. He LOVES wildlife tapes. He can't find any to hire. So I said I'd ask you. Do you know how he can rent/borrow wildlife tapes? He is so nice. So interested. Wants for his kids to be interested. If you could suggest anything I (& he!) will be so grateful. He only charged $5.00 instead of $11.00–$12.00 as usual!

Luckily I had already got out a little book!

The world has such wonderful people. It is NOT all bad. YOU are one of them.

Love,
Jane

10th July 1988

Dear Mrs Schwein,

Well — my thumb is almost better — I can't use it yet, it's still swollen, but it has healed. And I can get back, at last, to Gombe. I am not there yet — but I hope I will be at least in Tanzania by the time you get this letter.

I am writing about two things. Firstly, some of the things being done with the donation you sent. Secondly, a further need. But I must start by telling you about a visit I made to one of the big chimp labs — almost the biggest in the country. If you saw the 20/20 segment I did with Roger Caras, you will know it.* LEMSIP, just out-side New York.

I think you can probably imagine what it means for me to go to a lab? It's bad enough going to a zoo, even a good zoo. But only if I go, see with my own eyes, meet the people, can I try to help. The nightmares that follow must be coped with as best I can — and they certainly spur me to greater effort. So — I must describe this place, just a little.

The lab is run by a Dr Moor-Jankowski. Polish refugee — no, perhaps Hungarian. No matter. He is a medical doctor attached to New York University Medical School. The chimps (250 of them) are cared for by a most <u>unusual</u> man. Dr James Mahoney, a vet, and Irishman. He LOVES chimps. I mean, he really does.

Jim instigated a "Nursery." When the young ones must be taken from their mothers (2 years) they do not go into barren cages, in pairs, as in most labs. They go into a room with a carpet, windows, toys, a jungle gym — and <u>people.</u> People who <u>really</u> care. That is where I was taken. I sat with the 6 little ones for about 40 minutes. I was very impressed by the quality of care given by the "techni-cians."

Then — and I <u>wonder</u> if it was deliberate? — I was taken to one of the bleak, barren rooms, windowless, where some (8) of the adult males were housed in the traditional 5 foot × 5 foot, 7-ft-high cages. Usually, in a lab, the adult chimps hate people. They spit. Throw feces, try to grab you. These males were different. Yes — they performed their wild displays, making an AWFUL noise. But Jim talked to them and they quietened. They were not insane.

I never got further than the first one. He was called JoJo. His eyes looked into mine — puzzled (I read that in his direct gaze). Why was he here? Why must he stay there, month after month? He was so <u>gentle.</u> I would NEVER let a zoo chimp hold my hand. He held mine, groomed it, was so <u>grateful</u> that I stopped to pass the time of day. Long, bleak days, underground, nothing to do. And Jim, worked almost into the ground; not enough time.

Well, as JoJo fondled my hand, Jim, who had gone further along

---

* Referring to an ABC television news show.

the line, came back. He asked me something. I couldn't reply. He looked at me and saw the tears running into the mask I had to wear. Then he sat down (I was crouched low so as to be eye level with JoJo) and put his arms around me. "Don't do that, Jane — I have to face this every morning." Of course, that made it worse. I don't think I have <u>ever</u> had to fight for control as hard as I did then. I have never, ever, been through such an emotionally draining experience. (It was evening, I'd already had a lunch and given a speech in New York, and the hour's drive — oh, and a radio interview!)

Jim's wife is French. She told me that Jim comes home and, about once every 3 months or so, tells her he must quit. He can't stand it any longer. "But what will happen to the chimps?" he says, the next morning. So he stays. He is worn to a shadow. He never sleeps until after 2.00 a.m.

So — I was landed, that time, with a <u>double</u> nightmare. The chimps. And Jim. A <u>lot</u> of positive thinking was necessary. So —

Next month we start a "Kindergarten" for the little ones. Jim has found a woman already. She may get an M.A. out of it. She is a psychologist — as I had suggested. But is about 48, and has been to LEMSIP. She will teach the little ones some ASL signs — so they can ask for things, say what they want. Painting and drawing. They will learn that pressing different buttons, or levers, produces different results — a grape, a drink, etc. And, perhaps, the principle of video games (they would use a sort of "joystick" to move the cursor. I've seen it done). Coloured magazines to look at. And so on.

Next in the plan is to follow this through. Work once or twice a day with these same chimps when they are older and leave the nursery and have to live, in groups of 4 or so, in cages. Bare cages. And, finally, work with the prisoners in their metal prisons — JoJo and the others.

You see — a) it will help to alleviate the <u>terrible</u> boredom, b) it will make life more bearable for the staff who look after them — and the LEMSIP staff <u>all</u> care — Jim won't have them otherwise — c) there is <u>so much</u> that those wonderful chimps can <u>teach us</u> about their minds, how they work, what they think. All the different types of intelligence (at present all lost).

We have found a young man prepared to start work with the adults next month. He worked with Roger Fouts and the signing chimps. He may not be able to "take" the conditions. But he is going to try — he <u>desperately</u> wants to try. His name is John Lake.* If it works then he wants to get enrolled at New York University for a Ph.D. He is starting off on your money.

This is a scheme that could revolutionize the lab situation. I have written now to one of the big labs in Texas, where there are also some very humane people (I've not been there) and suggested this plan. And to the very big lab in Holland.

There is even better news at LEMSIP. Moor-Jankowski has <u>FINALLY</u> agreed to allow some of the chimps outside runs. Jim is struggling with construction costs — I think we should be able to get some of it done at COST price. Then their runs could be a bit bigger.

<u>AND</u> Moor-Jankowski has agreed that eventually, once the money has been raised, the adult chimps, in between their 6 month periods of testing, can go and live together on man-made islands.

You see, the chimps don't get sick of either hepatitis or AIDS — and those are the two things they are most used for. (They just keep the viruses alive in their blood. They test the vaccines.)

I am MUCH encouraged to find that in Europe there is a <u>real</u> determination to get <u>all</u> animals out of the labs. Better still, World Health Organization has firmly stated that, while its scientists perceived a <u>huge</u> demand for chimps for AIDS research a year ago, they now realized that "100s and 100s" were NOT necessary. Just a few. That is <u>such</u> a relief. Now one must, somehow, ensure that the same policy is adhered to in America — by my "friends" at NIH!!

Well. This has become rather long. I'm sorry. (All written with pen held between 1st 3 fingers!)

We have employed a new member of staff at the Jane Goodall In-

---

* Fouts eventually sent a student named Mark Bodamer, who set up an enrichment program for all of LEMSIP's chimps. According to Fouts (in his book *Next of Kin*), that program "was a great success, but, unfortunately, it was scuttled after Mark left." Some brave and independent people working in the laboratory tried to continue on their own after that.

stitute. Bob Edison. He has a special interest in lab animals. Is a psychologist. Turned down 5 job offers as top hospital administrator to work with us (for almost nothing!). Anyway, he is the person who will be organizing everything to do with the chimp lab issue. I am really delighted that he will be working with us on this.

Incidentally, my lobbying efforts on the Hill have been going rather well. And it seems that <u>despite</u> NIH, Fish and Wildlife may be going to come out in favor of reclassifying the chimpanzee as "endangered."

So — a lot of good things are happening. And if you'd like more details about the LEMSIP plan — drop me a line at Gombe.

Yours sincerely,<br>Jane

P.S. I encountered a version of the artificial "termite" fishing apparatus that, <u>at last,</u> is being widely used in zoos. (I designed a prototype in 1962!!) This one is perfect for lab chimps, is clamped to bars of the cage, & the "termites" (usually honey, or mustard or whatever) are put into test tubes. <u>So</u> simple. The zoo is making samples and sending them to LEMSIP and the Texan Lab for me. We sent 8 toy chimps to LEMSIP for the nursery chimps. I want to get some TV sets for the adults — probably video is best so one can select appropriate viewing material! And I'm looking for some suitable things that change shape when you switch on electricity. Don't know what you call them. That will give them <u>SOMETHING</u> to watch. Any ideas?

July 28, 1988

Dear Frank,

Well — it was good speaking to you last night. . . . I'm SO glad that your hip is behaving itself. That is wonder-ful news. It seems AGES since I saw you last. Hope to rectify that. One quick question. If I was able to visit for a day on 17 or 18 October, or alternatively, around mid-November, would you be there? Just to say hello to your students — and you of course! . . .

Now, close to my heart is the Workshop. As I told you, Dr. Moor-Jankowski of New York University Medical School was going to host the work-shop but, as I told you, we felt that "neutral" ground would be better. Someone suggested England, but this was vetoed on the grounds that the animal activists would demonstrate and disrupt everything. Then I spoke with you, and you suggested Tufts.* Well — it would be super if we could arrange that. . . . I'm not sure how many people. You have — well Andrew Rowan has — the list of people we had last time. Some of those should come again. Nice to have Schellekens himself, from Holland. I think he will work on the participant list. We MUST involve the NIH stronghold types on this next round. Senator Hatch said that he could arrange that for me. SO we may take him up on the offer.

The workshop has developed as a third major workshop. The first you know of. The second was in Amsterdam, following the TNO symposium on the use of non-human primates in medical research, at which I gave a paper. That workshop followed logically from the Washington DC one — we made recommendations at that one. At the second — what steps should next be taken to implement them? TNO is building its new chimps AIDS lab according to those recommendations, more or less.†

So the third takes us one step further. These are the recommendations, in general. This is how we propose to start implementing them. And now — to save effort, heartache — and, of course, dollars! — let us bring together a group of experts each of whom brings with him some concrete information. The BEST features of his lab. We do not gather to pull individuals or their labs to pieces. We come thinking that EVERYONE will have at least one positive contribution. Something that has been used at one lab or other — and WORKS. That is the key. Something good, already tried and tested. Something that works. (Even the infamous IMMUNO in Vi-

---

* This third workshop was hosted by the Tufts University School of Veterinary Medicine on May 10 and 11, 1989; Jane is writing here to Franklin Loew, dean of that school; Andrew Rowan was assistant dean for new programs.
† Unfortunately, TNO changed directors and policies before its enlightened plans could be put into effect.

enna has one good thing. Though I very much doubt that SEMA could contribute anything.)

Anyway, I have written to Huub Schellekens and given him your address. I thought that if you and he could start some kind of correspondence, then we could see where we were when I'm over in mid-October. Surely we can get together somewhere at that time.

What about funding? I think HSUS would put in some more. JGI can contribute something. (If they won't, I'll take some from my children's book fund!) TNO might well pay airfares and expenses — I'm sure they will — they have masses of EEC AIDS money. And the same will go for representatives of other labs, I should think. So it boils down to whether Tufts can provide meeting facilities, where participants could stay, and expenses for some of the participants, perhaps. Most, I'm sure, could come, and stay, under their own steam.

Well, that is about all I can contribute at this stage. Off to Gombe tomorrow maybe — only wait listed. It's really hard to get onto the planes these days. You need to know someone at Air Tanzania, and our contact has gone. But before signing off I want to ask you something. Can you tell me why NIH consistently defends SEMA? Why nothing, or virtually nothing, has been done to put things right, or righter, there? It seems so odd. I am assuming that you are aware of the violations that have been denied by NIH, and so on? I am really curious to know.

Enough. Have a wonderful summer. I hope the hip goes from good to better, and that I'll see you long before the year is out.

Love to you all,
Jane

10 December 1988

Dear Mary Lynn,

This is to wish you all a very happy Christmas. It is written from hot, steamy Dar es Salaam — which is fine right at this moment as it is raining and thus cool. But we are into the hot season, and there are millions of mosquitos to add to the general unpleasantness. And the sea full of seaweed which, as it is soaked in sewage, stinks! And the dogs covered in ticks — that actually thrive in the flea powder I brought from England! (I think they might well breed in it! I popped one into a little box with the powder, and he was fine the next day!)

There, having now painted such a grim picture, it is actually not so bad! There is a breeze a lot of the time, the trees are in full bloom — glorious red and yellow. There is a wild calling of sea birds, especially at night. My dogs (three, plus 2 of the neighbours') were so thrilled to see me, and are so faithfully welcoming and dear. It is lovely to be able to get up in the morning, slip on a dress, and be done with clothes. Bare feet instead of uncomfortable shoes. The beach to walk on (even if one does have to pick one's way between the seasonal seaweed, at least there's no oil and no litter). And the people in Tanzania are wonderful.

This has been a crazy year for me. I have been to America SIX times, West Germany twice, Austria twice, and once each to Sweden, Switzerland, Holland and East Germany. I have, of course, made many quick stop-overs in England as I rushed from continent to continent! And I have made the journey from London to Dar four times — am in the middle of the fourth spell in Tanzania right now. (When I saw you, I think I had done 2 USAs, 1 Germany, Sweden, and Holland.)

East Germany was most depressing. Somehow everything was grey and drab, and the outside of most of the houses was crumbling, with slates missing from the roofs. But worst was the actual boundary — high electric fence, long stretch of close mown grass, long stretch of ploughed up land filled with landmines, another stretch of close mown grass. And turrets with guns. And when a car leaves, the police search everywhere — they press on the seats, peer under the car and in the engine and the trunk. Just in case someone is hiding there.

I did more lobbying in Washington after I saw you — I got one extra trip there because of my thumb. Couldn't go to Tanzania as the doctor thought it might get infected, so I went back to Washington instead! It all seemed to be quite successful. At least, our petition to reclassify wild chimpanzees as endangered has been successful — so far, anyway, in that Fish and Wildlife have published a supporting Ruling. And we got an amendment into the NIH appropriations bill to the effect that chimpanzees are unique, and should only be used in medical research when really necessary.

Best news — the big shots in the AIDS research world have finally come out with the fact that chimps are NOT useful for AIDS research. A few are likely to be needed to test batches of vaccine. But whereas even this May some researchers were saying we needed "100s even 1,000s", this is no longer believed to be true. Reprieve for the chimps! Except that 87+ are already infected with AIDS virus and are thus "dirty" for life (unless a CURE is found). Also, so many millions of dollars have been poured into the chimp labs, as part of the national AIDS program — how will those labs justify their expenditure? Now that they have the chimps (and there certainly has been some stockpiling) what will they come up with to justify further grants to cover maintenance? That is a worry. However, we just have to take one step at a time.

We are very slowly making a difference in the labs. Two of them now have active programs to enrich the environment of the chimps — give them problems to solve, stimulate them, provide them with company. And I've persuaded 4 virologists to co-author a paper stating that it is NOT necessary to keep chimps in single cages, as is current practice. And two others, since then, have read the paper and told me they agree. These are internationally known figures, who also know the chimp scene. A real breakthrough.

Things at Gombe are going well and, as usual, we are still discovering fascinating new things. In May, Winkle died. She left three offspring — Wilkie, all but mature, Wunda, 9 year old female, and infant Wolfi, just over 3 years. Well, predictably Wunda adopted little Wolfi. She carried him during travel, she helped him up and down trees, she shared food with him, and let him into her sleeping nest. She tried to rescue him from potentially dangerous social situations. But over and above all this, it seems that she has actually produced milk for him. And this is really amazing when you realize that the female in the wild doesn't usually have her first baby until she is 12 or 13 years old! Of course, we can't prove that she has milk — but

Wolfi suckles for a few minutes every couple of hours (not just when he is in need of reassurance) and cries bitterly if she tries to stop him. Incredible.*

Unfortunately I can't make it to Gombe during this visit. All flights cancelled until further notice. And it is necessary for me to go to England for Christmas. Mum is, after all, 86 and as you may remember, has had open heart surgery. She seems like a 60 year old — copes with everything, drives a car, etc, etc — but something could always go wrong. Christmas always means a lot to my family. And so off I go. Shan't get to Gombe until end January. Still, there are people not only observing, but getting material on video. That is a relief.

I must close. The rain has just stopped, the wind has changed, and instead of rotting seaweed, the lovely scent of frangipani is blowing through my western windows. I look forward to seeing you all again next spring. And in the meantime I hope you and yours have a wonderful Christmas and that 1989 will be productive, successful, happy and, above all, healthy.

Love to you all,

Jane

P.S. I AM sorry that the printer messed up. I hope you will forgive the sudden change in print & the two words. We are running out of INK — and so many letters. To print AND yet to write!

8 July 1989

Dear Marta and Austin,

It is too long since I was in contact with you. It is time for me to give you something of an update. I am assuming you had your copy of the last newsletter (with the story of my thumb!). And there will, of course, be another newsletter. But not for a few months, so this is just a stop-gap! I'll start with what I've been up to in USA.

I am approaching the task of getting better conditions for chim-

---

* It turned out not to be true. Wolfi sucked on an unproductive nipple.

panzees (and, through them, for other animals too) via four different avenues:

a) Try for new legislation.

I just spent some of the busiest 10 days of my life lobbying on the Hill. Most of the appointments were set up by a young woman who was a legislative assistant for 4 years in Senator Ford's office. She is now married, but comes to town just to work for me (we pay her expenses, and it is certainly worth it — she really knows her way around, and she knows EVERYONE!). I saw just about everyone on the Agriculture Committee.

So far as I can tell things went well. Made some new friends. And I also saw the Secretary of Agriculture, for an hour. All of this can only help. How much good it will do remains to be seen.

b) Go into labs and talk with the people working there.

Only if people IN the labs WANT change, or at least totally understand why change must come, will we get anything done. It is so easy for a lab to somehow get out of complying with legislation. There are never enough inspectors, and of those that do make visits, not all really care themselves. And I cannot talk about conditions and the need for change unless I see with my own eyes what it is like. These visits are truly waking nightmares for me. But I go on doing it because it is actually beginning to make a difference. In one of the biggest labs, LEMSIP, things are still improving, as reported in the newsletter. And, I'm happy to report, NEW facilities are being designed MUCH, MUCH better. It is really beginning to pay off, this intense effort.

c) Expose injustices as widely as possible via the media — TV, radio, and the press.

The relationship I have with the media, and the coverage they are giving to the various things JGI is involved with, is excellent. And lots more things brewing. Big things. So that the general public can't help becoming more informed!

d) Work with children.

I just finished 8 little children's books, on different African animals. Describing one family, named individuals. Short text, coloured photos. Same publisher as The Chimpanzee Family Book. To be sold VERY cheaply, and in gas stations and chain stores etc WORLD WIDE. Those are for children of about 5 and 6. The animals are chimpanzees; baboons; lions; zebras; giraffes; wildebeestes; elephants; and hyenas. I am very excited about this little series. Then there is another series, for older children, with McMillan. Six books, with much more information. I only do the introductions, except that I wrote the chimp book (you'll immediately notice the difference!). They got a children's writer to write the others, and had them checked with experts. You would have been shocked if you'd seen the way the "writer" wrote them. Just awful. I had the MS's in Bournemouth, and Mum was even more shocked than I was. They are on chimps, hippos, elephants, lions, Californian sea otters, and giant pandas.

The little paperback, My Life with the Chimpanzees — which I do hope we sent you and if not please do let JGI know because we have hundreds — has found its way into so many classrooms. Several teachers have written to thank me for it, saying it's the first time they have had anything about animal testing, intensive farming etc in printed form that was suitable for the classroom, and that the children all got very involved with the issues because they were so fascinated by my life. . . .

My own personal news has not been too happy during the week since I got back to Dar. The worst is that my dear old dog Cinderella got very sick. It seemed she waited until I got back, though she can't have really. It turned out to be hepatitis and pneumonia, and I had to have her put to sleep yesterday, after some incredibly traumatic experiences with lousy vets, wrong treatments, and everything. Pretty well undid me, actually. I'd had her for 10 years, and she came into my life just after I lost Derek.

Then, four days ago, three days after I got back, I had a break-in. My house is right on the sand — the sea almost comes into the back-yard. The thieves came in a boat, it seems. They bent and removed two of the iron bars that are supposed to make the windows burglar proof! and removed three louvres. They took a computer, two outboard boat engines (one brand new) and, far the worst, between 30 and 40 recorded 8mm video tapes from Gombe. About one and a half years' work. . . .

They got in at about 4.15 a.m. — between the time when I had gone outside to see how my sick dog was and then gone up to read in bed until about 4.00 a.m., and the time when Prashant, who lives in the guest house, got up to make coffee at 5.00 a.m. because he was off to Zanzibar. At that time the waves were very high, almost in the garden. There are always a lot of loud and peculiar noises then — I'm always thinking there are burglars and peering. And I did actually hear these horrible creatures. I did peer through the window, but saw nothing and assumed it was Seranda (my now sole remaining dog) clambering onto the pile of chair cushions and knocking off some shells, as she often does.

Spent half of a day with the police, there and here. They reckon they might get the tapes back. We've offered a big reward. And put the news into the newspapers, and may, perhaps, get it onto the radio.

The atmosphere in Tanzania vis a vis conservation is excellent right now. The lead that the country has taken in the elephant situation has made everyone proud. There is no doubt but that Costa Mlay, the new Director of Wildlife, is a really good, sound person. And a NICE person. One story he told me illustrates that he really cares about animals. The first time we met I was telling him I'd stopped eating meat because I hated intensive farming. He told me that his daughter had gone off to Kenya, and there had bought some cages for broiler fowl. He was shocked. Said he would not have his family involved in such cruelty. That he would throw her out if she used them. She complained how much money the cages had cost. So he bought them from her, and trashed them!! Impressive, don't you think.

Well, that's about it. . . . Am hoping to leave for Gombe in four days' time. And stay there more or less until my trip in mid-August. I will try and call to say hello. And my number, between about 22 and 26 August, will be 202 362 1993.

With all best wishes,
Jane

And thank you.

30 May 1990

Secretary James Baker
Office of the Secretary
Department of State
Washington DC 20520
Dear Secretary Baker,

When we met in March, one of the topics that we discussed was possible NIH involvement in chimpanzee biomedical research in Africa. Geza Teleki has now put together the information concerning this issue that you asked for and it is enclosed with this letter. It is indeed good to know that we have your support in this matter.

In early September I shall be able to visit Zaire and follow through on your suggestion that I meet with President Mobutu. We are in touch with the Ambassador, and Conoco is being very helpful in taking me into Zaire and picking me up after the meetings. I cannot tell you how grateful I am that you took the time to set this up for me. I hope and believe that my visit, following your talks with the President, will really be helpful to the beleaguered chimpanzees of Zaire.

Thank you again, so very, very much.

Yours sincerely,
Jane Goodall, Ph.D.

# 11

❧ ❧ ❧

# REASON FOR HOPE
## 1987–1999

Is there hope for the rain forests of Africa? For the chimpanzees?
For Africa's people? Is there hope for the planet, our beautiful
planet that we are spoiling? Is there hope for us and our children
and grandchildren?

— *Reason for Hope*

JANE GOODALL'S MISSION expanded with the formal creation,
on May 25, 1988, of her British base of operations: the Jane
Goodall Institute (UK). The first letter of this chapter, written a
year before that event to Sir Peter Scott (British conservationist and
founder of the Waterfowl Trust), details the history of the Jane
Goodall Institute in the United States and also some of Jane's plans
for the British sister organization. Britain has never used chimpanzees in laboratories, and so JGI (UK) was free to concentrate on European and African projects unrelated to that issue. Instead, the
institute would aim to "increase public awareness," to establish research sites that might help resist forest destruction, to increase the
value of intact forests in Africa through "forest tourism," and "to
concentrate on educating children, too."

Both that first letter to Sir Peter and the third, to singer Michael
Jackson, touch on a problem that has plagued Jane Goodall since
even before she set foot on the beach of Gombe Stream in July of
1960: how to pay for it all.

From 1960 to the present, Jane Goodall has been committed to
sustaining (with buildings, equipment, and an expanding staff) various ongoing research programs at Gombe, paid for during the first

years by a few somewhat traditional grants and, of course, a decade of generous support from the National Geographic Society. After the mid-1970s, however, Jane largely gave up seeking funds from the usual agencies and turned instead to the public — the American public, mostly, who attended her regular lecture tours in great numbers. The nonprofit Jane Goodall Institute in the United States helped to organize those tours and later developed its own set of projects for raising additional money.

After the transformative Chicago conference of December 1986, when Jane decided in a burst of hopeful inspiration to reach out to the chimpanzees of the world, in captivity and in the wild, the fund-raising burden expanded as well. It would be an understatement to describe her mission of hope as "ambitious." While she was managing the "lab chimp" campaign (focused on the problems and situations of chimpanzees in U.S. laboratories and coordinated through her institute in the United States and the Washington-based CCCC), Jane was also becoming involved in several chimpanzee projects outside the States.

In large part, these additional projects would be supported through her American lectures and fund-raising by her U.S.-based institute. Further income was generated by three major books for adults — *Through a Window: My Thirty Years with the Chimpanzees of Gombe* (1990), *Visions of Caliban: On Chimpanzees and People* (coauthored, 1993), and *Reason for Hope: A Spiritual Journey* (coauthored, 1999) — plus an autobiography for children, *My Life with the Chimpanzees* (1988), and a multibook *Animal Family* series for children. Then there were the periodic gala events, such as the fund-raising dinner for one thousand guests that was held on May 6, 1991, in the ballroom of the Beverly Hilton Hotel, organized by a committee that included Johnny Carson, Phil Donahue, Jane Fonda, Gary Larson, Jimmy Stewart, and Ted Turner. Actor Jack Lemmon was master of ceremonies, and singer Michael Jackson was named honorary gala chairman. Disappointingly, Jackson failed to show up for the dinner, but he did provide a videotaped message as well as his famous white fedora, which was auctioned off on behalf of the Gombe chimps.

Jane had met Michael Jackson a couple of years earlier, and they seemed to have in common a powerful idealism and a love of children and chimpanzees. Michael, in fact, owned a young chimpanzee named Bubbles. Jane had by then concluded that, for ethical and practical reasons, individual people should not own individual chimpanzees. But they decided to overlook this difference of opinion. From the two letters to Michael in this chapter (written on July 8, 1989, and possibly early January 1992), we can see that Jane hoped he would support her work. She had once suggested that he write a song for animals and the environment, and he accordingly wrote "Heal the World." Jackson also offered to donate some of the royalties from the song, but in the end the donation never materialized — unfortunate, considering that his 1991 album including "Heal the World" sold 17 million copies.

In any event, with the creation of JGI (UK), Jane had a small organization and some resources in England with which to attempt to improve various European and African chimpanzee matters. Possibly the single most ambitious project from those years (addressed in some detail in the letter of May or June 1989 to Basile Sindaharaye, Minister of Tourism and the Environment) was the attempt to save Burundi's approximately three hundred wild chimpanzees from extinction. Jane proposed (a) support for an already existing conservation program (the Biological Diversity Project) to protect Kibira National Park, in the northern part of the country, (b) a research project to anchor a larger conservation effort for the wild chimpanzees scattered and hiding within rapidly disappearing forest remnants (the Rumonge Forest Reserve) to the south, and (c) a further plan to promote tourism in Burundi. Several local people had already been hired as monitors and trackers ("Chimpanzee Guards") to keep tabs on the elusive Rumonge chimps, and Jane planned to send a "most suitable young woman" named Charlotte Uhlenbroek to "initiate a preliminary pilot study of three months."

Charlotte Uhlenbroek arrived in Burundi not long after that letter was written and rented a small house in a small village on top of a big hill in Rumonge. She proceeded, with the assistance of a half-dozen Chimpanzee Guards, to look for chimpanzees, hoping to begin a habituation process that would make actual research possible. But whenever she happened to go on business into Bujumbura, Burundi's capital, Charlotte became aware of the presence of several "pet" baby chimps there, often kept in appalling conditions. Perhaps the worst case was that of Whiskey, a young male. Having outgrown manageable infancy, he was chained by the neck to a post in the old concrete lavatory cell of an auto mechanic's shop. There were several other heartbreaking cases, and since it was illegal to keep chimpanzees as pets, the authorities in Bujumbura agreed that confiscation was appropriate. Ten young chimpanzees were confiscated in a gradual and sensitive fashion, and Jane's institute financed the construction of functional temporary quarters, a "Halfway House" for the refugee animals. A detailed plan and budget were drawn up for a permanent sanctuary that, it was hoped, might someday become a centerpiece for tourism into Burundi. By the end of 1991, two JGI representatives stationed in Burundi were caring for up to thirteen orphan chimpanzees confiscated by the government, and the Halfway House had been officially opened.

Tourism probably could have made a difference, but the human problems were deep and ominous. Environmentally, Burundi seemed to be in an advanced stage of disintegration, both for the people and for the disappearing chimpanzees. The southern regions of the country, for instance, were stripped almost bare through a very rapid and ongoing process of forest clearance for agriculture. True, agriculture did sustain the crowded nation of 5 million people who survived on an average monthly income of roughly $14, but for how long would the same land support human numbers that were doubling every generation?* In addition, the peace of Burundi was threatened by a centuries-old division between the peasant Hutus and the pastoral Tutsis. Those divisions turned into antagonisms which, exacerbated in the twentieth century by an increasingly uneven distribution of wealth and political power, in 1972 exploded into the first of a series of bloody ethnic clashes. President

---

* Source: *1998 World Population Data Sheet* (Population Reference Bureau). As of 1998, Burundi's human population was doubling every 28 years; the average weekly income is based on per capita Gross National Product.

Pierre Buyoya, with whom Jane negotiated when she began working in Burundi, was intent on reducing ethnic tensions and modernizing the economy; but by the mid-1990s, Burundi and its northern neighbor, Rwanda, had begun unraveling in a horrifying series of pogroms and genocidal wars. As mentioned in the letter of July 12, 1994, the Burundi sanctuary was finally abandoned and the chimpanzees were airlifted to a Kenyan sanctuary, Sweetwaters, that was being developed in a JGI partnership with Lonrho Corporation of Kenya.

From her earliest moments at Gombe, Jane's vision of *Pan troglodytes* had always placed the particular ahead of the general. Intuitively, Jane saw the species as a gathering of precious individuals, and for the most part it has been the particular pathos of specific individuals that has moved her most decisively to act. Jane's mission and that of her institute quite naturally turned to rescuing identifiable individuals. One gets the impression that she tremendously enjoyed the adventure and drama of individual rescue operations, such as the transport of Milla (June 13, 1990, letter) from a cage in a Tanzanian hotel to a Zambian chimpanzee sanctuary run by a British couple, David and Sheila Siddle, and their "remarkable" Zambian associate, Patrick Chimbatu.

There were many such operations. Among the first in which JGI (UK) became involved, after its official birth in 1988, was the rescue of the Spanish beach chimps. Simon and Peggy Templar, an English couple living in Spain, had written to Jane several years earlier describing the exploitation of infant and young chimpanzees as photographers' props in the coastal resort areas of Spain and the Canary Islands. The baby chimps were typically smuggled out of Africa, dressed in children's clothes (with shoes forcing their feet into a human shape), then made docile with injections of hard drugs and coercive methods that included beatings and cigarette burns. When an unsuspecting tourist appeared, the little drug-addicted creatures would be thrust into that person's arms, creating a "cute" photographic tableau for which money might change hands. There may have been more than a hundred of those unfortunate animals at any one time, climbing into tourists' arms, posing, receiving their regular narcotic fixes; and when they grew out of the cute stage, at perhaps five or six years, they were sold or killed.

When the Templars first wrote to Jane, they had taken in one of those pathetic chimpanzees, whom they named Jenny. Although she had by then recovered from the worst physical and psychological symptoms of addiction and abuse, Jenny had also grown and become impossible to keep as a pet. At the time, a young woman named Stella Brewer was developing a sanctuary for orphaned chimps in the Gambia, West Africa, so Jane put the Templars in touch with her — and indeed, Jenny went to the Gambia and joined the chimpanzees there. The Templars, meanwhile, complained to the Spanish authorities about the ongoing abuse of infant chimps on the beaches. The authorities treated these complaints as a joke, while the photographers (or the criminal organizations associated with them) responded with death threats. Nevertheless, the Templars courageously continued to protest, took in more orphans, and ultimately transformed their own house into an ape refugee center. By 1986 they had nine chimps — growing, getting ever stronger and smarter and harder to contain.

Even before the formation of JGI (UK), Jane and some of her friends and associates were working on a solution for the Templars' nine apes. Jim Cronin, an American who had worked with captive animals for several years, envisioned a sanctuary in England that would rescue abused or surplus primates (from labs and zoos) and provide them with the best possible living environments, paying for itself by functioning as a well-managed public zoo. And so Monkey World in Dorset was conceived. It was partly financed and built by Steve Matthews, an expert in the construction of zoo enclosures. With the volunteered assistance of British veterinarian Ken Pack and some minor support from JGI (UK), Monkey World at last opened to the public, containing among its founding group of inhabitants the Templars' nine chimps. The newly established JGI (UK), meanwhile, assisted Cronin with his investigation into the larger problem — open abuse, smuggling, possibly an illegal traffic with the "retired" chimps. Jane also helped publicize the situation through press conferences and news releases and the production of a *Nature Watch* film ("Chimp Rescue") for European television.

Finally, in March 1990, Jane and Geza Teleki presented a report to the European Parliament and asked the European Economic Community for "help in chimp traffic matters throughout Europe."

Jane first met with U.S. Secretary of State James Baker at a private lunch given on March 11, 1990. Baker turned out to be a sympathetic listener as Jane enumerated several of her projects and plans. He seemed sincerely interested in helping, and since she had expressed particular concern about the chimpanzee situation in Zaïre, Baker agreed to mention the issue during his planned meeting with President Mobutu that summer.

Zaïre was and is (though now the Democratic Republic of Congo) a huge and possibly ungovernable country with a murderous colonial past and a monstrous postcolonial present. It stands at the very center of the human map in Africa; and because it contains the bulk of the second largest rain-forest formation in the world, Zaïre also stands at the center of the map of African ape distribution. The perhaps several thousand individual bonobos (once known as pygmy chimps) which constitute that species are found only there; and although the survey information remains sketchy, Zaïre quite possibly hosts most of the world's remaining wild chimpanzees. These apes were (and are) regularly eaten for food in that part of Africa, and Jane was beginning to observe from her usual haunts in East Africa the consequences of Central African bush-meat hunting: ape orphans being transported over the eastern Zaïrean borders into Uganda and Burundi to the north and Zambia to the south. Perhaps Mobutu would be interested in talking about the future of chimpanzees and conservation in his country.

Jane was also hoping to meet with Denis Sassou-Nguesso, president of Congo-Brazzaville, during an August 1990 trip to Central Africa.* The Jane Goodall Institute (UK) had become involved in Congo-Brazzaville two years earlier, after a British journalist publicized the horrific conditions in a "zoo" located in the coastal city of

---

* The actual name of this country is the People's Republic of Congo; but to distinguish it more readily from its giant southern neighbor (Democratic Republic of Congo), some people prefer to call it Congo-Brazzaville.

Pointe Noire. This place was more like a jail for animals. It was a rambling collection of very small concrete, steel-barred cages; the eight chimps inside them were in danger of starving to death. JGI (UK) quickly sent out a representative, Karen Pack (daughter of the veterinarian Ken Pack), who managed to turn the situation around. In the process, she discovered that Congo-Brazzaville was awash with chimpanzee orphans, helpless little creatures whose numbers were continuously replenished by the uncontrolled commercial hunting of all wild animals to supply the big-city meat markets.

Conoco, the Texas-based oil company, was exploring for petroleum in Congo at that time, and several top executives (including Roger Simpson, president of the Conoco subsidiary in Congo, and Max Pitcher, vice president for exploration) seemed interested in creating an alliance with JGI. They demonstrated convincingly that Conoco was operating in Congo under stringent, self-imposed environmental constraints, and they agreed to underwrite the creation of a Jane Goodall chimpanzee sanctuary on some of their concession land in the Pointe Noire area. Jane elaborated some of her ideas for that project in the letter of November 16, 1991, to Max Pitcher of Conoco. Congo-Brazzaville's President Sassou-Nguesso had by then guaranteed the government support necessary to begin construction. Among the first chimps to enter the completed Jane Goodall Institute Tchimpounga Sanctuary were the former victims of the Pointe Noire jail for animals (although one female, La Vielle, was by then so frightened of the world that she chose to remain inside her open cage). By July 24, 1995, after a follow-up visit, Jane was able to report back to her friends Paul Kase and Maureen Marshall that Tchimpounga was "the most utterly amazing place."

Congo's only other zoo, located in the capital city of Brazzaville, was distinctly better than the Pointe Noire animal jail, but still grim. Jane was particularly moved by the sight of poor old Grégoire, a depressed, emaciated, half-blind, almost hairless old ape who had lived inside the same barren environment, according to the sign outside, since 1944. Jane located some people in Brazzaville (British ambassador Peter Chandler and his wife, Jane, and Sylvie Menou) who were willing to bring food regularly to the Brazzaville chimps;

and the JGI (UK) imported a representative who found the perfect full-time keeper, Jean Maboto.

Meanwhile, the hoped-for meeting with President Mobutu in Zaïre never happened, as he was out of town, dealing with "village unrest" (which would turn out to be the beginning of the end for him in Zaïre). Still, in early September 1990, Jane crossed the river from Brazzaville and for the first time entered Kinshasa, the capital of Zaïre. She was accompanied by National Geographic photographer Nick Nichols and American ambassador William C. Harrop and his wife, Janet, and they were able to confer with several government officials. Jane and Nick Nichols also investigated some of the chimpanzee problems in Kinshasa and found the city full of orphans. Some had been taken by a biomedical research laboratory, where they became experimental subjects but were also fed well and given adequate medical care. Others had been dumped into the substandard Kinshasa City Zoo and also Mobutu's personal zoo at N'Sele. A woman named Graziella Cotman had charitably been feeding the eighteen N'Sele chimps, who were otherwise chronically underfed. Jane met Graziella during that first trip into Kinshasa, although they had begun corresponding a year earlier (letter of September 25, 1989).

Jane also gave a brief lecture to some interested people from the American community in Kinshasa. On the way to that lecture, her car passed one of the city's big open-air markets, and her eyes locked onto the pleading gaze of a tiny infant chimp for sale: tied by a short rope onto a cage of chicken wire, sweating in the heat, soon to die unless some sympathetic human with extra money happened to pass by. It was officially illegal to sell endangered species in that manner in Zaïre, but the law was mostly decorative. Still, it would have been inappropriate to pay for a baby chimpanzee in those circumstances, so the authorities were pressed to make an official confiscation. The following evening, flanked by a government minister on one side and a gendarme on the other, Jane cut the cord that bound Petite Janine* and handed her over to Graziella Cotman.

---

* Petite Janine became Little Jay after it became apparent that *she* was a *he*.

Within the year, newly invigorated government authorities had confiscated an additional seven chimpanzee orphans in Kinshasa, and they too were given into Graziella's care. Unfortunately, when Jane returned to Kinshasa in September 1991, the Zaïrean army began rioting and looting in the city. The situation was dangerous enough that all nonofficial foreign residents, including Jane and Graziella, were evacuated. Graziella, in fact, was forced to leave almost everything: her apartment, her job, all her possessions. But with the help of Ruth and Cedric Dumont, she brought out the eight orphans, who were soon placed in the Brazzaville Zoo; Graziella was then hired by JGI to take charge.

Mobutu was overthrown by Laurent Kabila (responsible for the 1975 kidnapping of four Gombe students), while a renamed Zaïre (the Democratic Republic of Congo) soon fell into a many-sided and seemingly interminable civil war. The chaos spread across the river into Congo-Brazzaville. The brewing trouble there is briefly referred to in the letter of July 12, 1994, where Jane describes being removed from a car at gunpoint on her way to see President Sassou-Nguesso. Congo-Brazzaville itself broke down into civil war, and thus all the chimpanzees in the Brazzaville zoo had to be rescued and airlifted to join many others in the Tchimpounga sanctuary near Pointe Noire, farther away from the centers of conflict. Graziella Cotman followed the chimps, and became the brave JGI manager of Tchimpounga, which today is caring for three times more residents than it was designed for.

Chimpanzee by chimpanzee, Jane Goodall and her institute became increasingly involved in an ongoing series of rescue operations in Africa, always with the defense that "each individual matters." But at what cost? Today, all three of humanity's closest living relatives, the three African great apes, are being decimated throughout their range by a multibillion-dollar European and Asian logging industry that has opened up roads into the deepest parts of the Central and West African forests, and thus works in concert with a highly efficient commercial meat industry. The loggers' roads allow hunters in and carcasses out, including the dismembered remains of chimpanzees, gorillas, and bonobos. Some have criticized Jane

Goodall's approach to the massive problems that threaten the very existence of wild chimpanzees in Africa. Is she in danger of saving a few individuals with humanitarian efforts while losing a conservation battle to save the species?

Still, one must start somewhere. One can never save a species in the abstract. Moreover, the various ape sanctuaries in Africa are not merely rescuing unfortunate orphans of the meat trade. By creating sites where chimpanzees and people can meet safely, the sanctuaries become educational centers. They provide employment for local people, creating an economic-based net of support for the apes. And finally, they can become focal points from which to begin larger land-preservation projects. Jane's defense of her involvement in African sanctuaries is, I think, well articulated in the letter penned in June 1998 to a friendly critic.

Along with financing the construction of the Congo sanctuary, Conoco also sponsored an educational exhibit about chimps that Jane had put together during the early 1990s, her "traveling chimp exhibit," described in the letter of July 11, 1991. The exhibit was carted around to several African cities starting with Jane's home — Dar es Salaam, Tanzania.

There the exhibit was formally opened by Julius Nyerere, Father of the Nation, at the start of Gombe 30 Wildlife Week. Jane had first arrived at Gombe on July 14, 1960; and the celebratory "week" from February 11 to February 15, 1991, in Dar was organized both to mark thirty years of continuous research at Gombe and to thank the nation of Tanzania for supporting it. The week's big events included formal parties, dinners, receptions, and other public functions supported and led by the governing elite of Tanzania; wildlife films shown at cut prices in the local theaters; a daylong seminar for the national park wardens; five radio programs in Kiswahili on chimpanzee behavior; and so on.

In addition, Jane visited all the secondary schools in Dar es Salaam and, with spirited assistance from Tony Collins (director of the Gombe baboon research), gave several exciting talks about her experiences with the chimpanzees of Gombe.

Jane had for some time been intending to work with children and young people, and so many young Tanzanians responded so positively to her talks in the schools that she founded during the week a "very very exciting children's programme" (July 11, 1991). She called the new organization Roots & Shoots, based on the image (as she described it in the January 1992 note to Michael Jackson) that children and young people can work rather like roots and shoots in approaching the seemingly unbreakable boulders and concrete barriers of the world's many problems: "roots creep quietly, everywhere, underground, making a firm foundation; shoots seem so new and fragile, but to reach the light they can move boulders, break concrete."

Roots & Shoots developed into a series of activist clubs with a strong emphasis on hands-on projects to help animals, people, and the environment. With seven hundred members in Dar es Salaam by the start of 1992, Roots & Shoots soon grew to include clubs "in Burundi, Congo, Angola. And UK, Germany, Belgium & Japan, as well as USA" (December 26, 1992), and from there to projects in Taiwan (October 2, 1997) and mainland China (November 18, 1998), as well as Dubai and "Russia — & even Albania" (June 26, 1999).

The Jane Goodall Roots & Shoots movement is currently supported by several thousand members in some twenty-five hundred clubs in sixty-five countries around the world. Growing and expanding and spreading — like roots, like shoots — it brings to mind a nature club known as the Alligator Society that Jane founded when she was a young girl. I believe it to be her deepest reason for hope, the project closest to her own wonderfully childlike, deeply mature vision of things. She is "Dr. Jane" to the children and young people of Roots & Shoots, and, rather like the wise old fantasy mentor of her childhood, Dr. Doolittle, she sees a world in which the dark glass of human isolation and limitation is broken through and shivered away, revealing at last a fuller reality, where strength is tempered by compassion and where a glorious light of knowing illuminates the awareness and spirit and worth of all living creatures, human and nonhuman. I have chosen to end this chapter

— and this book — with Dr. Jane's June 26, 1999, letter to members of a Roots & Shoots chapter at Prince Edward County Middle School in Farmville, Virginia.

\*      \*      \*      \*

17 July 1987

Dear Sir Peter,

When I was about 17 I wrote to you, begging you for a job of some sort. I was unlucky — at least, so I thought at the time. Thinking back on things, though, I believe you did me a great service. Had I come to you I should probably never have "found" the chimps!

Anyway, almost 40 years later I am writing with a different request.

In the late '70s some wealthy American friends, who wanted to help with the constant struggle to raise funds to keep the chimpanzee research going, set up a tax-exempt organization — the Jane Goodall Institute for Wildlife Research, Education and Conservation. Recently, with the help of a number of people, principally Gordon Getty, and since moving to our new headquarters in Tucson, Arizona, the institute has begun to spread its wings. We are not only raising money for Gombe, but also for ChimpanZoo — a project designed to increase our understanding of the flexibility of chimp behaviour; increase people's respect for chimps, not only as members of a fascinating species, but as unique individuals; and to improve their captive environments. 14 zoos in the U.S. are taking part. And in December we are organizing an international conference (funded by the NIH) as a result of which we hope to introduce new legislation to better protect chimps in the biomedical labs.

For a long time I have wanted to start a sister organization in England. And finally this is happening. Two good friends in London are working on the practical details and setting up a charitable trust: Karsten Schmidt of Baker & McKenzie and Guy Parsons of Peat, Marwick and Mitchell. Both will serve as Trustees.

And so I finally come to the point of my letter! We should be so honoured — and truly thrilled — if you would agree to join our board. We fully realize all the demands made on your time and energy and I promise that we shall never burden you with arduous duties. We are really asking for your blessing — for a token of your approval and good will.

The main purpose of the JGI in England, as I see it now, is to increase public awareness, as in the U.S., but to emphasize the truly desperate plight of chimpanzees throughout their range in west and central Africa. You know, only too well, the speed with which the great forests are disappearing. In addition to losing their habitat, chimps, in some areas, are hunted for food. And mothers are shot so that their babies can be sold — mostly for biomedical research. If we don't act soon, with a concrete plan, the chimps — in the wild — will be gone.

Already there is a plan. It sprang from a major conference on "Understanding Chimpanzees" held at the Chicago Academy of Sciences last November. To undertake survey and census work. To try to establish research in places where pressures on the land are not yet too great. To develop what I call "Forest tourism". The way I see it, we must habituate some of the shy and/or hard to see forest animals so that visitors, who will be on foot (or sometimes in little boats) will actually see things: monkeys, hornbills, forest antelopes — chimpanzees.

The forests represent great wealth to the African governments. If we want to save parts of them we must pay. We must compete with the timber merchants. Tourism brings in foreign exchange. Handled correctly, it brings international recognition and respect.

If the JGI in England is able to raise the funds, I would like to send people out to these forests. And those who go to help establish tourism don't even need degrees. They need experience with animals, love of nature, patience, patience, patience. (And physical stamina, along with a large portion of self-reliance.)

And I want to concentrate on educating children, too.

I am sending this letter via my mother, whom I believe you have met, so that she can enclose some materials that will give you some more information about JGI in the States. In England, of course, we shall adjust the newsletters, gear them for the British public. She will also send you some information regarding my fight for the lab chimps.

Let me close by saying that your paintings, your love of waterfowl, made a deep impression on me during my late childhood. I was truly inspired. I have continued to admire you, increasingly, for the tremendous impact you have had on people all over the world, awakening them to the great beauty and wonder of nature. It is because of my own personal appreciation and gratitude for what you have done, what you are doing, and what you ARE, that I hope so much that you will lend your name to our new venture.

With my very warm regards,
Yours sincerely,
Jane Goodall

[Probably May or June 1989]

Son Excellence Basile Sindaharaye
Ministre de l'Amenagement du Tourisme et de l'Environment
Bujumbura
Your Excellency,

In March 1989 I visited Burundi with the purpose of discussing ways and means of conserving your remaining chimpanzees. During my stay I drove to the Kibira National Park in the north and the Rumonge Forest Reserve in the south. I spoke with a number of people who were able to explain the situation and the need to develop research programmes that would, at the same time, save the relatively few chimpanzees from extinction.

As you know, I was also able to visit with President Buyoya and discuss these projects with him at length. I was very favourably impressed by the commitment of the President, and of all government officials with whom I spoke, to conservation issues.

With a view to initiating long term studies on the chimpanzees of Burundi it was agreed (a) that Chimpanzee Guards receive additional training at the Gombe Stream Research Centre in Tanzania (pending an official invitation from the Tanzanian Government) and (b) that I should try to locate suitable scientists from overseas to work with Burundi scientists to initiate the work.

Thus it gives me pleasure to say that I have contacted a most suitable young woman, Charlotte Uhlenbroek. She has lived in African countries and has spent time with me at the Gombe Stream Research Centre. I have utmost confidence in her ability to initiate, in cooperation with staff of the Biological Diversity Project and of the Kibira National Park, a sound research and conservation programme. Because I believe that it is vital to get such a project off the ground as soon as possible, I am proposing that my colleague, Charlotte Uhlenbroek, should initiate a preliminary pilot study of three months. During this time she will be able to ascertain the most suitable area for a further long term research effort. At the same time she will be collecting valuable data regarding the feeding and ranging patterns of at least one of the chimpanzee groups, providing additional training for the Chimpanzee Guards and establishing a working relationship with the inhabitants of the surrounding villages.

I believe that we have a source of funding for this initial three month project. I hope that, if money becomes available for a major research effort in Burundi, my colleague will be able to stay on and become a part of that initiative. . . .

I am very excited about this relationship with Burundi, and hope very much to meet you when next I visit. There is no doubt that if this plan is successful, tourism in Burundi will benefit. I have, as I promised during my last visit, been doing my best to promote Burundian interests while on my travels in USA and Europe.

I very much hope that we are at the beginning of a long and fruitful collaboration. And that we shall meet sometime during this year.

With my very best good wishes,

Yours most sincerely,
Jane Goodall, Ph.D.

8 July 1989

Dear Michael,

I really wanted to talk to you when I was in the States — but you have a different phone number. It was just that I wanted to say some words of sympathy because you had just looked at all that terrible, horrendous cruelty to animals on video. Anyway, I thought of you, and I admire you for having gone through with it.

Are we going to make a book of your song?

I have just finished 8 books for small children, on different animal families. They are going to be produced amazingly cheaply — they have superb colour photos, and plenty of them. And marketed through things like chain stores and gas stations for about a dollar. That is a project I'm very excited about, as I think it will carry the right message, "animals matter too", to thousands of children. If you and I did one together, it would reach millions, because of you, and convey a different sort of message than you alone, because of me. It could make a difference.

Think about it, Michael. (Think about me too — I just had to have my faithful and wonderful old dog put to sleep. She came into my life 10 years ago, just after Derek died. And there is no decent vet here — the one I got actually made her worse. I know that. And I also had a break in and lost various things like boat engines and a computer, which can be replaced, and 40 8mm video cassettes of chimp behavior, a year's research from Gombe, that cannot be replaced.)

25 September 1989

G. Cotman
c/o IGIP
Cooperation Allemande/Regideso
B.P. 691
Kinshasa 1, Zaire
Dear Chimpanzee Sympathizer,

I address you in this somewhat unusual manner because I cannot tell from your letter whether it should be Monsieur or Madame! Sorry!

I am also sorry I did not write before. Since I got your letter, which eventually arrived in Gombe and was collected by me in July, I have been to USA, England, Spain, Germany and Burundi! I now have ten whole days for catching up on correspondence, and trying to finish the sequel to In the Shadow of Man (which was translated as Les Chimpanzees et Moi in the French edition). I now only have 3 chapters [to go] — but I left the hardest ones to the end.

Your query regarding the chimpanzees in Kinshasa comes at a very good moment. There are chimpanzees in the same kind of situation in almost all African countries where chimpanzees still exist. Kinshasa is particularly bad. So much so, that I have a plan to visit, as soon as possible, to try to talk to various officials. I enclose a bit of information on the overall plan.

Your information is very useful. I hope to meet you, if there is an opportunity, when I finally come to Zaire. I shall keep you informed. In the meantime, it would be best if you wrote to me at The Jane Goodall Institute (UK), Mrs. Dilys Vass, 15 Clarendon Park, Lymington, Hants 8041 8AX. Mrs. Vass is our secretary and speaks fluent French. Thus she could translate your letter for me. (It took me a while to find someone to translate the last one. I regret I don't speak French.)

The more information you can find out about the number and whereabouts of chimpanzees in Kinshasa, the better. Thank you for writing, and good luck.

Yours sincerely,
Jane Goodall

P.O. Box 727
Tanzania
8 January 1990

Dear Neva,

Happy New Year! I do hope you and the family had a good Christmas. Mum and I were fine, but Mum's sisters, Olly and Audrey, were only just getting over that awful flu. And I only got back at 1.00 a.m. on Christmas Eve. After the most exhausting time at Gombe — first with the Geographic film team (more when I see you!) and then the treatment of the baboons. I have seldom felt so tired! Mum was utterly worn out after looking after Olly and Audrey, so we were very quiet and relaxed. And all recovered.

Anyway — finished the sequel to "Shadow" before New Year's!! Three years in the working (though as I only ever got two weeks or so at a time it was <u>actually</u> much less). It is called "Through a Window: A Quarter of a Century Watching the Gombe Chimpanzees." And you know something, Neva? — it's really only NOW — sitting on PA 009 to Miami and writing to you — that it has dawned on me — it is FINISHED!! Actually, I have been frantically doing the ACKNOWLEDGEMENTS and TWO appendices. And I only finished the last of <u>those</u> yesterday. And I have been selecting photos — and I am still doing that now! <u>BUT ALL</u> writing is DONE!! I wish you were here. I wish we were having lunch together in the Jefferson.* Perhaps we can do that again — in the spring. You arrange it, but let me treat you this time. I'd <u>like</u> to. By then we should be able to celebrate galleys — even PAGE proofs!!

Anyway, I have just been brought a nice glass of French white wine. So — CHEERS!

I'm enclosing a bunch of B & W negatives which I hope can have prints (usual 5 × 7) made from them. And just a few old colour slides that need B & W negs and prints made from them. I need, if <u>possible,</u> to be able to take them back with me on 21st January.

I hope (nothing to do with photos!!) that you will be able to come to the party organized by Geza. Which has to be 19th or 20th, which is, I think, a weekend. It is for people who <u>really</u> and <u>truly</u> help us. I <u>hope</u> Mum will be there. I hope I will be too!

Well — wine after a night spent <u>utterly</u> sleepless. At 2.30 a.m. I was drinking cocoa and eating chocolate biscuits and writing letters — business, of course — in the kitchen. And we left at 5.15 for the airport.

See you soon, Neva.

Love,
Jane

---

* A hotel in Washington near the National Geographic offices where Neva worked.

13 June 1990

Dear Secretary Baker,

I just thought you might like to hear, briefly, about my latest chimpanzee exploit. I have been travelling in the States and Europe for so long — mostly criss-crossing the United States on my spring lecture tour. And then doing things in UK, Spain, and France. Got back to Tanzania 10 days ago and set off on a crazy mission to take a chimpanzee who was born in the Cameroons from Tanzania (where she has been living, alone, since her mother was shot and she was rescued from a meat market) to a chimpanzee sanctuary in Zambia. There are no chimps in Zambia, but an amazing British couple, Sheila and Dave Siddle, who farm there, have been, for the past 7 years or so, looking after young chimps from Zaire, confiscated when poachers smuggled them over the border. More recently, people have been taking them chimps from all parts of the world.

You'll be interested to hear that, within the last two months, they acquired, first of all, two "Israeli chimps" (hand raised in Israel by two Israeli girls because their mothers would not care for them) and, only a week later, two "Arab chimps" — two chimps smuggled from Zaire into Uganda, smuggled from Uganda to Saudi Arabia, confiscated by the authorities (good show, that), and sent back to Uganda. There is nowhere there for chimps (yet) so they went off to the Siddles!

Anyway, my girl is 15 years old. She was left with this delightful couple in Arusha who did their best for her. But the usual story — when she was around 8 she had to be shut up in a cage. Where she has lived ever since. Does it sound odd to you if I say that she is probably the most charming adult female in captivity? Everyone fell in love with her when they got to know her. A British veterinarian flew out to tranquilize her for the journey, and she was picked up in a small single engine Piper Cherokee that came in from Zambia. I'm still not sure how we managed to survive the journey — we must have been overloaded. Indeed, the pilot was heard to murmur: "Well, I have flown once with the tail lower". Because Milla lived by the bar, and would imperiously summon her friends, as they passed, to bring her a beer or a coke. (If they chose wrong she would simply pour the drink onto the ground and demand a different one!) She had more than 8 per day! And so she weighs some 160 pounds (instead of about 75), and her crate weighed 190 pounds! And there were two pilots, as well as the vet and me.

However, we got there. A last bumpy truck drive and, late that night, after six and a half hours of flying, and two hours in trucks, and another hour or more waiting at airports. And, in the light of a hurricane lamp, Milla entered her new cage. She has to be introduced to the other chimps gradually because she doesn't know chimp language at all. Well, to cut a long story short, she got out of her cage the second day, and I had perhaps the most incredible time of my life (apart from Gombe) wandering around the Siddles' farm and outbuildings with a full grown female chimpanzee. Normally they are totally untrustworthy. Milla is unbelievable. She led us into the bush. Gazed with interest at the other chimps. Was interested, in fact, in everything. There is a remarkable Zambian there, Patrick, who for years has taken infant chimps into the bush. He fell in love with Milla too. And he said to me: "She is behaving as I would behave if I had been in prison for 8 years. Touching, looking, examining all the things that, for so long, have been out of reach". What a personality Milla has. She has made a deep impression on all of us.

I'm off to Gombe in a couple of days. Then back to Dar to receive this wonderful Dr. Martin Lazar with his first MediSend package (some $40,000 worth of medical equipment, that would be trashed in the States), to be handed over to the President for our teaching hospital here in Dar. And then Japan, then Britain, France, Germany, and Spain. Then over to New York, and so on to Congo and Zaire, to meet Mobutu — if he is still there! I shall, of course, let you know how I get on with that meeting. It can't make it worse for the chimps. I really believe that more are smuggled out of Zaire than out of any other African country.

Will close. Thank you, again, for your interest and, more, your support.

P.O. Box 727
Dar es Salaam
28 June 1990

Dear Simon & Peggy,

I have been hearing bits and pieces about you through the grapevine. I should so much have liked to come and visit you both, back at Can Miloca, after the hospital visit. But my life has been too utterly hectic. However, I have come to roost, in Dar, for two whole weeks. So at least I can write.

I just heard that little Chico — or is it Chica?, I am now confused — was just off to Monkey World, but that then something went wrong. I dare say I'll get the latest when I'm back in UK at the end of July. I wonder if you've seen the Nature Watch film yet? I missed it, but will see a copy when I'm home again. It got very good reviews — and people in the scientific world were impressed, which is good. In other words, it made a rational plea for help and understanding, not just an emotional one (although there were some very emotional bits in it).

Since I last saw you I seem to have been on a hectic race around the world! I hope that at least some of it will prove to have been worthwhile. Soon after I saw you I got to Tanzania for a visit to Gombe — not to be with my beloved chimps, but to help with a major effort to clear up a horrific, syphilis-like disease which has afflicted the Gombe baboons — and which, theoretically, could affect chimpanzees and humans. It required the darting and treating of some 150 baboons in three troops! Some undertaking! Fortunately we had Ken so it all went off well.

Then the real travelling began. From Gombe directly up the lake to Burundi, to check on the situation there (some 10 orphan chimps waiting for us to build them a sanctuary; a JGI student working on habituating one of three remnant chimpanzee populations as part of an overall plan to conserve the last of the country's rain forest). From Burundi, via Nairobi, to the Congo. My first visit there, all made very easy by the Conoco representative out there. We have many chimpanzees there who are also awaiting a sanctuary (and permission to build, from the government). But most exciting is the plan to create a huge national park in the south west of the country, in the most glorious forest, where there are not only chimpanzees and gorillas, but also all manner of other primates (as yet there has been no survey, so we don't even know what's there) and, of course, elephants and all the other forest creatures. Conoco is financing an eight month survey, starting in August, with a team of about 10 zoologists and botanists.

Then, after [a] press conference in Madrid, I rushed off to USA for a private lunch with the Secretary of State, James Baker himself! Just four of us. And he was very interested in what was going on in Africa, and said he wanted to help. And he has — at least, he's talked to President Mobutu of Zaire about the horrendous hunting and smuggling of chimps there, and arranged for me to meet the President in August. Which probably will do no good, but it certainly won't do any harm, either. Directly after that I went to Strasbourg to make a report to the European Parliament, and ask EEC help in chimp traffic matters throughout Europe. This was all well received. Whether it leads to any new actions remains to be seen! Then Munich, for a major lecture. Then Madrid again, for additional TV coverage. UK to finish the last shots on our Nature Watch film.

Then came a seven week endurance test. My annual USA spring lecture tour, made truly grim by the fact that I got bronchitis — of course during the very most hectic part of the seven weeks! But Fate dealt me good as well as bad experiences: one morning I awoke with no voice at all. Zero. I was due to give a lunch talk to the first gathering of the people in Dallas working to develop this great programme, MediSend (I'll ask that you be sent a brochure, as it is such a wonderful concept). Bob,* who was with me at that time, called to say that I would hardly be able to fulfill my obligations. Well, believe it or not, the lunch was being hosted, unknown to us, by one of America's top ear, nose and throat specialists!† He does Ronald Reagan, also top opera singers and rock stars!! He gave me

---

* Robert Edison, then executive director of JGI (US).
† Dr. Wayne Kirkham.

back enough voice to address the group in one hour! And then followed on with all kinds of medications. He also said that had I not gone to him when I did, I would probably have suffered permanent damage to my vocal cords!! (And not only was the treatment etc free, but he gave JGI $3,000 as well!!)

Then back to Tanzania, but fleetingly. Next came the exercise of getting a 19 year old female chimpanzee, Ludmilla — Milla for short — from Arusha, where she had been alone for 18 years since her mother was shot and she was rescued from a meat market in Cameroon, to the Siddles' in Zambia. We had to charter a small plane (single engine, 7 seater Piper Cherokee) and it was quite an adventure.

And then, at last, ten days in Gombe. But first I got malaria — soon over, but a real waste of time. And then I was bashed around by Fifi's son Frodo, our one and only rogue male. He is horrid to the other chimpanzees, too. Anyway, he stamped on me and hurled me off the trail, and made me angry (and also gave me a sore head!!). After my ten days here, catching up on correspondence, I go to Burundi (where I hear they are in a muddle and needing me!) for three days, then Japan for some conservation lectures and a lot of media. Then UK to sort slides and a lecture. Then New York for another lecture. And then, after two days in DC, by Conoco plane, with the Vice President for Explorations, to Brazzaville to meet with President Sassou-Nguesso, following which I nip over the river to meet with President Mobutu! Then visit the project in Pointe Noire. And then UK to do some promotion of the new book, the sequel to In the Shadow of Man. And then to Canada to launch JGI (Canada). And then book promotion in USA. And I refuse to think any further than that!

We are, incidentally, planning a Gombe 30 "Wildlife Week" in Tanzania after Christmas. Along with the Wildlife Division of the Government. It will be the biggest conservation event ever in Tanzania, and we have groups of fabulous people helping. The President himself will host a dinner at State House on the last day of the week.

So — you can see that I am not being exactly lazy! And, also, that things really do seem to be happening. But I have rambled on too long, and will stop now. I do hope you are both okay, and that we can all meet again soon. If you need anything, I hope you will let one or all of the "Three Chimpoteers" — Steve, Ken and me — know. We said we'd do anything to help. We meant that. And mean it.

With love to you both,
Jane

4 June 1991

FAX 44-403-41048
For Mrs June Blackburn, RSPCA
Dear June —

Well, here I am in Brazzaville. I spent all of yesterday afternoon at the zoo, with the Chandlers. They are really dedicated, caring people. Never fail to go twice a week — Monday and Thursday. And Sylvie Menou goes at the weekends.

First I want to say how grateful I am for the RSPCA donation. The cheque got held up in the bank — but came through this morning! Most of the money goes to pay our keeper, Jean Maboto. He is truly wonderful. He has a terrific relationship with the chimps, monkeys and many of the other animals. Talks to them. Gives adult ♂ chimp ChuChu the attention & grooming he needs <u>despite the fact</u> that ChuChu bit Sylvie.

Some of the chimps died of a peculiar disease — not identified. The 5 remaining are in good condition. <u>BUT</u> are all in solitary confinement. They need an expert to get them into <u>groups.</u> Gregoire looks like a real chimp now! His hair has grown back everywhere & is glossy & black. His eyes are bright. All the monkeys are fit — 4 are loose in the zoo grounds. Makes feeding difficult!! What a difference the Chandlers — & some money — have made! The mongooses, civets, jackal, birds are all doing well. And the pig. I took photos & will send you as soon as possible.

I am trying to get additional funding — from Terre Sauvage, Bardot Foundation, Aspinal, & USA zoos. (The 'Adopt a 3rd World

Zoo Chimp' idea.) We cannot <u>abandon</u> these animals. They matter. EACH ONE. The cages are mostly NOT tiny. They need painting, and FURNISHING. A chimp enclosure. (The Chandlers got some money for a cage for some monkeys.) I DESPERATELY HOPE THE RSPCA may grant at least <u>some</u> additional funds NOW. We have enough to last until mid-July.

Love,<br>Jane

P.O. Box 727<br>Dar es Salaam<br>Tanzania<br>11 July 1991

Dean Franklin Loew, D.V.M., Ph.D.
Tufts University
School of Veterinary Medicine
200 Westboro Road
N. Grafton, Mass. 01536-1895
Dear Frank,

Here is my autograph!* Isn't it time we worked some way for me to visit & earn my title? . . .

I seem to have been neglectful of writing. I am sorry, Frank. My life has got away with me recently. I seem to travel NON-stop. The USA part is about the same. But with JGIs in Canada & UK, those bits are more hectic. And the <u>African</u> part is very time consuming & exhausting! We now have projects or involvements in Burundi, Congo, Zaire, Angola, Uganda, Mali & Sierra Leone! I have not yet been myself to the last two, but they are coming up!

The important thing is that the visits I make do seem to make a difference.

Now have a "traveling chimp exhibit" — large photos, objects used by chimps as tools in different parts of Africa — <u>actual</u> tools,

---

* Jane was signing another year's contract for her 1988 and 1989 appointment as adjunct professor of environmental studies at Tufts University.

<u>actually</u> used. And various other things — graphics, interpretive texts in English, Swahili & French. Video tapes. Conoco is funding the gradual showing of this, one week per capital. Across Africa where there are chimps. I go with it, head of state (or closest we can get!) opens it, & we have a week of conservation awareness — kids bused in, radio & TV seminars, talks at schools — etc, etc. <u>Terrific.</u> Trying to do about 4 or 5 countries per year. This summer — Burundi, Zaire, Angola & Congo. Next year — Uganda, Gabon, Mali, Ivory Coast — and maybe one more. Cameroon, since right by Gabon.

So — that's keeping me busy! And a very very exciting children's programme — international. . . .

All the best,
Jane

The Birches
10 Durley Chine Road South
Bournemouth, Dorset BH2 5JZ
16 November 1991

Dear Max,

This is just a short note. It was terrific seeing you all, and so many Conoco people whom I have met before. I am beginning to feel really a part of the Conoco family. And such a nice family, too. In particular it was good to have a chance of talking to you, discussing Congo. And I thoroughly enjoyed the dinner with Diana and the other wives. For me, anyway, it was a lovely way to end the evening — and I caught my train easily and arrived home quite early — about 1.20 a.m.

I just wanted to put on paper the gist of what we talked about.

First of all, I would not feel happy about building a place for those chimpanzees too far away from Pointe Noire. This is partly for logistical reasons, partly for financial reasons. I don't think the keepers we have now, who are terrific, would want to move too far from Pointe Noire. Of course we could get others, but one of the two we have seems to be very good, and both know and love the chimps. And caring for the place, if Conoco is no longer there, would be difficult and expensive for JGI on its own. As you know, we ARE beginning to raise some money. But I feel very strongly that it is neither practical nor ethical to spend huge amounts of money on just a handful of chimps when there are so many others, equally needy, in other parts of Africa. Let alone the others in Congo.

I believe a really large sanctuary, jutting into the river, would first of all be very difficult to design because of the change in water levels during the year. Secondly, it would expose the chimps on three sides to poaching from the water. Very hard to protect them.

I believe that we need to stretch the funds that Conoco can make available to help not only a few chimps, but many chimps and other animals, AND PEOPLE.

I envisage a relatively small walled or moated or electric wired enclosure, big enough to include a few trees, big enough to contain 20 to 30 chimps. Where the chimps who have been captive will know a new kind of freedom. Not ideal — but even wild chimpanzees have to face many dangers and hardships. And at least we can continue to care for individuals who have, through no fault of their own, become dependent on their human owners.

Ideally, this is set within a national park. This area to include the most suitable part of the Conoco concession, and, perhaps, part of Chevron's also. Maybe some of the other oil companies. If it is a really big area, that would be terrific. If several corporations joined the effort, more money would be available.

This idea will:

a) Save natural habitat, some of which is unique, much of which is beautiful.
b) Save wasting the conservation effort that Conoco Congo has already invested in the area.
c) Conserve very many species of animals and plants, including chimpanzees and gorillas.
d) Offer jobs for many local people.
e) Offer an opportunity for developing controlled tourism, which, given the attractions of the coast, the historical and ar-

chaeological sites, could be very successful (and might help to prevent too much more spreading of eucalyptus plantations!).

f) Provide a stable environment for conservation education programmes, with the hope of involving other conservation organizations such as the World Conservation Institute (WCI), the conservation wing of the New York Zoological Society, and others, perhaps WWF.

g) By demonstrating a major commitment to and investment in a major conservation programme, persuade donor nations to set up some AID projects, particularly rural development programmes, especially agro-forestry ones.

h) Offer opportunities for scientific research. Which, in turn, is another method of focusing attention on the fascinating aspects of the area, as well as its problems.

So, that is how I would hope that we might be able to proceed, together and, as you say, with the cooperation of other organizations. . . .

Thank you again, Max — for all your support and interest, and for your time last week. I am so glad that that particular visit worked out so well. I hope your trip home was smooth and uneventful.

Please give my best to my many Conoco friends.

Love to Diana and you,

[Probably January 1992]

Dear Michael,

I'm typing this so you can read it. I'm sitting in my upstairs office in Dar es Salaam (which means Haven of Peace) looking out across the blue of the Indian Ocean. It is early on a Sunday morning and my son is still asleep, and our two dogs, also. They are curled up by my desk. I just took them out for a walk along the beach. (Where I was foolish enough to walk three days ago, the morning I got back, with my watch on. And a young thug came up with a large screwdriver which he pressed onto my throat, and removed my watch with his other hand!! If I'd made a commotion the dogs would have

come, but I had such a vivid mental picture of that screwdriver going into one of their eyes that I let him have his way. What is a
watch, after all.)

I played my children's organization "Heal the World" yesterday.
Of course, they loved it.

Did I tell you about them? We call ourselves Roots and Shoots —
roots creep quietly, everywhere, underground, making a firm foundation; shoots seem so new and fragile, but to reach the light they
can move boulders, break concrete. Good, symbolic name, and the
kids love it. We have 700 members in Dar es Salaam alone.

At the beginning of February we have a Wildlife Awareness
Week, here in Dar es Salaam.* With very many events, including a
students' congress — older children of 15 to 17 years old who are
the mainstay of Roots and Shoots. There are a great many events,
for children and for adults, during the week. The exhibit of chimpanzee tools from around Africa, with video tapes and photos. A
seminar about conservation and environmental problems. Various
competitions — art, poetry, essays and a quiz. A gala fund raising
dinner, with the President attending. And, on the final day, our very
popular Prime Minister will lead a walk, organized by Roots and
Shoots, to show our concern for the environment and to support the
young people in whose hands the future lies. The Prime Minister
will symbolically plant a tree at the end of the 10 kilometre walk.

After that week, I take the chimp exhibit and go to Uganda,
where a similar week is being arranged. Again, many events for children. And after that I take the exhibit to Burundi — for a similar
Wildlife Awareness week. And finally, a Week in Angola. The first
attempt to bring up the subject of conservation after the 15 year
civil war.

Michael, these events are making a difference. We have done two
already — last year it all began with the first one, here in Dar es Salaam. And then I did one in Congo.

Would you help me? You have written that beautiful song, Heal
the World. If you would just send a message (it would arrive in time

---

* That is, they were planning for the second such week, a year after the very successful Gombe 30 Wildlife Week of February 1991.

by DHL), preferably on video, but even on audio. Not professionally done — just a home video like the one you used to take of you and me in the mirror — did that come out, by the way? . . .

If you could just say something very simple. Like:

"Jane has told me that you are joining together to show that you care about the environment, and about animals. You know I do, too. I wish I could join you, but I am thinking about you. Jane wanted me to write a song for the environment, and for the animals. This is it."

You can say it better, but just something like that. You could add something about hoping that everyone would plant a tree for you, love an animal for you.

Even if it missed the Tanzania week, we'd get it for Uganda — but it would be wonderful for Tanzania. Where it all began.

Michael, everyone loves you here in Africa. The environment needs your help, so do the animals. And so do the children.

Please — I need your help, too.

26 December 1992

Dear Frank,

Always it seems that one of us owes the other a letter — This time it's I who owe one to you. I am going through a knee deep pile of correspondence, during a temporary lull in travel — & found a letter you wrote to me in July! You asked about Philadelphia Zoo. I don't know anything about it — except that they once had the oldest zoo chimp — but he died. Also they have one of the very very few colonies of <u>Drills.</u>* However, you made your mind up about that long ago! . . .

I am battling on with the lab issue. Another round of talks with the USDA about psychological well being. But more & more of my time is taken up with conservation in Africa & our young people's

---

* Drills *(Papio leucophaeus)* are a highly endangered species of forest-dwelling baboon currently found only in a small area of western Cameroon and eastern Nigeria, and on the island of Macias Ngeuma.

programme, which I began in Tanzania. "Roots & Shoots — the JGI Young Naturalists." <u>Roots</u> creep quietly underground & make a firm foundation; <u>Shoots</u> seem new & small — but to reach the light can move boulders, break apart concrete slabs. It is now growing — <u>beginning</u> to — in Burundi, Congo, Angola. And UK, Germany, Belgium & Japan, as well as USA. Most of these places — just little experimental plots! I've got into the International School network, which is fabulous: i.e. Brussels has 80 nationalities, Munich 60. And they spread all over Africa & the Middle East. I'm about to penetrate East Berlin!!

Gombe is fine — but that horrible Frodo, the one rogue male, really has it in for me & has spoilt Gombe for me.

Hope we meet in 1993.

Love to you & family,
Jane

27 May 1994

Dear Maureen and Paul,

I don't suppose I wrote to thank you for driving me around all over the place? I meant to, but somehow things got away from me as I rushed on from place to place.

Anyway, I can thank you <u>now.</u> I have 5 days, sandwiched in between Japan & a return to Africa. So I am trying to catch up on correspondence (which is actually impossible), and sort of organize myself for the coming two months. First Don Buford is joining us in the UK, & then, with Dilys Vass, the JGI-UK exec. director, we tour our Africa projects.* A crazy 3 week marathon — Kenya (a sanctuary); Tanzania (Dar es Salaam, Kigoma & Gombe); Burundi (sanctuary & research project); and Congo — sanctuary & coping with a zoo!!

Then Don & Dilys back to the UK, USA, & I have 3 more weeks in Tanzania. Hope to do some writing, and visit Gombe for more than 3 days!

---

\* Don Buford had become executive director of JGI (US); Dilys MacKinnon Vass was his counterpart in JGI (UK).

Japan was <u>excellent</u> because I think we are more or less set to launch Roots & Shoots. Over the years I've built up a great network — & the time has come to call upon those links that can help us to get the programme going. They are very enthusiastic, and I think the timing is <u>JUST</u> right.

I also visited Germany. There, also, I believe R & S is about to take off. We have a wonderful new contact who has decided to give a lot of time & energy to developing the programme, & to raising funds. Germany, potentially, is a good source of revenue for our projects in Africa.

Well — I just wanted to drop a quick note. I'm up in my room under the eaves, & two pigeons are on the window sill. They have turned the roof into a pigeon roost! Cozy, coo-ing sounds wake me each morning!

Thanks again, so much.

Yours ever,
Jane


12 July 1994

Dear Neva —

Herewith some films from my last Gombe trip. Could you send them to Bournemouth when done. I shall be in USA, but no longer coming to DC — not until September. But I'll <u>CALL</u> you and let you know what's going on.

Actually, things are moving quite fast. The trip with Don and Dilys was very good indeed. We began in Kenya, the Lonrho sanctuary. Then Dar es Salaam, Kigoma & Gombe. The little orphan chimps all have a fungus infection — hopefully being diagnosed now. We sent skin scrapings back to Germany with the German film team.

Gombe was SUPER — the film team & the 2 photographers — one French, one Swiss — very happy. The Swiss one, Karl Ammann, was getting photos for the National Geographic!

Burundi was tough. They live in real <u>fear.</u> In fact, Dilys receives, today, two little girls from one of my friends. Their parents were in tears every night — 1/2 at the thought that something might happen in Burundi, 1/2 at the thought of letting them go. It is very hard to get visas — I wrote a letter to the Brit. High Commissioner asking for visas for them to do Roots & Shoots stuff during the holidays. Then we'll see what is happening.

We got permission to move the 10 biggest orphans to the Lonrho sanctuary.

Then Congo — Gregoire still looking okay. Graziella Cotman, in Pointe Noire, doing a <u>SUPER</u> job with the 43 orphans. She is amazing. After D & D left on a Friday evening, I had a day in Brazzaville. The US Ambassador was very keen for me to see the President. Drama — I had to get to the Amb's residence. <u>BUT</u> . . . the President was having his 3rd meeting with the leader of the opposition — 3rd after the "cease fire." So — both sides found it necessary to make a show of strength. All roads towards the Palace were guarded by a <u>minimum</u> of 6 soldiers of each side — ie minimum of 12. All brandishing various types of weapons! Machine guns, rifles, pistols, revolvers! At one point soldiers stopped us, yanked open the car doors & got us out at gun point. They wanted the pick-up! (Opposition forces, non-uniformed!) Luckily a Congolese who was helping us came and talked them out of it! I got to the Ambassador & later, when meeting over & troops vanished, we had an hour long and very cordial meeting with the President!

We just had the first National Tanzanian Roots & Shoots Summit — in Zanzibar. It was <u>great.</u> 50 of us — from Kigoma, Kilimanjaro, Dar — & Zanzibar. Only 1-1/2 days, but well worth it. A <u>really</u> good meeting, opened by the Minister for the Environment.

Trip to the forest to see Zanzibar Red Colobus. Talks by the various representatives. Several by Dr. Jane! Above all, opportunities to meet & exchange ideas. It was about 50-50, teachers & students. And the students arranged <u>everything.</u> It was sponsored by a German organization — Artists United for Nature.

So, Neva. Please share this news with any of the JGI network you come across or think of. Like Susan, Rachel, Connie, Liz, etc. I've not written to any of them yet — only just back from non-stop travel. And the letter goes to you because of sending the films!

I arrive in UK on 28th July, USA on 3rd August. Leave USA on 12th or something. I'll definitely call.

My house is in the midst — still — of massive repairs! Roof done. Cess pit sort of done. Plumbing half done. Electricity done. But my room (where I'm writing) is piled with my belongings because the plumbers haven't finished messing with tanks above the cupboard! The veranda, where I usually work, is filled with Roots & Shoots!

My love to Bruce —

And you,
Jane

NOTE*** <u>ALL FILMS EXPOSED AT 400 ASA</u>

24 July '95

Dear Paul & Maureen,

I promised I'd write you a note from "darkest Africa". Now flying from Brazzaville to Pointe Noire — across some pretty "dark" Africa — lots of clear cutting & hunting going on below. A very noisy flight, and rather a long one.

Had a truly fantastic visit to Gombe. Spent time with Fifi, & my beloved Gremlin. Never even <u>saw</u> Frodo — of course, I was heart broken!! But the real thrill was the twins. Their mother, Rafiki (means "Friend") is <u>so so</u> competent. A boy & a girl. Not identical. Very different faces. Rock, AnnRoll. Ha! The choices were Ruff and Reddie (my idea), Ryme & Reeson, Riff & Raff. The Rock AnnRoll (which I also thought of) we chose because all the Tanzanians liked it. They didn't understand Ruff & Reddie — & how could one possibly translate!!

They are utterly adorable! Rock has a long white beard and moustache. AnnRoll has a sparse few white hairs on her chin. They are very active. Rock 3 times 'kissed' his sister. And I saw him take his first observed mouthful of solid food — banana!

My three Roots & Shoots "interns" arrived safely. They are so filled with enthusiasm and energy. We only had a week in Dar —

they certainly were thrown in at the deep end! We had immensely productive meetings with the British Council (who may fund 2 Tanz[anian] R & S co-ordinators for the next year, and one trip a month to a park on some kind of field experience). Also with the Peace Corps — (who may incorporate R & S programs & philosophy into their education programs). I left my 3 & 2 Tanz[anian] counterparts feverishly preparing an hour long presentation to the new batch of volunteers. The very last presentation in their training (6 weeks). With the street children group, also the orphanage. We had a R & S meeting — two actually, discussing ideas, accomplishments & plans for the future. And so on! It is working so well that I'm going to try to make it a permanent thing — two interns at any one time. Volunteers who will spend 3–4 months in Dar. With a reward of a trip to Kigoma — &, of course, a visit to Gombe! So if you hear of any students in the year between school & college, or older, let me know. We'll soon have a very precise idea of costs. But basically, air fare & food. They get a roof over their heads, & the R & S car. They go to schools, work with their TZ counterparts, etc. etc.

Now I've been working hard to get something similar going in the Congo. It will be hard to get the 'roof' part of it. At the moment, there is not really any R & S group. But the two young men who helped to launch R & S internationally, in 1992, are still interested, & I shall be meeting with them in Brazzaville on my way out.

LATER From the chimps sanctuary 'Tchimpounga'. This is the most utterly amazing place. Extraordinary. What is going on here does deserve to be shown to the world. We are right now trying to find a videographer who will come & film for a week.

To see 10 young chimps follow 2 Congolese men in blue uniforms onto the open plain, bordering the forest, all stop, each one be given a red cup of milk from a big blue bucket — except 2 that have bottles. Give back empty cup for refill. Then return when finished. Then all troop off into the forest for the morning. Amazing. Then 26 older chimps — same thing only they come out into the fenced in sanctuary after their night inside, and each gets a blue plastic mug.

Same thing — hand back for refills, return at end. Only <u>one</u> has a bit of bread hidden in pocket — he can only drink his milk if, at the same time, he drinks his bread!! After all milk drunk, another man arrives with large sack of pieces of French loaf. Each chimp gets one, some get 2. And then, on their own now, they go off to the forest for the day. Only the alpha ♂, 8 year old Maxillo, likes to patrol the boundary fence with a human. Well — with me!

And in the evening, similar but in their sleeping quarters. And instead of bread, big plates of fruit & at the end, before milk, big sticky balls of rice!

Well — enough. So much to do. Plans for clinic, school, R & S, reserve, tourists, solar pump etc, etc.

We'll stay in touch.

Much LOVE,<br>Jane

2.10.97

[Dear Paul and Maureen,]

Believe it or not, this hotel got its whole roof destroyed in a fire.* Still sell P.C's — & actually it still looks <u>almost</u> same. Fabulous time here in Taiwan. You'll hear soon. Just wanted to let you know I'm thinking of you. NOT MUCH TRASH anywhere. ONE minute scrap of gum paper in whole Nat Park!

Love,<br>Jane

[Probably June 1998]

Dear John,

I have just received your letter of 21 May. I appreciate the honesty and frankness, and I understand your position. Let me respond to some of the points that you have made.

The Jane Goodall Institute is (unfortunately) involved in caring

---

* Written on a postcard featuring a picture of the Grand Hotel in Taipei, Taiwan.

for a rather large number of orphan chimpanzees. The largest of our sanctuaries with 63 individuals is in Congo-Brazzaville. The others are in Uganda, Tanzania and Kenya. (Almost all the chimpanzees come from Congo-Zaire originally.) Kenya is not a range country for chimpanzees, and the 20 or so individuals there are mostly those which were moved from our facility in Burundi for safety reasons. (In Zambia, which also has no wild chimpanzees, Dave and Sheila Siddle, as you know, operate another large sanctuary for orphan chimpanzees many of which also originated in Congo-Zaire.)

Our JGI sanctuaries, in addition to providing care for the orphan chimps, serve a variety of functions. We hire as many local people as possible, and buy from nearby villages as much as we can. Thus we boost local economy. In Congo-Brazzaville we have raised the money for a small dispensary and primary school, as well as working with the government to protect a large surrounding area of forest savanna mosaic, home to a population of wild chimpanzees. When the country becomes more politically stable we hope that carefully controlled tourism will also help the local economy as well as bringing in foreign exchange to the central government.

Similar programs have been set up in Uganda and Tanzania. By helping local populations living around protected forest habitat to develop environmentally sustainable development programmes such as agro-forestry, giving women skills so that they can earn some money and education to improve their self-esteem (with the expectation that this will reduce the size of their families as has happened in other parts of the world), primary health care, AIDS education, family planning and some micro-credit [for] environmentally-friendly enterprise. Our best programme of this sort is in Tanzania, in the villages along Lake Tanganyika and around the tiny Gombe national park (27 villages). UNESCO is coming in with funding for clean water and hygienic latrines for these and other villages.

In these countries with populations of wild chimpanzees, the orphans serve as ambassadors of their species. We encourage visits from local people, especially school children, so that they can learn about the amazing qualities of chimpanzees — creatures living in their own forests whom they would not otherwise have a chance of knowing. The chimpanzees then become a focus for conservation education. Visitors knowing nothing about chimpanzees are invariably amazed when they spend time watching the orphans. Most of them have never imagined the complexity of chimpanzee behavior. They are delighted to see them kissing, embracing, holding hands, using tools and weapons, and the older ones caring for the smallest. The locals employed as keepers rapidly become absolutely captivated and are very proud to share their knowledge.

Chimpanzees can teach us, better than any other living beings, how blurred, after all, is the line between humans and the rest of the animal kingdom. This teaches a new respect, not only towards the chimpanzees themselves but, inevitably, towards the other amazing beings with whom we share the planet. Thus chimpanzees are excellent conservation teachers. They can perform this function in every country in the world.

In Kenya, the Sweetwaters Sanctuary is operated by Lonrho Hotels. As is the case in Uganda, the Kenya sanctuary pays for itself through tourist and visitor fees (except when flooded as a result of El Nino!!). A trust fund has been set up for money raised over and above that necessary for maintaining the operating expenses of the sanctuary. These extra funds will gradually build up until the capital is large enough to ensure that the chimpanzees can be cared for for life. In addition, money is to be generated for chimpanzee protection programmes in the range country or countries of origin.

I never wanted to become involved in caring for captive chimpanzees. Improving conditions in existing zoos, trying to help chimps in medical research laboratories — yes. Establishing and being responsible for orphans, especially in politically volatile Africa — no. But having learned from the chimpanzees for so many years, there was no way I could turn my back on abandoned individuals. That is how our first sanctuaries started in Congo and Burundi. But, from the first, I realized that sanctuaries would have to pay for themselves AND become conservation tools, to be used to encourage the local people, hunters and governments to enforce their own existing laws that make it illegal to hunt and sell endangered species (such as the great apes) without a licence. These laws exist in all countries that have become signatories to CITES, and these include most of the chimpanzee range countries.

I believe that the existing laws are sufficient as they stand IF they are adhered to. Enforcement will only come when the governments and officials responsible a) understand the law, b) understand the reason why such a law exists and c) feel that it is, in some way, worth their while to enforce the law. There is a law in the United States regarding the treatment of laboratory animals. It is almost worthless, because it is almost never enforced. This is true of many laws in many countries.

Thus our way has been to work on the ground, educating people, working with people and governments, encouraging enforcement of existing laws and demonstrating the practical value to both government and local populations of developing and enforcing conservation programmes. This is how we propose to deal with the situation in Angola (where the chimpanzee population is limited to the Cabinda area and is not thought to be very large).

Hopefully JGI-SA* will grow, and be able to assist in ongoing efforts to place dedicated conservationists on the ground in other chimpanzee range countries, to help them enforce or develop their own laws. I have made promising starts in many countries (Congo-Brazzaville,† Burundi, Sierra Leone and Angola itself) and been forced to quit because of political instability — yet I firmly believe that none of those efforts were wasted, and that some of the seeds sown, though they may lie dormant, will grow once conditions become more suitable.

Finally, I very much like your idea of bringing ape conservation into a more high profile in the UN agenda. We have been moving in this direction for some time (protect apes and their habitats and you automatically protect very many wild primate species). In mid-June a gathering of American primatologists will discuss some of these

---

\* The newly established Jane Goodall Institute in South Africa.

† Jane may have meant Zaïre. The project in Congo-Brazzaville was, and is, still working successfully.

issues. I have lobbied for chimpanzee welfare and conservation on Capitol Hill, and in the European parliament. I would very much like to sit down with you during my next visit to Johannesburg so that we can share our ideas. I think it would be an extremely fruitful and rewarding discussion.

Thank you very much for the careful consideration you have given to our project, and the critical points you have brought up. It shows how valuable it is for those who care to work together. Do let us keep in touch.

With warm personal regards,

Yours sincerely,
Jane Goodall, Ph.D.


[Postmarked November 18, 1998]

[Dear Paul and Maureen,]

I so miss you. 2 days in Beijing. Like a grain of sand falling in a super-saturated solution. It was AMAZING how the Chinese are clamouring for R & S. Timing PERFECT. And managed to climb to low turret of the Great Wall — just in time for sunset, drank glass of superb red wine. It was utterly freezing — so we nearly dropped the bottle & glasses! . . .

Much love,
Jane


26 June 1999

This is a letter to many people: Emily Grove, Victoria Kerr, Laura Donovan, Andrew Breckinridge, Jason Hatfield, Kate Murphy, Paul Peterson, Ashely DeMoth, Amanda Chandler, Milan Kidd, Diana Webber, Renae Hux, Nicholas Williams, Chris Ring, and Ellen Wilcox.

I wish I could write to each one of you separately. Alas, I do not have the time. But I expect you understand. But I did want to thank you all for writing. (You will find it hard to read this — I'm in a small plane and it is <u>very</u> bumpy.) I am on my way back from Gombe to Dar es Salaam — then to UK. It was when I got to Dar 8 days ago that I found all your letters. When this arrives, school will be ended I suppose, but I hope this will catch up with you one day.

Your letters were, each one of them, very important to me. As some of you noted, it <u>is</u> exhausting, trailing around the world non-stop. <u>BUT</u> to get letters like the ones you wrote — telling me that the message I left with you that day did, indeed, make some impact on your lives — well, that is what makes it all worthwhile. (I'd also like to congratulate you all on how very <u>well</u> you write & express yourselves. And congratulations to your teachers. You are an unusually articulate group of students!)

Gombe was wonderful. Even though I had to spend time with a film team, which is always very tedious. This is an IMAX film. The poor team had to carry this <u>incredibly</u> heavy equipment up & down steep, skiddy slopes, & through tangled undergrowth. They had been there 3 weeks. The stars of the film (so far) have been Gremlin & her family. Her brother, Gimble, the one survivor of Melissa's 1977 twins. Gremlin's eldest surviving son, Galahad (11 yrs), daughter (6 yrs) Gaia — and, of course, the twins, those adorable 10 month old girls, Gold, or Goldie, and Glitta. Goldie is a determined person, & never gives up. Goldie has a charming white beard & a little unruly tuft of hair on the top of her head. Gaia adores them. Her idea of heaven is to hold, groom or play with one or the other. (Very bumpy now!)

Fifi's infant, Flirt — born same week as twins — is twice as big. She gets double the milk I suppose. Also, Fifi always has big babies!

The film team will return next year to finish their work. They (me too) are praying the twins will be okay. I can't wait to see the chimps on the HUGE IMAX screens.

Also during ~~the past~~ two days, little groups of teachers (6 or 7 per group) have been led through the forest — as far as the waterfall, up to the peak. There were 90 teachers from 85 schools, from 5 regions of Tanzania. This was the very first national Roots & Shoots teacher workshop. If you knew how hard it is to accomplish something like this, you'd realize what an amazing job my R & S coordinators in Dar have done. Yared could tell you.* They even agreed to participate in the week-long workshop <u>without</u> "sitting" allowance, travel allowance, etc. They just got train tickets (those outside Kigoma region), food, & beds (in a secondary boarding school in Kigoma). Unheard of! All but 6 saw at least one chimp (extraordinarily lucky as each group only had 2 hours in forest). They visited one school, tree nurseries & agro-forestry projects. They learned how to use our new teacher manual. They had fun. Yesterday, their last day, I gave a talk. Then saw off those who had come by train — lots of pant-hooting from compartment windows to platform & back. It will take them 2 days to get to Dar. We flew over their train just now! It is exciting to think how many students will benefit from that workshop. UNICEF was so impressed they are funding my people to put on a Regional workshop in September to include teachers from the sadly very large refugee camps in the areas. From Burundi & Eastern Zaire — or the Democratic Republic of Congo as we should now call it — though there is nothing remotely 'democratic' about Kabila. There is still a Rwandan camp as well.

Roots & Shoots is growing. Now, in addition to a lot of interest in China & Dubai, I think we've found a way of starting off in Russia — & even Albania.

Anyway I look forward — very much — to hearing what you all do in your Roots & Shoots clubs. The best part of my work is to hear what is going on. All the ideas & plans — and how they are fulfilled. All the ways the world is always being made a better place for <u>all</u> life, for <u>all</u> individuals.

I hope you have/have had (depending on when you get this) a wonderful summer vacation.

Follow your dreams, work hard, have FUN.

Love,
Dr. Jane

---

* Yared Subusa was a Roots & Shoots member from Kigoma; he is currently working for a Ph.D. in the United States.

# EDITOR'S ACKNOWLEDGMENTS

I should like to thank a number of people who generously allowed me to examine their treasured correspondence with Jane Goodall, including most particularly her mother, Margaret Myfanwe (Vanne) Morris-Goodall, and her best friend from childhood, Sally Cary Pugh.

Other generous contributors of Jane Goodall letters to this and the first volume also deserve sincere and special gratitude: Neva Folk, Robert Hinde, Alison Jolly, Paul Kase and Maureen Marshall, Mary Lewis, Franklin M. Loew, Desmond Morris, Jean Nitzsche and the family of Ruth Davis, Anne Pusey, Emilie Bergmann Riss, Joan Travis, and Vivian Wheeler.

Thanks are due as well to the following institutions (and to responsible individuals within those institutions) for giving me access to files that included letters from Jane Goodall: the Houghton Mifflin archives at the Houghton Library of Harvard University; the L. S. B. Leakey Foundation archives (with help from Joan Travis); the National Geographic Society (and Neva Folk); the National Museums of Kenya's Louis Leakey archives (and Gideon Matwale as well as Mohamed Isahakia); the Stanford University archives at Green Library (and Pat White); and the University of Minnesota's Jane Goodall archives (and Anne Pusey).

Much of the background material for the chapter introductions was provided by helpful individuals to whom I am immensely grateful. They include, first, the immediate family of Jane Goodall — Mortimer Morris-Goodall and Vanne Goodall, Olwen Joseph, Judy and Pippit Waters, and Hugo and Grub van Lawick — who withstood with generosity and forbearance my relentless requests for information, documents, facts, and favors. And also, from among Jane Goodall's many friends, supporters, and colleagues: Petal Allen, David Anstey, Anthony Collins, Irven DeVore, Marie Claude Erskine, Susan Cary Featherstone, Neva Folk, Biruté Galdikas, Michael H. Goodall, David Hamburg, Brian Herne, Robert Hinde, Carrie J. Hunter, Alison Jolly, Mrisho Mpambije Kagoha, Jumanne Kikwale, Michael C. Latham, Jonathan Leakey, Richard Leakey, Mary Lewis, Franklin M. Loew, Kenneth Love, Dilys MacKinnon, Margaret Arthur McCloy, Eve Mitchell, Desmond Morris, Michael Neugebauer, Toshisada Nishida, Jean Nitzsche, Sally Cary Pugh, Gerald Rilling, Nancy Rillstone, David and Emilie Riss, Duane Rumbaugh, George and Kay Schaller, Mary Griswold Smith, Geza Teleki, Fiona Vernon, Vivian Wheeler, Richard Wrangham, Robert William Young, and Philip Ziegler.

Peter Matson, agent, and Harry Foster, editor, both deserve recognition for encouraging the idea of this book and helping see it through from start to finish. And manuscript editors Peg Anderson and Vivian Wheeler must be singled out and warmly thanked. Vivian gracefully combined her usual exacting standards and a particularly close relationship with the material of this book — she was a source of some of the correspondence and the editor of two of Jane Goodall's earlier books. Of course, a warm gesture of gratitude is due, as always, to those patient and faithful editors-in-residence: my wife, Wyn Kelley, and my children, Britt and Bayne.

Most of all, I feel obliged to acknowledge and to thank once again Jane Goodall's mother, Vanne, who among her many extraordinary qualities had the foresight and organization to save every single letter her prolific daughter wrote home over a period of nearly sixty years, thus providing nearly half the raw material for this epistolary self-portrait. Vanne was remarkable in so many other ways; and it is to her memory that this volume is lovingly dedicated.

# ILLUSTRATION CREDITS

Tool-using bird: Hugo van Lawick/NGS Image Collection
Jane and Grub in cage: Hugo van Lawick
In the beach house: Hugo van Lawick
Playing kickball: Timothy Green
Grub, George Dove, and Jane: Hugo van Lawick
Grub fishing: Jane Goodall
Portrait of Goliath: Hugo van Lawick
Hugo and Figan: Hugo van Lawick
Jane, Grub, and Louis Leakey: Leakey Foundation
Group of students with Jane: photographer unknown
Chimp threatening: Hugo van Lawick
Charging males: Hugo van Lawick
Flo, Fifi, and Flint: Patrick McGinnis
Derek and Wilkie: Jane Goodall
Grub and Derek: Jane Goodall
Grub and Wagga: Jane Goodall
Jane and Derek: the Goodall family
Derek with constituents: photographer unknown
Jane and Grub at Gombe: Kenneth Love © 1980
Jane and Dian Fossey: Leakey Foundation
Jane at Gombe: © Brian Keating
Jane and Julius Nyerere: photographer unknown
Jane and Professor Imanishi: photographer unknown
Jane and Secretary Baker: © National Geographic Society
With Gorbachev: Maureen Marshall
Roots & Shoots: Jane Goodall Institute
Evening relaxation: the Goodall family

# INDEX

The Jane Goodall Institute, grounded in Dr. Goodall's research, makes the connection between the health of one species and the well-being of all living things. Since 1977 the institute's research, conservation, and education programs have created a worldwide network of individuals committed to improving life on earth. For more information on the institute, please visit www.janegoodall.org or contact the JGI office nearest you.

JGI-USA, PO Box 14890, Silver Spring, MD 20911
JGI-UK, 15 Clarendon Park, Lymington, Hants, SO41 8AX
JGI-Tanzania, PO Box 727, Dar es Salaam
JGI-Uganda, PO Box 4187, Kampala
JGI-Canada, PO Box 477, Victoria Station, Westmount, Quebec H3Z 2Y6
JGI-Germany, Herzogstrasse 60, D-80803 Munich
JGI-South Africa, PO Box 87527, Houghton 2047
JGI-Taiwan, 6F, No. 20 Section 2, Hsin Sheng South Road, Taipei
JGI-Holland, PB 61, 7213 ZH Gorssel, Netherlands
Roots & Shoots-Italy, Via D. Martelli 14a, 57012 Castiglioncello (Li)